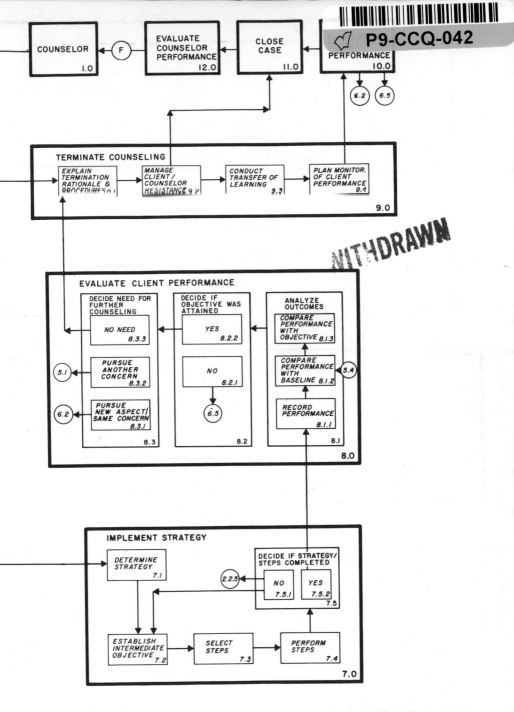

SYSTEMATIC COUNSELING

PREPARED BY }
— NORMAN R. STEWART
— BOB B. WINBORN
— RICHARD G. JOHNSON
— HERBERT M. BURKS, JR.
— JAMES R. ENGELKES

COLLEGE OF EDUCATION / MICHIGAN STATE UNIVERSITY

SEVENTH REVISION / MARCH 25, 1977

SYSTEMATIC

COUNSELING

Norman R. Stewart

Bob B. Winborn / Herbert M. Burks, Jr.

Richard R. Johnson / James R. Engelkes

Michigan State University

PRENTICE-HALL, INC., *Englewood Cliffs, New Jersey 07632*

Library of Congress Cataloging in Publication Data

Main entry under title:

Systematic counseling.

(Prentice-Hall series in counseling and human
development)
    Bibliography: p.
    Includes index.
1.–Counseling. I.–STEWART, NORMAN R.,
BF637.C6S95   158   77-24374
ISBN   0-13-880252-1

Prentice-Hall Series in Counseling and Human Development
Norman R. Stewart, *Series Editor*

Printed in the United States of America

10 9 8 7 6 5 4 3 2 1

Prentice-Hall International, Inc., *London*
Prentice-Hall of Australia Pty. Limited, *Sydney*
Prentice-Hall of Canada, Ltd., *Toronto*
Prentice-Hall of India Private Limited, *New Delhi*
Prentice-Hall of Japan, Inc., *Tokyo*
Prentice-Hall of Southeast Asia Pte. Ltd., *Singapore*
Whitehall Books Limited, *Wellington, New Zealand*

Contents

iii

Preface

One of the major voids in the literature of counseling is the absence of a comprehensive, detailed model that provides counselors with a practical theory for the entire counseling process. This book is an attempt to fill that void.

Students and practitioners of counseling have access to a wealth of information about theories and philosophies of counseling, the counseling relationship, interviewing skills, strategies for helping people, and the dynamics of behavior. Counselors are, however, severly handicapped by the lack of a unifying, inclusive, and concrete framework that shows *how* their knowledge, attitudes, and skills can be incorporated into a pragmatic and personalized approach for assisting clients.

It would seem that explicit models and directions for counseling would have evolved from some of the theories of counseling that currently exist. Unfortunately, most theorists have not provided extensive guidelines as to the sequence of procedures to be followed during counseling, the functions to be performed and the decisions to be made by a counselor, or criteria that can be used in evaluating the effectiveness of counseling. As Shertzer and Stone (1974, p. 240) point out, "Most theories seemingly consciously avoid clear prescriptions of what should be done in the counseling process." As a consequence, students and practitioners of counseling, while under the pressures of time, study, and work, are often required to devise idiosyncratic models for translating theory into practice and are forced to develop operating procedures largely through trial-and-error learning. In effect, they have to learn a counseling approach at the expense of their clients!

Systematic Counseling was written to provide counselor trainees, counselors, psychotherapists, social workers, and other members of the helping professions with detailed specifications for conducting the counseling process. We expect this systematic approach to relieve students and beginning counselors of the burden of deciding "what to do" during the different stages of counseling. It will not relieve them from using their intelligence, cognitive processes, knowledge, and human relations skills in creative and flexible ways to meet the requirements of individual clients. Rather, by following the step-by-step guidelines outlined in the blueprint and specifications, they should be better able to use their understanding of human behavior, their abilities, and their personalities to individualize counseling. We also expect that more experienced counselors will use the model of Systematic Counseling to gain additional understanding of how to proceed in counseling and as a means for evaluating and increasing their effectiveness as counselors.

We believe *Systematic Counseling* offers a new, interesting, and viable approach to the conceptualization and communication of the counseling process for the following reasons: (a) A flow diagram provides an easily understood and clear description of the entire process from the time a client referral is received by a counselor to the closure of the client's case, and (b) a manual of performance criteria makes it possible to evaluate the work of a counselor and the outcomes of counseling.

The graphic and schematic nature of the flowchart for Systematic Counseling (see Endpapers) enables one to form a gestalt of the complete process and perceive the relationships among the different parts of the counseling system. The flowchart shows the various functions that a counselor performs during each stage of counseling and the specific flow of information decisions, and actions that occurs throughout the process.

The Performance Criteria for Systematic Counseling (see Appendix A) include a set of standards for performing the specific counseling functions shown in the flowchart. Criteria are suggested for obtaining and processing information, making decisions, establishing counseling objectives, evaluating the performance of a client, and carrying out the various other tasks of a counselor. In addition, numerous examples are given to illustrate appropriate performance that will fulfill the criteria.

We have attempted to sequence the chapters of the book to facilitate the learning and practice of Systematic Counseling. The first four chapters give a broad and general description of the basic concepts that form the foundation of this approach to counseling. The flowchart and performance criteria are introduced with an explanation of how to read and use the flowchart.

Chapters 5 through 11 provide a detailed description and explanation of the procedures to be followed during each step and substep of the counseling process. Specific suggestions are given, and practical techniques are described to enable a counselor and client to carry out the procedures included in the flowchart in an efficient and effective manner. Numerous strategies are also suggested for assisting clients with specific kinds of problems and concerns. Chapter 12 describes reasons for and resistances to the development of counseling systems and suggests some uses of Systematic Counseling other than in one-to-one counseling.

Chapter 13 is a complete verbatim case study that demonstrates how a counselor carries out the entire process of *Systematic Counseling*.

In addition to the general organization of the chapters, which have been sequenced so that the reader can progress from the general to the specific in learning this approach, some additional aids for learning have been incorporated into the format. Each chapter begins with an overview of the topics to be discussed. This section is followed by an introduction which contains a description of how the content of the chapter is organized, the purposes of the chapter, and learning objectives for the reader. Each chapter also contains a summary that may be used by the reader to evaluate his or her basic understanding of the concepts contained within the chapter.

We developed a flowchart of *Systematic Counseling*, around which this book is organized, during nine years of collaboration while working together at Michigan State University. The experience the five of us have had as elementary, secondary, community college, college, and rehabilitation counselors; the experience we have had as counselor educators; and our training at Indiana University, the University of Iowa, the University of Minnesota, Stanford University, and the University of Wisconsin, has been synthesized into a system of counseling that can be used to deliver effective counseling services to clients. The flowchart has undergone seven revisions over an nine-year period as a result of feedback and suggestions made by counselors and supervisors who have used it. The model has not only been used by several hundred counselors and counselor trainees, but has also been subjected to professional review and criticism at workshops and professional meetings on numerous occasions. It has also been criticized and reviewed by systems engineers and out colleagues who are interested in a systems approach to counseling. Many of their suggestions have been incorporated into the model presented in this volume. We would welcome the suggestions of those who use this book so that an even more comprehensive, detailed, and useful model can be designed to assist counselors to better serve their clients.

As noted above, many individuals have contributed feedback and ideas during the development of this approach to counseling. We are especially grateful to our students, who have been both our severest critics and most steadfast supporters. We also appreciate the encouragement given us throughout the years by Stephen L. Yelon, the training we received from Leonard C. Silvern in systems analysis and design, and the opportunity extended to us by Robert C. Craig and other members of our Department at Michigan State University to incorporate a systems approach into our counselor training program.

N.R.S.

R.G.J.   B.B.W.

J.R.E.   H.M.B.

1

Introduction to Systematic Counseling

OVERVIEW

". . . counseling, like kissing, is so intrinsically interesting and satisfying that few bother to critically examine it (Thoresen, 1969, p. 264)."

This satirical statement calls attention to the lack of a disciplined research tradition in counseling. Probably the most important reason why counseling is so infrequently subjected to a critical examination is because, like kissing, it is a complex process that involves highly personalized relationships and requires— when done well—a high degree of skill. Because of the intricate human interactions and relationships which are involved, counseling has apparently been perceived as a process that is not amenable to rigorous analysis. Consequently, most counseling theories and models have been rather abstract and philosophical in nature.

The model of *Systematic Counseling* demonstrates that counseling is amenable to a relatively specific analysis. In this chapter, the basic components of the counseling process are identified and the relationships among them are described. Concepts derived from a scientific innovation known as the *systems approach* are used to design a model that shows how these basic components can be organized and managed in order to achieve a relatively stable counseling system.

INTRODUCTION

Organization

This chapter consists of four main sections. The first section describes the excitement and challenge provided by the counseling process and indicates why counselors must have an effective system to organize and guide their behavior. The second section consists of an introductory analysis of the basic components of the counseling process. This analysis is continued in the third section, where the sources and effects of errors that can occur during counseling are identified. In the final section, you will be introduced to the concepts of recycling and feedback. These concepts are used in the design of a counseling system to control for counseling error and to increase the probability of consistent and effective counseling outcomes.

Purposes

The major purpose of this chapter is to provide an introduction to some of the basic principles and concepts that form the foundations of Systematic Counseling.

Objectives

After studying this chapter you should be prepared to do the following:

1. State at least three reasons why counseling is a complex process.
2. State three advantages for having a counseling system.
3. Draw a diagram that shows the four basic components of the counseling process and their relationships.
4. Define the term *counseling error.*
5. Identify the sources of counseling error and give two examples of each.
6. Describe the effects of counseling error on (a) a counseling system and (b) counseling outcomes, and give two examples of each.
7. Define the terms *recycle* and *feedback.*
8. Draw a diagram that shows how the concepts of recycle and feedback can be used to attain consistent counseling outcomes.
9. State the reason why the model of Systematic Counseling was designed.
10. State the purpose for counseling.

WHY A COUNSELOR NEEDS A SYSTEM

We have found the work of the counselor to be tremendously exciting and challenging. Counseling is exciting because it provides us with the opportunity to have full-time careers which are focused on helping others. We find it to be emotionally and intellectually stimulating to assist someone to find a job, to make a decision, to locate valid information, to develop a set of values which make life more meaningful, to learn social behaviors that increase the quality of human relationships, to eliminate undesirable behaviors, or to resolve any of those thousand-and-one concerns that hinder people from leading more satisfying lives. In short, it is exhilarating to help people attain their personal goals through the counseling process.

Counseling is also exciting because this process involves highly personalized human relationships that are constantly changing and fluctuating from client to client. Those aspects of life which are the essence of our humanness are often intensely revealed to us during a counseling relationship. Love, loneliness, despair, happiness, confusion, fear, confidence, apathy, greed, survival, fantasy, passion, brutality, intelligence, ignorance, learning, and superstition—these are only a few of the human events which counselors are privileged to share with their clients.

Counseling is a challenge, not only because of the opportunity to assist someone to attain a personal goal, but also because it is a complex process. It is emotionally and intellectually demanding work that requires us to have a high degree of control over our own behavior, an extensive knowledge of human behavior, a sensitivity to human beings and their problems, and a large repertoire of technical skills. Moreover, not only must counselors perform many different functions, but they have to be able to carry out several functions simultaneously. For example, to develop and to maintain an effective, facilitative relationship with clients a counselor is required to attend to several functions concurrently. As Patterson (1969) points out, there are at least four conditions that must exist in order to have a good interpersonal relationship. A counselor must *actively* communicate by verbal and nonverbal behavior that one is listening to and understanding the client in an empathic sense, i.e., from the client's frame of reference. Concurrently, the counselor must demonstrate that the client is being received with nonpossessive warmth, i.e., "acceptance . . . as a person, regardless of behavior or other characteristics which may be unacceptable or unlikeable" (Patterson, 1969, p. 16). Throughout the counseling relationship, the counselor must also be genuine when interacting with the client, and he must also show a desire to work on a concrete level with the client's behavior and problems, i.e., to avoid ambiguity and abstractness in their relationship.

Along with providing the four conditions of a good interpersonal relationship a counselor must simultaneously perform even more functions. A counseling relationship does not develop in a vacuum or by engaging a client in irrelevant chit-chat. A counseling relationship is formed as the client and counselor work together toward developing a clear, concrete conceptual model of the client's behavior and problems. The counselor provides the conditions for an effective counseling relationship by obtaining information about the elements involved in the problem or problems that brought the client for counseling. This means that a counselor must listen carefully, sort through all of the verbal and nonverbal data given by the client, and relate these responses to his or her knowledge of human behavior—to a knowledge of human development, perception, learning, motivation, and personality. The counselor must also be alert to those environmental forces that influence a client's behavior such as the family, peer groups, and educational, economic, religious, and political institutions. At the same time, the cultural and subcultural mores and values held by the client must be understood and related to the client's problems and concerns. The counselor must also check out assumptions and hypotheses about the behavior of the client while developing a model that relates the important aspects of the client's behavior and environment to the problems at hand. Once the counselor and client can agree upon an adequate model, they can decide upon a goal and work to resolve or alleviate the problems or concerns.

This is an incomplete and overly simplified description of just a few of the many elements of human behavior and the counseling process to which the counselor must attend. However, even this brief description should convince you that counseling is a very intricate process. You may have asked yourself the question, "How does a counselor observe, remember, and synthesize the different messages communicated by the client and, at the same time, maintain those conditions of an effective counseling relationship that enables a client to trust and confide in the counselor?" The answer can be stated simply. The effective counselor has a *system* for organizing and guiding behavior while engaged in the counseling process.

A system of counseling can be thought of as a mental map or blueprint that a counselor consults while working with a client. The map or system enables the counselor to identify the different functions and stages of counseling, and to move from one stage to another as counseling progresses. The system then can provide a series of destinations or checkpoints so that one always knows where the counselor and the client are in the counseling process and where they must go if counseling is to be productive. The counselor does not have to devote an undue amount of attention to deciding on what the next steps in counseling should be. Instead, he or she can focus on the client's problems and behavior and on the relationship with the client. Thus, the counselor can assist a client to move systematically toward attaining the counseling goal.

All counselors have some type of counseling system to direct their counseling behavior. We have never encountered a counselor who did not have at least some general ideas about how counseling should be conducted. Currently, a wide variety of systems are in use by counselors. Some utilize a counseling system that is derived from a formal theory of counseling or personality. Others have an eclectic system based on components drawn from several theories or from their clinical experience. Some systems of counseling are based on scientifically derived principles of learning, while others are based upon "intuitive" systems which are dependent upon the hunches or subjective feelings of the counselor. Some of the systems used by counselors are quite complex with special vocabularies to describe the different stages and functions contained within the counseling process. Others are rather simple and naive, such as the system we call the "twenty questions" approach. The counselors who use this approach ask their clients a limited number of direct questions and then move to an advice-giving stage where they "tell" their clients how to solve their problems. Such a system has only two stages: (a) Ask questions, and (b) Give advice. Obviously, counselors who use such a system have a rather simplistic map to guide them as they work with the complexities of human behavior.

While all counselors use some type of counseling system, all counseling systems are not equally useful and effective in assisting individuals to solve their problems. In the next section, we will discuss the basic elements of the counseling process and how they are organized in order to have a viable model for counseling. The description of this model also contains several of the concepts that form the foundation of Systematic Counseling.

BASIC COMPONENTS OF THE COUNSELING PROCESS

The counseling process has four basic components. They consist of :

1. A counselor.
2. A client.
3. A counseling system.
4. The outcomes of the counseling system.

These components and the relationships that exist among them are shown graphically in Figure 1-1.

Two inputs into a counseling system are shown in Figure 1-1. These are the counselor and a client. The result of their interactions within the counseling system produces the outcomes of counseling.

Client Input

As a client, a person inputs or brings into the counseling system not only problems and concerns, but his or her entire *being*. This includes such qualities as physical health and appearance, genetic endowment, age, race, sex, socioeconomic status, prior learning history, motivational structure, environmental background, and a set of values which provides a host of opinions and attitudes about oneself and others. The particular way these characteristics and traits are organized and integrated makes the client an individual—a unique person. Thus, a counselor must be prepared to respond to the uniqueness of individuals.

Counselor Input

The counselor, too, brings personal problems and concerns, as well as a uniqueness as an individual. But the counselor also inputs certain skills, knowledge, and attitudes not usually possessed *in toto* by clients. One must be able to develop a sound human relationship with the client that is based on trust, understanding, and respect. This relationship must be established regardless of the client's behavior, attitudes, creeds, race, sex, or socioeconomic status.

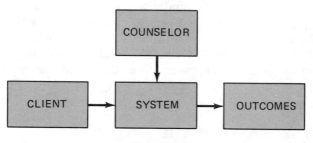

Figure 1-1.

The counselor must possess a self-awareness and self-discipline that permits control of his or her own needs and behavior while being empathic and objective about the needs of clients. A counselor also brings into a counseling system a knowledge of the psychological principles of human behavior, socioeconomic conditions, and a code of ethics established for the practice of counseling. In addition, one has the responsibility for being competent in the use of those tools, techniques, and strategies demanded by his or her system of counseling. These include such skills as observation, interviewing, testing, and the use of a variety of therapeutic techniques.

The Counseling System

The inputs made by a counselor and a client interact within the counseling system. The type of interaction that takes place depends upon the nature of the counseling system used by the counselor and the caliber of inputs made into this system by the counselor and client.

For example, a particular counseling system may not be appropriate for clients of a certain race or from a particular socioeconomic class. For other clients, the system may be adequate but one may not be able to control his or her own counseling behavior sufficiently to enable a client to move from one stage of counseling to another. The counselor may be "turned off" or "turned on" by a client and thus lose sight of professional responsibilities. A counselor may fail to make the type of inputs into the system that would make counseling a facilitative process.

The type of interaction that takes place within a counseling system also depends upon the input into the system made by the client. The client may not be sufficiently motivated to engage in those therapeutic tasks that are necessary for behavior change. Or, the client may be deceptive or dishonest in communications with a counselor. Some clients are "con" artists who attempt to use the counselor in order to manipulate some person such as a member of their family or a teacher. The client may also be "turned on" or "turned off" by cues in the counseling environment of which the counselor is not aware. These and numerous other client-inputs can hinder the work of the counselor when interacting with the client. We have found, however, that the great majority of client-inputs can be used to the advantage of the client if the counselor utilizes a counseling system that has the capability of providing guidelines for working with a wide range of clients, and if the counselor has the appropriate skills, knowledge, and attitudes to input into the counseling system. It is the primary responsibility of the counselor and not the client to provide the necessary conditions for effective human interaction.

Counseling Outcomes

The last basic component of the counseling process is the output or outcomes of the interaction between the counselor and client that have taken place within the counseling system used by the counselor. Any time counselor and client engage in the counseling process there is some kind of outcome as a product of their interaction. This is the "payoff" of the counseling process and the counselor's "moment of truth."

The outcomes of counseling can be positive or negative for the client. For the client who attains the goals established during counseling, the outcomes represent a rewarding experience. Perhaps the client has made a decision that will change some aspect of his or her life. The client may have obtained information that will help in getting a job. Or, perhaps the client has learned how to control fear of certain social situations. But, what about the client who experiences negative outcomes?

Actually we know very little about what happens to clients who experience detrimental effects from the counseling process. Such effects are rarely reported in the professional literature. We can infer, however, from our knowledge of human behavior some of the possible consequences when negative outcomes are produced. For some clients the counseling experience may represent one more failure in their attempts to solve personal or environmental problems. This may reinforce previously learned attitudes of inadequacy in terms of coping with the problems of living in our society. Such clients may leave the counseling experience feeling confused, depressed, or apathetic. Others may become angry and frustrated over their inability to obtain assistance in resolving their problems. They may engage in antisocial or unproductive behavior in order to relieve their feelings of hostility or frustration. It is also possible that counseling may produce outcomes that intensify the nature of the client's problems without providing the means for eliminating or decreasing the stimuli or responses that generated the problems. In other words, a client may terminate counseling and be more troubled, confused, or disorganized than before the process began. Rather than receiving help, the client may have only learned that the problems are more complex or severe than they had originally appeared to be.

Perhaps in our inferences about some of the possible consequences of negative counseling outcomes we have overly dramatized their effects. It may be that many clients merely accept such results without any adverse behavioral effects. Until more evidence becomes available, we believe that counselors should be constantly aware of the possible negative effects that can be produced by counseling. Furthermore, they should attempt to decrease the possibility of negative outcomes by understanding and controlling many of the elements that give rise to *error* during the counseling process.

SOURCES AND EFFECTS OF COUNSELING ERROR

Error, as we shall use this term, refers to the mistakes in perception, reasoning, memory, and behavior that are made by either the counselor or the client during the counseling process. Probably most of the errors of this type are made unintentionally. Regardless of the degree of deliberation, however, they tend to occur when one or both participants in counseling fail to give due regard to the consequences of their behavior, or are negligent of their personal responsibilities as a client or counselor. In addition, some counseling errors can only be attributed to ignorance and ineptness. These mistakes are usually so flagrant that they can be called blunders.

Obviously some misunderstandings, imprudent decisions, mental lapses, and inappropriate behaviors are relatively minor and only slightly hinder a client's progress during counseling. Such mistakes probably have only a small influence on the outcomes of counseling. However, major errors in perception, reasoning, memory, and behavior cause counselor-client interactions within the counseling system to be erratic and nonfacilitative. In other words, major counseling errors produce *instability* within the counseling system being used to guide the counselor's professional behavior. A system that is not or cannot be stabilized produces inconsistent counseling outcomes. Error, regardless of its source, makes it less likely that clients will attain positive benefits from counseling. Rather, it increases the probability of having clients experience negative outcomes.

The effects of counseling errors when they are left unrectified are shown schematically in Figure 1-2.

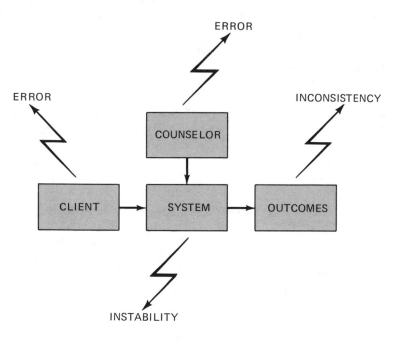

Figure 1-2.

Client Error

Perceptual error, erratic reasoning, forgetfulness, and contradictory behavior are to be expected of individuals who seek counseling. Anxiety, suspicion, hostility, excitement, passivity, or any number of other affective states may cause clients to think, feel, and respond in a defensive manner. Some clients may be quite unrealistic in their interpretation of the environment and their behavior. Others may be unable to communicate accurately their concerns and feelings. In other words, it is the rare client whose input into counseling is completely objective, logical, undistorted, and free of error.

Client error, then, is an integral and fixed part of the counseling process. In fact, without it counseling would be a rather simple procedure. Counselors would only have to be concerned with preventing their own mistakes and blunders. Thus, counseling becomes a more complex and demanding process when both client and counselor errors are introduced into the system.

Counselor Error

One major source of counselor error involves the counselor's failure to control his or her own personal behavior. For example, a counselor may establish an effective counseling relationship at the beginning of an interview, but then may neglect to maintain the same kind of relationship throughout the interview. Perhaps the language, physical appearance, or problem of the client are found to be objectionable. Regardless of the reason, this kind of error produces instability in a counseling system.

Instability is also generated when a counselor becomes overly involved emotionally in a counseling relationship and therefore fails to observe important relationships that exist in a client's behavior patterns. The counselor may, in some instances, over-identify with a client's point of view and lose some degree of objectivity. Emotional involvement may also cause a counselor to be dishonest in communications with a client.

Some counselors who lack self-discipline become moralistic when the values of their clients do not agree with their own. Others are so surprised or shocked by the behavior exhibited by some of their clients that they forget or neglect to use the counseling skills which they possess. Another common error of self-control occurs when counselors become so wrapped up in their own problems and concerns that they fail to observe the subtle cues being communicated by the verbal and nonverbal behavior of clients.

A second major cause of counselor error is unsystematic behavior. This refers to counselor behavior that is ambiguous, unorganized, and lacking in continuity. Such behavior is often demonstrated by counselors who are advocates of abstract, eccentric systems of counseling (intuitive systems, for example) that provide few guidelines for organizing and managing the counseling process. Such counselors are usually opposed to the concept of systematic counseling procedures for theoretical or philosophical reasons.

Most counselors use a system that provides specific guidelines for systematic counseling procedures. They may, however, forget or neglect to follow the methods prescribed by the system. For example, some counselors may be intimidated by certain types of clients or counseling problems and may perceive some clients as authority figures. If such clients are assertive in their social behavior, the counselor may ignore procedures for counseling and surrender the management of the counseling process to the client. Such clients could be influential people in the community or individuals who are considerably older than the counselor. They could be students whose parents occupy positions of power. They could be militants or members of powerful street gangs, or possess any of a number of individual or group identities that cause the counselor to abandon a systematic approach.

Clients who present sexual, drug, racial, and other similar problems may also intimidate some counselors. Such counselors may be so fearful of working with these problems that they neglect to use systematically the principles of counseling that they have learned.

Time pressure due to heavy caseloads is another reason why some counselors are inconsistent in their use of a system of counseling. They may rush to gather information about a problem without clearly identifying just what the problem is. In their hurry to move their clients through the counseling process, they neglect many important behavioral cues and have an incomplete understanding of the scope of a client's problem. The counselor may also yield to the temptation to advise or prescribe without knowing exactly what objectives the client wants to reach as a result of counseling.

Regardless of the reasons for unsystematic counselor performance, the consequences of being unsystematic are quite clear. These have been aptly summarized by Ford and Urban (1963, p. 27):

> If one does not have a systematic scheme, a series of problems follow. One does not know to which of a myriad of events one should attend. Without system there are no explicit criteria by which to determine what is relevant and what is irrelevant for one's purposes. The observations recorded will be related or unrelated in some unknown fashion. As a consequence, what one does is likely to be as unsystematic as the observations on which the action is based. Accurate generalization from occasion to occasion is highly unlikely, since there is no known order in the events from which the generalization is to be made.

Instability in the System

We have previously described how client and counselor error can produce instability in a counseling system. We will now examine some causes of instability that are the result of inadequate system design. Unfortunately, this type of instability is innate to the system and can only be corrected through revision or redesign of the counseling system.

You will remember that a system of counseling can be thought of as a blueprint or mental map that a counselor uses to organize and guide professional behavior during the counseling process. A system of counseling, then, to be useful in assisting clients from a broad, heterogeneous population, must comprehensively identify and describe the various functions to be performed by counselors and clients. In addition, the system must indicate the optimum sequence or stages in which these functions should be carried out. The design of a useful system, in other words, must include an adequate technology that specifically and parsimoniously points out what counseling functions should be performed, when and by whom they should be accomplished, and how well the functions must be carried out. Without the guidance and direction of a well-developed technology of counseling, a counseling system will be unstable. A counselor is forced to rely on trial-and-error procedures or chance to guide the management of the counseling process. In a sense, one must attempt to discover a new technology for each counseling session. Although at times a counselor may be successful, such procedures are inefficient, often insufficient, and usually unproductive.

The design of a system must also include a technology for controlling the errors that counselors and clients input into a counseling system. A counselor must be able to monitor continuously what is going on in the counseling process so that adjustments in the system can be made when there are breakdowns in relationships, communication, decision making, perception, or any of the other elements of the process. Criteria for effective counselor-client interactions and performance must be available to enable one to evaluate the performance of both the client and oneself during counseling interviews. Adjustments can then be made on the basis of the discrepancy between *actual* performance and the criteria that have been established for effective performance. If such a technology is not a part of the design of the system, a counselor has only intuition to rely on to keep the system stabilized and productive of positive counseling outcomes.

Inconsistent Counseling Outcomes

Counseling is often described as one of the *helping* professions. Our professional mission is to assist people to attain those personal goals which will result in positive changes in their lives. When we fail to help, inconsistent counseling outcomes are the result and the effects of our efforts do not coincide with our professional purpose and intentions.

The counselor, not the client, must bear the major responsbility for inconsistent outcomes. Clients do contribute error to the counseling process. They may make it difficult for counselors to establish effective interpersonal relationships. They may describe their problems in an ambiguous manner or refuse to communicate. They can be obstinate, seductive, or hostile. Regardless of the kind of client error, however, professional counselors (ideally, at least) are trained to be effective even when these conditions are present. We are expected by the public and our clients to know the limits of our competencies and to make appropriate referrals for those individuals whom we are unqualified to assist. It is assumed that professional counselors can establish effective personal and environmental conditions for counseling. Above all, we are expected to be skilled in the use of some systematic procedure or system that is useful in assisting a wide variety of clients to obtain the positive benefits offered by the counseling profession.

One of the most critical issues facing the counseling profession today is how to match the promises of counseling with the actual outcomes. How can counselors become more accountable to their clients and to the public? As a result of increased expectations from the people they serve, counselors are now beginning to look for ways to improve the effectiveness of their practice and to decrease the frequency of inconsistent counseling outcomes.

RECYCLING, FEEDBACK, AND CONSISTENT OUTCOMES

All counseling systems are designed to produce consistent outcomes. That is, ideally *all* clients should attain positive results from their counseling experience. The kinds of outcomes the counseling process should produce and the systems technology that is available to increase the frequency of such outcomes are shown schematically in Figure 1-3. Unfortunately, we have not arrived at a stage in the development of counseling psychology so that the attainment of this ideal goal is possible. It is possible, however, for a counselor to decrease the frequency of errors made in attempting to help clients. We do have the knowledge and technology to enable us to control for instability in a counseling system and to correct the errors we make as we interact with our clients. Counselors can significantly increase the number of clients who achieve positive outcomes by learning how to identify, avoid, and manage many of the sources of error and instability that occur during the counseling process.

A system and technology that can help you to become a counselor who can be of assistance to a significant number of your clients will be fully and specifically described in later chapters. Following is a broad perspective to introduce two significant concepts that, when properly used, can tremendously influence the consistency of counseling outcomes.

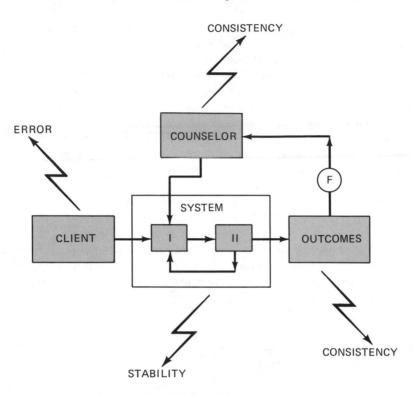

Figure 1-3.

The schema depicted in Figure 1-3 shows that client error is accepted as a fixed condition that will be demonstrated to some degree by all clients. It is to be expected that the problems and concerns experienced by individuals will create errors in perception, reasoning, memory, and behavior. Thus, a counselor must be prepared to use the counseling system to cope with the error.

The input from the counselor should be relatively consistent. The counselor has been trained or has learned from experience to control personal behavior so that his or her inputs into the system are consistent with professional purposes. In addition, the counselor can make use of two technical concepts to maintain system stability by preventing or correcting counseling errors. Refer to Figure 1-3 as we describe how these concepts are used.

Notice that the counseling system contains two small rectangles. Imagine that they represent the stages of counseling that make up this system. The relationships among the stages are shown by the arrows. The initial interactions between client and counselor take place within Stage I as each makes an input into the system. Assuming that counseling progresses beyond the first stage, interactions of a different type begin in Stage II. If error is recognized during Stage II, the counselor can *recycle* to Stage I and attempt to correct the error. The arrows from Stage II back to Stage I symbolize the recycle concept. For example, a counselor may discover during the second stage a misunderstanding of the nature of the client's problem which had been previously discussed in Stage I. It is therefore necessary to recycle or return in the system to a previous stage and the appropriate counseling functions in order to obtain more, or exact, information about the client's problem. Although not shown in this simple diagram, it should be pointed out that there can be several recycling loops both within and among the various stages and functions of the system.

The process of feedback is used to *control* or *stabilize* a system in order to obtain consistent outcomes. It is symbolized in Figure 1-3 by the arrows and lines that contain an encircled F. Feedback signals a need for change within a system. This concept should be easily understood if you consider the function of the thermostat that we use to control the temperature of our homes. This device can regulate the temperature of a residence by controlling the amount of heat produced by a furnace. The thermostat detects a drop in the temperature below a predetermined point and sends a signal to the furnace so that more heat is produced.

In Figure 1-3, information from counseling outcomes is fed back to the counselor. The counselor can use this information to compare outcomes with the criteria for acceptable system performance and output. If the outcomes are unacceptable, changes can be made in counselor behavior and/or the design of the counseling system in order to increase the consistency of the output of the system.

A counselor, for example, may find that some clients want to become more assertive in social situations but rarely achieve this objective. Recycling — repeating existing strategies—has not sufficiently improved counseling outcomes. After reviewing tapes of the interviews with such clients, the counselor may conclude that the strategies being utilized for helping clients become assertive are ineffective. One may, as a result, begin a search of the professional literature to learn of more appropriate ways to assist individuals with this type of problem. One may also decide to attend a workshop or class to obtain specific training in counseling unassertive clients. Or, a counselor may request instruction in the necessary skills from a qualified colleague.

Colleagues, supervisors, and other qualified members of the helping professions can, and should, be used by a counselor to evaluate the effectiveness of one's counseling practice. These individuals can often be more objective in comparing counseling outcomes with criteria for performance. They can also be a valuable resource for locating the source of error or instability and for suggesting preventive or remedial procedures.

Only one feedback loop is shown in Figure 1-3. Other feedback loops, however, could be a part of the design of a counseling system. As with recycling loops, they can be located within and among the various functions and stages of the system. It is possible to design a system so that there are controls over each step of the counseling process. Such a design is probably unwarranted, however, and would make counseling a very tedious and slow process. Therefore, feedback loops usually are placed only at critical points in the counseling process so the counselor can be informed about the adequacy of the outcomes of counseling.

The concepts of recycle and feedback occasionally become confused, since both are used to maintain the stability of a system. You should have no difficulty with these concepts if you remember that feedback signals a need for behavior or some function in a system to be *changed* if the system is to be stabilized. Nothing is changed when recycling occurs. Certain counseling functions or procedures are only *repeated* in order to gain additional information or to provide additional opportunities for a client to learn certain behaviors.

Systematic Counseling was designed to provide a model of the counseling process that, when used appropriately, will increase the consistency of counseling outcomes. It is an approach in which the various aspects of the counseling process are clearly identified and organized into an optimal sequence designed to resolve a client's concerns efficiently as well as effectively. It incorporates the concepts of recycle and feedback for controlling counseling errors, as well as a number of other concepts which have been generated by a remarkable innovation that has come to be known as the *systems approach.* The events and developments which led to the conceptualization of the systems approach will be discussed in the chapter to follow. In addition, the developments and rationale which led to the design of the model of Systematic Counseling will be presented. Then, beginning with chapter 4, the model, procedures, and technology of Systematic Counseling will be described in detail. As you become proficient in using the procedures and technology of Systematic Counseling, we believe that you will also find counseling to be tremendously exciting and challenging. In addition, you will be making an important contribution to our society as you help individuals attain outcomes that are consistent with their desires and the promises of the counseling profession.

SUMMARY

The purpose of counseling is to help individuals attain those personal goals which will result in positive changes in their lives. The counselor who consistently helps people to reach such goals recognizes that the task is complex. The counselor knows that, to be effective, he or she must observe, remember, and synthesize the various messages communicated by a client and, at the same time, maintain those conditions of a facilitative relationship that enable an individual to trust and confide in a counselor. The counselor also understands that the complexities of human behavior and the counseling process require the use of an *effective counseling system* to organize and guide one's behavior while counseling.

A counseling system can be thought of as a mental map or blueprint that enables a counselor to identify the different functions and stages of counseling and to assist a client to move from one stage to another as counseling progresses. A viable counseling system, then, must include a technology that specifically and parsimoniously describes what counseling functions should be performed, when and by whom they should be accomplished, and how well the functions must be carried out. In addition, the system must include a technology for controlling the errors made by a counselor or client so that the system remains in a stabilized condition that is capable of producing positive counseling outcomes.

In this chapter, diagrams were used to describe how the basic components of the counseling process can be organized and managed to achieve a relatively stable system. The concepts of recycling and feedback are basic to such a design of the counseling process. While both of these concepts are used to prevent or correct for instability within a system, each has a different function. Recycling involves the repetition of counseling functions in order to correct for counseling errors. Feedback signals a need for changing behavior or redesigning the functions performed by the client or counselor so that mistakes made during counseling are either corrected or prevented. These and other concepts to be described in future chapters were developed as a result of a scientific innovation known as the systems approach. They serve as the theoretical and technological basis for Systematic Counseling.

2
Philosophical Foundations of Systematic Counseling

OVERVIEW

Systematic Counseling is based on a relatively recent scientific innovation known as the systems approach. This approach can be generally described as a process for designing and testing conceptual models or systems. A basic tenet of the process is that problems and events should be conceptualized as wholes (systems) which function as a result of the organization and interrelations of the various parts which make up a whole. A system can be analyzed to identify the parts of a system and to determine how these parts are related to one another and to the system itself. A system can also be created by using the process of synthesis to identify and relate parts to one another in such a way as to form a new whole. These are some of the concepts and processes which were used in developing the model of counseling discussed in this book. An explanation of these concepts is given in this chapter. The primary focus of the chapter, however, is on the philosophical assumptions which underlie Systematic Counseling.

INTRODUCTION

Organization

A model of the counseling process based on the concepts and methodology of the systems approach is a recent innovation in the counseling profession. This chapter provides an introduction to the concepts, terminology, and basic assumptions associated with the systems approach and describes how and why this schema was used in developing Systematic Counseling.

The chapter has two main sections. The concept of a system is defined in the first section. The second section describes the concepts, values, and assumptions which form the rationale for Systematic Counseling.

Purpose

The main purpose of this chapter is to explain the theoretical and philosophical foundations on which Systematic Counseling is based.

Objectives

Upon completing this chapter it is expected that you will be prepared to do the following:

1. Identify three ways in which the definitions of a system presented in this chapter are similar to each other.
2. State the definition of a system that is considered a benchmark of Systematic Counseling.
3. List the seven criteria used by the authors of this book in identifying an appropriate model of the counseling process.
4. State five reasons why a systems approach was used in designing and testing the model of Systematic Counseling.
5. Explain why Systematic Counseling represents a synthesis of the scientific and humanistic points of view.
6. Describe how the graphic analog or flowchart for Systematic Counseling can help increase a counselor's accountability to clients.

SOME DEFINITIONS OF SYSTEM

Systems approach, systems engineering, systems research, operations research, and systems analysis are descriptors currently being used to identify a scientific innovation that has led to what has been called the "new technology" and the "Second Industrial Revolution" (Bertalanffy, 1968, p. 4). Since World War II, this remarkable innovation has been extensively used in the design, operations, decision making, and evaluation functions of business, industry, and government. It has provided a new conceptual framework for research and theorizing in many of the basic and applied sciences. Yet, even though the systems approach[1] has had a significant impact upon the thinking of many leaders in science, technology, and management, it is relatively unknown to those who work in the applied behavioral sciences. We believe this to be especially true

---

[1]We will use *systems approach* as a generic term to include the various descriptors that identify the systems concept.

for practitioners of counseling. It seems, therefore, appropriate at this point to define the concepts of a system and introduce you to some of the basic terminology and symbols used in systems thinking. Some of the philosophical assumptions underlying the systems approach and Systematic Counseling will become apparent as you study the fundamentals of this new approach which holds great promise for advancing our knowledge of counseling and other behavioral sciences. Since our discussion here will be limited to selected definitions, concepts, and events associated with systems theory and methodology, you are urged to consult the references section of this book for a more complete exposition of the subject.

The word *system* is most likely familiar to you as it is to most Americans. However, this familiarity may in itself create some difficulty in understanding the technical and scientific meaning of the systems approach since the word may appear trite and its descriptive power may have become diffused.

"System" attained almost instant popularity in the speech of the American public. The mass media made it possible for millions to be repeatedly thrilled by the words, "All systems are go!" as astronauts achieved the objectives of the Mercury, Gemini, Apollo, and Apollo-Soyuz space programs. The expression was associated with technological success. The rhythm and conciseness of the sentence were appealing and so, "All systems are go!" took its place among the many other clichés used by Americans to sterotype behavior and events.

Not only has system become a hackneyed word through its popularization, but it has tended to become a symbol that elicits emotional responses along a pleasure-displeasure continuum. We know, for example, a number of music lovers who view their stereo systems with unabashed pleasure. True stereo buffs can talk enthusiastically for hours about how they have organized turntables, amplifiers, speakers, and other assorted electronic gear into systems that produce the ultimate in sound. Then there are those proud alumni who talk happily about the merits of the educational systems which they attended, or the gambling afficionados who delight in explaining their systems for breaking the bank at Las Vegas.

On the other hand, system has become a synonym for "establishment" for many individuals. Powerful negative emotions are expressed when system is identified with the civil, military, political, religious, and industrial establishments of this country. "The system must be destroyed through revolution!" "The system must be changed!" "We have to work within the system!" Expressions such as these cause the word system to be linked with certain philosophical positions and it becomes a shibboleth. It symbolizes for some members of our society the impersonal and dehumanizing aspects of our world.

Let us now turn to some recent definitions of a system that will add a new and more precise dimension to the term. As you might expect, a number of definitions have been authored and these reflect the professional or academic interests of the authors. We have purposefully selected the definitions presented below to demonstrate the wide range of interest in the systems approach. They will serve not only to help you acquire an understanding of the specialized meanings of the word "system," but will also show a convergence of ideas from a number of different disciplines toward the systems concept. The following definitions represent the thinking of scientists who have specialized in management science, systems engineering, sociology, psychology, and education.

A system is an organized or complex whole; an assemblage or combination of things or parts forming a complex or unitary whole (Johnson, Kast, & Rosenzweig, 1963, p. 4).

A system is an integrated assembly of interacting elements, designed to carry out cooperatively a predetermined function (Gibson, 1960, p. 58).

A system is a collection of entities or things (animate or inanimate) which receives certain inputs and is constrained to act concertedly upon them to produce certain outputs, with the objective of maximizing some function of the inputs and outputs (Kershner, 1960, p. 141).

The kind of system we are interested in may be described generally as a complex of elements or components directly or indirectly related in a causal network, such that each component is related to at least some of the others in a more or less stable way within any particular period of time (Buckley, 1967, p. 41).

A system is an assembly of components that perform together in an organized manner (Rabow, 1969, p. 2).

A whole which functions as a whole by virtue of the interdependence of its parts is called a system (Rapoport, 1968, p. xvii).

A system is a set of objects together with relationships between the objects and between their attributes. Objects are simply the parts or components of a system, and these parts are unlimited in variety. Attributes are properties of objects. The relationships . . . are those that "tie the system together" (Hall & Fagen, 1968, pp. 81-82).

An organized assemblage of interrelated components designed to function as a whole to achieve a predetermined objective (American Association of School Administrators Commission on Administrative Technology, 1969, p. 171).

The word "systems" connotes the whole, the combination of many parts, a grouping of men and machines, the assembling together of components or subsystems to accomplish a task (Ramo, 1969, p. 12).

You will note that even though they were written by scientists from several disciplines and for different purposes, there are some remarkable similarities among these definitions. First, there seems to be general agreement that a system is always a *whole* (assembly, collection, network, set). This indicates that a system is always some unity with specific boundaries. It is a totality. Even though a system may be very complex, as with the human body or a metropolitan city, it can still be perceived and conceptualized as a single, specific configuration. Second, the *whole* is always defined as being composed of *parts* (components, objects, things, elements) that are related to and interacting with one another. This points out that the parts of a system are organized in some manner. They are not merely arranged in some random or haphazard order. There is some logical design, an *organization* of relationships among the parts and the whole. Third, several of the definitions indicate that the purpose of a system is to accomplish a task or reach an objective. This means that some degree of *stability* or *order* must exist within the system if it is to serve its purpose. There must be some means for *controlling* the different functions that operate within a system so that the performance of the system is relatively consistent. Otherwise, as is sometimes the case, the system will be undependable or erratic. For example, you may have on occasion ignored those signals from your nervous system that serve to control your bodily functions. To your distress, you may have found after overeating or excessive drinking that your performance was very inconsistent or erratic for the next several hours or even days.

Some systems do outlive the purposes for which they were designed. In some instances obsolete systems are supported and maintained by the societal forces of tradition, ritual, tribalism, and vested interests. While it is possible to design a self-destruct component into a system, the same societal forces mentioned above would negate the practical value of such a function in most systems.

A more concrete illustration of the common elements or similarities that exist among the different definitions of a system may be seen by examining Figure 2-1. This model of the counseling process represents a *whole*, with the boundaries of the whole being clearly shown. Within the whole, the different *parts* of the system are identified and *related* in an *organized* manner. Symbolically, the arrows ($\rightarrow$) represent the relationships among the parts of the counseling process. *Control* within the system is represented by the symbol F for feedback. The model shows that information from the evaluation of counselor performance is fed back to the counselor so that, when necessary, the counselor can change or alter the appropriate parts of the counseling process to stabilize the system and thereby obtain a more consistent output from the counseling process.

The definition of a system that we will use for purposes of this book incorporates the elements found to be common among the several definitions of a system that we have considered. The definition was conceived by Silvern (1965) who describes a system in this way:

> A system . . . is the structure or organization of an orderly whole, clearly showing the interrelations of the parts to each other and to the whole itself (Silvern, 1965, p. 1).

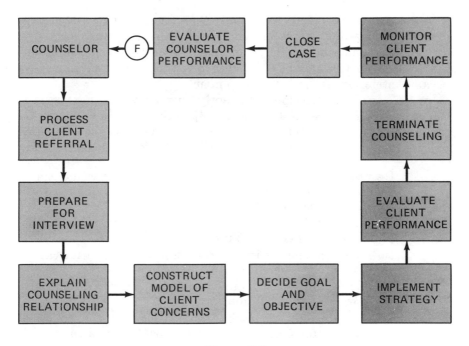

Figure 2-1

We selected this definition of a system as one of the principal benchmarks of Systematic Counseling, not only for its inclusion of the essential elements of other definitions, but also for its simplicity and utility. Silvern, through a rigorous choice of words, has concisely and clearly explained the concept of a system without using the technical jargon that appears in several of the other definitions. Furthermore, his definition has the property of universality. It is not a definition that is restricted to one discipline, profession, or purpose. It can be used to describe physical, biological, social, and psychological systems as separate entities or as parts of some greater whole or suprasystem. Its scope is broad enough to include human, machine, and interactive (human-machine) systems. In other words, Silvern's definition provides the utmost flexibility in describing the concept of a system while clearly circumscribing the boundaries of the concept. It is this characteristic of his definition that permits the generalization of the systems approach to a vast field of endeavors including the behavioral sciences and counseling.

SYSTEMS APPROACH TO COUNSELING

In this section we will set forth our reasons for selecting a systems approach to counseling. We will attempt to do this by stating our values, assumptions, and schemas for counseling as succinctly and honestly as possible, but first, it may be of interest to you to learn how and why we became interested in the systems approach.

In 1967, we had become sufficiently dissatisfied with our basic counselor training program to make a major effort toward seeking ways to make improvements. We began a search for a model of the counseling process that could meet several criteria. The model we sought would:

1. Be a tangible map of the counseling process that would enable counselor trainees to efficiently and effectively learn an appropriate framework for counseling,
2. Be applicable both as a training model and as a model for the practicing, professional counselor,
3. Be appropriate for use in providing assistance for a wide variety of clients from different environmental backgrounds,
4. Be appropriate for use in providing assistance with an extensive range of concerns and problems,
5. Provide both the counseling supervisor and the counselor trainee with unambiguous criteria for evaluating a counselor's performance,
6. Provide a method for objectively assessing the outcomes of counseling, and
7. Provide the means for clear and unambiguous communication between counselor trainees and counselor trainers.

We were unable to locate an existing model that satisfied all or even most of these criteria and so began a search for the appropriate tools and skills for designing a model that could meet these criteria.

The systems approach was first drawn to our attention by reports of the successful application of this method in science, business, and government. (We will discuss some of these applications in Chapter 3.) After considerable study of systems theory and the methods of systems analysis used by people from several disciplines including sociology, political science, psychiatry, and psychology, we concluded that this approach hold the potential for providing the type of counseling model that we desired.

A Methodology

One of the primary reasons we selected the scientific approach to systems is that it provides the best methodology currently available for designing and testing a model for counseling. The model of Systematic Counseling was developed by using a specific method of deductive reasoning (described by Silvern, 1965). The counseling literature and our own experiences as counselors were analyzed to determine the functions and components of the counseling process. We then used a specific method of inductive reasoning (Silvern, 1965) to synthesize these functions and components as described by a graphic analog or flowchart model. This model was tested in the laboratory using simulation techniques and then field tested over a period of seven years by counselor trainees in real-life counseling sessions. Design errors were observed and feedback for revising the model was received from counselor trainees and their supervisors. These operations were recycled until a high-fidelity model was obtained that could be used effectively and consistently by counselors to assist clients from the real-life environment. Approximately 700 counselor trainees and 50 different supervisors participated in the field-test operations.

Conceptualizing a Whole

Humanists, being advocates of a holistic point of view, have criticized scientific psychologists for having an atomistic approach to the study of people. Humanists believe that a person should be studied as a "whole" rather than in small units such as reflexes or sensory stimuli. We support this belief. A model developed with a systems approach shows clearly the relationship of the parts of the model to one another and to the whole model itself. This permits the scientist to study an individual component of a model while maintaining a clear perspective of the relationships that exist between the component and other parts of the model. This can be done without losing sight of how the component relates to the entire model.

Being able to maintain a holistic perspective of a model and its parts enables a designer to modify, add, or delete various parts of the model to bring about a more effective design. This also makes it possible to update and upgrade the model as new knowledge, feedback, and innovations in counseling are generated. For example, it has been demonstrated (Super, 1970) that computers can assist clients to make vocational decisions, and to explore educational and career opportunities by providing vocational information. A model based on a systems approach allows a designer to display how and where such a counseling technology would relate to different parts of the counseling process as well as to the whole model itself.

As Rapoport (1968, p. xxi) has pointed out, the modern systems point of view shows "promise of reestablishing holistic approaches to knowledge without abandoning scientific rigor." Thus, the systems approach offers the possibility of bringing the humanistic and scientific branches of applied psychology closer to each other.

A Technology

Counseling is an applied behavioral science. This means that the practice of counseling involves the application of scientific knowledge, i.e., *a technology*, of human behavior by a counselor or counselor substitute (as in computer-assisted counseling) or by both, to the practical purpose of assisting one or more people with their concerns.

The term "technology" is rarely found in the literature of counseling, even though the bulk of the writings of counseling theorists and trainers is devoted to describing the style or method a counselor will use in applying certain concepts, techniques, and procedures when working with clients. For example, Kemp (1971, p. 8), when describing the basic concepts of existential counseling, is really discussing a technology of counseling in part when he states: "To know the counselee is to relate to him in his totality, to grasp his being." Or, when Patterson (1969, p. 20) writes that "counseling or psychotherapy is a method of behavior change in which the core conditions (or the relationship) are the sufficient conditions for change to occur," he is describing a technology of counseling based completely on the ability of a counselor to provide clients with empathic understanding, nonpossessive warmth, genuineness, and concreteness or specificity.

Counselors have long known that the success of their practice and their reputations for being able to change behavior depends upon having an adequate technology for dispensing and prescribing assistance. Since the dawn of civilization the tribal or community priest, witch doctor, shaman, or sorcerer has developed elaborate technologies for providing "assistance" to clients. Verbal incantations, symbols, mystical objects and signs, magical practices, and rituals have all been used to make their treatments acceptable and relevant to people who came to them for help. Grotesque masks and clothing, ceremonial dances, and exorcism of demons and evil spirits were all useful tools and part of their technology of clinical practice. Some of these ancient technologies, in perhaps a more sophisticated form, are still being advocated by some of the more "mystically" oriented counseling theorists.

The technologies of counseling range from those that depend primarily on the presence and verbalizations of a counselor to complex procedures that utilize laboratory-derived principles of behavior. In addition, there is a technology developed by advocates of a nontechnology. Apparently a large number of counselors and psychologists of the humanistic school are theoretically and philosophically opposed to the application of any form of a technology of human behavior. It was to such individuals that Kelly (1969), who was himself a humanist, appealed when he asked that they not abandon technology. He writes that a technology for humanistic psychology is required if humanism is to realize its objectives and avoid turning into classicism. His appeal is summed up by the following words:

> Humanistic psychology needs a technology through which to express its humane intentions. Humanity needs to be implemented, not characterized and eulogized merely (p. 55).

A systems approach to counseling, as expressed in Systematic Counseling, provides a technology in the form of a flowchart model that indicates a basic and optimal sequence of functions and operations that the counselor should perform. A simple, direct, and easily learned language is used to guide the counselor and client through the counseling process. In addition, when the counseling process is considered in holistic terms, the model of Systematic Counseling provides an umbrella under which any prior technology of merit, or any which may be produced in the future, can be incorporated and used as needed.

The technology for the systems approach to counseling which we have utilized relies heavily on scientific psychology, i.e., on research that has been replicated and verified. Specifically, we advocate the use of a technology based on those principles of learning which have been operationally defined and empirically validated. We do not know of any reputable counseling theorist today who would state that learning is not a central element of the counseling process. Until recently, however, few theorists had bothered to do more than just acknowledge counseling to be a learning process. Most have avoided an in-depth discussion of learning other than to state that when counseling is successful, clients will obtain "insight" about themselves and the nature of their problems. The available scientific data in the area of learning generally have been disregarded.

Currently there are a number of principles of learning, as we will point out in the chapters to follow, that have been validated through research in the scientific laboratory and in experimentally controlled studies of counseling and therapy. This is not an issue among psychologists. For example, Bugental (1967), a humanist and antibehavioralist, acknowledges that scientific psychology has clearly shown that certain principles of human learning can be effectively demonstrated. His principal objection is that these principles will be used to control and dehumanize members of our society.

We share the concern of Bugental. Obviously, any technology of counseling can be misused, just as any tool or concept invented by people can be used to their detriment. London (1969) has shown how *all* forms of counseling and psychotherapy are used in attempts to control human behavior. Indeed, counselors, therapists, social workers, and others who attempt to assist people with their problems *cannot* avoid the problem of controlling behavior.

In the hands of unscrupulous or unethical counselors, a technology based on scientific principles of learning, just as any other counseling technology, can be employed in ways which are inappropriate and harmful to clients. It also seems likely that some counselors may misuse principles of learning because they are unaware of how learning occurs or do not consider the effects that learning can produce. This could be due to a lack of training or because they hold certain philosophical convictions. However, these are ethical matters for which appropriate guidelines and the means for policing the practice of counselors and therapists should be, and are, established by professional associations and governmental agencies.

While acknowledging the potential dangers involved when any counseling technology is employed, we think it is important to stress the positive benefits which can accrue to clients when scientific principles of behavior are used ethically and systematically to prevent and remedy their concerns and problems. We advocate that a holistic viewpoint be taken with regard to when and how technologies for changing human behavior are to be utilized. The "whole" of the problem and its various interrelated parts should be considered. Research should be undertaken to determine if certain technologies of counseling and therapy *do* produce dehumanizing effects when applied in an ethical and responsible manner. If they do, the question should be investigated as to whether these effects apply to all segments of our population or to only certain groups of individuals. In addition, we believe that equal consideration should be given to the potential harm or dehumanization that can occur when scientific principles of behavior *are not used* because of some ideological preference or naiveté on the part of the counselor. In short, while there has been a great outpouring of rhetoric of an emotional and philosophical nature from rather limited or prejudicial perspectives, there has been little research conducted to provide factual data about the dehumanizing or humanizing effects of counseling technologies.

Behavioral Humanism

Thoresen (1971) has proposed that the counseling profession become engaged in efforts to synthesize behavioral theory and technques with humanistic goals and concerns. Under the rubric of behavioral humanism, he urges that the literary and philosophical concepts of humanism be translated into behavioral terms or human response categories. We have found that a systems approach to counseling with its holistic emphasis makes it possible, in fact mandatory, to bring about such a synthesis.

Later in this book, as you study Systematic Counseling, you will learn how to translate abstract, humanistic concepts into behavioral terms. At this point, through the use of examples, we will only demonstrate the importance of operationally defining such concepts. Suppose a client comes to you and states a desire to become more self-actualizing. Obviously, self-actualization can be defined in an infinite number of ways. The counselor cannot assume that all clients possess a common definition of self-actualization. Therefore an important, and we believe humane, function that a counselor must perform is to assist the client to arrive at an idiosyncratic and behavioral definition of self-actualization. For one client, self-actualization may mean locating a job that provides sufficient monetary rewards so that one can spend weekends water-skiing and fishing at a lake 200 miles from home. For another client, to become self-actualized may involve decreasing the frequency of cynical or satirical remarks made to individuals at social events—remarks which in return cause people to ignore the client. For a woman, self-actualization may involve divorce from a husband who prevents her from having certain friends. A member of a minority race may define self-actualization as being able to purchase a home anywhere one chooses.

Most, if not all, of the humanistic concepts such as love, warmth, autonomy, freedom, responsibility, and authenticity, are amenable to operational definitions of an idiosyncratic nature. Thus, the concepts valued by humanists as descriptors of the subjective, covert experiences of the individual person can be incorporated into a systems approach to counseling.

Accountability

When one agrees to work with a client toward the resolution of a problem, a counselor automatically becomes *accountable* to that client. This means that the counselor assumes certain ethical and professional responsibilities. The counselor should be able to produce data in such a form that the client can objectively evaluate the outcomes of counseling and the services which the counselor has provided. In a broader sense, counselors are also accountable to their employers—schools, colleges, or agencies—and the general public for the manner in which they discharge their responsibilities.

Likewise, counselor educators engaged in the professional preparation of counselors are accountable to their trainees, to the employers of counselors, and to the general public. They are responsible for producing counselors who, in measurable terms, can demonstrate that they possess certain counseling skills and can perform the functions required by the counseling process. Hence, the ultimate responsibility for accountability rests with counselor educators who select, train, and endorse their graduates to the public.

A systems approach, by definition, provides the means for counselor educators and counselors to be accountable to their publics. A system was previously defined as " . . . the structure or organization of an orderly whole, clearly showing the interrelations of the parts to each other and to the whole itself (Silvern, 1965, p. 1)." Using this definition the organization of the system for attaining a specific goal must be clearly communicated to the users of the system. Not only must the separate functions and operations performed within the system be clearly shown, but the interrelationships between functions and the system itself must be described in unambiguous terms. Clear and unambiguous communication is a prerequisite for any system that is designed to enable users of the system to be accountable to themselves and others.

This is achieved in the model of *Systematic Counseling* by the use of a graphic analog or flowchart to depict the counseling process. The flowchart model (see Figure 1-1 for a simple example) represents an improvement in communication over the purely narrative models such as those represented by verbal monographs or books. Communication is greatly enhanced when human actions, decisions, and information processing are shown in graphic form and described in a relatively simple language derived from a combinations of words, numbers, and symbols. The use of this type of model is a first step toward increased accountability, as it permits counselor educators and counselors to communicate with their publics in a direct and simple manner without resorting to a complex jargon or secret vocabulary which is open to myriad interpretations.

Since the model of Systematic Counseling is presented in a concrete, tangible form, it is available for visual study and inspection. *Nothing is hidden.* The weaknesses as well as the strengths of the model can be easily perceived and criticized. It can also serve as a standard or criterion against which other models of the counseling process can be compared.

Consumers, whether they be clients or counselor trainees, have a discernible model which can be used as a means for pointing out any discrepancies between what is promised and what is actually delivered by counselors and counselor educators.

In future chapters we will discuss several functions included in the model of Systematic Counseling that *require* a counselor to be accountable to clients. These include: (a) the stating of a client's objectives for counseling in behavioral and measurable terms, (b) an evaluation of a client's performance as one attempts to attain stated objectives, and (c) the use of performance criteria developed for the model of Systematic Counseling to evaluate how well a counselor carries out counseling responsbilities.

MODELS AND MUSIC: A SUMMARY

In this section, we have stated our reasons for selecting a systems approach to counseling. We know that these reasons alone do not constitute a convincing argument for all professional counselors and counselor trainees. Some, after acknowledging the validity of these reasons, are still critical of the model. This criticism seems to focus on what they describe as the cold, mechanical nature of the flowchart for Systematic Counseling. For these individuals, the act of describing the counseling process in numbers, symbols, and words on a single sheet of paper appears to downgrade the human elements of counseling.

We want to emphasize that the flowchart model *is* a cold, inanimate object and the functions depicted in the model can be performed by a counselor in a mechanical, artificial manner. To use the flowchart effectively, a counselor is needed who also is skillful in: (a) making clients feel accepted as people of worth and dignity, (b) helping clients to feel that they are being understood by an empathic individual, and (c) being sensitive to the wide variety of ways that clients express their needs and concerns.

An analogy may also help. A sheet of music is a cold, inanimate object or model that contains only lines and music notation. This sheet of music can be used by a skillful musician to produce beautiful sounds for our enjoyment. One could, of course, play an instrument or sing in a very mechanical way. In fact, musicians usually do perform in a mechanical fashion until they have received sufficient training and practice. We hope that this analogy helps you to understand the purpose for the flowchart. We also hope that you will learn to use it in a skillful manner so that you can provide your clients with effective and accountable counseling services.

3

Historical Foundations
of Systematic Counseling

OVERVIEW

Since the systems approach is a recent and relatively unknown innovation in the behavioral sciences, we think it is important to provide you with information about the historical foundations of Systematic Counseling. A few of the major events and people who played a part in the development of the systems approach are described in this chapter. The information contained in the previous chapter and this one should provide you with an adequate understanding of the philosophical and historical foundations of Systematic Counseling. This knowledge will also assist you to use the model of Systematic Counseling more effectively.

INTRODUCTION

Organization

This chapter consists of two major sections. A general discussion of some of the major historical developments of the scientific systems approach is presented in the first section. The influence that this approach is having on several disciplines is also emphasized. The second section describes the brief history of the application of the systems approach to problems presented by counseling and guidance services.

Purpose

The major purpose of this chapter is to provide the historical foundations and context of Systematic Counseling.

Objectives

After studying this chapter you should be prepared to do the following:

1. State the purpose of general systems theory.
2. Name two important functions served by general systems theory.
3. Name at least three disciplines in which developmental work in general systems theory has been done.
4. State the functions of an operations research team.
5. Describe at least two specific situations in which operations research has been conducted.
6. Name the three events which occurred between 1946 and 1950 that enabled scientists to conceptualize a systems approach to their work.
7. Explain the importance of SAGE and the early NASA projects such as Explorer I and Mercury in the development of systems engineering.
8. Name the person who apparently was the first to describe the use of the systems approach in counseling and state why he and his associates were preoccupied with man-machine systems.
9. List at least five uses of the systems approach in guidance and counseling that do not necessarily include man-machine systems.

THE DEVELOPMENT OF THE SYSTEMS APPROACH

The history of the systems approach, although brief in terms of time span, is complicated to trace because of the vast number of related theories, models, and projects generated by this approach in a host of disciplines and technical fields. The explosion of knowledge in this area has been so great that several volumes would be needed to adequately trace all of the developments. Therefore, we have arbitrarily concentrated on three areas in order to provide a brief overview of the evolution of the systems approach. These are:

1. General systems theory
2. Operations research
3. Systems engineering

The systems approach, as it is known today, has been shaped by the developments in each of these areas. Concepts from each have been influential in the development and design of Systematic Counseling.

General Systems Theory

Bertalanffy, a biologist, is usually credited (DeGreene, 1970, p. 14; Khailov, 1968, p. 47; Kremyanskiy, 1968, p. 77) with introducing the idea of general systems theory in 1937. He noted the structural similarity of mathematical expressions and models used in biological, behavioral, and social sciences (Bertalanffy, 1968, p. 13). He felt that these similarities or isomorphisms were being ignored by science. Furthermore, he believed it was possible to develop a higher generality for science (a general theory) from these similarities which could serve as a foundation for the specific theories already developed by the various branches of science. General systems theory would thus, ideally, bring about the eventual unification of the various sciences.

The purpose of general systems theory, then, is to identify the common ways in which the components of different systems are organized or inter-related. Principles or concepts that apply in a universal way to several specific theories could then be investigated. Such a general theory would, of course, enhance communication across the various sciences and provide a holistic rather than a reductionistic approach to scientific knowledge. This purpose is concisely expressed in the following description of the major functions of the Society for General Systems Research.

> Major functions are to: (1) investigate the isomorphy of concepts, laws, and models in various fields, and to help in useful transfers from one field to another; (2) encourage the development of adequate theoretical models in the fields which lack them; (3) minimize the duplication of theoretical effort in different fields; (4) promote the unity of science through improving communication among specialists (Bertalanffy, 1968, p. 15).

The requirements that a general theory of systems should satisfy have been pointed out by Mesarović. These are:

1. The general theory should be general enough to encompass different types of already existing specific theories. It should, therefore, be sufficiently abstract so that its terms and concepts are relevant to specialized theories. Clearly, the more abstract statements have a broader content but, at the same time, they carry less information regarding the behavior of any particular system. The general concepts must emphasize the common features of all the systems considered yet neglect the specific aspects of the behavior of any particular system. The real challenge in developing a general theory is, therefore, to find the proper level of abstraction. The concepts must have wide application, while the conclusions which they lead to must

provide sufficient information for proper understanding of the particular class of phenomena under consideration.

2. The general theory has to have a scientific character in the sense that its concepts and terms must be uniquely defined within the proper context. If the general theory is to be of any help in solving scientific and engineering problems, it must not rely on vague, ill-defined, almost poetic analogies. The basis for the general theory must be solid so that its conclusions have practical meaning for real systems. . . .(1964, p. 3)

Mesarović's statements suggest that a general systems theory would serve an integrative function for the amalgamation of the concepts and research of several theories which fall within a given class of phenomena. The need for such an overarching general theory has been discussed by Rapoport (1968, p. xxi), who points out how the trend toward narrow specialization in science has posed a threat of an "avalanche of 'findings' which in their totality no more adds up to knowledge, let alone wisdom, than a pile of bricks adds up to a cathedral."

Any serious student of psychology realizes the appropriateness of Rapoport's comment when he attempts to read and synthesize the voluminous amount of literature produced by this one discipline. The applied behavioral scientist, and especially the practitioner, desperately needs a general theory of human behavior which has the capability for organizing and relating current and future knowledge within an overall framework. A general systems theory of human behavior could serve to integrate and synthesize the knowledge produced by the disciplines of anthropology, economics, history, human ecology, human physiology, philosophy, psychology, and sociology. At the present time it is impossible for a counselor, as one practitioner of an applied behavioral science, to utilize all of the potentially useful information from these disciplines in attempting to understand and assist clients.

In addition to amalgamating the knowledge from various disciplines, a general systems theory would also serve an equally important heuristic function. Certainly, as data are organized and related during the process of synthesis, new relationships and understandings of a particular phenomenon often become apparent. For example, Charles Darwin formulated his theory of organic evolution after five years of study and observation during his famous voyage aboard the *Beagle*. Darwin apparently noticed similarities and relationships during his observations of natural phenomena that led him to conceive of a theory of natural selection. This theory continues to serve as a catalyst for advancing our knowledge of people and nature in a number of different disciplines. General systems theory, in a similar but more encompassing manner, could serve as a heuristic stimulus for further development of scientific thought, more effective methods of investigation, and improved understanding of people and their environment.

As several writers have indicated (Bertalanffy, 1969, p. 36; Gray and Rizzo, 1969, p. 26; and DeGreene, 1970, p. 25), we are only at the beginning stage in developing a general systems theory. However, a great deal of developmental work has been done in several disciplines. We have already mentioned the work of Bertalanffy, whose work has been influential in many fields and especially in biology and psychiatry. The following examples will illustrate the scope and influence of general systems theory in several disciplines.

Sociology.   Buckley (1968) views society or the sociocultural system as a complex adaptive system which is open and subject to change. He has outlined a model for such a system which he believes can unite some of the more recent sociological and social psychological theories.

Archaeology.   Clarke (1968) has created a general model for the organization and relation of archaeological activities. His model starts with an archaeological segment of the real world. This sample is subjected to experimentally controlled contextual and specific observations from which an hypothesis or model is constructed. The model or hypothesis is then tested against the latest observation samples for goodness of fit. Propositions about the real world based on the archaeological segment are then synthesized.

Human Factors Engineering and Psychology.   The works of DeGreene (1970) and Gagne (1962) contain several models and concepts derived from systems theory which are applied in the fields of human factors engineering and psychology. In the terminology of that period, such topics as man-computer interrelationships, man-man and man-machine communications, concepts of training, motivation, and job performance are considered.

Political Science.   Easton (1965) views political life as a set of interactions that establish and maintain the boundaries of a system which is a part of, and surrounded by, other social systems. The political system is seen as an open system which, if it is to survive, must have the capability of obtaining adequate feedback about its performance in order to adapt to environmental conditions.

Psychiatry.   This is a discipline which has given a great deal of attention to general systems theory. Gray, Duhl, and Rizzo (1969) have reported that general systems theory is an important conceptual framework for scientific thought in the areas of communication, cognition, information, human growth and development, the environment, social change, and psychotherapy. Grinker and his associates (1956) have also made important contributions to psychiatry and the behavioral sciences as they have moved toward the development of a unified theory of human behavior based on concepts derived from several behavioral systems.

Cognitive Activity. Laszlo (1969) has endeavored to develop a scientific theory of the mind based on the concepts of general systems theory. His intent is to construct a map of the basic structure of cognitive activity. He states that the exploratory phases of his work suggest that a basic regulatory structure underlies the phenomena of the mind and of human interrelations. This regulatory structure is believed to be similar to the servomechanisms used by cyberneticians.[1]

While the above examples do not represent a comprehensive survey of the total field, they do demonstrate that general systems theory has had a significant impact on a number of scientific disciplines in a relatively short period of time. In addition, general systems theory was only one aspect of the change in scientific thought that followed World War II. A number of closely related theories and concepts, although with different emphases and terminology, were in the process of development at approximately the same time. The more important developments are:

1. *Cybernetics*, based upon the principle of feedback or circular causal trains providing mechanisms for goal-seeking and self-controlling behavior.
2. *Information theory*, introducing the concept of information as a quantity measurable by an expression isomorphic to negative entropy in physics, and developing the principles of its transmission.
3. *Game theory*, analyzing in a novel, mathematical framework, rational competition between two or more antagonists for maximum gain and minimum loss.
4. *Decision theory*, similarly analyzing rational choices, within human organizations, based upon examination of a given situation and its possible outcomes.
5. *Topology* or relational mathematics, including nonmetrical fields such as network and graph theory.
6. *Factor analysis*, i.e., isolation by way of mathematical analysis, of factors in multivariable phenomena in psychology and other fields (Bertalanffy, 1962, p. 3).

These parallel developments, while not in the same category, do share much in common with general systems theory and are a part of the

[1]A complete and technical discussion of general systems theory as it has been utilized by the theoreticians mentioned in this section may be found by consulting the references section of this book.

systems approach. As you know, the concepts developed by cyberneticians and by information, game, and decision theorists have made possible the tremendous post World War II advances in Western technology.
These developments, along with general systems theory, share a common
interest in the structure or organization of the parts that constitute a
system and the influence of these parts upon one another and on the
system itself.

Operations Research

While the search goes on for a universal or general theory of systems,
the more visible and dramatic advances in the systems approach have
occurred in the applied sciences such as engineering and management.
Quite often these advances have been made without the benefit of theory
as scientists have been forced to respond to real-life problems on a short-
term basis. As DeGreene (1970, p. 38) has stated, theory has often followed after observation and experience with actual problems and cases.
Operations research, as an applied science, had its origin as a result of
such a set of circumstances.

According to a monograph by the Air Ministry (1963), the term
"operational research" was coined in 1938 by A.P. Rowe, who was
superintendent of one of the early projects to utilize the technique of
operations research in response to tactical and strategical military
problems presented to Great Britain prior to and during World War II.
The term is a most appropriate descriptor. The work of operations
research is usually performed by a multidisciplinary team of scientists
who work closely with personnel who have the responsibility for the real-
life operations of a certain project or activity. The functions of the
research team typically involve a study of the operational requirements
of the project and then a scientific analysis of actual operations through
the use of data from real-life environments. Alternative models for
achieving the purposes of the project are developed which provide the
base for comparing and predicting the value, effectiveness, and cost of
each model. On the basis of this information, conclusions are drawn and
recommendations made to the people who are charged with making decisions for the project.

One of the most distinctive features of operations research is that the
input for the analysis of the requirements and operations of a project and
the development of alternative models for decision-making comes from
individuals who vary in their training and scientific backgrounds. This,
plus the input from personnel engaged in the actual operations of a project, increases the probability that all aspects of a project will be considered during a research operation. Such procedures point out the
holistic nature of operations research.

The United States Department of Defense became aware of the development of operations research in Great Britain during World War II and established teams of operations research analysts within each branch of the armed services. These were continued in the postwar period, and during the tenure of Robert McNamara as Secretary of Defense, operations research as a part of a total planning-programming-budgeting system (PPBS) was installed in the Department of Defense. President Lyndon Johnson was so impressed with McNamara's work that he announced in 1965 that PPBS would be required in all federal agencies and departments (American Association of School Administrators Commission on Administrative Technology, 1969, p. 29).

In the postwar period, leaders of American business and industry were quick to perceive that the procedures for analyzing military operations would be appropriate for the analysis of business and industrial operations. In fact, a strong foundation for the implementation of operations research in this country had been developed prior to World War II. Frederick W. Taylor, in the early 1900s, had conducted experiments in which he analyzed and measured work output and studied the use of wage incentives for increasing the productivity of workers. He used the results of these investigations to develop the principles of what he termed scientific management. In addition, the prewar development of accounting techniques, time and motion studies, statistical quality control, aptitude testing, and the Hawthorne experiments had prepared the business world for operations research (Roy, 1960, p. 19).

The methods of operations research mentioned in previous paragraphs have been applied to a myriad of business and industrial operations. Operations research is now, more often than not, the basis for management decisions in regard to manufacturing, marketing, and distributing operations. The research ranges from studies of the operations of checkout procedures in supermarkets and the buying habits of customers who buy from mail-order houses to studies of the total operations of an entire industry (Davidson & Roy, 1960, pp. 786-843).

The concepts and procedures of operations research have enabled scientists to develop techniques to provide decision makers in government, business, and industry with recommendations based on scientific data. This suggests the possibility of using the concept of operations research for developing or applying existing techniques to operational problems of counseling and other applied behavioral sciences. Game theory, for example, is already being used by counselors to assist individuals who are attempting to choose careers or resolve conflicts. Game theory, as used in operations research, was originally developed to study probable outcomes or payoffs when different strategies are used by decision makers. It may be possible to adapt several of the other techniques of operations research. In short, this particular contributor to the systems approach has the potential to advance our understanding and improve the operations of the counseling enterprise and other helping services.

Systems Engineering

As Roy (1960, p. 21) points out, the origin and development of systems engineering are not as well defined as operations research. It seems that systems engineering is the product of a gradual convergence and synthesis (which is still continuing) of a number of scientific concepts and developments which came to fruition immediately after World War II. Operations research and the basic engineering and technological capabilities were already present at that time. General systems theory was being seriously discussed and explored by a number of scientists. Then, beginning in 1946 with the completion of the first electronic computer, several important events occurred in a short span of time. Wiener published *Cybernetics* in 1948, which contained his ideas of control (feedback) and communication theory. In 1949, *The Mathematical Theory of Communication* was published by Shannon and Weaver.

The computer greatly expanded the size and complexity of problems and projects which scientists and engineers could undertake. A computer, in a relatively short period of time can perform calculations and solve problems that men working with ordinary calculating machines could not solve in a lifetime. The computer and the new theoretical concepts of cybernetics and communication theory opened new vistas for scientists and engineers as they began to perceive how various components could be related by means of feedback, communication networks, and information flow. Churchman (1968) suggests that such events helped to broaden the outlook of scientists and they began to understand their work as a "systems approach." They saw the need for interdisciplinary teams that could analyze problems and then design, construct, and evaluate the systems to solve the problems. These scientists also saw the value of general systems theory and operations research and adopted many of the functions, theories, and tools of these related fields. They used them, however, for a different purpose; the theories and tools were used to design and develop new systems rather than for the analysis of the ongoing operations of a project, business, or industry.

Systems engineers received the opportunity to put their new ideas into operation in 1953 when the U.S. Air Force authorized SAGE, the semi-automatic ground environment air defense system. This was the first large-scale system which related numerous components to one another in a complex, computerized communications network which covered much of Canada, the United States, and adjacent oceans. In the early 1950s, systems engineers were primarily concerned with the "hardware" and machine aspects of systems design and development as they worked on

SAGE and other similar projects. This was also the period when systems engineers and operations research teams gained experience in working with systems concepts and theories. They also developed and refined the needed tools and techniques for working with the problems associated with large and complex systems such as SAGE, PPBS management systems, and NASA programs such as Explorer 1 and Project Mercury.

During the 1960s, the people who were engaged in systems work became concerned with the relationships and interrelationships between men and machines, software and hardware components, and the human factors that were interwoven with systems design and development. Some began to perceive interrelated components as "total systems" irrespective of whether the components were human or nonhuman. After the successes of the extremely complicated Gemini and Apollo space programs, it now seems a natural evolvement that some systems researchers and theorists would turn their attention to civil and social systems. They began to perceive of the problems of pollution, urban decay, race, education, environmental quality, government, poverty, and human relations as interrelated systems—as "complex combinations of many social, psychological, emotional, cultural, and economic factors with technological facets" (Ramo, 1969, p. 9). It also became apparent that the analysis of such problems and the design, development, and operation of systems to solve them would require personnel from many different disciplines who were trained to perceive problems and their solutions as wholes—as systems. This is how operations research, systems analysis, systems engineering, systems research, and other related fields came to be known as the "systems approach" and how people who use the theories, concepts, and tools of this approach came to be called "systems scientists."

THE DEVELOPMENT OF THE SYSTEMS APPROACH IN THE COUNSELING PROFESSION

The possible application of systems concepts to counseling was a by-product of the development of training programs by systems scientists. A number of behavioral scientists had assisted in the development of military training programs during World War II. In the postwar period, their services continued to be needed as weapons and defense systems became more and more complex. The successful operation and maintenance of such systems demanded that personnel be selected, trained, and given work environments that would enable them to meet the specifications and requirements of the system.

Behavioral scientists, especially human factors engineers and educational, experimental, and industrial psychologists, were called upon to do the basic and applied research on which to base the training programs for those who would operate the increasingly complex and technologically sophisticated military systems. They also provided input into the design of systems in terms of the requirements of the human components of the systems. Research training and development (R&D) organizations were established by the armed forces or contracted to universities and private corporations to study the relationships and interactions of man-machine systems and to develop procedures for improving the design and performance of military systems. Some of the more notable of these organizations were the Air Force Personnel and Training Research Center, the Army Human Resources Research Office operated by The George Washington University, the American Institutes for Research, and the Systems Development Corporation.

It was inevitable that the spin-off from these R&D centers would begin to influence civilian education and training as the concept of "instructional systems" evolved and as advances were made in educational technology.[2] Educators became aware of the systems approach as psychologists accepted academic appointments in colleges of education and departments of psychology where they began to teach and continued to research the skills and concepts they had developed while working on military projects. Private corporations also became interested in applying systems concepts to problems of elementary and secondary education. Systems Development Corporation, for example, developed CLASS (Computer-Based Laboratory for Automated School Systems). This instructional system provided for automated, individualized instruction that was linked to a computer that gave instructional directions to students, presented questions, and gave immediate knowledge of results of student performance (Saettler, 1968, p. 278).

CLASS is of special interest for the counseling profession. Cogswell (1961) wrote a technical paper for this project entitled, "Proposed Systems Simulation Research Studies for CLASS: The Counseling Function." This paper possibly marks the first occasion when the systems approach and counseling are linked together.

Cogswell's initial paper was followed by a report (Cogswell, 1962) of an analysis of the counseling and pupil personnel data processing functions of a large school district in southern California. He was interested in evaluating the application of systems techniques in an educational setting and in generating hypotheses for systems research in the counseling function. His analysis revealed a number of problems related to counseling which the school district was experiencing. The analysis also served as a basis for formulating hypotheses for systems research in counseling.

[2]A more complete discussion of the concepts and events leading to the development of training research and the systems approach in education may be found in: Gagné (1962), Glaser (1965), and Silvern (1965).

Specifically, he outlined designs for systems research studies which would investigate the possibilities of : (a) increasing the frequency of teacher use of diagnostic and grouped data collected by counselors from the student population, (b) using automated interviewing techniques and programmed learning for the diagnosis and treatment of student learning problems, and (c) providing data to counselors on the day-to-day learning performance of students to facilitate the possibilities of preventive counseling. A computer-based system was seen as the principal vehicle for achieving his research objectives.

Cogswell and Estavan (1965), in collaboration with Loughary, Friesen, and Hurst (1966), later designed a model for computer-assisted counseling which simulated a counselor's behavior in assisting students with educational planning. The model was developed after an analysis was made of the behavior and decision rules used by a high school counselor who was experienced in assisting students with this type of planning. Computer programs were developed for an automated cumulative folder appraisal system and for an automated educational planning interview. A pilot study involving 40 ninth-grade students was then conducted to evaluate the automated systems. The results of this study indicated that when the computer appraisal program was compared with the appraisal behavior of two human counselors, no significant differences were found on 75% of the appraisal statements. Points in the computer program were also located where modifications could be made to produce even greater similarities between the appraisal behavior of humans and automated procedures. The reactions of students to computer-assisted counseling varied widely. However, an attitude questionnaire administered to the students indicated that the overall trend was in a positive direction. The investigators concluded that automated appraisal and interviewing procedures for counseling could be developed, but that additional study was needed to determine how to integrate computer-assisted counseling into actual counseling practice effectively.

The early history of the application of the scientific systems approach to counseling shows a strong preoccupation with man-machine systems. Specifically, the pioneers in using the systems approach to solve problems related to the counseling function were concerned with developing useful and effective man-machine relationships and interactions in order to attain some of the objectives of counseling in a more efficient manner. This preoccupation is understandable, as systems scientists were interested in developing computer-based educational systems which would individualize instruction for students regardless of the variation in individual differences.

The interest in man-machine counseling systems has continued to the present day. As we shall show later in this chapter, the concept of a systems approach to the counseling function has evolved to include models that are basically human systems. While models such as *Systematic Counseling* have appeared, research and development of human-machine counseling systems has continued to grow and flourish. This is a healthy situation for the counseling profession, as these two emphases are complementary.

A number of computer-assisted vocational counseling systems have been developed and are in various stages of experimentation or operation at a number of school systems and institutions of higher education around the nation. While these systems require the interaction of a human with a computer, other systems have been developed that utilize "software" such as documents, programs, and media of various types. GUIDPAK, developed at the University of Oregon under the direction of Loughary and Tondow (U.S. Office of Education, 1969), is such a system. This system provides materials to assist students to obtain information about entry level job opportunities, multimedia materials on career development, materials that show local entry job and training opportunities, and data that enable a counselor to monitor student progress within the system.

The research and development of man-machine counseling and guidance systems continue to be a significant and promising application of systems concepts. However, in the mid-1960s, a new dimension was added. A small number of counselor educators and researchers began to discuss how the systems approach could be used to analyze and design counseling and guidance systems and subsystems that did not necessarily include man-machine relationships and interactions. For example, Loughary (1966) outlined how school counselors, with the appropriate training, could use the systems approach in improving many aspects of a guidance program by following the procedures listed below:

1. Define operationally the problem to be studied, and make a statement of desired outcomes.
2. Determine the limits of the system to be investigated and its general relationship to subsystems.
3. Determine the objectives of the system being studied.
4. Identify components of the system being studied.
5. Develop system flow charts.
6. Continue system component analysis.
7. Provide feedback of findings to those working in the system in order to verify and clarify the way in which the system functions.
8. Develop new system or modification of existing system and methods of evaluating the new system.
9. Test new system (p. 29).

Thoresen (1968a, 1968b) in papers presented at the annual meetings of the American Personnel and Guidance Association and the American Educational Research Association, called on counselor educators and researchers to reconceptualize counseling and counselor training programs. He advocated the use of the systems approach for the analysis and design of models of the counseling process and counselor education that would be more responsive to the complexities of human problems.

More and more members of the counseling profession became aware of the potential of the systems approach for the analysis and design of human systems as information about this innovation was disseminated in the counseling literature and at professional meetings. Others were becoming apprised of developments in systems research by their colleagues in educational psychology and technology who were hard at work designing instructional systems. Few counselors or counselor educators, however, possessed the necessary training and skills to use the concepts of the systems approach in designing models for improving counseling services. This obstacle was partially overcome in 1969 when a five-day training institute was held to teach counselors and counselor educators the theory and practical skills for using systems techniques. Thirty-four counselors and counselor educators were selected to attend this training program, which was held under the sponsorship of the American Educational Research Association. The objectives of the program were as follows:

1. To develop participants' understanding of concepts and principles of systems research;
2. To increase participants' familiarity with application of systems research principles;
3. To improve participants' skills in using systems techniques;
4. To foster in participants favorable attitudes to systems research (Ryan, 1969, p. 1).

The program was apparently received with enthusiasm, as similar training sessions were sponsored by the American Educational Research Association during 1970 and 1971. In addition, the American Personnel and Guidance Association sponsored such a training program prior to its 1970 annual convention. In more recent years, workshops on the use of the systems approach in counseling and guidance have been sponsored by the Bureau of Guidance of the New York State Department of Education and several university departments of counselor education.

It is important to note that a group of counselor educators (D.G.Hays, R. E. Hosford, T.A. Ryan, N.R. Stewart, C. E. Thoresen, and B.B. Winborn) worked as an instructional team with a systems engineer (L. C. Silvern) to conduct the workshops. The skills and concepts of a systems scientist were integrated with those of counselors and counselor educators to produce a training system for a special audience.

A number of systems models for counseling, counselor education, and guidance programs have been developed since the first AERA training program in systems research. For example, Hays (1969) produced a flowchart model for designing a school district testing program. Yelon (1969) used a systems approach to design a model for one part of the counseling process. He displays the process of using observation for hypothesis testing in order to arrive at an appropriate therapy or treatment strategy for a particular individual. He points out that this model may be used for the instruction of counselor trainees as well as in actual counseling. This is an excellent example also of the design of one subsystem that would be contained within the larger whole or system of the counseling process.

Hosford and Ryan (1970) have designed flowcharts of a generalized model for developing counseling and guidance programs which are compatible with the environments in which they function. They point out that several benefits can accrue from using their model:

> Communication within the profession and between the profession and others involved in counseling and guidance can be facilitated. The obligation for accountability can be satisfied. Weaknesses, gaps, missing links in a system working against wholeness, strong interrelationships, compatibility, and optimization can be pointed up. Increased creativity and innovation can be achieved. Improvements in the total system, strengthening of functions, and tightening of interrelationships among functions can be realized through the provision for continuing evaluation in light of previously defined behavioral objectives (1970, p. 230).

The use of a systems approach by members of the counseling profession has had only a very brief history. The models described above as well as others (Thoresen, 1969b; Campbell, Dworkin, Jackson, Hoeltzel, Parsons, & Lacy, 1971; Stewart & Fiedler, 1971; Pierce, Ripp, Thelander, Tonetti, & York, 1972; Stewart, 1972; Stewart, Jensen, Leonard, & January, 1972; Cook, 1973) have been developed within a short period of time. They represent our first attempts to systematically analyze and synthesize counseling systems in which human functions are clearly identified and related to one another and to the whole itself. We can expect that future models will demonstrate better design and higher fidelity of simulation to the real-life environment as counselors and counselor educators continue to work with the concepts of the systems approach.

SUMMARY

The systems approach has a relatively brief history, having come into existence after World War II. It is not a clearly defined discipline, as it is an amalgamation of several related theories, concepts, and operational procedures. In this chapter, three of the more important areas that contributed to the development of the systems approach were described. These are general systems theory, operations research, and systems engineering. In addition, the development of the systems approach in the counseling profession was discussed.

In the next chapter the distinguishing features of Systematic Counseling are presented and a flowchart model of this process is introduced. You will become acquainted with the special symbols and vocabulary that are used to describe the counseling process. You will also be introduced to the Performance Criteria that are used by counselors to evaluate their effectiveness as systematic counselors. In Chapter 4 you will begin to learn how to conceptualize counseling as a whole. You will learn how the various parts of the counseling process relate to one another and to the whole itself. You will be learning how to use a map of the counseling process to organize and direct your behavior while engaged in the counseling process.

4

The Systematic Counselor at Work

OVERVIEW

A dichotomy is sometimes drawn between theory and practice. Skeptics have often remarked, perhaps with justification, "Your idea sounds good in theory, but will it work?" Some approaches to counseling have languished because they have failed to show how their basic rationale may be applied in an actual counseling situation. Others have failed to endure because they have consisted of isolated and fragmented techniques without a unifying rationale.

The point of view taken in this book is that "There is nothing so practical as a good theory." Conversely, one way to find out whether a theory is "good" is to note the ease and effectiveness with which it can be applied. The basic rationale for a systems approach to counseling has been presented in the first three chapters. The primary intent of the present chapter is to provide the linkage between that rationale and the overall sequence of procedures utilized in Systematic Counseling.

INTRODUCTION

Organization

This chapter consists of three main sections. The first section reestablishes your perspective by reviewing the nature of Systematic Counseling and contrasting it with other approaches which are sometimes labeled "systematic." The second section describes a flowchart outlining the Systematic Counseling process and tells you how to read the flowchart. The third section acquaints you with the Performance Criteria used to assess the counselor's progress throughout the Systematic Counseling process.

Purposes

The overall purposes of this chapter are (a) to explain what Systematic Counseling is, and what it is not; (b) to describe the specific steps and procedures of Systematic Counseling as presented by a flowchart model; and (c) to introduce the Performance Criteria used to guide and assess the progress of the Systematic Counselor.

Objectives

Upon completing this chapter it is expected that you will be prepared to do the following:

1. Specify two ways in which Systematic Counseling differs from other "systematic" approaches.
2. Define Systematic Counseling and specify its scientific bases.
3. State five ways in which a flowchart is superior to a narrative outline as a means of communication.
4. Name and list in correct order the 12 subsystems of the Systematic Counseling process.
5. Trace on the detailed flowchart for Systematic Counseling the entire counseling process from receipt of client referral to evaluation of counselor performance.
6. State definitions of special terms used in this chapter, including *flowchart, system, subsystem, LOGOS, point-numeric code, level of detail, function, descriptor, signal path, collection dot, recycle, feedforward,* and *feedback.*
7. Explain symbols used in the flowchart for Systematic Counseling.
8. Indicate the relationship between point-numeric codes of varying levels of detail.
9. Explain the importance of evaluating counselor performance against behavioral criteria.
10. State the Performance Criteria for each of the subsystems and functions in the Systematic Counseling process.

PERSPECTIVE

The rationale for a systems approach to counseling was presented in Chapters 1, 2, and 3. Moreover, a particular application of the systems approach—known as Systematic Counseling—was introduced. However, before we proceed to a detailed description of this process, it may be helpful to reestablish our perspective by reviewing what Systematic Counseling is, and what it is not. Let us begin by considering two inappropriate uses of the term.

Pseudosystematic Approaches

You will recall that all counselors—even those with little or no training—use some sort of "system," whether they realize it or not. Counseling behavior is not random. Rather, on the basis of their training, the conditions under which they work, and a host of other factors, counselors tend to develop perferred ways of behaving. Once developed, these modes of behavior tend to be repeated, i.e., they become "systematized." Counselors, like most other people, are creatures of habit. If we were to observe their behavior with a large number of clients, we would probably find that they tend to handle certain categories of clients and problems in much the same way from one case to the next. Thus, in this sense all counseling might be termed "systematic counseling."As you will see shortly, however, this is clearly *not* what is meant by Systematic Counseling.

Another questionable use of the term "systematic" occurs in reference to formal, well-established approaches in which global steps or procedures are set forth to guide the counselor in practice. Thus, in an approach labeled by Patterson (1973, p. 124) as "one of the few really systematic approaches to counseling," the counselor's major steps are to (a) establish an atmosphere of permissiveness, (b) encourage the client to free associate, (c) reward the client for talking, (d) handle the transference, (e) help the client to label feelings, and (f) teach the client to discriminate by attaching appropriate verbal cues to stimulus patterns. While such an approach is obviously more "systematic" than the one described in the previous paragraph, it is quite different from Systematic Counseling as used in this book.

Systematic Counseling

What, then, is *Systematic Counseling?* And what sets it apart from other, more or less "systematic" approaches?

Definition. Systematic Counseling is *an approach in which the various aspects of the counseling process are clearly identified and organized into a sequence designed to resolve the client's concerns efficiently as well as effectively.* Note the emphasis upon deliberate *design* of a system in which the parts are *clearly identified* and *organized.* The intent of organizing the parts into a particular sequence is to increase the likelihood that counseling will be not only effective, but *efficient* as well. Such an approach goes well beyond the notion that all counselors use some kind of system. Likewise, it transcends those approaches in which major procedures are simply listed and described, with little attention to efficiency, detail, and interrelationships among the parts of a system.

Scientific bases.   Unlike other approaches, Systematic Counseling represents a synthesis of three scientific approaches—learning theory, systems analysis, and educational technology. Learning theory and the principles of behavior modification provide the theoretical and experimental base. Systems analysis provides the organizational framework, and educational technology is the source of methods and materials.

Distinguishing features.   There are several specific features of this approach which, when taken in combination, serve to distinguish it from other approaches to counseling:

1. Counselor and client establish a mutually agreed-upon objective for counseling and then work toward the attainment of that objective.
2. The objective is stated in terms of specific observable behaviors.
3. The counselor directs specific learning experiences designed to help the client attain the objective.
4. As suggested in the definition of Systematic Counseling, an attempt has been made to identify the elements of the counseling process and to place them into an optimal sequence. It should be stressed, however, that while this sequence is considered ideal for most situations, flexibility is provided for situations which deviate from the usual.
5. In this approach, counseling is viewed as a *learning process.* Through counseling, the client learns new ways of obtaining information, new ways of making decisions, and new ways of responding to the environment. Moreover, the client learns how to apply these learnings to other situations beyond those concerning the original problem.
6. The counselor uses a wide variety of resources in terms of strategies, techniques, and people in helping the client to attain the objective for counseling. Besides such "standard" counseling techniques as listening, reflecting, clarifying, asking questions, summarizing, and furnishing information—nearly all of which are strictly verbal in nature—the counselor uses a number of additional techniques and strategies as well. For example, the client may be asked to observe a model of the

desired behavior, whether live, audiotaped, or videotaped; it may be arranged for a client to visit a place of business; behavior contracts or other forms of contingency management may be implemented; counterconditioning or role playing may be utilized. Most of the latter procedures are not limited to the verbal medium. The counselor also frequently involves significant others in the client's environment (e.g., teachers, parents, and peers) to observe client behavior and dispense reinforcement for appropriate client responses.

7. Monitoring and evaluation of both client and counselor performance are built-in aspects of this approach to counseling.

8. Systematic Counseling incorporates a self-corrective mechanism by which results from evaluating the counselor's behavior are fed back to the counselor to help in working with other clients.

Limitations.   Finally, it should be noted that Systematic Counseling, as presented throughout this book, is a format for individual, one-to-one counseling. We have deliberately chosen to focus upon this skill because it is central to other counselor functions. One skilled in Systematic Counseling, for example, could design adaptations for its use in group counseling, consultation, and guidance systems management, since many of the same procedures and strategies would probably be involved. Exploratory work in these areas is currently in progress.

Reader Transition

Up to this point you have been reading general introductory material. Now it is necessary for you to make a transition from a passive to an *active* role. We have previously presented the rationale for the development of a Systematic Counseling model and suggested the utility of such a model. It would be ideal if we could communicate everything about the model to you in brief, but accurate, fashion. Unfortunately, this is not possible, since the model is very complex.

In order to facilitate communication, we will need to rely heavily upon a "language" or form of communication that may be new to you. The complex relationships among the large number of counselor actions contained within the model can be communicated more succinctly and precisely through the use of a *flowchart* than through a lengthy and cumbersome narrative that would be needed to convey the same information.

The section that follows presents in considerable detail the rules, conventions, and symbols used in the Systematic Counseling flowchart. Because an understanding of this new language is essential to the remainder of the book, this section should be studied carefully.

FLOWCHART FOR SYSTEMATIC COUNSELING

Now let us look closely at this unusual means of communication. Actually, it is not completely new. You have encountered it before in Chapters 1 and 2, where simple flowcharts were used to illustrate major aspects of the systems approach. But what *is* a flowchart? Let us begin by offering a definition. As used throughout the remainder of this book, a *flowchart* is a graphic, sequential description of the actions, decisions, and flow of information in the counseling process. The flowchart enables the counselor to grasp the overall scope of the procedures involved in the counseling process and to follow a planned, economical sequence of tasks in counseling.

But why use a flowchart at all? Why not use a narrative outline instead? Actually, the flowchart offers several advantages over the outline. First, because it is *graphic* in nature, the flowchart enables one to express relationships, not only among elements which are topically related or adjacent, but among those which are far removed as well. Second, the flowchart makes it possible to express *unusual* relationships among elements, including the concepts of *recycling, feedforward,* and *feedback* (these terms will be explained later in this chapter). Third, the flowchart is more convenient and economical. Since it constitutes a form of "shorthand," it is possible to express on a single page a complex set of interrelationships which would require many pages of narrative. Fourth, since the flowchart constitutes a visual "picture," it is easier to remember than a verbal description. Finally, once one has acquired practice in reading a flowchart, it is possible to read and grasp the relationships involved much more quickly than in a comparable narrative presentation.

Reading a Simple Flowchart

A complete description of the *detailed* flowchart for the Systematic Counseling process will be provided later in this chapter. However, let us begin by examining the simpler version in Figure 4-1. The entire chart is a model or representation of a *system*—the Systematic Counseling process. Each of the rectangles is a *subsystem* or component of the system. In combination, the various subsystems and their interrelationships constitute the overall system. The temporal sequence in which the various subsystems fit within the overall system is indicated by the numbers found in the lower right-hand corner of the rectangles, and by the arrows.

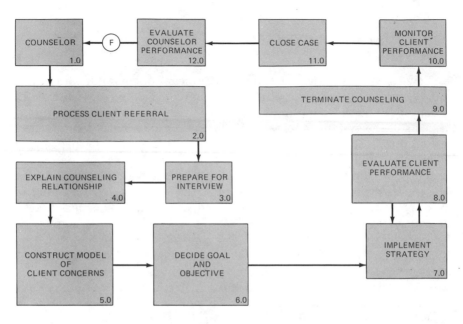

Figure 4-1

We start with the counselor (Subsystem 1.0), who comes to the counseling process with certain basic qualifications. Succeeding aspects of the flowchart show what the counselor does. The first step is to process the client referral (2.0). The counselor next prepares for the initial interview (3.0). During that interview, the counselor explains the counseling relationship (4.0). The counselor then engages the client in a discussion of the client's concerns and contructs a model or picture of those concerns (5.0). Next the counselor decides with the client what the goal and objective of counseling will be (6.0), and implements a strategy (7.0) designed to attain the objective. Then client performance is evaluated (8.0). If the objective for counseling has *not* been attained, it is necessary to reimplement the strategy (7.0) and then evaluate client performance again. Once the objective has been attained, the counselor terminates regular contact with the client (9.0). Next, the client's performance is monitored for a reasonable period of time (10.0) and the counselor then proceeds to close the case (11.0). The counselor's performance is then evaluated (12.0), and the information resulting from this evaluation is "fed back" to the counselor (as indicated by the symbol F) to help produce a better job with subsequent clients. Understanding the simple flowchart will help in reading the more detailed flowchart.

**Reading the Detailed Flowchart for
Systematic Counseling**

As you can see, reading a simple flowchart is rather easy, requiring little more than following the numbers and arrows, and reading the printed labels. However, interpreting a more detailed flowchart such as that used in the actual practice of Systematic Counseling requires an understanding of certain additional terms and symbols. The "language" underlying the flowchart has been termed LOGOS by Silvern (1969). LOGOS is an acronym based upon the expression, "*L*anguage for *O*ptimizing *G*raphically *O*rdered *S*ystems." As Silvern has pointed out, LOGOS is a graphic language which includes certain shapes and symbols, as well as words and numbers. Let us now look at some of the terms and symbols with which you will need to be familiar.

You already know that the overall chart represents a *system*. Moreover, you have learned that each of the large rectangles is a *subsystem*. Note that each rectangle in Figure 4-1 is designated by a *point-numeric code*, i.e., a number which shows (a) the location of the component within the overall sequence of the system and (b) the *level of detail* of the component. Levels of detail and their corresponding codes may be illustrated as follows (adapted from Silvern, 1969):

Level of Detail	*Code*
First	1.0
Second	1.1
	1.2
	1.3
Third	1.3.1
	1.3.2
Fourth	1.3.2.1.
	1.3.2.2
	1.3.2.3
	1.3.2.4
	1.3.2.5
nth	. . . . etc.

Subsystems represent large segments or components of Systematic Counseling. Accordingly, they are coded at the first level of detail, ending in zero—i.e., 1.0, 2.0, and so on. For example, in Figure 4-2 the COUNSELOR is the first subsystem, coded 1.0:

Figure 4-2

Other subsystems consist of major portions of the counseling process, such as processing the client referral, preparing for the interview, and explaining the counseling relationship.

As used in this book, a rectangle coded at a further level of detail (second, third, or fourth) denotes a *function*. A function is a relatively specific action, object, or informational component of a subsystem. In Systematic Counseling, functions typically show the sequence of specific counselor actions within a larger segment or subsystem of the counseling process. For example, in Figure 4-3, RECEIVE REFERRAL (Function 2.1) is coded at the second level of detail. COUNSELOR OBSERVATION (Function 2.1.1) is coded at the third level of detail, as are Functions 2.1.2, 2.1.3, 2.1.4, and 2.1.5. Finally, RECORDS (Function 2.1.1.1) is coded at the fourth level of detail, as is ENVIRONMENT (Function 2.1.1.2).

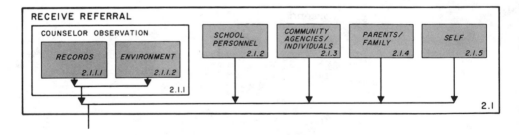

Figure 4-3

The words which label a particular subsystem or function are known collectively as a *descriptor*. Thus, in Figure 4-4 the descriptor for Subsystem 3.0 is PREPARE FOR INTERVIEW, while the descriptors for Functions 3.1 and 3.2, respectively, are ARRANGE FOR APPOINTMENT and REVIEW AVAILABLE DATA.

Figure 4-4

The arrows on the chart are known as *signal paths*. Each signal path carries information in the direction shown by the arrowhead.

A *circle with a point-numeric code inside* is a shortcut means of showing a relationship between two relatively distant functions, as opposed to connecting them directly with a signal path. This prevents cluttering the flowchart and makes it easier to read. See Figure 4-5, taken from the detailed flowchart for Systematic Counseling:

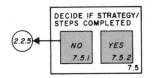

Figure 4-5

This diagram signifies that if a NO decision(7.5.1) continues to be reached after repeated attempts to complete the strategy and steps, it is then appropriate to move to ASSIST IN LOCATING APPROPRIATE ASSISTANCE (Function 2.2.5). Correspondingly, Function 2.2.5 would appear at a relatively distant point on the flowchart with a circled input from 7.5.1, as shown in Figure 4-6.

Figure 4-6

These two short signal paths, each terminating in a circled code, take the place of a long conventional signal path which would otherwise clutter the flowchart.

A *collection dot* is a symbol indicating that all data from the various parts of a particular function are to be "collected together" or summed and then carried as a unit to the next function. Consider the example shown in Figure 4-7.

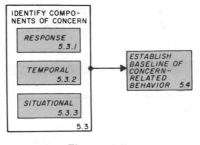

Figure 4-7

The absence of signal paths *within* Function 5.3 signifies that there is no prescribed sequence in which the three components—5.3.1, 5.3.2, and 5.3.3—must be performed. Therefore, it is not possible to designate a particular component from which the output to Function 5.4 should originate. Hence, a collection dot—at the beginning of the signal path—is used to indicate that, regardless of the order in which the components are performed, the information is summed and then carried from 5.3 as a whole to 5.4.

Recycling is the process of repeating one or more previously performed functions and/or subsystems in order to meet an established criterion. Recycling is continued until the standard has been met or until it is determined that it cannot be met. (See Figure 4-8.)

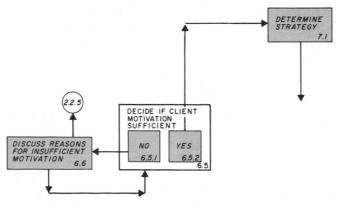

Figure 4-8

In Function 6.5, the counselor must make a YES or NO decision. If the decision is YES (6.5.2), the counselor moves on to the next function (7.1).

If the decision is NO (6.5.1), it is then necessary to move to 6.6, discuss reasons for the client's lack of motivation, and return again or recycle to 6.5 and make another YES or NO decision. If, after repeated attempts the client is still insufficiently motivated, the counselor moves to 2.2.5 (indicated in the circle), and initiates a series of functions leading to termination of the counseling contact.

Feedforward is a term applied to a signal path showing an output from a subsystem to a succeeding subsystem, *where there are one or more Intervening subsystems which are unaffected by that signal path.* This relationship is illustrated in Figure 4-9.

The critical point to note is that the feedforward signal path (with the circled "FF") goes directly from 2.2.4 to 4.3.1 without passing through subsystem 3.0. This indicates that the conditions specified by the counselor to the referral source are "stored away" by the counselor for subsequent use when explaining the purpose of counseling (4.3.1) to the client. However, these conditions have no effect upon the intervening subsystem (3.0). The sequence of counselor *actions* is to perform 2.2.4 and then 3.1, as shown by the regular signal path.

A *feedback* signal path is one which shows output from a subsystem and input to a *preceding* subsystem. Such a signal path creates a closed loop and controls the output of the preceding subsystem to which it extends. Feedback is illustrated in Figure 4-10.

Note that in subsystem 12.0 the performance of the counselor is evaluated. The information resulting from this evaluation is then fed back (as indicated by the signal path with the symbol "F") to an earlier subsystem, COUNSELOR (1.0). This information controls the subsequent output of subsystem 1.0, since the counselor's behavior with the next client will be affected by the results of evaluating performance with the present client.

Now that you know what a flowchart is and have been introduced to the language of LOGOS, let us look in detail at the complete flowchart for Systematic Counseling (see Endpapers). On the chart, trace the activities of the counselor throughout the counseling process.[1] While the various subsystems are briefly summarized in the following sections, they will be treated at greater length in other chapters. It should be remembered also that the counseling sequence described here will typically consume a minimum of two counseling interviews, and in many cases more.

---

[1] As you proceed through the flowchart, you will note that the counselor must make decisions from time to time. Since the primary intent is to show the *sequence* of steps involved in Systematic Counseling, the criteria for making decisions will not be emphasized at this point. Guidelines for those decisions, coded in accordance with the flowchart, are contained in the Performance Criteria for Systematic Counseling (Appendix A). Further uses of the Performance Criteria are described later in this chapter.

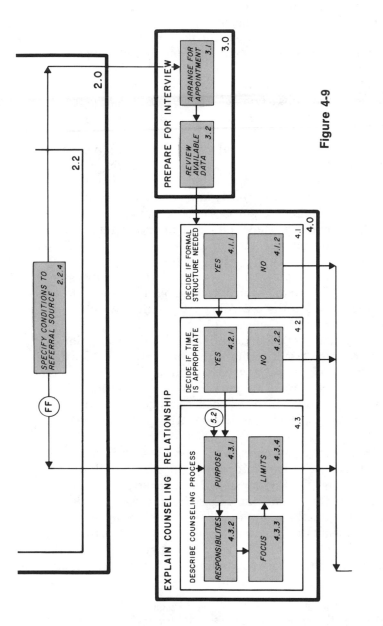

Figure 4-9

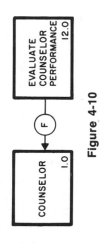

Figure 4-10

Counselor (1.0).   In Systematic Counseling, as in other approaches, we start with the counselor as the main functionary. The counselor as represented in this subsystem is not only one who has certain professional knowledge and skills, but also one who possesses fundamental attitudes and ethical beliefs which are important in counseling.

Process client referral (2.0).   The first specific subsystem with which the counselor is concerned is that of processing the client referral, as indicated by the signal path extending from 1.0 to 2.1. The referral may originate in a number of ways. It may be based upon observations made by the counselor (2.1.1), by other school personnel (2.1.2), by community agencies or individuals (2.1.3), or by the client's parents or other family members (2.1.4). In some instances, the client may initiate the referral directly (2.1.5).

Regardless of the source, the counselor then analyzes the appropriateness of the referral (2.2). The first step in this process is to collect data concerning the reasons for the referral and the circumstances involved (2.2.1). The counselor then examines the data (2.2.2) and on the basis of this analysis makes a decision (2.2.3) as to whether the referral is an appropriate one to accept. If it is decided to accept the referral (2.2.3.1), the counselor then specifies to the referral source the conditions or ground rules under which the acceptance is made. Any such conditions stated to the referral source are then "stored away" by the counselor for subsequent use in explaining the purpose of counseling to the client (indicated by the circled "FF" or "feedforward" on the signal path from 2.2.4 to 4.3.1).

However, the counselor may for various reasons decide *not* to accept the referral (2.2.3.2). In such an event, the counselor helps the client to locate appropriate assistance from other sources (2.2.5). Contact with the client is then terminated (9.0).

Prepare for interview (3.0).   Let us now return to the more usual case in which the counselor has accepted the referral (2.2.3.1) and has specified the conditions of acceptance to the referral source (2.2.4). The counselor next prepares for the initial interview with the client (3.0). An appointment is arranged (3.1), and the counselor reviews any available data on the client (3.2).

Explain counseling relationship (4.0).   At the time of the first interview, the counselor usually explains the counseling relationship to the client. First, it must be decided whether a formal explanation (structure) is needed (4.1). Assuming that formal structure is needed, the counselor must then decide whether the present time is an appropriate one in which to provide structure (4.2). The counselor may reach a YES decision (4.2.1), or a NO decision (4.2.2). If structure is deemed necessary but is postponed, it must be provided later, as in 5.2 (indicated by the circled

4.3.1 to the right of Function 5.2), or when deciding goals for counseling (6.0), or at the termination of the first interview.

If it is decided that structure is necessary and that it should be performed at the usual time (near the beginning of the interview), the counselor then proceeds to describe the counseling process (4.3). There are four main aspects to be covered in the explanation: the purpose of counseling (4.3.1), the respective responsibilities or roles of the counselor and client (4.3.2), the focus of counseling (4.3.3), and the limits under which counseling is conducted (4.3.4).

Construct model of client concerns (5.0). The counselor then proceeds to construct a model or mental picture of the client's concerns. First, the various concerns of the client are identified (5.1). Next, counselor and client select a concern to focus on in counseling (5.2).

Once a concern has been isolated for immediate attention, the counselor then identifies the components of that concern (5.3). There are three components to be identified. First, the response components must be specified (5.3.1), i.e., what the client does or how the client reacts in the problem situation. Second, the temporal components are identified (5.3.2), i.e., when the behavior occurs, how long it has occurred, and whether there is a pattern or sequence to the problem. Finally, the situational components of the concern are focused upon (5.3.3), i.e., where or under what circumstances the problem becomes apparent.

In the next function (5.4), the counselor formally establishes a baseline or benchmark of the client's concern-related behavior. This baseline provides a succinct description of the relevant aspects of the problem behavior, lays the groundwork for the behavioral objective subsequently to be developed, and provides a convenient benchmark against which the behavior of the client can be assessed as counseling proceeds. Accurate recall of such data is especially critical later in the counseling process when, in 8.1.2, the client's performance is compared with the baseline (as indicated by the feedforward signal path extending from the bottom of 5.4).

A precept of Systematic Counseling is that most,if not all, maladaptive behavior is maintained by certain reinforcing consequences. In order to help the client break the pattern of maladaptive behavior, the counselor attempts to identify the reinforcers which maintain the problem behavior (5.5) so that they can be eliminated or perhaps applied in other ways to motivate more adaptive behavior.

In Function 5.6 the client is asked to verify the counselor's perception of the concerns. The client must verbally agree that the counselor's model is essentially accurate. If this agreement cannot be obtained, it is necessary to "recycle" to IDENTIFY CONCERNS (5.1) and go back through the various functions in subsystem 5.0 to identify and resolve the discrepancies between the counselor's and the client's model of the concerns. Not until this agreement has been reached may the counselor move to subsystem 6.0.

Decide goal and objective (6.0).   In this subsystem the counselor's first task is to decide whether or not a goal can be established (6.1). Ordinarily, a YES decision will be made (6.1.1). However, if a NO decision is made (6.1.2), it is necessary to discuss the need for goals in counseling (6.7). The counselor then recycles to 6.1 and again determines whether the client is willing to establish a goal. This process may have to be repeated several times. In this regard, despite the fact that the client has verified the counselor's model of the client's concern, it is conceivable that the client's reluctance to establish a counseling goal reflects a fundamental misunderstanding about the nature of the problem. For this reason, provision is made for the counselor to recycle from 6.7 to IDENTIFY CONCERNS (5.1), as indicated by the circled 5.1 immediately below 6.7. If, after exhausting the possibilities mentioned above, the client still refuses to work toward an objective, the counselor must then "in-put" or move to ASSIST IN LOCATING APPROPRIATE ASSISTANCE (2.2.5), as shown by the circled 2.2.5 beneath 6.7, and pursue operations to terminate counseling contact with the client.

Assuming, however, that the client agrees to establish a counseling objective (6.1.1), the counselor then helps the client to determine the desired goal (6.2). This involves a specification by the client as to what the ideal outcome or resolution of the problem might be.

Knowing what the client wants to accomplish, the counselor must now decide whether he or she has the professional capabilities, interests, and resources necessary to help the client work on an objective related to the desired counseling outcome. Assuming that a YES decision is made (6.3.2), the counselor and client then proceed to establish a specific learning objective for counseling (6.4).

The learning objective includes a highly specific statement of desired outcomes and the attendant conditions under which those outcomes are to be demonstrated, including definite time limits. The counselor should therefore make a final check to determine whether the client is sufficiently motivated to work toward the objective as stated (6.5). If the client indicates readiness to move ahead and decide upon a strategy for reaching the learning objective, the counselor makes a YES decision and moves on to subsystem 7.0. If, however, the client is not sufficiently motiviated, the counselor moves to DISCUSS REASONS FOR INSUFFICIENT MOTIVATION (6.6), then returns to 6.5 and again assesses the client's level of commitment. This recycling process continues until either a YES decision is reached, or it becomes apparent that the client is definitely lacking the necessary motivation. In the latter case, the counselor then moves to 2.2.5 (indicated in the circle above 6.6) and assists the client in locating appropriate assistance, after which termination operations are conducted.

Implement strategy (7.0).   Assuming that the client *is* sufficiently motivated, the counselor now moves to the performance of operations designed to help the client attain the learning objective. The first step in this subsystem is to determine the counseling strategy (7.1). The choice is to be made from one or more of the following: learning new responses, motivating behavior change, and becoming self-directed. These strategies will be defined and explained in detail in subsequent chapters.

A meaningful learning objective can seldom be attained in an economical and efficient manner if it is approached from the beginning as a global entity. It is usually necessary to analyze the objective and set up a program of interim or subobjectives, the progressive attainment of which will lead to the ultimate learning objective. The counselor therefore proceeds to establish one or more intermediate objectives (7.2).

After the intermediate objectives have been agreed upon, the counselor and client then select immediate operational steps (7.3) to accomplish the intermediate objectives. The next function involves the actual performance of the steps which have been agreed upon (7.4).

Following the performance of steps, the counselor must decide whether the strategy and the accompanying steps have been completed (7.5). If a YES decision is made, the counselor then moves to the next subsystem (8.0). If a NO decision is made, it is necessary to recycle to ESTABLISH INTERMEDIATE OBJECTIVES (7.2), repeat the sequence from 7.2 to 7.5, and again decide whether the strategy and steps have been completed. If a NO decision continues to be reached after repeated attempts, it is then necessary to move to 2.2.5, help the client locate appropriate assistance, and proceed to terminate counseling contact. Only after a YES decision has been reached may the counselor move to subsystem 8.0.

Evaluate client performance (8.0).   The first major function in this subsystem involves an analysis of the outcomes of counseling (8.1). Here, the counselor must first record the performance of the client (8.1.1), preferably in writing. The performance is then checked against the baseline or presenting level of concern-related behavior (8.1.2) as previously determined in Function 5.4. Next, the client's performance is compared with the objective for counseling (8.1.3). The counselor then decides whether the objective has been attained (8.2). If a NO decision (8.2.1) is made, it is necessary to recycle to 6.5, determine whether the client's motivation is sufficient, and proceed from that point forward.

If the decision is YES (8.2.2), the counselor must then decide whether the client needs further counseling (8.3). Here, there are three possible decisions. It is conceivable that, when asked about the possible need for further counseling, the client will decide to pursue a new aspect (8.3.1) of the same general area of concern as that of the objective which has just been accomplished. In such an event, the counselor recycles to 6.2, determines a desired goal, and proceeds through the flowchart from that point forward. A second possibility is that the client will indicate a need for further counseling, but on an altogether different concern (8.3.2) from that of the objective which has just been accomplished. In this case, the counselor must recycle to 5.1 (indicated by the circle to the left of 8.3.2), clearly identify the new concern, and proceed from that point forward. The third possibility, of course, is that the client will indicate that there is no need whatsoever for further counseling at this time (8.3.3). In that event, the counselor proceeds to subsystem 9.0.

Terminate counseling (9.0). After the objective has been attained and there is no apparent need for further counseling, the counselor proceeds to terminate regular contact with the client. First, the rationale and procedures for termination are explained (9.1), and any client or counselor resistance to termination is resolved (9.2). Next, the counselor conducts transfer of learning (9.3), emphasizing how the strategies and skills learned during the counseling process can be applied by the client to future problems. Finally, in 9.4 a plan is established for monitoring the client's performance for a reasonable period of time after the termination of counseling.

Monitor client performance (10.0). Since the client may have trouble sustaining the improvement attained in counseling, it is usually advisable to make a performance check from time to time. The procedure for doing so will follow the plan previously established in PLAN MONITORING OF CLIENT PERFORMANCE (9.4). If the client encounters difficulty, provision is made for recycling to DETERMINE DESIRED GOAL (6.2) or to DECIDE IF CLIENT MOTIVATION IS SUFFICIENT (6.5).

Close case (11.0). The process of closing the case may vary somewhat from client to client. If the referral has been judged inappropriate, or if the normal counseling process has broken down at some point, the counselor will first help the client locate appropriate assistance and will then close by going directly from MANAGE CLIENT/COUNSELOR RESISTANCE (9.2) to CLOSE CASE (11.0).

Typically, however, the process of closing the case will be conducted after the client has demonstrated continued successful performance during the follow-up period (10.0). Here, depending upon the nature of the plan for monitoring the client's performance, the counselor will conduct a brief "wrap-up" session with the client and will then complete interview notes and other records concerning the case.

Evaluate counselor performance (12.0). Next, the performance of the counselor is evaluated. In a sense, self-evaluation is a continuous part of the counselor's activity throughout the counseling process. Nevertheless, an especially appropriate time for evaluation has been set aside in this subsystem. Evaluation of counselor performance may be accomplished in a variety of ways. The counselor may engage in introspection and may also seek the help of others in evaluating counseling performance, including the client, fellow counselors, teachers, supervisors, and others who are familiar with the case.

In the next and concluding step, the information resulting from the evaluation of the counselor's performance is transmitted or "fed back" (as indicated by the circled "F" between 12.0 and 1.0) to the counselor to help in the development of improved methods so as to be more effective and efficient with the next client. This closes the loop and completes the cycle, thus emphasizing the self-corrective nature of the Systematic Counseling process.

PERFORMANCE CRITERIA FOR SYSTEMATIC COUNSELING

The flowchart provides a basic road map for the counselor's guidance in completing the various procedures and tasks in Systematic Counseling. Like most maps, however, the flowchart is more concerned with what to do than how to do it or how well it should be done. The counselor needs additional help. For example, how does one decide whether to accept a referral? How should one explain the counseling relationship to a client? How does one establish a baseline of the client's concern-related behavior? The flowchart directs the counselor to determine a counseling goal, but how is this to be done? How does one know when a goal has been appropriately stated? These and many other questions must be faced and resolved if the counselor is to know how to proceed. For this reason, a set of Performance Criteria has been established to supplement and clarify the procedures noted on the flowchart.

Importance of Behavioral Measures

As noted earlier in this chapter, it is important that the client's objective for counseling be stated in terms which are observable and measurable. Only in this way can it be subsequently known whether the objective has been attained. Similarly, it is important that the counselor's behavior be measured against criteria which are behavioral. Clear specification of these criteria not only enables the counselor to know how to proceed, but also facilitates the evaluation of performance during and after training.

The Criteria

The complete Performance Criteria have been included as Appendix A. Since the criteria are largely self-explanatory, they will not be treated in detail in this chapter. However, certain highlights will be emphasized.

It will be noted that the criteria are subdivided according to the various subsystems of the counseling process. Thus, the criteria for COUNSELOR (1.0) are concerned primarily with certain basic attitudes which the counselor should possess.

Since PROCESS CLIENT REFERRAL (2.0) is the first subsystem which involves counselor activity, let us look in detail at some of the criteria. After indicating the source of the client referral, the counselor must present evidence in Function 2.2.1 that data were collected concerning the reasons for the referral. Note that the kinds of evidence considered appropriate have been listed here for the guidance of the counselor. Note further that the evidence must be listed directly on the form, and that a space is provided in the rectangle for the supervisor or other person monitoring the counselor's performance to indicate whether the evidence is adequate. If the evidence is not adequate, the supervisor will indicate in what ways it is deficient and the counselor will be expected to make corrections accordingly.

Next are listed the criteria for ANALYZE DATA (2.2.2). Here, the counselor must identify the problem and its attendant conditions in writing, using behavioral terms. Again, specific examples are given to guide the counselor in the description, and space is provided for the supervisor to record an evaluation. Note that the same basic format is followed for the remaining functions of subsystem 2.0 and throughout the Performance Criteria, concluding with EVALUATE COUNSELOR PERFORMANCE (12.0). (At this time you should take a few moments to read through the remainder of the Performance Criteria.)

Using the Criteria

The Performance Criteria may be used in two closely related ways—as a training aid and as an evaluation tool. For the student or counselor who wishes to learn the procedures of Systematic Counseling, the Performance Criteria—in conjunction with the flowchart—provide a basic means of direction and evaluation.

As a training aid, the Performance Criteria constitute a written "model" of appropriate performance to be emulated by the trainee or counselor. The criteria also contain a built-in mechanism for feedback on the quality of the counselor's performance; the counselor tries to respond in accordance with the model, the performance is checked against the model by the supervisor, and suggestions are then made for improvement. Subsequent efforts are again checked against the model. Thus, the Performance Criteria provide a basic vehicle for shaping the counselor's behavior.

In the counselor education program at Michigan State University, the criteria are used primarily in prepracticum and practicum courses. In the counseling procedures course prior to the practicum, each student is required to play the role of counselor in a number of complete tape-recorded counseling cases. In conducting these cases one must adhere to the flowchart and must complete the counselor's portion of the Performance Criteria. These tapes and the Performance Criteria are then submitted to an instructor who reviews the tapes and marks the supervisor's evaluation in the boxes on the form.

A similar procedure is followed in the counseling practicum. One set of criteria sheets is used for each client counseled by the student. Prior to meeting with the supervisor for a tape review session, the student completes the starred portions of the criteria covered by the taped interview submitted for critique. The supervisor then completes the evaluation in the boxes on the form while listening to the tape, and returns the form to the student. In places where the performance is not rated adequate, the student must make appropriate modifications in the next interview with the same client. Additional portions of the form are completed by the student prior to presenting the next taped interview for critique, after which the supervisor again makes written comments, returns the tape and form a second time, and so on. This procedure is repeated until the case has been completed.

A counselor who is not enrolled in a formal training program but who wishes to utilize the procedures of Systematic Counseling can follow much the same procedure, reviewing interviews and, with the aid of the Performance Criteria, critiquing one's own counseling behavior. One may, of course, enlist the aid of others, such as fellow counselors, to observe and make ratings on the criteria. More will be said about evaluating counselor performance in Chapter 11.

SUMMARY

This chapter has provided an overview of the procedures, tools, and techniques of Systematic Counseling. This unique approach has been described and differentiated from other "systematic" approaches. The major steps in the counseling process have been presented, and the related flowchart and Performance Criteria have been introduced.

Systematic Counseling is an approach in which the various aspects of the counseling process are clearly identified and organized into a sequence designed to resolve the client's concerns efficiently as well as effectively. As a synthesis of learning theory, systems analysis, and educational technology, Systematic Counseling differs markedly from other approaches which are sometimes labeled "systematic."

Systematic Counseling is organized into 12 subsystems, beginning with the counselor as a person and extending through 11 major operations outlining what the counselor does in one-to-one counseling. Information resulting from the evaluation of the counselor's performance is fed back to the counselor to assist in dealing with future clients.

The various aspects of the counseling process may be represented graphically by the flowchart for Systematic Counseling. The flowchart helps one to grasp the overall scope of counselor responsibilities and to follow a logical sequence of tasks throughout the counseling process. Understanding the flowchart requires a mastery of certain terms and symbols provided by the language of LOGOS.

Supplementing the flowchart as a basic means of direction are the Performance Criteria for Systematic Counseling. The Performance Criteria provide the counselor with a written model of appropriate behavior and facilitate the evaluation of counselor performance. While the criteria were constructed for use in a formal training program, they may also be used for evaluation in on-the-job settings.

As you have seen, this chapter has a strong didactic orientation intended to acquaint you with the broad scope of the Systematic Counseling process. But what might the Systematic Counselor actually *say* and *do* in dealing with a specific client? Illustrative answers to this question are provided in subsequent chapters, and a complete case transcript is included in Chapter 13.

5

Preparing for Counseling

OVERVIEW

The preceding chapters of this book have been designed to provide a description of the foundations of Systematic Counseling and to survey the principal aspects of this counseling system and technology. Beginning with this chapter, you will be studying the specific operations and functions performed by counselors as they assist clients to work through the counseling process in order to attain their counseling goals and objectives. You will be studying the professional competencies and skills that are demanded of counselors if they are to use the model of Systematic Counseling for the benefit of their clients. You will also learn specific operations and procedures for the first three subsystems of this model so that you can assist a client to be prepared adequately for counseling.

Some of the functions performed by a counselor may be unexpected ones. We would like you to remember that the model of Systematic Counseling has been conceived as a whole system. Each part of the system is important and contributes something to the total output of the system. You may at first find it somewhat awkward and frustrating to perform some of the functions. However, remember that it is usually difficult to perform well when first learning a new system. It takes much practice to gain confidence and skill in using the model of Systematic Counseling, just as it does when learning a new musical skill, sport, or academic subject.

There are two basic components in the counseling process—counselor and client. Additional subcomponents or functions are necessarily performed to establish, maintain, and terminate the counseling process. Because so many functions must be performed, the counselor may tend to overlook some and disregard others. Systematic Counseling serves as an organizational aid to the counselor in effectively managing the functions that must be performed in counseling.

This chapter provides a detailed coverage of the functions in the initial stages of counseling. The flowchart for Systematic Counseling presents the probable sequence of functions in counseling. As you study the flowchart, you will note that the subsystems covered in this chapter extond from COUNSELOR (1.0) to PREPARE FOR INTERVIEW (3.0).

INTRODUCTION

Organization

There are *three* major topical divisions in this chapter. The initial section presents the counselor as the main functionary in the counseling process. The seven conditions of an attitudinal state of readiness for counseling are explained, and individual interaction skill-building activities that facilitate both verbal and nonverbal aspects of counseling are described. The second section presents a set of procedures for processing a client referral. The third section describes how to prepare for the initial counseling interview.

Purposes

The general purposes of this chapter are (a) to help you understand the initial phase of the Systematic Counseling process; (b) to help you understand the interrelationships which exist within this initial phase; and (c) to provide a set of model procedures which will facilitate your preparation for counseling.

Objectives

Upon reading this chapter it is expected that you will be prepared to do the following:

1. List and distinguish among the four major sources of environmental referrals for counseling.
2. List the five considerations in determining the appropriateness of the referral.
3. List the two functions involved in preparing for the interview.

THE COUNSELOR (1.0)

You will recall from your study of the flowcharts in Chapter 4 that the model of *Systematic Counseling* is composed of 12 subsystems. The other 11 subsystems indicate that the counselor is responsible for providing direction and continuity for the counseling process while carrying out the different functions associated with subsystems 2.0 through 12.0. These operations demand that a counselor be able to demonstrate certain attitudes, skills, and knowledge in order to assist a wide range of clients to attain positive outcomes from counseling. In the following section, we will describe a set of conditions which, when synthesized by a counselor, will facilitate the counseling relationship and process in the different subsystems of Systematic Counseling. The basic interviewing skills required of a counselor will be described in a later section.

Professional Competencies

1. A counselor must respect the worth and dignity of a client regardless of the client's behavior, attitudes, creeds, race, sex, age, or socioeconomic status.

Most counselors work in educational settings or for governmental agencies that are supported by public funds. They are expected, indeed obligated, to assist individuals from widely varying backgrounds who display problems of a myriad nature. Obviously, then, counselors should strive to manifest an attitude of respect for every client, as bias and prejudice can hardly facilitate the counseling relationship and process.

Unfortunately, all of us have learned at least some irrational attitudes of hostility toward some other peoples. If we are aware of these, we can take steps to control our behavior so that the counseling relationship can be made as facilitative as possible. At the same time, we should attempt to change our value systems so that we can grow to respect the worth and dignity of an increasingly larger number of people. For example, a counselor may feel that anyone on drugs is a menace to society and should, therefore, be incarcerated. Such a counselor could report his or her feelings to a client with drug problems and offer to help the client locate a counselor who could be of assistance. Another alternative for this counselor is to perceive drug usage as a societal problem rather than one of individual wrongdoing. The counselor may then be able to change negative feelings toward particular clients. The client may be respected as a human being in need of help to resolve a drug problem.

Some of us are unaware of, or deny to ourselves, the fact that we possess certain biases and prejudices. We are unaware of the detrimental effects that such insensitivity may be having on a counseling relationship. Some cues that may signal that a counselor has prejudicial attitudes are: boredom during interviews, inattention to the verbal and nonverbal behavior of a client, lack of enthusiasm or fear of working with certain clients or certain kinds of problems, the use of sarcastic or stereotyped responses, and the display of various forms of direct or subtle hostility. Counselors who are alert to such cues can examine their value systems and, when necessary, attempt to change them. Change may be brought about by engaging in learning experiences such as counseling or values clarification groups, or by deliberately seeking opportunities in the environment to interact with individuals who arouse prejudicial attitudes. One of the most useful ways we have found to be sure that we are respecting the dignity and worth of our clients is to constantly remind ourselves that it is a privilege to enter into a counseling relationship with another person—any person.

2. *A counselor must work to develop a facilitative relationship with a client.*

Respect for an individual, discussed in the previous paragraphs, is one of the principal characteristics of a facilitative counseling relationship. It is so important that we have described it as a single competency. There are, however, other important dimensions of a facilitative counseling relationship.

It must be remembered that a counselor has the responsibility for developing an adequate relationship with the client. It is the counselor who must create an environment that encourages a client to have confidence in the counselor, to feel free to discuss concerns openly and honestly, and to understand that the counselor sincerely desires to be of assistance. Too often we have heard counselors and counselor trainees rationalize their inability to help clients by blaming clients for their unwillingness to establish effective relationships. Such counselors may have been deficient in establishing an effective environment for counseling with these particular clients.

With many clients, facilitative relationships can be achieved during the first few minutes of the initial interview. Those who have attained sufficient confidence in themselves and others are often secure enough to discuss their concerns candidly almost from the time that they first meet the counselor. These clients are also usually well motivated to seek help from counseling. With other clients, facilitative relationships often evolve over a period of several interviews. Such clients may not be motivated to seek counseling, but have been referred to a counselor by a teacher, parent, employer, governmental agency, or similar source. They may be unaware of the purposes for counseling and be fearful of the counseling process. Others may distrust or lack confidence in professional people who offer counseling or similar services. Regardless of the reason, the length of time taken to establish an effective relationship is an excellent cue to how clients have learned to relate to many adults, to the severity and duration of their problems, or to the lack of professional competencies by the counselor.

The nature of assistance being sought by a client is also an important determinant of the time it takes to develop an adequate relationship. A counselor can usually develop appropriate relationships easily with most clients who are attempting to make vocational or educational decisions. Ordinarily it is more difficult and requires more time to develop relationships with clients who have problems that they feel are to be kept hidden,—e.g., sexual, racial, social, drug, or alcohol problems. These clients often find it difficult to disclose their thoughts and feelings until they are assured through the counselor's behavior that they are in an understanding, confidential, and safe environment.

A facilitative relationship has the best chance to evolve when a client is given the opportunity to learn that a counselor is competent, can be trusted, and respects the client as a person of worth and dignity. In other words, as counseling progresses the counselor must teach a client to have confidence in their relationship and the counseling process. The counselor does this concurrently, and throughout the process, while performing the other functions required by the counseling process.

A facilitative counseling relationship is perceived by a client as a whole. A client does not usually view or label the empathic, respectful, and congruent behaviors of a counselor as separate entities, but rather gains a whole impression of confidence and trust in the counselor. Thus, the establishment of a relationship with a client is dependent upon the sum total of a counselor's verbal and nonverbal behaviors— i.e., the statements made by a counselor and *how* these statements are made, upon listening skills, body posture, movements, and facial expressions. An effective relationship requires a counselor to synthesize these behaviors into a whole that is seen by a client as a helping relationship.

You probably have already synthesized and demonstrated many, if not all, of these verbal and nonverbal behaviors at certain times with certain people. With close friends, we often establish facilitative relationships. Recall for a moment one of the occasions when a friend engaged you in a serious discussion. You probably were attentive and listened carefully. You may have shown that you were listening by looking at your friend and generally keeping eye contact. You would want a friend to feel that his or her statements were important to you, so you would make comments, body movements, and facial expressions to communicate such understanding. Depending upon the topic being discussed, you may have been physically close to your friend and communicated your understanding by touching him or her with your hands. You would not be phony with such a person; you would be truthful and objective in an empathic manner. By these actions, you would have communicated respect and trustworthiness.

We believe that the dimensions of a facilitative counseling relationship are the same as those of a facilitative relationship between close friends. The principal differences are that you are free to choose your friends, and the purpose of interactions between friends is often not directed toward the goal of resolving a problem. Most counselors are not free to choose their clients, and the only purpose for facilitative counseling relationships is to assist individuals to reach their counseling goals.

We have observed that such concepts as respect, empathy, nonpossessive warmth, genuineness, and concreteness have the highest probability of being actualized into a facilitative relationship when a counselor consistently synthesizes the following: (a) undivided attention to both verbal and nonverbal behavior; (b) accurate listening; (c) a repertoire of verbal and nonverbal communication skills; (d) empathic truthfulness and objectivity; (e) self-control of behavior and emotions; (f) eye contact that is comfortable for the client; (g) physical closeness that is comfortable for the client; and (h) a friendly, welcoming, unpretentious, and relaxed manner.

How can you determine whether you are making progress toward attaining an effective relationship with a client? There are several important cues. As a client learns to trust and have confidence in a counselor, the client usually becomes more visibly relaxed and finds it easier to discuss his or her concerns. The level of self-disclosure of personal or intimate information becomes more appropriate to the type of assistance being sought. Contradictory and exaggerated information becomes less frequent. Eye contact between client and counselor becomes more prolonged. Pretentious mannerisms begin to drop out of the client's behavior, and he or she tends to become more objective about problems. More and more self-control over behavior and emotions is evidenced by the client.

If none or few of these cues are manifested in the client's behavior during the first or second interviews, you should first evaluate your own behavior to determine if you are demonstrating the behaviors that lead to an appropriate relationship. If you are not, then you should discuss with the client the observations that led you to judge that a facilitative relationship is not present. In most instances an empathic discussion of your observations will lead to an improved relationship.

3. *A counselor must always assist a client to examine the biological, environmental, and psychological dimensions of what he or she is thinking, feeling, and doing.*

We pointed out in Chapter 1 that a client brings to counseling a unique integration of biological, environmental, and psychological qualities in which his or her problems or concerns are embedded. A high school girl, for example, may be teased by classmates for having a severe case of acne. If the teasing persists over a long period of time, she may learn to avoid her peers, develop unsatisfactory social relationships, feel worthless and lonely, fail to achieve up to her ability in school, or learn a host of other debilitating behaviors. Thus, a biological difficulty can bring on a wide range of environmental and psychological problems.

A counselor should possess a good general knowledge of the typical and irregular influences that these biological, environmental, and psychological dimensions can have on the development and maintenance of behaviors. This knowledge then becomes the basis for assessing the unique organization of these qualities in the life of a client. The counselor combines this general knowledge with what is learned during interviews from the verbal, nonverbal, cognitive, affective, and psychomotor responses of a client. In addition, a counselor will often find it necessary to obtain additional knowledge by observing the client and consulting significant people in the environment.

When a client is assisted to examine all three dimensions, the client and counselor will have a more complete understanding of the factors responsible for a client's concern. Thus, a more accurate model of the concerns can be constructed. Too often, we have observed counselors who focus on the psychological influences of behavior to the exclusion of the biological and environmental. Generally, these counselors fail to construct an accurate or helpful model of the client's concerns.

4. *The personal needs of a counselor for reinforcement must be continually examined to determine if the counseling relationship is fulfilling those needs at the expense of client progress toward goal attainment.*

Continuous reevaluation of a counselor's motivation to serve clients must occur to prevent inappropriate, if not negative, outcomes from the counseling process. Some counselors apparently find it rewarding to assume a "mothering" or "fathering" role with their clients. They seem to gain satisfaction from dependent relationships. Others appear to have sexual needs that are directly or indirectly fulfilled at the expense of clients. Some seem to be in the counseling profession primarily for financial gains, to solve their personal problems, or for the prestige of the position. A few seem aloof, noninvolved, and uncaring in their relationships.

Nurturing, protecting, and supporting clients are therapeutically appropriate at certain times in the counseling process. Encounter, focusing responsibility for behavior on the client, not coming to the rescue of a client, and counselor self-disclosure of personal problems are also appropriate procedures in certain situations. Our concern lies in the motivation of a counselor when assuming certain roles or using certain techniques and procedures. If a counselor is nurturing a client because it makes the counselor feel good, or if a counselor asks most clients to describe their sex lives regardless of the nature of their problems, then we question the legitimacy of the counselor's motivation.

5. *A counselor must be an adequate social model of the counseling profession.*

You have probably heard several disparaging remarks made about individual counselors. We have made such remarks ourselves in several places in this book. Whether deserved or not, counselors receive considerable criticism from clients, parents, teachers, administrators, government officials, and the general public. Almost every week someone tells us how a counselor "screwed up" some aspect of his or her life. Rarely do we hear people applauding those counselors who have helped clients obtain positive benefits from counseling. In our society it often seems that negative reports are the only ones to be communicated. The tragic aspect of such criticism is that many negative reports are essentially correct. Many clients do receive mediocre assistance. Many potential clients, upon learning of this criticism, are probably discouraged from seeking assistance with their concerns.

As in many areas, critics can easily stereotype the entire counseling profession on the basis of the ineffectual performance of a few counselors. We have known, for example, several black educators who have stated that blacks should not be counseled by whites, and they can cite several legitimate cases of unethical and unprofessional counseling of black people by white counselors.

We believe that much of the criticism should alert counselors to become extremely aware of their roles as social models. Any perceived incompetency is often generalized by individuals to the entire counseling profession. We can overcome negative criticism only by working toward making ourselves, as individual counselors, more accountable to our clients and the public by subjecting our work to rigorous evaluation and then taking steps to improve our performance where needed. We will always make errors in counseling due to the complexity of human behavior and the counseling process. We can, however, decrease the number of errors and increase our effectiveness in assisting more clients to receive positive benefits from our services.

6. A counselor must be thoroughly familiar with a system of counseling that provides an adequate technology for assisting clients and evaluating the results.

A counselor may respect his or her clients, be able to develop facilitative relationships, help them to examine the different dimensions of their behavior, and be legitimately motivated to provide assistance, *yet still be unable* to assist very many clients to attain the goals they seek. It is our view that such a counselor lacks one vital competency. The counselor lacks a complete understanding of a total system of counseling *or* is using a system that lacks a technology that sufficiently describes the functions to be performed during the counseling process.

A counselor trainee must repeatedly practice a system and technology of counseling during role-played and other simulated counseling conditions. The trainee must practice until the system and technology are so completely understood that they feel as comfortable as an old pair of favorite shoes! Then, when face to face with an actual client, the trainee will feel relatively confident that he or she will know what, when, and how to perform the various functions of the counseling process. If the five competencies previously mentioned are also demonstrated consistently, the trainee or counselor will very likely be or become an appropriate social model for other members of our profession.

7. *A counselor must pursue a continuing education program throughout her or his career.*

A counselor's education must not cease at the termination of formal education if his or her counseling effectiveness is to be maintained and improved. Today, many opportunities exist for counselors to continue learning about human behavior and the counseling process.

One of the most valuable and productive methods for gaining additional skills is to study your own taped interviews. Each client can increase your knowledge of human behavior and the counseling process if you will carefully evaluate each case and note how you can increase your counseling competencies. Other counselors can also be asked to assist in evaluating your skills and to make suggestions for avoiding counseling errors.

You should also give high priority to the study of your own behavior. There are excellent workshops, courses, and books that can help you increase your self-awareness and self-control.

Many counselors have found it very beneficial to deliberately seek opportunities to learn more about the customs, values, and behavior of different ethnic, racial, and sexual subcultures in our society. The differences among people from various income, occupational, and age groups can also be studied. Becoming involved with people from all types of backgrounds is one of the best ways to study and change, if needed, your own biases, prejudices, values, and behavior.

You can keep current with new developments, knowledge, and research in the behavioral sciences by becoming a member of professional organizations and reading their journals. These organizations often provide skill-building workshops prior to or after their national conventions. State branches of these groups also provide workshops during the year at the local level.

These are only a few suggestions for obtaining additional training. There are many other opportunities such as university courses, independent reading, and in-service programs. For the benefit of your clients and yourself, however, we suggest that you develop a program for your professional growth that is based upon a good evaluation of your counseling behaviors. Then, you should locate those materials, courses, colleagues, or instructors that can assist you to gain those personal skills that you need.

Basic Interviewing Skills

In addition to the professional competencies described in the preceding section, a counselor must have a good command of basic interviewing skills in order to effectively use the model of Systematic Counseling. In fact, without effective verbal communication, a counselor cannot expect to demonstrate respect for a client and establish a facilitative relationship.

We conceptualize basic interviewing skills as having six components. The first is the interview setting and getting started. This involves the physical environment, greeting the client, inviting the client to participate in the interview, maintaining eye contact, and demonstrating proper counselor posture. The second includes the problem focus to be utilized in counseling. The third component focuses on identifying an important theme for counseling. The problem theme for counseling is the topic of the fourth, while the fifth component involves directing the theme toward a goal. The sixth component concerns managing counselor-client interactions, which includes four major interactional techniques: restatement, maintaining tension during the interview, interpretation, and managing pauses and silences.

The first five interview skill components are concerned with general considerations that are important in effective interviewing. The sixth component involves a study of the specific words that can be used to communicate the areas and directions of the interview with a client.

THE INTERVIEW SETTING AND
GETTING STARTED

A counselor may increase the likelihood of helping the client by attending to five physical and interactional factors that are vital to beginning the interview.

1. Physical arrangements. The physical features of a counselor's office are the least important variables in determining whether or not one will be successful in assisting clients. A skillful counselor can be of help in most any type of setting, providing it is private and has a minimum amount of furniture. We will focus, therefore, only on that arrangement of furniture which is most valuable in promoting a good relationship between the counselor and the client.

Two comfortable chairs are a basic requirement for a counselor's office. Typically, there is also a desk or table. The important thing, however, is the placement of the chairs. If only chairs are used, they should face each other and the counselor's chair should be positioned to facilitate leaning forward and touching the client.

When a desk or table is used, the client's chair should be placed by the side of the desk. The desk should not serve as a barrier between the client and the counselor. Again, the counselor should be near enough to lean forward and touch the client if and when it is appropriate.

The reason for these arrangements is to provide an intimate atmosphere so that the client will develop a sense of trust in the counselor. The closeness of the counselor helps to indicate a person who is attentive and willing to be of assistance.

2. Greeting and seating the client. Most individuals appreciate being extended a warm and friendly greeting. Statements such as, "Hello, won't you come in ? My name is Tom Jones. Would you like to take the chair next to my desk?" are appropriate. Shaking hands is usually acceptable even with junior high school students, although local custom dictates how this would be received. The counselor should also greet a client with a smile or with a relaxed, noncritical facial expression.

The reason for such behavior when greeting and seating a client is to help the client feel at ease. The client should be made to feel the counselor's respect for the client as a unique person, rather than as just another individual.

3. Inviting the client to participate in the interview. Getting an interview started would appear to be a rather simple task. *It is.* Many inexperienced and poorly trained counselors, however, go through an elaborate ritual for five or ten minutes before asking clients to indicate why they have come for counseling. Such counselors discuss the weather and other inconsequential topics in order (they think) to set the client at ease. Such "small talk" may lead the client to believe that the counselor is avoiding any discussion of the client's problem. Such behavior may divert the client from discussing the important reasons that prompted this visit to the counselor's office. The client may try to please the counselor by continuing to discuss topics presented by the counselor or use them to avoid discussing anxiety-producing material. In short, a client will usually respond to whatever opening leads are given by a counselor.

Simple statements such as, "How may I help you?" or "What would you like to discuss today?" are usually appropriate to open an interview. Of course, if you initiated a contact with a student, teacher, or parent, you would begin by stating the reason for the interview. For example, "I asked you to come in today to discuss your progress in the sheltered workshop," or "I asked you to come in to discuss your son's progress this semester."

4. *Maintaining eye contact.* Counselors usually maintain eye contact with their clients. Eye contact helps build a personal relationship between two people and indicates that the counselor is not embarrassed or afraid to approach a problem. It also permits the counselor to observe nonverbal behavior exhibited by the client.

Occasionally, eye contact will make a client uncomfortable. When this occurs, the counselor should maintain contact only for a few seconds at a time until the client is more at ease. You do not want clients to feel that they are being examined under a microscope.

The counselor may find an occasional need to divert eye contact from the client in order to concentrate. The counselor should take care not to look away from the client while the client is discussing topics of personal concern. Such behavior may suggest to the client that the counselor is embarrassed or critical.

5. *Demonstrating proper body posture.* The counselor should be relaxed, but at the same time, attentive to the client. A good posture for the counselor is one of leaning forward toward the client and maintaining eye contact. Such posture assists in developing an intimate counseling atmosphere. It indicates that the counselor is interested in the information that the client is presenting. Further, the counselor's posture should be mobile, allowing freedom of movement and ability to use the body to assist in communication.

The Problem Focus

Another consideration in getting started in an initial interview with a client is that of determining the nature of the problem focus during the counselor-client interaction. If directions are not given during an interview, the client may tend to ramble and there is the possibility that important data related to the problem may be ignored. Since most individual counseling is relatively short-term (three to six interviews), it is necessary that the counselor assist the client to focus on important themes or topics of concern. Wolberg (1967) calls this the principle of *selective focusing.* Selective focusing is the process of identifying an important theme in the client's verbalizations, focusing the client's remarks around this theme, and directing the theme into a goal-directed channel. The counselor should also be alert to the nonverbal cues that are related to the discussion of the problem.

Identifying an Important Theme

The counselor listens and observes as the client presents a problem. As the client talks, the counselor tries to identify the important themes of client verbalizations by examining the preoccupations of the client.

What does the client choose to discuss, and how strong is the emotional significance that the client attaches to the topics? Identifying themes is made somewhat easier by grouping the major preoccupations of clients. Clients tend to have problems that cluster in one of three areas. These are:

1. *Existing environmental difficulties.*   Problems in this area constitute the bulk of an individual's preoccupations. Clients, for example, will discuss what aspects of the environment assist in gratifying their needs and what causes them to have satisfactory relationships with others. Clients also talk about how the environment hampers their daily lives. They will indicate the sources of frustration and conflict that interfere with their plans and schedules. Remember that most problems encountered by clients are caused by environmental difficulties and can be considered developmental problems.

2. *Difficulties caused by inappropriate learning.*   Many clients find that their attitudes and habits are in conflict with those of other people. Clients may find that habits of dependency, aggression, detachment, perfectionism, and complusive ambition interfere with social relationships at work, at home, and at school. These difficulties can be considered remedial problems. That is, the existing inappropriate behavior is maladaptive in that it does not result in a lessening of conflict or frustration.

3. *Persisting childhood difficulties.*   The last group of preoccupations consists of those difficulties *which have persisted over a period of time.* We think of these as originating in childhood. They consist mainly of unresolved fears, guilt feelings, and immature behavior patterns.

You may find it easier to identify important themes in a client's verbalizations if you think of classifying them into one of these groups: environment, developmental learning, and remedial or childhood problems.

Focusing on a Theme

Once a theme has been identified, the counselor has to direct the client's verbalizations so that they focus on the theme. Usually the client has feelings associated with the theme which should be identified and discussed. The most effective use of the interview occurs when the client is assisted to talk at length about a limited number of topics. Only a certain amount of data can be retained at any one time, so the counselor must help the client focus on data that relate to the theme of personal preoccupations. The counselor does this by refocusing on the central theme each time the client strays or rambles. Such leads by the counselor as, "You were telling me about why your father doesn't understand you," or "Can you tell me more about your difficulties in math class?" will help control the flow of client verbalizations.

Directing the Theme Toward a Goal

The principal purpose of counseling is to assist a person to alter behavior to meet a goal or objective that the client and counselor both believe is worth attaining. This could be a career or educational goal, or a goal for improving one's social skills. Goals may also be established to remove environmental difficulties, inappropriate behavior patterns, or guilt feelings that were developed in childhood. Regardless of the specific problem presented by the client, the counselor always and continually directs the interview into a goal-attaining channel.

After the main themes of the client's verbalizations have been identified and these themes have been explored in enough depth to provide the counselor with an understanding of the client's self-perception and his or her environment, the stage is set for discussing counseling goals. Then, leads such as the following will be helpful:

> "As I understand things, you want to stop daydreaming when you should be studying?"
> "What you want to accomplish in counseling is to select a training school for either drafting or auto mechanics?"
> "You want to decide whether to go to college or enter the armed services?"

Such leads will produce further discussion of the specific goals that a client wishes to establish for altering personal behavior.

Managing Counselor-Client Interaction

The final area of focus in basic interviewing skills is the counselor's sensitivity to three techniques that may be used in facilitating the client's discussion of concerns, as well as a technique for managing silences and pauses. Sometimes in a counseling interview there is discussion of numerous topics that are unrelated to the client's problems. Clients do not always talk easily. Some lack the verbal skills to express their concerns. Other clients do not trust the counselor enough to verbalize freely their personal ideas and feelings. When a client has threatening ideas or feelings, there may be some resistance to further discussion, as evidenced by "clamming up." Therefore, it becomes important for the counselor to have a number of techniques to maintain the flow of client verbalizations:

Restatement. This technique involves putting statements of the client into different words to bring the client's attention to certain aspects of the verbalizations that may have escaped notice. The technique also is used to point out specifically what the client may find difficult to verbalize. It can also be used to help a client focus on feelings or important themes in the verbalizations. The following example will demonstrate the effective use of restatement:

> *Client:* "I'm not sure why kids in my class don't like me. I know I'm kinda sensitive about failing last year and I've had a couple of arguments with the teacher. That doesn't seem to be enough to have all of the class against me."
>
> *Counselor:* "For some reason the students in your class don't seem to care for you, and the only things you can think of that might cause this situation is your sensitivity about failing and some disagreements you've had with the teacher."

Maintaining tension in the interview. The client must be motivated to work actively toward achieving a goal in counseling. Being overly relaxed does not promote active client involvement in the counseling process. Some clients want to dump their problems and let the counselor take the responsibility for finding solutions. The counselor has to be alert to such situations and take steps to maintain an optimum amount of tension during the interview.

Tension can be created by focusing on provocative topics, by asking challenging questions, and by silence. For example, the counselor could say, "Do *you* really want a job?" or "I'm getting the feeling that you want me to do all the work."

When a counselor uses silence to increase tension, the client is made to become uncomfortable. This discomfort may cause the client to respond spontaneously to the situation. A counselor must also be aware that silence may be interpreted as rejection or hostility by the client and, therefore, must be used with discretion.

There is a danger of creating too much tension in the interview. The client may develop an active dislike for the counselor and the counseling process. If this situation occurs, the counselor must be prepared to offer supportive counseling to lower the state of tension within the client. For example, the counselor might say, "I could see that you were getting angry because I wouldn't talk. It's okay to get angry in here. The important thing, however, is for us to communicate, and we were just not getting anywhere."

Interpretation. This technique is used by the counselor when presenting a hypothesis about the client's behavior to the client for mutual consideration. The purpose of interpretation is to prompt the examination of possible relationships or meanings of client behavior from new perspectives. However, interpretation must be presented in such a way that the client feels free to reject it if so desired. It does little good to insist that a client accept the counselor's hypothesis. Usually the interpretation is preceded by such phrases as, "I wonder if . . ." or "A possible explanation might be . . ." or "One way of looking at this that occurs to me is . . ."

Managing pauses and silences.   Pauses often occur during counseling while the client thinks through some of the ideas that have been brought out during the interview. On some occasions the client will pause to reorganize thoughts. Such pauses are to be expected and should not be interrupted. When they continue beyond a moment or two, the counselor can focus the content of the interview by: (a) repeating the last word or last few words the client has used, (b) restating the content of the last few statements made by the client, or (c) asking a question about the material that has been under discussion.

Periods of silence, beyond a moment or two, may occur for at least three different reasons. First, early in the interview the client may be embarrassed or threatened by the counseling process. In such an event, the counselor can take steps to relieve the tension by providing reassurance and structure. Second, silence may mean that a particular topic has been worked through and the client is wondering what to say next. And third, the client may be thinking over what has just been said. In these situations the counselor should wait for the client to continue until it becomes obvious that the client is waiting for some response from the counselor.

Silence may also mean that a client is experiencing difficulty in expressing some feeling or idea. Shyness or concern about confidentiality may be an issue. In these situations, the counselor should help the client verbalize by making such statements as, "It's sometimes difficult to discuss certain things," or "How can I help you talk about the things concerning you?" or "I'm wondering if you are afraid that I will discuss your concerns with people outside of this room?"

Silence is likely to follow intense emotional discussions. In these situations, the counselor should maintain an understanding silence until the client has recovered somewhat from the emotional strain.

Finally, some clients don't have the social skills needed to carry on long discussions with adults. They may have learned to express their feelings and thoughts in very few words, or they may have learned to depend on others to initiate and take responsibility for directing the flow of verbalization. In these situations the counselor will have to be patient. One can either attempt to help the client gain the social skills necessary for effective communication, or accept the behavior of the client and rely on nonverbal cues to help provide direction for the counseling process.

Long periods of silence are infrequent in most interviews when the counselor is adequately trained. When silence is a hindrance to further progress in the interview, the following steps are suggested by Wolberg

(1967, p. 414). These suggestions have been modified to make them appropriate for a counseling setting.

1. To break a period of silence, the counselor may focus the client's attention by saying, "You find it difficult to talk," or "It's hard to talk."
2. If no reply, the counselor may say, "I wonder why you are silent."
3. Thereafter, the counselor may remark, "Perhaps you do not know what to say next."
4. Then, "Maybe you're trying to figure out what to say next."
5. This may be followed by, "Perhaps you are upset."
6. The next comment could be, "Perhaps you are afraid to say what is on your mind."
7. Finally, if silence continues, the counselor may say, "I wonder if there is something about me that makes it difficult for you to talk."

In those rare instances when the client remains silent, the counselor should say, "Why don't we just sit here for a while, and maybe you will be able to tell me what you have been thinking." After a reasonable length of time, the counselor can attempt again to break the silence. If this is unproductive, the counselor should gently dismiss the client with the assurance of availability at some future time if the client would like to try again. The counselor should communicate a feeling of patience and a willingness to work with the client.

You have now studied the basic competencies and skills needed by a counselor to carry out the functions shown in the flowchart for Systematic Counseling. In the next section of this chapter we will discuss functions and subfunctions involved in processing client referrals.

PROCESSING CLIENT REFERRALS (2.0)

Subsystem 2.0 shows five major sources from which counselors receive their clients. These are: (a) counselor observations; (b) teachers or other school personnel; (c) individuals or agencies within a community; (d) parents, family members, and friends of the client; and (e) self-referral. Each of these sources makes a determination of whether or not to refer an individual to counseling on the basis of observation, feedback from others, direct contact, or records that exist on the individual.

A flowchart for Process Client Referral (2.0) is presented in Figure 5-1. This flowchart should be reviewed and followed as our discussion now shifts to the variety of referral sources.

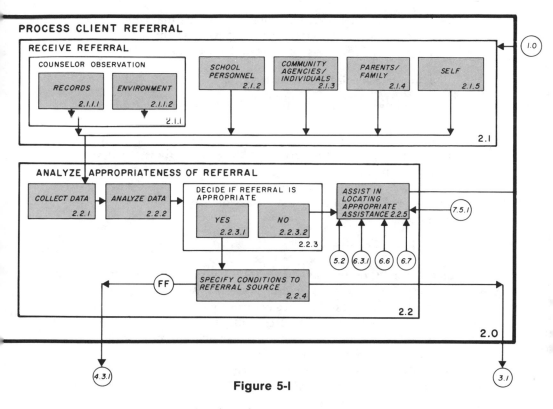

Figure 5-I

Counselor Observation (2.1.1)

Counselors spend varying amounts of time observing individuals in the halls, school cafeteria, and classroom; reviewing school or agency records; and discussing individuals with teachers and other professionals. From these observations and record reviews, the counselor may identify individuals who should be invited to see a counselor because of poor interpersonal relations, poor study habits, poor grades, lack of a sense of educational or vocational direction or commitment, a disability, or other difficulties.

School Personnel (2.1.2)

Teachers, administrators, and other professional and support staff may also identify individuals in need of counseling assistance. The individual who is a frequent discipline problem in the school may be referred for assistance in changing maladaptive behavior. The inattentive student, the handicapped worker, the hyperactive student, or the student who has had a recent significant change in behavior may also be referred to the counselor. Any behavior of an individual which is causing problems either for the individual or those with whom there is personal contact may be ample cause for referral to a counselor.

Community Agencies/Individuals (2.1.3)

Counseling referrals can come from a number of social agencies and individuals within the community. Social agencies such as departments of social services, child welfare clinics, and the probate court often work with clients for whom counseling may be appropriate for at least some aspect of their problem.

Public health nurses, family physicians, pastors, employers and other individuals in the community may also identify those who may profit from counseling.

Parents/Family (2.1.4)

Difficulties may be perceived in the home more readily than in any other setting. Consequently, a parent, sibling, other family member, or friends may decide that difficulties confronting an individual necessitate counseling. Although the home is frequently used by an individual to test new behaviors, occasionally the behavior causes difficulties for that individual or others with whom there is close contact.

Most referrals, except those made by the counselor and those who refer themselves, are accompanied by a letter of referral or a telephone contact explaining the reason why it is felt that counseling is necessary, or by an oral report of the conditions which led to the referral. Additional data that the counselor should collect and analyze might be found in an agency case file or a cumulative record. From such data the agency counselor can get some indication as to the types of difficulties the client has had in school, what the job history is, what disability exists and when it occurred, specific job training, rule infractions which have been committed, noncurricular activities, or a student's curricular and academic standing. The counselor should also contact the referral source to clarify the information received.

Whether the referral is appropriate or not, the counselor should inform the referral source as to what may be expected as a result of counseling. If the counselor decides not to accept the referral, some assistance should be given to the client or referral source in locating appropriate assistance. In this sense, then, the counselor becomes the referring agent.

The term "referral" denotes the action of the counselor in transferring the client to a different counselor or agency for treatment. The decision whether to refer, treat, or drop the case is a difficult one. There have yet to be developed specific guidelines which will readily offer the counselor easy answers to the question, "Should I drop the case, refer it, or begin treatment?" The decision is a subjective, professional one and is often difficult.

Several guidelines are available. They are particularly involved with the ethical and legal aspects of behavior changing. One guideline is contained in the Ethical Standards of the American Personnel and Guidance Association. (APGA, 1974):

> Section B.10. If the member is unable to be of professional assistance to the counselee, the member avoids initiating the counseling relationship or the member terminates it. In either event, the member is obligated to refer the counselee to an appropriate specialist. (It is incumbent upon the member to be knowledgeable about referral resources so that a satisfactory referral can be initiated.) In the event the counselee declines the suggested referral, the member is not obligated to continue the relationship.

This guideline reflects the importance of evaluating the competencies of the counselor and the agency for whom one is working.

Also available are several guidelines which are somewhat more specific in nature. The following considerations provide a guide for the counselor in deciding whether to refer, treat, or drop the case.

1. Is there a need? The decision must be made as to whether the problem behavior is of such nature that it requires changing.
2. Is the client interested? The behavior change will be easier if the client is interested in modifying some behavior.
3. Are time and facilities available? A preliminary outline of a possible treatment plan should provide the data necessary to decide whether the counselor has available the requisite time and facilities for implementing a possible treatment plan.
4. Can a contractual agreement be reached? Such an agreement is necessary if the decision to treat the client is made. The agreement of individuals to be used as necessary behavior mediators must be obtained. These individuals may include parents, siblings, school personnel, community members, classmates, and the individual whose behavior is to be changed.
5. Am I, as a counselor, professionally qualified to work with this client?
6. Do I have any personal inadequacies that would make it impossible to work effectively with this client?
7. Is there another individual or agency that would be better able to help this person?

These considerations may well include consultations with the individuals involved as well as other professionals. The seven questions listed above should provide a framework within which the counselor can decide whether an individual client should be referred to someone else, terminated, or counseled. If the counselor should decide to accept the client, the client should be informed of the types of assistance to be provided the client, how long it may take, and what additional information and involvement from the referring person or agency is needed.

The critical decision which must be made in processing client referrals, subsystem 2.0, is whether the referral is appropriate or not. You may find it helpful to read a portion of the case presented in Chapter 13 to see how Juanita's counselor carried out the functions involved in processing a client referral. These pages specifically present all relevant data which could be considered part of processing a client referral. This section of the case relates the situation as perceived by the teacher, Ms. Holt, and told to Mr. Adams, the counselor. All dialogue between the teacher and counselor is part of the referral process.

Perhaps a few examples of subsystem 2.0 would be helpful. Consider an individual who walks into the counselor's office and is visibly upset and crying. Obviously, the RECEIVE REFERRAL function (2.1) has already been completed, since the client is in the office. The next function to be performed would be ANALYZE APPROPRIATENESS OF REFERRAL (2.2). Here, the counselor may gather data about the client on which to decide the appropriateness of counseling for the client. The client may blurt out the problem, thus allowing the counselor to analyze the self-report data on the spot, or the counselor may have to probe and clarify until a mutual understanding regarding the nature of the concern is established. Typically, this counselor-client interaction would not occur until the IDENTIFY CONCERNS function (5.1).

Typically, the client processing procedures performed in subsystem 2.0 would involve referred clients rather than those who decide to drop in of their own accord. In such cases the counselor would not meet with the client until the first interview when the counseling relationship would be explained (4.0). In light of this more typical procedure, consider an individual referred by a teacher because of classroom behavior problems. In this situation, the counselor would consult with the referring teacher to collect all appropriate data regarding the "classroom behavior problems." The counselor would also consult available records, and other sources of information which have been collected. The counselor would review and analyze the data in light of the competencies that the counselor has and determine the appropriateness of the referral (2.2.3). If the counselor decides that the referral is appropriate, he or she would contact the referring teacher and specify the conditions under which the client will be seen by the counselor. Perhaps the teacher would find out that the counselor will see the client only about some of the client's concerns and will refer the client to some other professional for treatment of the other concerns. It might be necessary to remind the teacher of the

confidential nature of counseling. The referring teacher should understand what is to be expected of the counselor-client relationship. The
counselor would then proceed to arrange for an interview with the client
(3.1) and review the available data (3.2) prior to the first client contact.
Although other procedures may be necessary to accommodate a specific
client, those presented above are appropriate in most cases.

Once all the data have been gathered from the referral source and the
conditions have been specified to the referral source, the counselor is
ready to proceed with the next subsystem, PREPARE FOR INTER-
VIEW (3.0).

Preparing for the Interview (3.0)

Once the client has been referred to the counselor and the counselor
has accepted the referral as being appropriate, it is necessary to prepare
for the initial interview. Two functions must be performed in this subsystem: review existing data and arrange for an interview time. These are
shown in Figure 5-2. Between the time when a client is accepted and the
first interview, additional information may be obtained regarding the
new client. Accepting a referral serves to focus the counselor's attention
on a particular individual who probably has a cumulative record folder
including test scores, grades, anecdotal reports, health reports, and a
variety of other information which may or may not be relevant to the
counselor's work with this client. The counselor should develop
hypotheses concerning the client's problem from analyzing the data in
the cumulative record folder. Data may also be provided by the school
psychologist, the school social worker, other counselors, teachers, community agencies, or professionals in the community. This list is not
meant to be exhaustive, but exemplary of the various sources of information which may be considered by the counselor when preparing for the initial interview.

Figure 5-2

When reviewing information about the client who is having difficulties
in the classroom or on the job, the counselor may wish to look for information regarding how the client has interacted with teachers and supervisors in the past. "Has this been a problem before?" There may be some

concern with academic achievement. "How well has the client kept up with fellow students or workers?" "How well does the client read?" Reading two years or more below grade level may make one ill-equipped to meet the challenge of work. If corroborative data exist for the present problem, the counselor should determine how long this has been a problem, and the frequency of the problem until now. This type of information assists the counselor in understanding a client's background more completely before interviewing the client. Moreover, gathering information prior to seeing the client will help to save time during the interview itself.

The counselor who has a reasonable understanding of the client's background should contact the client and arrange a time which is mutually acceptable to both for the initial interview. If a client is a self-referral, and time is available, the appointment can be immediate. The counselor should find an opportunity, however, to review quickly any records that are available.

The Case of Juanita in Chapter 13, illustrates the way in which subsystem 3.0 could be performed in counseling. The counselor, Mr. Adams, has sent a call slip to Juanita, reviewed her cumulative record folder for some background information, and is prepared to see her the next morning.

SUMMARY

Counseling services can be no better than the counselor who delivers them. A counselor who is knowledgeable about sound practices and sensitive to individual needs is essential to this, as to any other, counseling approach. Considerable practice is required, however, to blend knowledge and sensitivity and to use both in working with clients.

The first specific task performed by the counselor with regard to any case is the processing of the client referral. Counselors receive requests for service from several sources. Among those who might refer a client for counseling are (a) other school personnel, (b) individuals or agencies in the community at large, and (c) parents or other family members. Clients may also refer themselves for counseling, of course. On other occasions, a counselor may observe individuals in work or play settings, believe that counseling would be beneficial, and ask them to visit the counseling office. After considering a given case, the counselor may decide that a particular counseling case is an inappropriate one to handle. In such an instance, a client will be helped by the counselor to find appropriate assistance from other sources.

Once a counselor accepts the referral, the process of preparing for an interview begins. This involves arranging for an appointment and reviewing any available data concerning the client. After processing a client referral and preparing for an interview, the counselor is ready to initiate the counseling process, as described in the next chapter.

6

Initiating the Counseling Process

OVERVIEW

The importance of carefully laying the groundwork for counseling cannot be stressed too much. In the initial meeting with a client two factors are of immediate concern. The concerns of the client must be transmitted to the counselor in an open, unmasked way that allows for clarity of understanding on the part of the counselor. At the same time, the client has every right to know what to expect from the counselor and the nature of their relationship. This chapter presents a step-by-step procedure for meeting both of the above expectations. To enhance the learning process, we encourage you to follow the flowchart of Systematic Counseling, as presented in the Endpapers and also to read the case of Juanita presented in Chapter 13. This case presents a word-by-word account of how a counselor works with a client and provides a detailed example of each step in the counseling process.

INTRODUCTION

Organization

Two major topics are discussed in this chapter. Section one presents the skills utilized in opening an initial interview. Section two discusses how to construct a model of the client's concerns. The summary that follows should prepare you for the next phase of systematic counseling—the process of deciding on a mutually acceptable goal toward which the client, with assistance from the counselor, can work.

Purposes

The general purposes of this chapter are (a) to help you understand the value of providing an overview of what happens in counseling, (b) to provide a model for presenting this overview to the client, (c) to help you understand the rationale for focusing on specific client problems, and (d) to provide a means by which you can assist clients in constructing a clear view of their concerns.

Objectives

Upon reading this chapter it is expected that you will be prepared to do the following:

1. List and explain three considerations in deciding whether an explantion of the counseling relationship is needed.
2. List and give a rationale for the four points included in an explanation of the counseling relationship.
3. Identify and explain nine of the eleven basic components in initiating the establishment of a relationship.
4. List and explain two counselor skills that assist in identifying client concerns.
5. Explain the importance of selecting a single concern upon which to focus in counseling.
6. Name the three components to be covered in assessing the concern.
7. Define the term "baseline."
8. Identify maintaining reinforcers within a problem context.

EXPLAINING THE COUNSELING RELATIONSHIP (4.0)

After the available data on a new client have been reviewed and an appointment time has been determined, the counselor and client will meet for the first time in an interview situation. There has been considerable controversy regarding the need to structure and define the counseling relationship explicitly. Some say that the relationship develops better and more naturally if structure remains implicit and is not provided by the counselor at the outset (Rogers, 1951). Others say that counselors should structure explicitly. According to Loughary (1961), two purposes for explicit structuring by the counselor are: (a) to help the client gain realistic expectations about the counselor and counseling and (b) to give the client some idea of what is involved in counseling methods and purposes. The authors of this text firmly believe that explicit structure should be provided to all new clients, since it is their civil *right* to know what can be expected from counseling as practiced by their counselor (4.1). Once it has been determined that formal structure is needed (4.1.1), the counselor must decide the best time to provide it (4.2). If a client seems anxious, unsure, hesitant, or insecure, the counselor should provide structure immediately, as described in Function 4.3. On the other hand a client may readily begin sharing a concern, and thus the provision of structure at this time would be an intrusion upon the client's desire to share the concern. If this is true, the counselor may provide structure at some later time in the initial interview.

Before the counselor formally explains the counseling process, two questions are asked, i.e., "Is formal structure needed?" and "Is this the appropriate time?"

A YES decision as to whether formal structure is needed is based on the following criteria:

1. All referrals from referral sources (2.1.1–2.1.4) should be provided with formal structure.
2. All self-referrals (2.1.5) who are being seen by the counselor for the first time should be provided with formal structure even though they have been previously counseled by another counselor.

Criteria for a NO decision include the following:

1. The client has been seen previously by this counselor, when structure was provided, *and*
2. The client responds immediately when invited by the counselor to discuss concerns.

A NO decision concerning need for formal structure moves the client and counselor directly into Subsystem 5.0, CONSTRUCT MODEL OF CLIENT CONCERNS.

A YES decision concerning need for formal structure is followed by another decision as to whether or not this is the appropriate *time* to establish formal structure. It is important to remember that the timing of structuring is flexible. It may be done initially, sometime during the first interview, or at the conclusion of the initial interview. A YES decision that it is the appropriate time to formally explain the counseling process is based on the following criteria:

1. A 2.1.5 (self-referral) client does not respond to the invitation of the counselor to discuss concerns and/or shows signs of anxiety

such as blushing, shifting weight in the chair, looking away
from the counselor, gripping the chair tightly, wringing hands,
playing with objects, and slow, hesitant speech.

2. All clients from referral sources (2.1.1–2.1.4) should be provided
with formal structure unless they begin talking after being
seated and without being cued by the counselor.

The criteria for a NO decision concerning the appropriate time for
structure include the following:

1. A 2.1.5 (self-referral) client responds immediately when invited
by the counselor to discuss concerns. Then, structure is usually
provided during Subsystem 5.0, CONSTRUCT MODEL OF
CLIENT CONCERNS, or at the termination of the initial interview.

2. A client from referral sources (2.1.1–2.1.4) begins to discuss
concerns without being cued by the counselor.

A NO decision about establishing structure at this time also allows the
client and counselor to continue directly into Subsystem 5.0,
CONSTRUCT MODEL OF CLIENT CONCERNS. A YES decision on
these two decision points indicates the need to establish formal structure
at this time, as an initial function.

Many clients come to counseling with vague notions concerning the
purposes of counseling, such as "just talking things over" or perhaps
"getting some advice." Actually, clients are not without some justification in viewing counseling in this manner, since many counselors have
not clearly established the purposes of counseling in their own minds,
and therefore cannot clearly communicate their purposes to others.

DESCRIBING THE COUNSELING PROCESS (4.3)

How does one describe the counseling process? One approach is to explain the framework or structure within which a counselor works with a
client. In Function 4.3, DESCRIBE COUNSELING PROCESS, this
framework is communicated to the client by talking briefly about four
aspects of counseling (See Figure 6-1). You will note that in structuring,
the counselor defines *purpose, responsibilities, focus,* and *limits* with
regard to the counseling process.

The counselor may need to provide more than one explanation of the
counseling relationship during the course of working with a given client.
Restructuring should be used whenever the client seems to have forgotten the intent of counseling. For example, in selecting a concern for
counseling (Function 5.2), clients may ask the counselor to decide rather

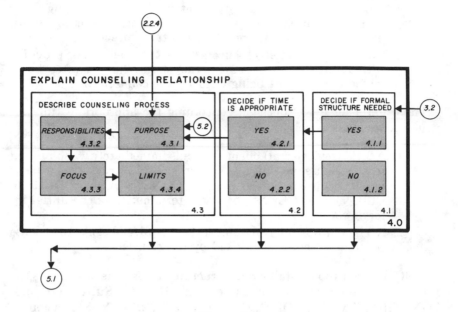

Figure 6-1

than accepting the responsibility themselves. At this point, the counselor reviews the responsibilities of the counselor and client, indicating that the counselor expects the client to make the decision. Any indication that the client is confused about or does not understand the counseling process should serve as cues for the counselor to restructure.

In structuring, as in all other phases of the counseling process, we are aware of the need to adapt a language that is suited to the age and comprehension level of the client. The wording of counselor responses used in this text as examples may be suitable for only some of the clients with whom you work. Others would find our vocabulary either too difficult or too condescending. As you read the counselor responses used here, think of the people with whom you work and practice appropriate wording for this clientele.

Purpose (4.3.1)

The purpose of counseling is to build a relationship wherein the client can receive help in dealing with the normal concerns that occur in the course of human development as well as be provided with immediate assistance in problem solving. Counseling is also designed to help clients develop problem-solving skills that can be utilized in dealing with problems that are faced following the termination of the formal counseling relationship. We stress with the client that counseling is essentially a learning situation wherein one can develop more effective ways of coping with some of the problem situations that occur. While counseling often deals with the normal concerns with which all people are faced, this does not minimize the importance of the client's problem. The problems are very real and extremely frustrating to the person involved, even though they may appear minor to others. The purpose of counseling might be explained as follows: "The purpose of counseling is to assist you with the things that concern you or those that interest you. Some individuals want to make decisions about what to do after high school. Others may need help with school problems, subjects, and teachers. Some have problems in getting along with others, such as classmates, parents, marriage partners, or their boss at work. The purpose of counseling, is to help you cope with your concerns."

Responsibilities (4.3.2)

Within the counseling process, both the counselor and client engage in certain activities. The counselor should communicate the responsibilities of both participants. It is essential that the client understand what can be expected of the counselor. The counselor can be described as a professional person who provides assistance to the client by listening to concerns, observing the client, and interacting with the client. More specifically, it should be noted that the counselor will assist the client in specifying concerns and suggesting courses of action. Moreover, the counselor at times will also provide support for the client. In communicating this information to the client, the counselor would perhaps mention that counseling provides a "safe" environment in which to try out new behaviors.

It is also essential that the counselor inform clients of their responsibilities. Primarily, the client describes and discusses concerns and participates in the interview by providing the counselor with needed information. The client should also understand that, although the counselor will provide assistance to the client, the responsibility for carrying out assigned tasks as well as the responsibility for making decisions and carrying them out remains with the client.

An example of how a counselor might state the responsibilities would be: "My job as a counselor is to listen and try to understand how you feel and think about things. I won't make decisions for you, but together we may come up with some things for you to consider in making a decision. If you make a decision, I will help you find ways to carry it out. Your part in counseling is to help me understand how you feel and think. You also have to make decisions and carry out the tasks that need doing before you can reach your goals."

Focus (4.3.3)

If counseling is to be of maximum effectiveness, the client must also understand that the process will focus on one specific concern with the intention of bringing about an overt change in behavior. In order to bring about this change in behavior, a specific objective will be established and agreed upon by the client and counselor. This objective will describe what the client will be doing as a result of counseling.

While formal structure is provided to many clients, *implicit* structure is also provided throughout the counseling process. The counselor can provide leads that are designed to maintain focus on the current problem. Both verbal and nonverbal reinforcements can be used to develop appropriate client behavior in the interview. For example, the counselor can use postural movements as a device to encourage clients to pursue a particular subject area. Moving closer or leaning toward the client will tend to reinforce whatever behavior the client is engaging in at the time. By the same token, withholding reinforcement for inappropriate client behaviors, such as rambling talk during the interview, can serve to move the client's attention to more meaningful material. While formal structuring would occur during the early stages of counseling, if not at the outset, implicit structuring would be used as needed throughout the process.

An example of how the counselor might state the focus of counseling would be: "In counseling we usually focus on establishing a specific objective or target to shoot for. We'll undertake just one objective at a time, but may cover several before our work together is finished."

Limits (4.3.4)

The last area to be discussed concerns the limits of the counseling relationship. In discussing this area with the client, the counselor should communicate to the client that they will deal only with certain types of problems, primarily those that are typical of most people. Most client concerns are developmental problems encountered in the process of living. Counselors must know the limits of their training and skill. Those problems indicating serious maladjustment should be referred to a psychologist or psychiatrist. In the typical school setting or agency it must be made clear to the client that participation in counseling is voluntary. The client cannot be compelled to participate, even though the client may have been referred to counseling by school authorities, parents, or agencies. The client is responsible for describing concerns to the counselor, and unless the client is willing to participate actively in counseling, the counseling process will not be productive.

One of the limits that should be communicated to the client concerns access to information. Counselors should carefully point out their obligation to maintain the confidentiality of the information transmitted in the interview. Should circumstances arise wherein it would be useful to the client to involve a third party in the process, disclosure of information derived in the interview would only be made with the client's prior permission and would be limited to the information that the third party would need in order to help the client. The only time a counselor should break confidence is when the client is in danger of harming self or others. The best policy when in doubt is to consult with other professional people concerning the maintenance of confidentiality. Some schools or agencies may have policies restricting the degree of confidentiality. A counselor must be aware of any such restrictions on confidentiality and must communicate these restrictions to the client.

The counselor is also limited by the amount of time that can be spent on any one problem with any one client. The specific time limits will vary with the particular setting in which counseling is conducted and with the individual client. In many counseling situations, the counseling process will involve three or four interviews of approximately 25 to 50 minutes' duration. Obviously, more interviews can be scheduled if needed. Other interviews, for purposes of evaluating progress and monitoring client progress, are usually of 5 to 15 minutes' duration.

A counselor stating the limits of counseling might speak the following: "In counseling, we have several limits within which we work. First, I limit the people with whom I work to those who have developmental problems and refer those who have serious maladjustments to those who specialize in this area. Second, you volunteered to come here, and your continuation of counseling will be strictly voluntary. Third, we both have time constraints. I typically see people three or four times, and each session runs from 25 to 50 minutes. However, I can see you more often than this if it is needed. Finally, I want to stress that our communication is confidential. I will talk with no one about our conversations unless I have your prior approval. One exception: If human life is in danger, I would have to break this confidence. . . . Do you have any questions?"

If the decision has been made to structure immediately, this process will probably take about five minutes. After structuring, the counselor must be concerned with identifying the client's concern. Remember that, at all times, the counselor is working to establish and to maintain a good working relationship with the client.

An ongoing debate has focused on the area of building a good working relationship in counseling. Some writers indicate that the relationship must be built first with empathy, genuineness, unconditional positive regard, understanding, acceptance, communication and other conditions

(Rogers, 1951; Tyler, 1969) before any meaningful interaction related to the client's concern can be undertaken. The authors take the position that the process of building a relationship is not an isolated initial phase of the counseling process, but rather a continuously developing realization of the individual's concerns, the counselor's competence and willingness to deal with those concerns, and the counselor's confidence in working with the client. In this text, however, the process of directly building a relationship will not be stressed. Instead, the assumption will be made that the relationship continues to build as a simultaneous function of the concern-related interaction between counselor and client.

How might Subsystem 4.0 be operationalized in a client-counselor interaction? Two examples may help clarify how it is done. In the case presented in Chapter 13, Juanita is willing to discuss her concerns, and the counselor responds accordingly. However, if the client is not willing to express a concern, the counselor may use structuring to help the client learn about the counseling process. The following dialogue is an example of client-counselor interaction.

CO.: Perhaps it would help if I shared my basic beliefs about counseling with you.

CL.: OK.

CO.: Fine. The purpose of counseling, as I see it, is to help you work on things that concern or interest you. Some individuals may want to make decisions about jobs, school curriculum, post-high school training, or selecting a mate. Others need assistance with working on relationships with parents, friends, peers, or supervisors. Whatever is important to you will become our purpose in counseling.

CL.: It sounds like I decide what we're going to work on.

CO.: That's right. My job as a counselor is to listen and understand how you think and feel about the concern. Together we'll generate ways for you to work on the concern.

CL.: Sounds OK, but what do I do?

CO.: Your job is to help me understand what you think and feel about your concern. You will need to provide me with information, make necessary decisions, and perform any tasks necessary to reach your objective.

CL.: It just seems hard to get a handle on what my concern is.

CO.: Frequently that's the case. We usually try to focus on a specific target that you would like to accomplish. Sometimes this target or objective is only a small part of your concern, yet gradually we will work on more and more parts until we have resolved your concern.

CL.: I see. You mean we'll just take one step at a time?

CO.: Exactly. One other thing. I want you to know that counseling is voluntary. You may quit whenever you wish. The interviews are private; that is, I won't discuss you and your problems with anyone else without your prior permission. . . . Our interviews usually last about thirty minutes. It usually takes about five sessions to resolve a typical problem, sometimes less, sometimes more. . . . Now, what questions do you have about counseling?

CL.: None, I guess. It seems pretty clear.

Although the counselor's structuring remarks may be tailored to the specific concern of the client, the basic procedure should be as presented. Again, the key components to be communicated are: purpose, responsibilities, focus, and limits of counseling.

CONSTRUCTING A MODEL OF CLIENT CONCERNS (5.0)

Prior to deciding upon a goal or intended outcome for counseling, the counselor needs to understand the concerns and pressures that the client brings to the counseling situation. The client is encouraged to explore several aspects of his or her life and environment that might be of concern. From the several concerns that might be initially explored, one is selected for detailed consideration. Others may be explored at a later time, but the counselor and client both have limits pertaining to how much information they can handle at a given time and therefore need to study a single concern at some length. In addition to selecting a specific concern, other steps in the process of model-building include assessing qualitative and quantitative dimensions, examining forces that might encourage the continuation of the response of concern, and verifying that the counselor and client view it in the same way and to the same degree.

IDENTIFYING CLIENT CONCERNS (5.1)

In the process of identifying client concerns, the counselor continues to build a good working relationship with the client. In building this relationship, he uses verbal and nonverbal techniques and employs, to advantage, the physical arrangement of the interview setting. The counselor must elicit sufficient information from the client regarding each concern, if there is more than one, so that the best selection of a concern for counseling can be made. You will find it helpful to refer to Figure 6-2 throughout this discussion of Subsystem 5.0, CONSTRUCT MODEL OF CLIENT CONCERNS.

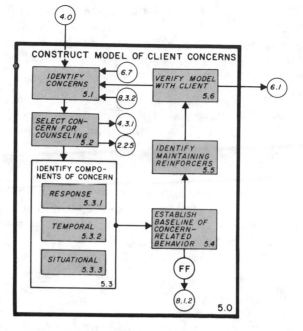

Figure 6-2

Considerable time variation occurs in this function. Some clients have a simple, straightforward concern which can be quickly and easily understood. When a single concern exists, the focus for counseling is easily established. Other clients have multiple and complex problems, and it may take considerable time and skill to come to an understanding of them. Identifying important themes in a client's remarks will be useful in identifying specific problems.

The two major skills used by the counselor in identifying concerns are listening and probing. Listening is used to understand the problem, while probing is used to elicit additional clarifying information regarding the problem and to detect additional problems. Typically, the probing should be done by using open-ended questions, rather than questions which can be answered by a simple "yes" or "no" response.

Although the selection of a concern for counseling may seem difficult, it is relatively easy if the counselor has thoroughly identified the client's concerns. A counselor typically begins to identify a client's concern by asking "What seems to be concerning you today?" or "How can I help you?" Both of these leads are broad, open-ended questions that allow the client as much latitude as possible to begin identifying concerns. Occasionally a client will find such a question too broad to handle, so the counselor may have to be somewhat more specific in a second question, e.g., "What, about your relationship with Kevin seems to concern you?" The counselor continues to probe until satisfied that the general concern is of central importance to the client and the client is willing to provide the necessary information for the full exploration of that concern. A careful blending of questions with empathic listening provides the necessary ingredients for successful identification of the client's concerns.

SELECTING A CONCERN FOR COUNSELING (5.2)

When the counselor is satisfied that the client has talked freely about various concerns and that further general exploration is unnecessary, the counselor turns the client's attention to the task of selecting the single concern that is of most immediate importance. Occasionally, a client will present a single concern and insist that no other concerns are present at that time. More frequently, a client has several concerns of greater or lesser importance that are tentatively considered. Which should the counselor focus upon? Selection may be made in terms of the concern's immediacy, its complexity, or its intensity.

Some concerns are more immediate than others. If the counselor wishes to focus on job training but the client has no place to sleep, it would be better to help secure lodging first. Concerns also vary in terms of complexity. Usually the more complex the problem, the more difficult it is to resolve. It may be better to focus on less complex problems first and, when they have been resolved, begin working on the more complex ones. This will allow the client to experience success and to gain confidence in the counselor, which may be a very important prior condition for working on more complex concerns. Finally, concerns may vary in intensity. The intensity of a client's feelings about a problem is probably one of the best indicators of the concern upon which the client and counselor should focus.

Each counselor, depending on the client and the concerns, may wish to develop personal criteria for helping a client select a concern for counseling. Interview time is used most effectively when the client talks at length about a limited number of topics. Because the client forgets, wishes to avoid further discussion, becomes anxious, or merely wanders, the client does not always continue to explore the identified concern. Only through a continued attempt to focus on the concern does the counselor bring the client back to the central theme. Some of the following might be helpful leads for the counselor: "You were telling me about why your father doesn't understand you. . . . " or "Concerning your difficulty in meeting strangers, you were saying. . . ."

A client's verbalization at any moment has both *content* and *feeling*. *Content* refers to the objects, actions, or information to which the client refers. However, content may be less important than the essential attitudes (*feeling*) concerning the content. For example, a client may say, "I drove here from St. Louis last night and nothing happened." *Content* refers to the act of driving from a given point at a given time of day without incident. But this particular comment seems rather uneventful. Why, then, did the client make this comment? Perhaps it indicates the accomplishment of something which seemed unattainable. The counselor should therefore focus upon whether the comment reveals primarily the client's *feelings* and whether the client may wish to elaborate.

As the counselor attempts to help the client focus on a concern, a conscious effort should be made to differentiate between *content* and *feeling*. Note the following examples:

> "Perhaps we could get back to your problem with assignments." (Content)
> "You said you would keep the appointment, but it makes you angry." (Feeling)

The presence of both feeling and content can be readily seen in the last lead. A bit of content is presented (appointment), but the underlying feeling (makes you angry) is emphasized. Use of this type of response not only returns the client to the selected concern, but involves the client more deeply by tying in personal feeling or attitude about what is being said. A *feeling* response helps to push the client toward further self-exploration.

IDENTIFYING THE COMPONENTS
OF THE CONCERN (5.3)

A client's concern may be viewed as having *response, temporal,* and *situational* components. This categorization helps the counselor analyze a concern in terms of the questions *What? Where? When?* and *How?*

Response component (5.3.1)

To identify the response facets of the problem, a counselor must learn *what* the concern is, *how* it is manifested, and *what effect* this concern has on the client's life.

A counselor should help the client to describe responses in terms which are observable and measurable. If, for instance, a client tells the counselor, "I feel just lousy," the counselor would have a difficult time setting up a strategy to deal with decreasing or eliminating a "lousy" feeling. On the other hand, if the client says that this "lousy" feeling is of concern because of an inability to choose a suitable college, one can more readily see possible strategies for handling the concern. Similarly, the manifestations of worrying (for example, time spent thinking about the problem, less time spent studying, lower grades, or parents' nagging) are all observable and measurable responses.

Once responses have been specified, the counselor next identifies the specific effects of worrying upon the client's life. When a client says that this "lousy" feeling makes life dull and blue, one doesn't really have a grasp of the effects of the concern. If, however, the client says that worrying about an appropriate college has cut down study time by an hour each day because of daydreaming, or that parents "bug" the client for 20 minutes each day, the counselor has a clear picture of the effects of worrying upon the client's life.

Temporal Component (5.3.2)

The second step in exploring a client's concern is to examine the temporal aspect. This is, *when* does this behavior occur, for how long has it occurred, and finally, is there any sequence to the behavior? To a *when* question, a client might say "All the time," but further exploration may reveal a much more precise breakdown. The client might tell us that it occurs when driving to and from work. This answer specifies concretely *when* the behavior occurs. The counselor might pose the question, "How long has this occurred?" A response such as, "Oh, for a long time now," doesn't give us a specific answer. Going somewhat further, we might get responses such as "For the past month" or "Since I received my PSAT scores last Monday." The counselor might ask, "Is it getting better or worse?" in order to learn whether the client is experiencing progress or decline with regard to the concern. Responses might be, "Yeah, I used to worry about it every day, but now I only get concerned once a week, maybe," or "Something like this used to bother me only when I was new on a job, but now I get jumpy after two or three days."

Situational Component (5.3.3)

The counselor's third task is to explore the situational aspect. That is, *where* or under what circumstances does this concern become apparent? The client may initially reply, "When I'm with the gang," or "Anywhere." After close examination, however, it may turn out that the problem occurs only in the dorm when somebody in the group starts smoking pot. This response answers the question, "Under what circumstances or under what influences or pressures does this behavior manifest itself?"

When the client and counselor are able to verbalize the response, temporal, and situational components of the concern, they have a sound basis for proceeding with counseling. It is very difficult to select and implement a behavior-change strategy without knowing the present concern-related behavior of the client. The counselor identifies components of the concern in order to develop a baseline of concern-related behavior (5.4).

Intensity

The components of the concern provide highly specific information about the nature of the client's difficulty. It is now known that the client elicits a certain type of behavior in certain situations and at certain times. Additional information the counselor should have is related to the intensity dimension of behavior.

Two basic concepts of intensity are frequency and duration. *Frequency* refers to the number of times a given behavior occurs. For example, if a student has been called to the principal's office five times, the frequency is five. *Duration* is defined in two ways. First, it refers to the length of time over which a given behavior has occurred. Thus, the frequency of five visits to the principal's office may have been for a duration of one week, one year, or the entire number of years during which the student has been in that school. A second definition of duration is the length of time a behavior continues at each occurrence, in this case the length of each visit to the office. Some visits may have been relatively short, perhaps five to 10 minutes, while others may have been rather long, 30 to 45 minutes.

Another example of frequency and duration involves a male who has been hospitalized for three weeks with a job-related injury. He reports that before the accident he and Peg had a great relationship, but during his hospitalization he has not had a visit from Peg and her only phone call was for just two or three minutes. His concern, obviously, is his girl friend's sudden lack of interest in him. Two frequencies are revealed: "Peg has made no hospital visits," and "Peg has called only once." The duration measures are: "During a three-week period" for visits and "For two or three minutes only" for the phone call. The prevailing condition, apparently, is his job-related injury and hospitalization, although the counselor would want to examine other aspects of their relationship to determine whether or not the injury merely provided the means for severing a relationship that was more fragile than the client presumed. The use of frequency and duration allows the counselor to have a much better grasp of the concern's magnitude. Without the probing and specificity that produced the above information, the counselor might have heard only from the client: "I guess Peg doesn't care about me much anymore."

ESTABLISHING A BASELINE OF
CONCERN-RELATED BEHAVIOR (5.4)

Adequate assessment of the client's concern with regard to the behavior, the situation, and the temporal component, as well as the frequency and duration of the behavior, provides the counselor with a measure of the client's functioning at the onset of counseling. This measure is called a baseline and can be used as a point of comparison throughout counseling to indicate whether or not progress is being made. The specific function in Systematic Counseling is Function 8.1.2, COMPARE PERFORMANCE WITH BASELINE. Thus, an individual who came in to stop smoking and was consuming 20 cigarettes a day when the counselor determined the baseline may find that, after completing counseling, only five cigarettes are being smoked each day. This result can dramatize the effect of counseling.

Occasionally, a counselor may cover each of the specific components of the concern carefully with the client, but find that the client's comments provide little specific, quantifiable data. When this occurs it may be helpful to set up a data-gathering device to validate empirically the current level of problem behavior in terms of the response, time dimension, situation, or intensity.

Two useful devices for obtaining accurate baseline data are the behavior chart and the behavioral log. The behavior chart is a graphic representation of the frequency of a specific behavior. Data for the chart can be jotted down, or a unit counter or other device can be used to record instantly the occurrence of the specified behavior. Figure 6-3 contains a chart on which the tallied daily behavior can be entered to determine the patterning of the behavior in question.

The data presented in Figure 6-3 help the counselor and client to identify where the problem seems most evident. For example, it can be seen that the client seems to improve each day of the week until Friday. These data suggest further investigation into the differences between Thursday and Friday to better understand the problem.

A second data-gathering device for establishing a baseline is a behavioral log. A behavioral log is like a diary in which the client enters all significant aspects of the specified behavior for a given period of time. Information logged might include the date, time, setting, event that transpired, client's reaction, and client's desired reaction. Usually a one-week period is adequate to determine the baseline for components of the concern.

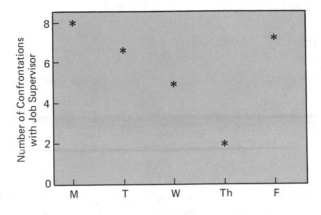

Figure 6-3

With both of these techniques, focusing upon a specific behavior tends to increase the accuracy of the report. In some instances the client may be introduced to the chart and/or log early in the counseling process and make self-assessments of behavior. Making a chart or log gives the client a greater sense of involvement, and the improving results in charted form may provide encouragement for the client.

IDENTIFYING MAINTAINING REINFORCERS (5.5)

After the components of the concern have been identified and the baseline has been established, the counselor is sufficiently knowledgeable about the concern to begin working toward the resolution of the difficulty. However, problem resolution demands more than just understanding the problem; it is necessary to focus on the forces that have allowed the problem behavior to continue. These forces are termed maintaining reinforcers. In other words, what benefit does the client derive from keeping the concern-related behavior? If the client knew why this behavior persisted, counseling might not be necessary. The client's inability to detect maintaining reinforcers suggests that the counselor may also have difficulty in identifying them, and this is often the case.

Examples of maintaining reinforcers are numerous. A disabled male's behavior of fondling women at work may be maintained by the attention received from women who feel sorry for him. An elderly woman may frequently talk of her backache and thus enlist help from sympathetic children. A female may manifest excessive crabbiness in order that her roommate avoid her, thus providing desired privacy. Poor work performance may be maintained by sympathy from the supervisor.

The essential question to be asked about the concern-related behavior is, "What is 'in' it for the client?" Answers to this question provide clues as to why the behavior continues.

Once the maintaining reinforcers have been identified by the client and counselor, strategies for changing the behavior in the desired manner will be more easily formulated. Planning a behavior change strategy for the person with poor work performance, for example, might entail finding more positive behaviors which would elicit the desired attention from the supervisor. Without knowing *why* the worker exhibits poor performance, the counselor might well conclude that the worker lacks skill and might develop an inappropriate strategy for change.

Our focus up to this point has been upon collecting and processing information that will allow the counselor to develop a mental image or model of the client's concern. The model in final form concerns a specific behavior with which the client is seriously concerned and which has been both quantitatively and qualitatively defined. Further, the counselor has attempted to determine the maintaining reinforcers involved. All of these counselor thoughts, however, may not yet have been shared with the client, and this is the counselor's next task.

VERIFYING THE MODEL OF CLIENT CONCERNS (5.6)

Throughout the development of the model of client concerns, the counselor has been listening, probing, and making hypotheses about the components of the client's problem. Now that the counselor has a picture of what the concern entails, the final step in the process of model construction is to determine whether or not this picture is an accurate one from the client's vantage point.

The counselor's task, then, is to verbalize this model to the client and allow the client to amend, delete, or approve the model presented. Are there any discrepancies between what the counselor says and what the client thinks and feels?

The counselor might begin by explaining to the client a need to clarify what the client has said so that they can both proceed with the same background knowledge. For example, the counselor might say: "Jack, let me go back for a minute and review what you have been telling me. Listen, and let me know if I understand your problem correctly." The counselor then briefly reviews the interpretation of the client's problem, making certain to include:

1. *what* the concern is.
2. the *response* component.
3. the *temporal* component.

    4. the *situational* component.

    5. the *maintaining* reinforcers.

While presenting the above interpretation, the counselor must be alert to responses from the client. Response signals may be more nonverbal (head shaking, scowling) than verbal ("No, that's not it."). If a response is detected during the interpretation, the counselor may test this perception by a question such as, "How am I doing so far?" If client response is positive, the counselor may proceed. If not, it may be necessary to seek client assistance in clarifying misconceptions of the counselor. Are the counselor and client both talking about the same concerns? Did the counselor understand correctly the concern on which the client wished to begin working? If the answers to these last two questions are "No," the counselor reviews the concerns identified (5.1). This would allow the counselor to better understand the basic concern and then proceed to "repair" the remainder of the model before seeking verification once more. Therefore, the point is that accurate understanding and summarization of the concern is the key to providing accurate verification of the concern.

Perhaps the following examples of a poorly conducted verification and a properly conducted one would help to clarify the intent of this function. First, let us consider a poor verification. Eric is a high school senior who has never dated. The information he has communicated to the counselor has been focused on his need to decide on a college. He has given hints of a dating problem in discussing concerns, but the counselor has lost it among all of the college selection concerns being presented. The counselor now states, "Eric, if I understand you correctly, you must decide on a college by April 1 of next year. You have been trying to decide for the past six months, with little success. As a result of our working together, you would like to select a college to attend next year." Eric's response might be, "Well, Ms. Zambrowski, I am concerned with selecting a college, although I'm really hung up right now on wanting to date this particular girl, but don't feel comfortable asking her out." At this point the counselor, sensing she has missed the client's major concern, would explore his dating problem more carefully, then make appropriate adjustments to other aspects of the model developed.

Next, consider a well-conducted verification of the model of a client's concern. Sharon is in the eighth grade and concerned about her parents' impending divorce. The counselor states, "Sharon, from what you've told me, it seems that your parents may be separating in the near future, based on threats you've heard each one make. You may then be forced to select whether you would live with your mother or with your father. You love them both and don't want to hurt either one. You also realize some of the consequences so that you can make a good decision in light of the situation." Sharon's response is, "Mr. Nakano, I don't like to hear what you're saying, but you understand the problem. I can't think of anything you've missed." At this point, the counselor and client can proceed to DECIDE GOALS FOR COUNSELING (6.0), since verification of the model has been successfully completed.

In some instances, the counselor may perceive no response signals that would suggest a lack of mutual accord. Nonetheless, at the end of the interpretation the counselor needs to test this perception. "You've been silent. Does this mean I'm with you or not?" If the client response is unquestioningly positive, the counselor can proceed to work with the client in DECIDE GOALS FOR COUNSELING (6.0). Counselors having any doubt as to whether or not the model of client concerns is accurate should recycle, as previously suggested.

SUMMARY

Successful counseling practice is based upon the concurrent development of two types of understanding. On the one hand, counselors attempt to create a relationship of trust and understanding with each client. Concurrently, they develop a comprehensive model or "picture" of client concerns.

At some time during the initial interview, counselors describe the process commonly used in counseling as one vehicle for establishing a sound relationship with the client. Elements of the process identified are the purpose of counseling, the respective responsibilities of both the client and counselor, the focus or convergence of attention upon one concern at a time, and the limits within which counseling is conducted. This shared understanding of the counseling process provides a sound foundation for the development of mutual trust that is so essential in counseling.

Along with developing a comfortable working relationship with clients, counselors are concerned, during the early phases of counseling, with helping clients to "tell their story." Clients are encouraged to relate their concerns so that specific details are considered, and an assessment is made of how often and under what circumstances the concern is displayed. Counselors can determine whether or not their perception of the concern is shared by clients, relating their understanding to the client for verification. If their perception is inaccurate or imprecise, counselors can then direct client attention back to the areas in question and explore them more carefully.

Once a counselor has explained the basic essentials of the counseling relationshp and worked with a client to develop a model of expressed concerns, both counselor and client are ready to begin working toward an acceptable goal and a strategy that can be used in attaining it. The next chapter is concerned with ways in which counselors can help clients in establishing goals and developing strategies.

7

Goals and Strategies
for Counseling

OVERVIEW

Goals and developing plans to attain them are the focus of this chapter. Prior to goal-setting, the counseling process has been concerned with learning about clients, their concerns, and their environment. Now the emphasis shifts from the past and present behavior of the client to behaviors or responses that the client would like to learn to make as the result of counseling.

A three-step translation process is used throughout the goal-setting process. First, the counselor helps the client to view his or her concern in terms of a desirable goal that might be reached through counseling. Next, the counselor and client consider the desired goal within the constraints imposed by the client's circumstances and environment. From this review they develop a learning objective that is both attainable and measurable. Third, the learning objective is broken down into a series of intermediate objectives and steps that are arranged to maximize the likelihood that the client will attain the goal established. Examples and illustrations are provided to assist you in understanding each step in this process.

INTRODUCTION

Organization

This chapter has two main sections. The first section presents the process through which concerns are converted into learning objectives or targets for the client and counselor to focus upon during the process of behavior change. The second section presents an overview of the process steps taken in conducting a change strategy.

Purposes

The general purposes of this chapter are : (a) to present and describe the sequence of counselor actions necessary to establish goals and learning objectives for counseling and to implement strategies for reaching these goals and (b) to provide practical suggestions and examples concerning the performance of this phase of the counseling process.

Objectives

After reading and practicing the procedures presented in this chapter, you should be able to do the following when considering a counseling case:

1. Specify reasons for setting goals in counseling.
2. Distinguish between goals and learning objectives.
3. Discuss reasons why a counselor might not wish to continue handling a counseling case.
4. Write or verbalize a learning objective.
5. Describe the similarities and differences between a learning objective, an intermediate objective, and a step.
6. Discuss the utility of *sequenced learning* in the helping process.

DECIDE GOAL AND OBJECTIVE (6.0)

Establishing a goal toward which the client and counselor are to work is a process and not an event. Clarification of the client's concern has been completed in the previous subsystem (CONSTRUCT MODEL OF CLIENT CONCERNS, 5.0). In the process of establishing the goal, counselor attention is directed initially at client willingness to participate in this process (DECIDE IF GOAL CAN BE ESTABLISHED, 6.1). If the client seems to be willing, the counselor next explores the hoped-for outcomes of counseling (DETERMINE DESIRED GOAL, 6.2) before translating the desired but perhaps lofty ambitions into attainable terms (ESTABLISH LEARNING OBJECTIVE, 6.4). This process is presented schematically in Figure 7-1.

THE RATIONALE FOR GOAL-SETTING

The previous chapter was concerned with the exploration and verification of client concerns. In some instances talking about concerns with someone who is understanding and helpful may be enough. More often,

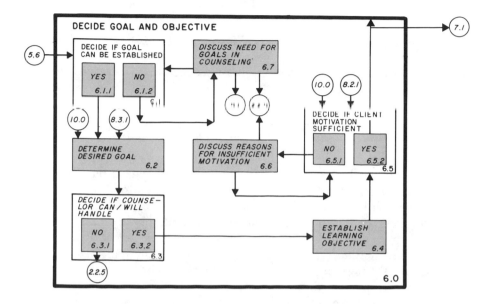

Figure 7-1

this step is only an antecedent to alteration that is needed in the social environment or range of response options available to the individual. Occasionally, a man deeply concerned about his marriage may be sufficiently relieved from "talking it through" that no further assistance is desired. More likely, however, talking will be helpful only in allowing the client and counselor to understand the focus of concern. Further talking becomes circular, and the "rehashing" beyond the point of identifying the concern and the conditions that surround it only produces added anxiety and guilt. What may be needed is some means of altering the circumstances surrounding the marriage (e.g., problems in living with in-laws or husband and wife working different hours) or the response options available (e.g., reducing the frequency of hostile remarks or providing a more adequate income).

Goals Direct Learning Activity

An initial step in any learning process is the setting of goals or statements of intent that will direct the learning activity. Research has shown that the more precisely the goal is stated, the more likely the learner is to attain the goal (Walker, 1970). This rationale has direct application in counseling. An early task of the counselor is to assist the client in identifying goals that will direct client learning activity. Setting goals assists the learner in several ways. Each of these will be explored and illustrations given.

1. Goals are targets.   Stating a goal in specific terms helps us to direct our thought and work toward a given end. Setting a goal involves more than stating where we're headed; it involves specifying where we hope to be when we finish. Whether our goal is "passing the test" or "overcoming a fear," we are setting our energies in motion toward reaching a specified end. Were we to say, "I don't like what I'm doing," we might be voicing a need for change, but what change would we like to make?

2. Goals are motivators.   Goals are most motivating when they are explicitly stated and are readily attainable. Vague goals usually fail to spark our enthusiasm. We would tend to be motivated to "learn five essential social skills," but might feel uninspired to "become more gracious socially." Likewise, immediate or short-term goals tend to motivate us toward them, while remote or long-term goals may be left undone. "Using the XYZ method this morning" and "learning the four-step review process today" are immediately attainable goals. Longer term goals such as "improving grades during fall term" or "selecting a career area sometime this year" can too easily be put off and even forgotten as competing goals such as "earning $10 for Saturday night" command our attention.

3. Goal attainment is rewarding.   Experimental studies have shown that, as a goal is approached, effort is increased (Gordon, 1963). When a goal is nearly complete, it is very difficult to distract the learner from reaching the goal. The closer the goal, the greater is its pulling power. Extrinsic rewards represent an obvious reason for desiring completion, but goal attainment provides intrinsic rewards as well. The knowledge that "I did it," "I *can* do it," or "that task is finally over" is rewarding in itself. Further, if goal attainment has been a pleasant experience, the reward of completion makes us want to move on and set higher standards or attempt to reach new goals. Because we all like to experience success, the knowledge that we have set a goal and reached it is rewarding.

4. Goals provide for planned change.   In the helter-skelter existence that many of us experience, we sometimes see that change is needed. We may have the best of intentions about making changes. We would like to do this more often or stop doing that. But we never quite get ourselves into motion. A person may have some feeling that change is needed, but may need help in clarifying the alternative goals that are available. Goals provide a way for us to consider changes that we would like to make, record them in writing if need be, and then work toward effecting the change we desire. However, goals are no panacea.

Decide if Goal Can Be Established (6.1)

Within the Systematic Counseling model the first step in the process of converting concerns into learning objectives is to determine whether or not the client is willing to become committed to goal-directed behavior. As is done in other chapters of this book, the descriptors and point-numeric code for each counselor function are included within parentheses so that the functions described within the text can be identified within the flowchart model.

The first decision that the counselor makes within Subsystem 6.0 (DECIDE GOALS AND COUNSELING OBJECTIVES) is to determine whether or not the client is willing to make a commitment to a goal in counseling (see Figure 7-2). At this point the counselor is not concerned with the specifics of a goal. Rather, the counselor is making a decision, perhaps through a single direct question and the response received, as to whether the client is indeed ready to continue with the counseling process (DETERMINE DESIRED GOAL, 6.2) or whether additional time should be taken to DISCUSS NEED FOR GOALS IN COUNSELING (6.7).

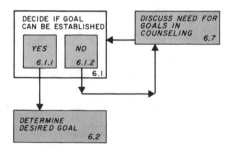

Figure 7-2

If the client understands the meaning of a goal in counseling and is willing to begin discussing such a goal, the client and counselor can begin this process (6.2). If, however, the client is hesitant to set a goal, the counselor should then discuss the need for goals (6.7).

The counselor's task is a mental one of deciding whether the client is willing or unwilling to make a commitment to a goal. This process should be a short one which can be facilitated by the counselor's considering three questions:

1. Does the client have an idea of what he or she would like to be able to do as a result of counseling?

2. Is the client curious to see what the next step will be?
3. Is the client willing to work along with the counselor on a goal?

If the answers to these questions are "yes," the counselor will DETERMINE DESIRED GOAL (6.2). If the counselor feels that the client is not ready to set a goal after considering the responses to the above questions, the client will be asked to DISCUSS NEED FOR GOALS IN COUNSELING (6.7).

Discuss Need for Goals in Counseling (6.7)

Clients, for any of a number of reasons, may be hesitant or unmotivated to set counseling goals. The Systematic Counselor believes that goals are necessary before the counselor can go further in the counseling process. Until the client concurs, no further "progress" can be made. Rather than viewing this client response as obstinance, however, the counselor can take this resistance as a signal that the client has some reason for not wishing to go further at this moment. More understanding on the part of the client, the counselor, or both is needed before the impasse can be broken.

In taking time to explore the reasons for client reluctance to goal-setting, the counselor may find that the client:

1. Is not anxious to work on this particular concern because it is too threatening at the moment.
2. Doesn't believe that the concern is really important enough to work on at all.
3. Needs time and understanding to think through just why he or she is in counseling.
4. Doesn't understand the purpose of goals and why one now needs to be established.
5. Wonders what some typical goals might be.
6. Would like to know more about how the counselor generally works.

Through listening, inquiring, and encouraging, the counselor can determine the reason for the client's reluctance. Usually the counselor can then focus the discussion upon the client's unwillingness to set a goal. If, for example, the counselor has learned that a male client doesn't want to work toward a goal because he doesn't understand what some typical goals might be, the counselor can provide the client with examples of several goals which seem to fit this client's particular problem. The closer to the client's own concern the examples are, the quicker he will understand the counselor's point.

Or, a client may report unwillingness to work on a goal because the prospect of behavior change is too threatening right now. The counselor may be most useful at this point by acting as a supporter and reinforcer to encourage some new attempts on the client's part.

Some clients may be too content with the present situation to want to change their ways. The counselor, in these instances, may need to help clients to look at their behavior and see the consequences involved in changing or not changing.

Once the source of client reluctance has been identified and discussed, the client will usually be ready to DETERMINE DESIRED GOAL (6.2). Occasionally, however, clients may still be unwilling to commit themselves to the task of goal-setting. At this point the counselor has at least three alternatives.

The *first* alternative is for the counselor to consider whether another reason for hesitation or resistance might exist. The counselor could discuss this matter with the client much as was done with the prior cause of resistance. The counselor should be wary, however, of the possibility that the client may be manipulating the counselor into long discussions in order to avoid action steps.

A *second* alternative is that the counselor may not be the best source of assistance and the client may realize this. Any of a number of factors related to skill, perceived life style, age, sex, race, and speech may cause the client to be unwilling to work with the counselor. The counselor then can ASSIST IN LOCATING APPROPRIATE ASSISTANCE (2.2.5). Specifically, the client can be helped to locate and set up an appointment with a different counselor or agency.

A *third* and final alternative involves the termination of counseling. If all the discussion has been fruitless and the client has no interest in seeing another counselor or visiting another agency, then the counselor has no alternative other than to terminate the counseling process with the client.

In Systematic Counseling emphasis is placed on the importance of doing more than just discussing a concern without taking steps to alleviate it. Some clients, however, are only interested in discussing their concerns and really don't want to change their circumstances. A counselor response of continuing to focus upon the concern and not moving on to goal-setting after the concern is mutually understood merely reinforces the client's pattern of response and never allows the possibility of action that would relieve the situation. When this pattern of client-counselor interaction occurs, the counselor is advised to terminate counseling on the grounds that he or she cannot be a source of help if the client is unwilling to engage in a process of change. This possibility of termination (9.0) in some instances acts as a motivating force. When faced with a choice of acting or receiving no further counselor attention, the client may choose to act.

Determine Desired Goal (6.2)

Clients often are able to describe what it is that they don't like about their circumstances, but are unable to suggest what they could do to improve them. A person may describe in vivid detail a state of loneliness but have never thought to become involved in some task or social interaction that is rewarding.

In some instances, however, such a change cannot be readily identified. A male who describes himself as being a chronic worrier may tell the counselor that above all else what he would like to become is an honor student, not a nonworrier. For him, being an honor student would give him the status and feeling of self-worth that he desires. Lacking this, he may be given to excessive worry. His expressed concern, excessive worry, can be eradicated when he experiences academic success. The counselor who fails to determine the outcome the client desires from counseling and focuses professional energies upon helping the client to reduce his incidence of worry might not succeed either in relieving the concern or meeting the client's goal. Focusing upon academic improvement might well do both.

Concerns may suggest goals, and goals may alleviate concerns. Converting a client concern into a goal that might be pursued in counseling is a creative task. The assumption that the concern will always suggest the goal can be erroneous. However, what other options does the counselor have? Involvement of the client in this task and the joint effort of both toward finding an appropriate goal are needed. The experience of the counselor and self-searching on the part of the client may both be needed before an appropriate goal for counseling can be found.

In some instances the concern suggests the goal that might be pursued. A client who has difficulty socializing may establish a goal of being accepted by others. However, another client who displays antisocial behavior may have a good reason for doing so and may really wish to spend more time alone.

Juanita, the client in the case presented in Chapter 13, was concerned because she didn't have any real friends at school. She wanted to get to know other kids better, but was afraid they might reject her. Somewhat later, when determining her desired goal, she said, ". . . I suppose I would like to be able to talk easily with other people and make myself interesting enough so that I could establish good relations with anyone that I wanted as a friend." (Cl 55)

Let's look at some other stated concerns and the desired goals that might result from them.

1.	*CONCERN*	*Feeling guilty about the way I treat my mother.*
	GOAL	To talk with her without losing my temper.
2.	*CONCERN*	*Feeling as though I'm worth nothing, totally inadequate.*
	GOAL	To maintain steady employment.
3.	*CONCERN*	*Always being picked on by others.*
	GOAL	To stop being sent to the principal's office for fighting on the school grounds.

Concerns, don't necessarily suggest the goals that might be set. Given a verified model of client behavior, the counselor may want to encourage the client to dream a little; to think about a desired job, skill, or personal habit; to become untangled from the pressures of daily life and consider what the client would like to do or become. During this process the counselor should be only minimally concerned with realism. The wished-for state of the client may provide important data for the counselor to use during later phases of the counseling process.

The counselor can use numerous leads to get the client to "dream a little" about the goal to be reached through counseling. An appropriate counselor lead would be, "Just think about where you'd like to be . . . what you'd like to be doing . . . what you'd like to see changed as the result of our work together." Impossible as the dream may seem at the moment to the client, it provides valuable data to both client and counselor concerning a goal that the client would really like to attain.

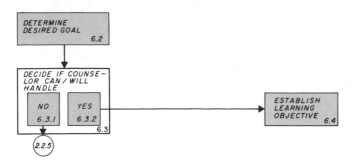

Figure 7-3

Decide if Counselor Can/Will Handle (6.3)

At this point the counselor knows a great deal about the client's past and present behavior and the desired goal for bringing about change. The counselor might wish to reconsider, at this time whether or not it is appropriate to continue working with this particular person within the present circumstances (See Figure 7-3). The counselor may briefly reflect upon four practical considerations: (a) the counselor's own skills and resources, (b) the appropriateness of this concern to this office or agency, (c) the amount of time needed and the amount the counselor has available, and (d) ethical considerations of the counselor in continuing to work with this client.

The helping professions have developed a number of specialists, of whom the counselor is one. In working with students the counselor may find one who might better see the college financial aids officer, one who should be encouraged to discuss a personal concern with the family welfare worker, and a third who should be referred to someone with greater skills in counseling or psychotherapy. Hopefully, the analysis of data prior to seeing the client will have identified those who should be referred. In some instances, however, it is possible that the counselor might become rather involved with a client before realizing that another person or agency would be more appropriate.

Few counselors find that they have adequate time to meet the demands that surround them. Deliberate steps must be taken to make certain that services are available to all, and yet those who desire them are given sufficient time to attain the outcomes they set for themselves in counseling. One guide for doing this is for the counselor to limit the type of case he will handle and to establish time limits for contact (see Appendix A, 6.3). Another source of concern is whether or not the counselor is overcommitted. The goal established may demand more counselor time than is available. To become overloaded may jeopardize both this client and others with whom the counselor is currently working.

Ethics may cause the counselor to question whether to continue assisting the client with the identified outcome. One client may wish to learn leadership skills in order to start a riot. Another might wish to involve the counselor personally in a questionable activity. A third might like to explore reasons for religious belief. Dependent upon further details and the specific situation, the counselor might decide that continued involvement would be ethical or unethical, appropriate or inappropriate.

Specific criteria for making the decision of whether or not to continue with a particular client are given within the Performance Criteria (see Appendix A, 6.3).

Establish Learning Objective (6.4)

Allowing the client to dream a little, to "think big," or to disclose a secret ambition is a productive activity. The data generated from considering goals in this light is valuable to the counselor and may open new horizons for the client. Too often the remedy we initially consider when in a dilemma represents too conservative a change and we wish at a later time that we had been more ambitious in pursuing what we really wanted, but thought impossible.

Following this process of dreaming, realism is introduced. The counselor next considers with the client how they might agree upon a target or counseling outcome that is indeed attainable (see Figure 7-3). The counselor may need to remind the client that their time together is relatively limited and that any outcome they agree upon must be something that they both believe can be accomplished.

Because counseling is basically a learning process, the outcome toward which the efforts of both client and counselor are directed is termed a learning objective. There is an important distinction between a goal and a learning objective: The goal suggests a direction and an ambition, but may well be beyond the capacity of the client and counselor to achieve; the learning objective, however, not only indicates a focus and a direction, but also specifies a standard that both consider attainable before counseling is completed.

The focus of the counselor and client in establishing a learning objective is upon the new responses or patterns of responses that must be learned by the client to attain the desired outcome. This is not to imply that the individual's only response to stress is modification of his or her own behavior. Social activists will suggest that the social environment might well need modifying. Certainly one of the counselor's responsibilities is helping to make environments conducive to positive human development. In working with a client whose family situation (or job, or classroom) prevents the achievement of legitimate goals, the counselor might help the client to change this environment. In another instance a client might be assisted in learning to maximize the opportunities within a restrictive environment. The counselor and client, of course, might give some attention to both of these alternatives. Even if the client chooses to try to bring about environmental changes, the accomplishment of this objective usually involves the acquisition of personal skills and responses that can bring about such changes.

Many problems of adolescents have to do with family situations over which youths have little control. One possible response to such a situation would be to help the adolescent to cope with a continuing unpleasant situation. Another approach would be to help the client learn some responses which might reduce family friction and lead to improved relationships. In either case the client will have to learn new responses.

To say that most if not all solutions to psychological problems necessitate a change in the client is not to imply that the client is at fault. It merely recognizes the fact that the client is concerned and anxious to do something about the situation. No one else is likely to be as motivated to work toward change as the client. However, the client's actions may well be directionless and unrewarding unless assistance is received from a professional helper. Counselors, with their experience in identifying obstacles to change, can be very helpful to clients.

Establishing a learning objective greatly clarifies the purposes and needs of the client. Occasionally, the client's goal is stated as desired changes in behavior. Examples: "I would like to quit smoking" or "I want to have better control of my temper." More often the goal is stated in terms of the rewards that the new response might bring. Example: "I would like better grades . . . more friends . . . a steady job." Here the learning objective must be thought of as the new or improved responses that would be required to accomplish these goals.

Learning objectives must be tailored to the individual. For example, two people who want to accomplish the same goal of acquiring friends might define friendship in quite different ways and want quite different outcomes because of the specific types of interactions they value with others. Let's look at some desired goals and learning objectives:

GOAL	LEARNING OBJECTIVE
To have friends.	To learn to express myself to at least one other fellow worker while taking a lunch break on the job so well that a worker comes to sit by me at least twice within a week.
To maintain steady employment.	To learn constructive responses to criticism from work supervisors so well that an observer reports that I have made no hostile responses during a two-week period.
To stop being sent to the principal's office for fighting on the school grounds.	To learn alternate ways to handle hostility so that I will engage in no fighting on the school grounds during a three-week period.

You will note that in each of the three learning objectives derived from goals there is (a) an identification of the desired *behavior* or *response,* (b) a specification of the *criterion* or *standards* of minimum acceptable performance, and (c) a description of the important *conditions* that should exist when the behavior or response is emitted. Specifically, the first client wants to learn the behavior of being able to express oneself to at least one other fellow worker. The standard established for knowing whether or not this expression is effective is that it will be done "so well that a worker comes to sit by me at least twice within a week." Further, conditions are defined that suggest when the expression of oneself will take place. In this instance the condition is "while taking a lunch break on the job."

In each of the above examples, the learning objective was established because the client and counselor believed that it represented the best of several possible alternatives for reaching the client's desired goal. Other learning objectives might have been suggested to accomplish the same goals. Several possible learning objectives might be generated in the counseling session before the client and counselor agree upon one. More than one learning objective may have to be accomplished in order to attain the desired goal. In this case some priority among objectives will have to be established, for it is generally preferable to work on one objective at a time. Above all, the learning objective must be clearly understood by the client and counselor. This objective will then be "fed forward" to EVALUATE CLIENT PERFORMANCE (8.0) and a comparison of client performance will be made with the objective established (8.1.3).

Target Behavior. Establishing an objective that meets the needs of the client is vitally important. Several clients might indicate that they have an identical goal, but the target behavior that each client must alter in order to reach the goal would be quite different. For example, several clients might indicate that they were having difficulty in establishing satisfactory social relationships with members of the opposite sex. One client might specifically indicate a desire to overcome stuttering caused by extreme anxiety. Another might report no particular anxiety, but a general lack of skill in conversing and appearing attentive. A third might indicate that his own aggressive acts toward females caused them to respond negatively. For each client a different target behavior has been identified.

Target behaviors should be specific. Statements such as "making him aware of his behavior" and "helping her feel comfortable" are too vague to indicate exactly what the client and counselor might focus upon. The following statements, however, all indicate the specific behavior change that the client hopes to achieve through counseling: (a) increase the frequency of contacts with strangers, (b) discriminate between insensitive and hostile remarks, (c) decrease the number of self-references in conversation, and (d) respond calmly.

Standards. Although the above statements indicate the target behaviors, they do not indicate *how well* or for *how long* the behavior is to be displayed. Establishing a *standard* or *criterion* specifies how well or for how long the target behavior is to be displayed. Key phrases that are often helpful in stating a standard or criterion are " . . . so well that . . . ." and " . . . so much that . . . ." For example, how much should the client increase the frequency of contacts with fellow workers? It is, of course, an individual matter. The client and counselor can decide what *standard* or what level of contact frequency the client would attempt to attain. In one instance it might be decided that "The client will increase the frequency of contacts with fellow workers so much that she speaks to each worker each day" or "so much that he has conversations of two or more minutes' duration with at least four workers." Either standard would set a minimum acceptable level for contact. When that level is met or exceeded, the client has accomplished what he or she wished to do through counseling.

Some varied forms and illustrations for the statement of standards are:

Form	Illustration
Specific time period	for twenty minutes daily. once daily for two weeks.
Specific degree	on four of five occasions. with less than a 10% error rate.
Task accomplishment	until the project is completed. until the instructor approves.
Change of personal state	without crying. while remaining relaxed.

Conditions. Identifying the target behavior and the standard or criterion of acceptable performance are two elements of a learning objective. The third concerns the conditions or limits that surround the performance of a behavior. A timid speaker may have no difficulty in an empty auditorium, but become flustered before a large audience. A student may have no difficulty doing homework in a quiet sanctuary, but may have a problem concentrating with several active siblings running about.

A learning objective, then, takes into account not only the target behavior that is to be performed and the degree to which it is to be performed, but also the conditions that will prevail when the behavior is performed at the conclusion of counseling. In the above examples, some steps may be taken to desensitize the speaker and the student to the environmental distraction, but to remove the audience or dismiss the family is unrealistic. Both are going to be present, and the learning objective must reflect this fact. Performance of the behavior under the conditions stated and to the degree specified suggests that the client has completed the objective established for counseling.

A suggested format for the statement of counseling objectives is first to specify the conditions (if any), then the learning behavior, and finally the criteria. Presume that a person reports being lonely and has decided that one way of combating loneliness would be to increase the number of acquaintances encountered during the twice-daily bus rides to work (or school).

Conditions	When (you are) riding on the bus . . .
Learning behavior	. . . begin and continue a conversation with another person . . .
Criteria	. . . *so well that* you can recall the person's name, occupational or educational setting, and two interests or hobbies.

Collectively, the counseling objective would be: When riding on the bus, begin and continue a conversation with another person *so well that* you can recall the person's name, occupational or educational setting, and two interests or hobbies.

Decide if Client Motivation Is Sufficient (6.5)

The time and energy expended by both client and counselor throughout the counseling process are considerable and cannot be regarded lightly. The effort involved in the process of identifying concerns and selecting goals for counseling is relatively small when compared with the time and energy that will be expended during the implementation of strategy. For this reason a checkpoint has been inserted into the counseling process following ESTABLISH LEARNING OBJECTIVE (6.4) so that the counselor can determine whether the counseling relationship should be continued, should be clarified, or should be terminated.

Specifically, the counselor needs to select one of two alternatives. Either the counselor can safely assume that the client is motivated and therefore can begin to IMPLEMENT STRATEGY (7.0), or sufficient doubt exists concerning the client's motivation that the counselor may wish to pause, consider the matter with the client, and when motivation is insufficient, DISCUSS REASONS FOR INSUFFICIENT MOTIVA- TION (6.6) and perhaps subsequently to ASSIST IN LOCATING AP- PROPRIATE ASSISTANCE (2.2.5). This series of actions is shown in Figure 7-4.

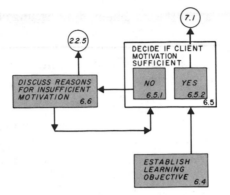

Figure 7-4

The decision of whether to undertake a particular strategy or to select other courses of action rests with the counselor. Like other decisions in Systematic Counseling, this judgment is made after a candid discussion of alternatives with the client. In some instances the counselor may be so confident of the client's motivation to continue that the counselor can make the decision almost instantaneously. On other occasions, doubt may exist concerning the level of client motivation. Because of the deci- sion's importance, the counselor is urged to err on the side of caution and discuss client motivation when doubt exists. In borderline cases, the counselor may devise two or three leads to elicit the extent of client motivation and make a decision on the basis of the client's response. An example follows:

CO: You've mentioned how busy you are. Perhaps we should con- sider for a moment whether you really have time to continue in counseling.

CL: Oh . . . I'm always short of time. . . . I guess I complain a lot about my lack of time.

CO: . . . And continuing counseling would cut into what time you *do* have.

CL: Yeah, but I'm not *that* busy. I really want to continue counseling. . . . I think I can really benefit.

Not much doubt exists as to this client's commitment. A few counselor leads have clarified the matter, and the counselor can begin to IMPLE-MENT STRATEGY (7.0). Let's alter the example a bit, however, and consider another possibility:

CO: You've mentioned how busy you are. Perhaps we should con-sider for a moment whether you really have time to continue in counseling.

CL: Oh . . . I'm always short of time. I seem to get involved in things and then wish I had the time for something else.

CO: And counseling . . . is this a commitment you wish you hadn't made?

CL: Well, I don't know . . . I'm not sure . . . I'm a little confused as to just how much I'm really going to get out of it.

No great sensitivity is needed to detect that this client is not fully com-mitted. The counselor would initially DISCUSS REASONS FOR IN-SUFFICIENT MOTIVATION (6.6) with the client. Some clarification might result in the client being quite committed to continuing. Or, the clarification process may be a rather extended one in which the counselor will have to refer back to the initial selection of concerns and discuss the benefits and costs of counseling in light of the stated concern and the probability of being able to do something about it. The result of this dis-cussion, however well handled, may be that the client desires to ter-minate counseling and the counselor then will ASSIST IN LOCATING APPROPRIATE ASSISTANCE (2.2.5).

Use of the term "costs" seems appropriate when one considers sources of low client motivation. Among the "costs" to the client may be one or more of the following:

1. Time is being expended in traveling to the counselor's office and participating in counseling.
2. Money may be expended (e.g., time lost on job, transportation costs).
3. Participation in counseling is probably anxiety-producing.
4. Risks of various types may be involved that the client doesn't wish to cope with.
5. Participation in counseling may be unsettling and make the client's life less comfortable than it was.
6. The client may be asked to discuss matters or perform tasks outside the interview that are personally embarrassing.

Individuals will give quite different weights to the various costs, dependent upon their personality and life style. One client may find a risk to be insurmountable and withdraw from full commitment to counseling. Another, faced with a much greater risk, may accept it as necessary and remain committed.

Cues indicating lessened motivation may be subtle. The counselor may be aware of a change in motivational level and yet may be unable to specify why motivation seems to be lessened. In determining whether or not the client has sufficient motivation to implement a strategy, the counselor has *three* basic measures of commitment that can be used. The counselor can proceed to implement the strategy if:

1. The client has verbally agreed that the established objectives are appropriate.
2. The counselor and client have discussed the client costs involved (e.g., time, money, risk, anxiety, embarrassment).
3. The client has verbalized commitment to work with this concern after a discussion of costs.

IMPLEMENT STRATEGY (7.0)

The core of the counseling process is contained within this subsystem. Any change that is to take place, any decision that is to be made, any knowledge that is to be gained will most likely occur as the result of the client and counselor's efforts in this phase of the counseling process. For this reason it is likely that IMPLEMENT STRATEGY will take more time than all the other subsystems combined. It may, in fact, take nearly all of the counseling time. Another important point should be stressed. Unlike the other subsystems, which are designed to be performed with comparative uniformity from client to client and from concern to concern, IMPLEMENT STRATEGY will differ greatly in both *time* (number and length of interviews) and *tasks* (client assignments during and between interviews). The client's learning rate, the complexity of the concern, and the strategy selected all contribute to this great diversity in *time* and *tasks*.

Constructing a model of client concern (5.0) provided knowledge of the client's past and present behavior with regard to the selected concern. With the establishment of the learning objective (6.4), the counselor and client both have agreed upon the goal that will be reached before counseling is concluded. At this moment it may seem that a great distance exists between the client's present and desired behaviors. The counselor's next task is to introduce the process that will bridge this gap (see Figure 7-5).

The process for effecting this change is called a strategy and is a comprehensive plan. When we think of learning to ride a bike, taking a trip to Europe this summer, or building a beach house, we know that a great many small steps are necessary to complete each part of the task and

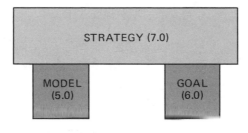

Figure 7-5

that the completion of each part is essential to reaching our goal. Much the same process is involved in developing a counseling strategy. Using the trip to Europe as an analogy, we originally plan to "just go to Europe and have a good time." We then learn that many challenges face us in our preparation for the trip. One phase might be termed "making transportation arrangements," another "customs and legal requirements," and another "making arrangements for care of house and pets." We already have several phases identified, and we haven't even left! To continue our analogy, we have an objective, "taking a trip to Europe this summer," and have identified some of the intermediate objectives that it will be necessary to complete if we are to make the trip at all. Further, we can immediately realize that "customs and legal requirements" are only a statement of intent. To do this we will need to complete a great many small, specific steps such as having pictures taken for passports, applying for passports, applying for an international driver's license, and so on.

Much the same process is involved in counseling. We start with a learning objective and develop a comprehensive strategy or plan that will take the client and counselor from the present circumstances to where they wish to be at the conclusion of counseling. Similar to planning the trip to Europe, this includes identifying the necessary intermediate objectives that will help in attaining the learning objectives, and then selecting the steps or specific actions that are necessary to reach each interim point or intermediate objective (see Figure 7-6).

The general model for IMPLEMENT STRATEGY (7.0) is presented in Figure 7-7. In addition to the selection of a strategy, identification of intermediate objectives, and selection of steps, provision is made for both counselor and client to perform the steps that they have been assigned. Further, a check is made to DECIDE IF STRATEGY/STEPS COMPLETED (7.5). If either the strategy is incomplete or the steps have not been completed, the counselor would usually recycle to review the intermediate objectives established (7.2) and proceed from there with the completion of the strategy. The counselor might find, for example, that intermediate objectives had not been completed because they were too

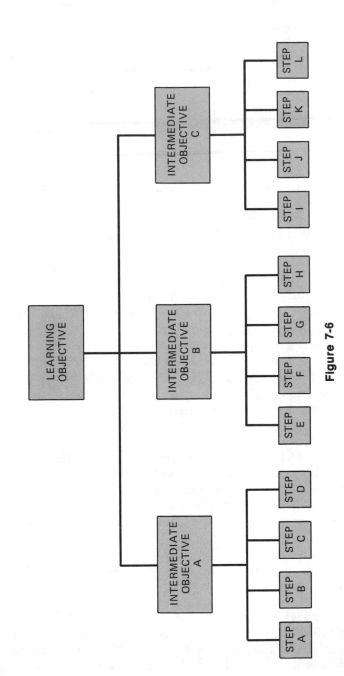

Figure 7-6

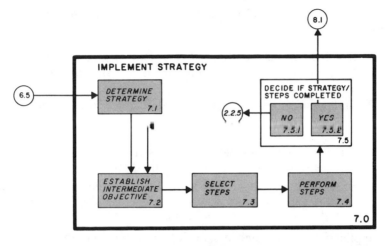

Figure 7-7

difficult. The next step would be to review them with the client and make adjustments so that the difficulty could be reduced. The client would then attain the intermediate objective through work over a longer period of time.

In searching for a strategy the beginning counselor sometimes selects one that is highly complex and may far exceed the needs of the client. If a practical, uncomplicated strategy can be found, it will reduce the amount of time the client needs to spend in counseling and probably produce more predictable results. Such a process, *sequenced learning*, is described in the section that follows.

Sequenced Learning

A primary procedure to employ in effecting behavior change is called sequenced learning. It is not a strategy, per se. Rather, it is a set of principles that may be used independently or in combination with strategies such as reinforcement, extinction, and decision-making. (These and other strategies will be described in the chapters that follow.) Because of its comparative simplicity, sequenced learning is a procedure that should be given first consideration. Simply stated, sequenced learning is an arrangement of learning steps of manageable size which lead from responses the client is now capable of making to those that can be made when the learning objective is attained.

A history of failure makes it difficult for an individual to learn new or modified responses. Minimizing the chance of failure and maximizing the probability of success is a key part of any learning experience. Success generates enthusiasm and continued effort, while failure leads to discouragement and abandonment of the learning endeavor. To promote learning and minimize failure, the following steps are generally applicable:

1. Divide learning into manageable steps arranged in a sequence.
2. Make the first step one that the client can manage with little effort.
3. Make each succeeding step small enough so that the client is capable of attaining it.
4. Attempt to make each step small, but not so easy or trivial that the client will consider it worthless.
5. Involve the client in developing learning activities.
6. State each step clearly so that client and counselor will know what is expected and whether or not the step has been completed.

An application of sequenced learning may be seen in the strategy employed in the following case. A male client who has sustained an injury in an auto accident has been left with a slight but permanent limp. Embarrassment about his handicap contributes to his seeming lack of motivation to go out and seek employment following his convalescence. He wants a job and recognizes the need to overcome the anxiety he feels in situations in which others might notice his limp.

GOAL	*To find steady employment*
Learning Objective:	To eliminate or reduce anxiety in social situations.
Suggested Initial Learning Steps	1. To go to a section of town with heavy pedestrian traffic and for 20-30 minutes observe people and the variety of ways in which they walk and how much notice they attract.
	2. To go to a shopping center where he is unlikely to meet an acquaintance and walk around for an hour noting any special reactions to the limp.
	3. To visit a friend and in the course of the conversation tell the friend about the accident and the leg injury.
	4. To take a walk around the block in his neighborhood.

Any one of the above might be chosen as an initial learning step, depending upon what might be reasonably expected from the client. Other learning steps would be arranged to build upon the initial experience. The sequence of steps should help the client to feel more at ease in going anywhere he chooses and to be as comfortable with people as he had been before the accident.

As you work with different clients and varied concerns, a number of types of sequences may be applicable. Each will be described briefly.

Natural or Logical Sequence. When sequencing learning, first determine whether a natural or logical order might best be used. In learning decision-making skills, for example, one learns to generate alternatives, to gather information, to assess probable outcomes, and finally to make a tentative choice. One step may be no more difficult than the next, but each step leads to the next in a logical sequence.

Sequences Increasing in Complexity. Complex learning objectives can be accomplished by practicing initially under simplified conditions that increase in complexity in subsequent learning trials. Simplification can be accomplished by reducing the number of environmental cues to which the client must attend, by intensifying those environmental cues, and by focusing on just one new response to be learned at a time. One having difficulty in handling criticism, for example, might narrow his or her focus from handling general criticism to dealing with one kind of criticism from a particular source, such as criticism of work performance by a supervisor. A sequence can then be developed that gradually adds varying types of criticism from the supervisor, varying types from several authority figures, and so forth.

Sequences Increasing in Frequency or Duration. Often the learning objective is not to acquire a new response but to make an existing response occur more frequently or for longer periods of time. A student may wish to study for longer periods of time, or a mother may wish to increase her use of praise in order to encourage her children. In these cases the response can be practiced at a frequency rate or for a period of time within the client's present capability and be gradually increased until the goal is reached.

Sequences Decreasing in Frequency or Duration. Habitual responses can be reduced or eliminated through the use of a learning sequence that reduces the frequency or duration of the response. Watching TV, daydreaming, and worrying, for example, can be reduced or eliminated by gradually decreasing the time involved in the activity. Smoking, swearing, and crying can be decreased or eliminated by practice in restricting these responses to a gradually decreasing frequency of occurrence.

Sequences Increasing in Anxiety-Producing Stimuli. Learning responses in which anxiety plays an important part can be sequenced so that initial learning and practice take place in a nonthreatening situation, perhaps a role-played situation with the counselor. In subsequent trials, situations holding progressively more potential threat may be attempted. The client's contribution is vital in helping to suggest and order the learning steps in ascending order of anxiety and difficulty.

For those clients who know or who can easily be helped to see the steps necessary to attain their learning objective, who are able to take the first step, and who are sufficiently motivated, *sequenced learning* may be all that is needed. Many clients, however, can't see clearly what is needed to solve their problem. Others have fears that inhibit learning. Still others find it difficult to make a sustained effort toward a goal. For these clients, sequence learning can be helpful, but it is not enough. Additional strategies, such as those that are described in the chapters that follow, need to be called upon.

An example of a counselor using sequenced learning with a client follows. Kelly reports that she needs to spend at least one hour per night on math in order to succeed. However, she finds many distractions while studying and seldom studies math for more than 10 minutes. With the counselor's assistance, she identifies the time and location that would be most conducive to study. She then attempts to study for at least 15 minutes on three consecutive nights. Her times per night were actually 22, 15, and 27 minutes. The counselor suggests that the minimum expectancy be increased to 25 minutes and be increased again whenever the existing standard has been met or exceeded for three consecutive nights. She is to continue this process until she can consistently study math for one hour each time she needs to.

Determine Strategy (7.1)

The choice of a strategy that is appropriate for a given purpose is dependent upon the skills possessed by the counselor and the specific needs of the client. Several basic strategies that will assist the counselor in working with a wide range of client concerns are presented in the next three chapters. Within these chapters, presentation is made and examples given in sufficient detail so that the counselor should know how to employ strategies for increasing the likelihood of a response, decreasing the likelihood of a response, and assisting the client to learn new responses.

From the model developed and the learning objective established, the client and counselor can readily determine the change that is desired. If the counselor feels competent to use only one means for changing a client's behavior, no choice as to strategy need be made. However, that one strategy might be unpromising for use with all clients. Knowing several possible means of effecting change increases the likelihood that the counselor can use a strategy that will help a given client.

Which strategy would work best with a particular client seeking a given goal? In deciding which strategy to implement, the counselor considers the goal sought by the client, any available objective or subjective data concerning client motivation and willingness to participate in a lengthy or shortened procedure, and the counselor's own familiarity with various strategies that might meet the client's need. At this vital point the counselor may wish also to consult a colleague or professional reference to obtain additional help in developing a plan that fits the circumstance.

For ease of communication, the examples used in this chapter demonstrate the use of a single strategy. In practice, however, the client and counselor may agree that several strategies are needed in order to attain the chosen learning objective.

Establish Intermediate Objectives (7.2)

The counselor frequently finds that the client wishes to change a behavior that is complex. Oftentimes the gap between the client's entry behavior level (ESTABLISH BASELINE OF CONCERN-RELATED BEHAVIOR, 5.4) and the learning objective is large. When this occurs, the client will find it difficult to complete the learning objective successfully because he or she needs some intermediate goals that can be attained in less time (see Figure 7-8). If the client had to wait until the learning objective was completed before feeling some degree of success, it might be difficult to maintain motivation. In some cases, several subgoals must be completed before one can attempt the learning objective.

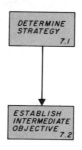

Figure 7-8

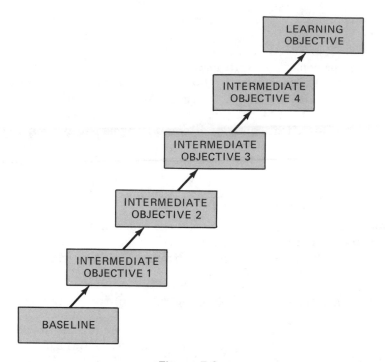

Figure 7-9

In developing subgoals care must be taken that the emphasis upon behavioral specification does not encourage the selection of inconsequential learning objectives. The counselor must also be certain that objectives are not beyond the client's reach.

In form, intermediate objectives are identical to learning objectives. Both state an explicit behavior, a criterion or standard, and the conditions that are to exist when the behavior is exhibited. Only in degree are they different. As illustrated in Figures 7-9 and 7-10, there are two ways of conceptualizing the use of intermediate objectives. In Figure 7-9, the intermediate objectives are a series of sequential steps or approximations leading to the learning objective. These successive substeps are of graduated difficulty and reduce the possibility of client failure to a minimum since each substep requires skills that are within easy range of the client.

To illustrate the use of sequential intermediate objectives, let's assume that a person knows how to initiate contact with others, but is extremely shy and makes fewer contacts than he or she desires. Because the skills of initiating conversation are known, the counselor can consider a series of simulations of social interaction that will initially be nonthreatening. As each simulation is completed, the client can undertake a more difficult

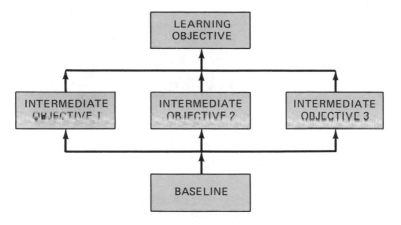

Figure 7-10

simulation. The ultimate objective would be to have the client engage in a simulation that is very much like the real-life environment.

The use of sequential intermediate objectives may not be applicable to the behavior change desired by some clients. Rather, the client may need to engage in learning activity in a number of related areas. This situation is depicted in Figure 7-10. A client who has had limited success in obtaining employment, for example, may need to work on such diverse activities as (a) finding employers with job openings, (b) discriminating between appropriate and inappropriate behaviors to exhibit during a job interview, and (c) obtaining supportive references from past employers. The particular order in which these objectives are completed is not important, but the completion of all is necessary before the client attempts a job interview.

In some situations both of the approaches shown in Figures 7-9 and 7-10 may be integrated. A client may complete the three intermediate objectives for obtaining employment and still be far from ready to face a job interview. A series of simulations may be needed to prepare the client for the real task of being interviewed for a job. The client may be composed when talking with a mild-mannered interviewer, but may become angry and aggressive when faced with dehumanizing language and racial epithets. A series of simulated interviews of increasing intensity may be necessary before the client is able to maintain appropriate interview behavior when faced by a hostile interviewer.

Select Steps (7.3)

Both intermediate and learning objectives are targets that are established to give direction. But how can they be reached? *Step* is the term used to designate a specific task that the client can do in order to

Figure 7-11

reach the established target. Some steps that might be taken by a client seeking employment are: observe a fellow worker, obtain cost figures, read want ads, find out the name of an electronics firm, ask a friend for information about working conditions, write down each incident as it happens.

As shown in Figure 7-11, steps are selected immediately following ESTABLISH INTERMEDIATE OBJECTIVES (7.2). As the counselor and client consider how an intermediate objective might be attained, they may generate a great many possible steps that could be used. The steps can then be placed in some order whenever it seems necessary to accomplish one before attempting another. In this process of sifting and sorting, some steps may seem too large and may need to be divided into two or more specific acts. As work on the steps continues, the client may give evidence that some steps can be skipped.

In the case presented in Chapter 13, Juanita and her counselor developed a number of intermediate objectives and steps that would be performed to complete each objective.

> *Intermediate Objective: Make contact with two potential friends (one Latino and one non-Latino).*
> Steps: a. Make a list of desired characteristics in a friend; rank in order of desirability.
>   b. Make a list of potential friends; rank in terms of possession of desired qualities.
>   c. Initiate conversation with two potential friends at top of list.

Perform Steps (7.4)

Much time has now been spent by the client and counselor in planning the acts that the client will undertake in gradually moving toward the learning objective. Finally, the client and counselor can begin *to do* something. While much of the doing will be the responsibility of the client, the counselor may also be involved in the *doing* process. For example, a female client may be attempting to alter her social behavior. During a given week she has agreed to work on a number of specific steps that will start the change process. One of the steps, however, might involve her counselor in observing her during the week and then reinforcing her attempts at behavior change. Both the counselor and the client, then, may perform steps. Assignment of who is to do what is accomplished during the planning process (SELECT STEPS, 7.3).

Arduous as the planning process might seem, PERFORM STEPS (7.4) is the single function within Systematic Counseling that produces behavior change. All of the other functions are involved with planning and assessing outcomes. It is only logical, then, that the greatest time commitment of the counselor and the client is given to this vital function.

Decide if Strategy/Steps Completed (7.5)

As steps are completed satisfactorily some means must be used for determining whether, in fact, the entire strategy has been completed. This is accomplished through the counselor's reference to a YES/NO decision concerning both steps and strategy (see Figure 7-12). The completion of all steps requires that the counselor also ask if other parts of the strategy (for example, other intermediate objectives) have been completed. When both steps and strategy are completed, the counselor is ready to begin the process of evaluating client performance (8.0).

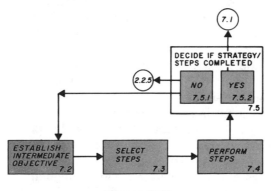

Figure 7-12

If the counselor finds that more steps remain to be completed, the client and counselor are redirected to the unfinished tasks and they plan together as to how and when they might be accomplished. If they have been completed unsatisfactorily, the existing steps should be examined to determine whether some revision is needed to make them more readily understood, easier to accomplish, or more meaningful for the client.

In the case presented in Chapter 13 Juanita's counselor reviewed the strategy that had been developed and then asked, "Now, have we done all of those things?" Juanita referred to some remedial steps that had been necessary and then replied:

CL 338: Yes, I think I have. I can't think of anything that was left out.

CO 338: I can't either, Juanita. (pause) Now, let's see if we can record very specifically how you're doing at this point. . . .

The words of the counselor's final response indicate that the process of evaluating client performance (8.0) has already begun.

Repeated failure to accomplish either steps or strategy may force the counselor to consider with the client whether or not another source of assistance might be preferable and/or desired by the client. If another source is preferred, the counselor then abandons the strategy and proceeds to ASSIST IN LOCATING APPROPRIATE ASSISTANCE (2.2.5). Referral to another source of assistance may result from the realization that the client's concern is of greater magnitude than originally determined, thus requiring skills and/or time the counselor cannot provide.

Superficial or inappropriate performance or the client's failure to perform steps may result from difficulties caused by lack of clear communication or tasks of inappropriate difficulty. If the client doesn't understand the purpose of the strategy or feels no ownership of it, motivation is understandably lessened. The strategy and steps may not seem sufficiently relevant to the client's concern to maintain client motivation. If the steps are too difficult or not sufficiently challenging, the client may not be motivated to accomplish the assigned tasks. Failure caused by situational factors such as attempting to visit employers when a car is in disrepair may be corrected through finding alternate modes of transportation or altering the steps.

Because PERFORM STEPS is the single most important function in the Systematic Counseling process, care must be exercised both in planning the strategy and steps, and in deciding upon actions to take when steps are not performed adequately. DECIDE IF STRATEGY/STEPS COMPLETED provides a checkpoint for the counselor so that client progress can be monitored on a weekly basis and clarifications and adjustments can be made as they are needed. Only when all steps and all parts of the strategy are completed satisfactorily does the counselor begin to EVAULATE CLIENT PERFORMANCE (8.0).

SUMMARY

Determining the goal and strategy to be used are important steps in the Systematic Counseling process. During this phase of the process the counselor and client are concerned with making three translations. First, they must find a means of translating the concern that was previously identified and discussed into a goal or target toward which their efforts in counseling might be directed. Next, they examine this goal and convert it into a form that is realistic and operational, yet explicit and quantifiable. This statement is called a learning objective.

Using the learning objective as a basis, the counselor and client next begin to build a strategy that will bridge the distance between the client's current behavior and the desired outcome. As a strategy is being considered it is often obvious that the client needs some subgoals to point toward during the early stages of the change process. The third translation entails setting intermediate objectives that are addressed to specific tasks to be attained or skill levels to be reached.

Sequenced learning, because of its simplicity, is a procedure that should be considered before other more elaborate counseling strategies. Sequenced learning is an arrangement of learning steps of manageable size which lead from responses the client is now capable of making to those he or she wishes to be able to make prior to terminating counseling. Other strategies will be described in the next three chapters.

8

Strategies for Learning New Responses

OVERVIEW

Prior to considering strategies for assisting your clients, you should know them quite well. They have trusted you with their problems, their concerns, and their hopes. You should know something about the kinds of things they want to achieve, the type of persons they want to become, and the obstacles that stand in their way. They are counting on you to assist them. What can you do to help them achieve their goals?

The next three chapters describe actions that you can take to assist your client. Chapter 8 describes modeling and simulation strategies for helping clients acquire and practice effective responses. The use of reinforcement and extinction strategies in counseling is described in Chapter 9. Chapter 10 explores a number of ways to help clients become more self-directed through effective decision-making and self-management skills.

In the normal nonsystematic way in which people learn to respond to their environment and to one another, many individuals fail to acquire appropriate ways to deal with certain situations. Some find it difficult or impossible to express their ideas or feelings to others. Some lack the skills required to initiate social contacts. Others cannot respond adequately to criticism. And others lack any number of responses required for maximum effectiveness in dealing with life's encounters. Frequently these learning deficits can be attributed to the absence of adequate examples to follow or to inattention to examples even when they were available. Many individuals develop characteristic ways of responding to situations based upon extremely limited, if not totally inappropriate models. Parents with response deficits themselves often pass these inadequacies on to their children by serving as poor models to follow. Even the presence of adequate examples does not ensure that they will be perceived and emulated, since many different models—some appropriate and some not—compete for attention and influence.

Inadequate models are but one of several causes for learning deficits. Failure to learn appropriate responses may be due to insufficient encouragement during early attempts to acquire new behaviors or to the occurrence of some embarrassment, punishment, hurt, or failure which has inhibited responses or even produced withdrawal from the learning situation. Thus, for a variety of reasons, important responses which should have been acquired are not well learned or are absent entirely from the response repertoire of many individuals. An important job of the counselor is to help clients learn responses that: (a) have never been acquired, or (b) haven't been learned well enough to be effective, or (c) have been inhibited and whose absence presents problems of concern to the client. Modeling procedures provide counselors with ways to help individuals acquire new responses and learn of the possible rewards to be realized from new ways of responding.

Once the client has observed appropriate models and knows more effective responses, the client must have opportunities to try them out and develop skill in using them. Clients need opportunities to try out several alternative responses and to develop those that are suitable. Because it is often uncomfortable or even frightening to try out new responses in actual social settings, counselors often use techniques that allow clients to rehearse a response and to develop some skill in using it prior to attempting it in an actual situation. Simulation is one such technique.

INTRODUCTION

Organization

This chapter has two major sections. The first, on *social modeling*, will help you to identify those problems in which modeling might be useful. Also considered is how to find or develop appropriate models and how to use models to effect changes in the responses of clients. The second major section of this chapter presents the use of *simulation* as a way of providing clients with practice opportunities in safe, manageable settings.

Purposes

The general purposes of this chapter are to help you learn two counseling strategies, modeling and simulation, that have been effective with a wide variety of problems. The chapter will also provide a rationale for the use of these techniques and help you choose the one most suited to the counseling problem at hand.

Objectives

After reading and practicing the techniques presented in this chapter, you should be able to do the following when presented with a counseling problem:

1. Determine whether or not modeling would be an appropriate strategy to use.
2. Identify or develop appropriate models.
3. Help clients learn more effective responses by observing models.
4. Determine whether or not simulation would be appropriate to use.
5. Develop a simulation to allow a client to try out and evaluate a new response.

SOCIAL MODELING

Anyone who has recently learned to drive a golf ball, knit a scarf, cast a flyline, decorate a cake, or any other such skill will be aware of how helpful it is to observe a skilled performer. Being *shown* how to do it is usually much more effective than being *told* how it should be done. Imagine the difficulty of trying to teach a child to tie his shoe using only verbal instruction. The relative ease of communicating a desired behavior through demonstration as opposed to verbal instruction is apparent to those who have tried to assemble some new purchase, relying solely upon the manufacturer's written directions. How much easier the job would have been if someone else had demonstrated the assembly first. So it is with many who come to see that the solution to a personal difficulty necessitates learning new responses. *How much easier it is to learn the new response when there is a model to follow.* It is here that counselors can assist by helping individuals select and use models effectively.

An important way in which individuals learn to respond to situations is by observation of others. Complex motor behaviors, involved verbal patterns, and subtle social skills, as well as a variety of emotional reactions to social and other environmental stimuli, can be learned through observation (Bandura, 1969; Bourdon, 1970). Some of this learning is intentional, with deliberate attempts made to demonstrate the desired responses and to encourage practice by the learner until the responses are mastered. Learning is more frequently incidental, however. Often the learner informally observes individuals in the environment as they respond to a variety of people and situations and unconsciously incorporates these responses into his or her own repertoire.

While teachers, coaches, and others interested in instruction have long used demonstrations as aids in teaching, observational learning is a relatively new tool for counselors. Interest in modeling has been stimulated most recently by the research and writings of psychologist Albert Bandura (1969) and by those who take a social learning approach to personality development and have applied observational learning phenomena to counseling (e.g., Hosford, 1969; Krumboltz & Thoresen, 1969, 1976).

The study of observational learning has been conducted under many different names—vicarious learning, observational learning, imitation, modeling, and role-playing. The term *modeling* is in current use in counseling and refers to the process in which a performer or model demonstrates a response to be learned by an observer. Live models can be used to demonstrate the desired responses in actual or in role-played situations, or symbolic models can be presented through film, videotape, printed pictures, written descriptions, or any combination of these. Counseling uses of modeling usually include observation of the model being rewarded for his response as part of the learning demonstration. This encourages the observer to match the response when faced with the same or a similar situation. To further motivate learning, imitative responses by the observer are rewarded or reinforced as they approximate the modeled performance.

Children, particularly before they have developed language facility, are highly dependent upon observational learning. The development of oral language skill itself is largely accomplished through imitation. Parents are powerful models in the youngster's early years, both because observational learning is especially important at this age and because there are few other models for young children to observe. Youngsters' mannerisms, voice patterns, and emotional and social responses are often carbon copies of those of a parent. Parents as models can transmit to their children social skill or ineptness, self-confidence or timidity, friendliness or hostility, and many other alternate ways of responding in given situations. Incidental learning from observation of a model is often more effective then deliberate attempts to teach responses to children through the use of other approaches. It has been noted frequently that children more often follow parents' examples than their exhortations. Many parents have been amused or embarrassed to see their behavior replicated in great detail by their children.

Parents, of course, are not the only models available, especially as the youngster matures. Older brothers and sisters, friends, teachers, personalities from sports or entertainment, as well as characters from TV, movie, or literary fiction are all models with the potential to influence response patterns.

Observational learning is not restricted to children. Adults also learn through observation, but with some difficulty. This difficulty is due in part to the complex maze of previously learned perceptual, cognitive, and behavioral habits and emotional responses that inhibit further observational learning. The learning of new responses becomes increasingly complicated in adults by the necessity of having to unlearn older, firmly ingrained responses. Skiing instructors, for example, spend a great deal of time teaching novices to lean and move in a manner which is contrary to that which previous learning has taught them is the "natural way." An individual desiring to learn to initiate social contacts may have learned avoidance responses that interfere with learning the new social skills. The reservoir of perceptual, cognitive, and response habits, as well as the inhibitions which have been shaped by the adult's long learning history, account for many adults' seeming lack of spontaneity, unwillingness to take risks, and lack of readiness to learn. Adults, however, can and indeed do learn to acquire new skills, be more effective in their social contacts, give up old habits, or acquire new ones. Observation of models plays a part in this learning.

Modeling has an important function in learning by communicating to the learner a view of the complete response to be learned, the components that comprise the total response, the consequences that are probable, and the environmental context in which the response is performed. A model demonstration shows the learner the response to be acquired more accurately and vividly then words can convey.

Uses of Modeling in Counseling

Modeling has a number of uses in counseling. Counselors can use modeling to help clients: (a) learn new responses, (b) engage in previously inhibited responses, and (c) eliminate or reduce inappropriate responses.

Learning new responses. Bandura (1969) makes a distinction between the acquistion of a new response and the performance of the response. Logically, he maintains that a response must be acquired before it can be performed. Those who emphasize reinforcement in learning are dealing with performance rather than with acquisition. Reward or reinforcement increases the likelihood that a response will be performed only if the response exists within the individual's repertoire.

The acquisition of a response possibility can be produced through observational learning in which neither the model nor the observer is rewarded. Once a response has been acquired through observation of a model, some incentive may be necessary to encourage its performance.

Observing a model being rewarded for exhibiting the desired response increases the likelihood that the response will be performed by the observer. Rewarding the observer for matching the modeled response will further increase the likelihood that he will exhibit the response in the future. A reward can encourage the performance of a response, but only if the response has been acquired and is in the individual's repertoire.

The distinction between acquisition and performance may seem to be trivial since we are ultimately concerned with performance, but the distinction has important implications for counselors. Failure of an individual to exhibit a given response may mean that while the individual has the response capability, reward contingencies for this person have been such that performance of the response has been discouraged. On the other hand, it may mean that the response hasn't been acquired in the first place, and no amount of reinforcement will produce the response until it has been acquired as a possibility. This suggests that the counselor needs to assess whether or not the response capability exists before undertaking a program to encourage its performance through some incentive program. For example, a person who has not explored career possibilities may know how to go about it but be unmotivated to do so. This suggests a reinforcement counseling strategy, to be described in the next chapter. On the other hand, the client may have considerable interest in seeking vocational information but not know how to find the information needed. Lack of this response capability suggests a different counseling program. It is quite possible, of course, that the individual lacks both the motivation and the know-how. In this case the counseling approach must provide for both acquisition and performance.

An individual who wants to learn a new response pattern needs to have a good idea of what that new response is. He or she needs to know what the verbal, behavioral, and situational elements are and how they relate. A word description might serve as a model; pictures might model the response even better; and a live demonstration might serve as the best model when complex response acquisition is involved. For example, a person wishing to learn how to write a letter may be helped as much by reading basic rules and seeing model letters as by a demonstration. If the responses to be learned are alternative ways of dealing with hostility, however, the individual may need to see a model demonstrate a variety of responses in order to observe the relationship of verbal, behavioral, and situational elements. A written description would be ponderous and confusing.

The probability that a response will be performed depends to some extent on the learner's awareness of the probable outcome of the response. This awareness may come directly from experience in the same or similar situations or indirectly through observations of others and the consequences of their responses. Modeling can be used to demonstrate the positive consequences of a response. This will tend to encourage the performance of a response already in the individual's repertoire. For example, presume that a woman knows how to ask questions or otherwise participate in a group discussion, but doesn't because she has never been rewarded for past attempts to contribute. A model who demonstrates such participation and is strongly reinforced for her contribution can demonstrate for the observer the reward consequences which the observer herself has never directly experienced. In this fashion, modeling extends experience vicariously without the threat of failure. The vicarious learning of reward contingencies has been demonstrated by research and practice to be effective in motivating the performance of a variety of responses.

Engaging in previously inhibited responses.   While the above discussion has dealt with cases in which an individual lacked a given response or lacked motivation to perform it, there are problems of another type in which the person has both the response capability and an understanding of the desirable consequences of performing the response, yet still cannot exhibit it. This difficulty may frequently be caused by direct or vicarious experiences in the individual's learning history that have associated fear, embarrassment, anxiety, pain, or failure with the response and inhibited its performance. Modeling in such cases can demonstrate the absence of real threat in performing the behavior. Often it is necessary to illustrate the lack of negative reactions of others to the response in order to overcome previous experiences which have socially inhibited the response. For example, an embarrassing experience in speaking before a group may have an inhibiting effect which makes an individual, though otherwise capable of public speaking, feel uncomfortable before groups and actively avoid such future experiences even while knowing well the desirability of being able to talk before an audience. In another example, the discouragement of being turned down when applying for a job may make an individual reluctant to seek employment vigorously even though he or she knows very well how to go about it and wants a job very much. Many avoidance responses are not the result of lack of knowing appropriate behaviors, but of inhibitions learned through some unfortunate previous experience. Modeling which demonstrates the positive rewards and lack of aversive consequences of a response can disinhibit the response in the observer.

Fears of riding in elevators, taking part in group discussions, asking a girl for a date, or initiating a conversation are typical of this kind of inhibition. The individuals know what to do but just can't bring themselves to do it. Modeling in these cases can demonstrate not only the desired responses but also the consequences of the responses. The individual learns to anticipate a favorable consequence, where previously he or she has feared some unknown or imagined negative result. Modeling permits vicarious learning of the rewarding consequences of behavior where established avoidance reactions have prevented this from being learned directly or where the initial learning steps are nonrewarding or even unpleasant. Imagine trying to teach a young boy to ride a bike or to roller skate and expecting him to continue trying in spite of suffering falls and minor hurts, were the child not convinced that bike riding and skating are fun. And how does he know these activities are fun? He has seen others enjoying themselves in these activities. He learns vicariously that riding or skating along on wheels is not only possible for those like himself, but is fun as well.

Through modeling, individuals who have apprehensions or fears that prevent them from trying new behaviors can be shown the positive consequences of such activities and the lack of real threat involved in engaging in them.

Eliminating or reducing inappropriate responses. Modeling also can be used to demonstrate undesirable behavior in order that a person might identify and alter it. Normally, individuals learn to avoid actions which have obvious undesirable outcomes, but they have greater difficulty making this connection when the consequence of their actions is subtle or long delayed. Cues which help individuals discriminate between appropriate and inappropriate responses may be weak or difficult to perceive in complex social situations. For example, a man who completely dominates conversations may be totally unaware of the negative effect he is having on others. Courtesy demands that his listeners smile and give other outward signs of interest and attention and do their best to conceal their real feelings. A perceptive person might see that the "listeners" are not really listening, would like a turn to talk themselves, and are annoyed with the speaker. The complexity of human interaction, however, can obscure subtle social signals which, if perceived, could modify behavior. Some individuals have not learned to be finely attuned to the reactions of those around them and therefore miss subtle or concealed communications which could guide their actions.

Modeling allows focus to be placed upon any of several cues that may be relevant. Weak but relevant cues can be intensified and extraneous cues reduced through modeling until the learner is able to discern the appropriate stimuli. Focus can then be placed upon learning to perceive the cues in increasingly complex situations until the learner can detect the cues and react to them in the real-life situation. In the example of the conversation dominator, the initial model presented may have to be an exaggerated one in which those in the conversation group are obviously annoyed with the speaker. The observer would be asked to look for and interpret the reactions of the model listeners. In subsequent modeled conversations the listeners' responses could be more disguised until the observer could pick up very subtle cues. The ultimate criterion would be whether or not he could perceive and react to those cues in his own social interactions.

Modeling is a useful technique for counselors who often need to help individuals learn new ways to deal with situations. Through modeling, observers can acquire entirely new responses or new patterns of existing responses. The observer may know and be able to exhibit all of the required parts of a response pattern, but it is the pattern itself which is unique and must be learned. Learning to be a better decision maker might be an example of putting together a new pattern of existing behaviors. The individual may be capable of performing all the decision-making skills of generating alternatives, gathering relevant information, estimating probable outcomes, and choosing a tentative course of action, but their sequenced application to a problem may be novel and have to be learned. Modeling is useful in learning a single response or a complex pattern of behaviors.

In some instances the necessary responses are present and can readily be performed in one situation but not in another. Social skills which an individual can demonstrate in small groups may need to be applied when encountering larger groups; assertiveness exhibited with close friends may need to be displayed occasionally to others; or the ability to plan and organize enjoyable activities may need to be applied to accomplish necessary but unpleasant tasks. Modeling can help produce transfer of learning by demonstrating the behaviors to be learned in a variety of settings and circumstances.

Requirements of an Effective Model Presentation

Models can be presented in various ways and with differing degrees of fidelity. The fidelity of a model presentation refers to how faithfully it represents the real-life situation. The highest degree of fidelity is attained by observing people in a natural setting who are unaware that they are serving as models. A counselor may ask a client with an uncontrollable temper to observe an actual conflict situation involving someone he or she knows who can better handle anger. This would be an example of high fidelity model use. Lesser fidelity can be demonstrated with a model and another person role-playing typical anger-provoking situations to show how frustrations could be handled. The role-played situation could be presented on film with some further loss of fidelity. A written description of the same situations would have even lower fidelity.

The live model in a real situation offers high fidelity, but it has disadvantages. Only activities which are performed openly can be observed in a natural setting, and even then the observation may be difficult to arrange. Also, observation in a natural setting not only provides all relevant elements but also may present many nonrelevant and distracting elements. The learner may not be able to discriminate between the relevant and irrelevant elements.

Some sacrifice in fidelity is often warranted in order to ensure ease of management and control of stimulus elements. The questions to be answered when selecting a mode of model presentation are: (a) what modes are available, and (b) what degree of fidelity is necessary to convey the important stimulus elements? A predominantly verbal skill (being interviewed by a prospective employer, for example) could be modeled with written descriptions or transcripts of actual job interviews. While the actual words used in such interviews could be conveyed in a written transcript, it would be difficult to communicate facial expressions, eye contact, gestures, and other nonverbal cues present in the interview itself. The tone of voice would be lost in the written model. Are these nonverbal elements important? They may or may not be important, depending upon what interpersonal skills the client already possesses. For some the written model may be sufficient; for others a higher fidelity of presentation may be necessary. An audiotape of the interview, a sound movie film, or a live performance are possible modes of presentation. In practice, until counselors have available a film or tape library of models demonstrating a variety of desirable responses in social situations, observation of live models in natural settings or role-played situations will generally be employed.

In any model presentation the response to be learned and the situation variables in which the response is to occur should be clearly communicated to the observer. The nature of the response and the degree of sophistication of the learner will determine the choice of model. The counselor must determine whether or not the particular client will be able to duplicate the response after being exposed to the model. If not, the counselor must find ways in which the model can be presented that will enable the observer to make a matching response.

In selecting a model, it is important to identify the relevant responses and situational cues. In social interactions, the words exchanged between people may be the relevant responses. The tone of voice, the nonverbal communication signals, and the environmental setting may also provide important cues. Relevant aspects of the interaction are dependent upon the particular problem and must be determined before an adequate model can be identified. When this has been done, a model is chosen or developed that exhibits the responses to be learned in a relevant context.

For observational learning to take place the learner must focus on the essential elements in the modeled response. *Preorganizers* are helpful in this regard. Preorganizers are attentional cues presented before the observation that identify for the observer the important elements being modeled. They focus the learner's attention upon cues that should be looked for and are a reminder that the observer will be called upon to reproduce the performance. Attentional cues can be supplied during the modeled performance through commentary, stop action, exaggeration of important aspects, and reduction of extraneous elements in specially prepared model presentations. The learner must know which elements should be observed and that he or she will be asked to reproduce the model's performance.

Sources of Models

The client as his or her own model. In discussing a problem with a client, the counselor may learn that the client can remember at least one occasion in which he or she performed well in the problem situation. A vivid description by the client of the context in which the problem occurred and the response that dealt successfully with the situation could serve as a model for future behavior. Perhaps responses now used effectively in one area of life can be applied to an area in which there is a problem. Sometimes a model can be developed by having clients record their responses and the results. The most effective responses can be identified and compiled into a model for future behavior. By using the best current responses as a model, the client can compare other responses and engage in a self-corrective process.

The counselor as a model. The counselor as a person is not presented as a model for the client to follow. Instead the counselor enacts those responses desired by the client in a deliberate role-played encounter with the client. The counselor plays the person the client would like to become. The portrayal of the model can be changed under the client's direction until it indeed becomes a model acceptable to the client. The counselor might present several alternative ways to handle the same situation and allow the client to choose one most suitable as a model to follow.

Environmental models. There are several possible sources of models in the client's social environment. The client may know someone or be able to recall someone previously known who exhibits the behaviors desired. If the client has observed the model well and can vividly recall enough of the relevant details, the recollection and description of the responses may serve as an appropriate model. If observation has not been adequate or if memory is vague, it may be necessary to arrange to have the client make careful observations focusing on the important environmental cues and the model's response to them. The counselor and the client may have to seek out appropriate models in the client's family, friends, and work or school associates. In some cases it may be necessary for the counselor to arrange an observation of a model unknown to the client. Perhaps many observations will have to be made of a number of possible models until an appropriate one for the client is found. In some instances no person may be found who represents all aspects of the model desired. Behaviors exhibited by several models may have to be synthesized to develop a model for the client to follow in the situations which have caused difficulty.

None of the above discussion should be taken to suggest that it is desirable for a client to try to become another person in all respects. What is suggested is that when ineffective responses causing serious concern have been identified, sources of alternative response patterns exist in the environment. A suggested sequence for replacing an ineffective response with a more effective one is to: (a) observe a number of models; (b) try out, imitatively at first, potentially more productive responses; and (c) adopt those which enhance the individual in the attainment of his or her goals.

Symbolic models. Symbolic models are presented through words or media rather than through observation of live performers. A model can be presented using movie film, videotape, audiotape, filmstrips, pictures, cartoons, and verbal descriptions.

Still or motion pictures can be symbolic models with or without accompanying verbal description. Videotape with motion pictures with sound can produce high fidelity symbolic models. Research by Bandura (1969), Hosford (1966), and Krumboltz and Thoresen (1964) indicates that these symbolic models can be effective in observational learning. Whether they are as effective as live demonstrations depends upon their ability to convey all the necessary stimuli in the particular case.

Modeling Procedures in the Counseling Process

Modeling is a counseling strategy. It is a means of changing client responses. It is an effective strategy for working with *some* clients concerning *some* problems. As the counselor considers how to assist the client to move toward the desired counseling outcome, the counselor may wish to consider several strategies. The nature of the outcome desired and the counselor and client's resources will help to determine which of several possible strategies might be effective. Modeling seems best suited to problems which have one or more of the following conditions:

1. The client doesn't know the response that will achieve a goal. EXAMPLE: She wants to be liked, but doesn't know specifically what is required to be likeable.

2. The client doesn't know the conditions which should cue a proper response.
   EXAMPLE: He likes to joke with friends but misses cues which should tell him that he is carrying the joke too far.

3. The client doesn't know the reward potential of the response.
   EXAMPLE: She doesn't know the positive reaction people have to a smile.

4. The client has had a bad experience which has inhibited some response and made it unlikely that he will attempt to perform it. EXAMPLE: He has been punished at home for disagreeing with adults and cannot voice a dissenting opinion in school with a teacher present.

Any of the above problem types might respond well to modeling, but before settling upon a strategy some questions must be answered. Can the relevant aspects of the response and its consequences be effectively communicated verbally without a higher fidelity model? There is rarely a clear "yes" or "no" answer to this question, but if verbal instruction is sufficient to enable the client to try the new response, higher fidelity modeling may be unnecessary and inefficient. One must also ask whether or not suitable models exist or can be developed.

Once it has been determined that modeling procedures are to be used, several steps may be necessary to select or develop appropriate models. First, available models, real and symbolic, need to be reviewed and the most appropriate model selected. Both suitability of the model for the objectives of the client and the model's availability for observation by the client are matters to consider in the selection of a model.

If appropriate environmental models are not identified and symbolic models are not available, a model may be developed by the counselor and client. The model might be produced in a series of role-played performances in which the counselor and client alternately play the model role which develops as each contributes to its character. A written model might be created by listing the characteristics and examples of ways the model might respond. Once developed on paper, the character could be brought to life through role-playing as an actor brings life to a script.

To maximize the effectiveness of observational learning, the observer should know specifically what to look for in the model demonstration. There is often the need for organizers to help order observations and to focus attention on the appropriate situational cues, modeled responses, and their consequences. This preparation for observation is especially important when environmental models are used in a natural setting in which many irrelevant and even distracting responses will occur. Cues which the learner should observe will depend upon the specific counseling problem, but in general the observer will be looking for answers to questions like the following:

1. What precipitated the model's response?
   a. What was the situational context?
   b. What were the social stimuli?
2. What was the model's response?
   a. What was said?
   b. What was the manner of speech?
   c. What did the model do?
3. What were the consequences of the model's response?
   a. How did others react?
   b. How did the model seem to feel about the experience?

This is a general set of preorganizers. Specific ones should be developed for each counseling case because of differences in individuals. One client's attention may be directed to the response of others to the model's performance. Another's focus may be upon the events which precipitate the model behavior.

The observer should be in a position to see and hear all relevant aspects of the modeled response and the situation in which it occurs. It is desirable to record observations as they occur or immediately afterward. For maximum generalization of learning, the response should be observed a number of times as it is performed by different models in a variety of appropriate situations. If the response is complex, it may be necessary to observe its performance more than once while focusing upon a single aspect each time. Repeated observations of other aspects would then follow until all parts of the response had been observed.

For observational learning to be maximally effective, it is desirable for observers to attempt to match and rehearse the response as soon as they have seen it modeled. When it is difficult or impossible to try to match performance immediately, some value has been found in having the client covertly rehearse the response. That is, the client mentally goes through the response to be learned. When observation in a natural setting is used, covert rehearsal may be the most practical way to practice a response initially.

Role-play rehearsals represent another way of matching model responses. Such rehearsals are helpful because they allow the new behaviors to be tried in a safe environment, one step at a time, until some facility is gained. Practicing a response in the counseling session allows the counselor to reward responses which approximate the modeled performance. When some confidence has been gained in the new responses, they can be practiced in the least threatening of several suggested situations in real life. A continuous cycle of observation followed by attempts to match may have to be conducted until enough appropriate responses are learned to make the response sufficiently effective in the real world.

Case Example. A case will be presented to illustrate the use of modeling in counseling. In the case of Mark, the counselor used a symbolic model on video tape. Notice what conditions existed that suggested modeling as a counseling technique, how the model was chosen, how the model was used, and how the client learned to match the model performance.

Mark, a sixth-grade boy, was referred to the counselor because his teacher felt that he was too quiet. "He never volunteers to take part in class discussion, yet he seems to know the answers when I call on him." His ability and achievement test scores were above average, and he generally did well in school.

In talking with the student, the counselor learned that Mark liked school, knew that he was more quiet than others, and felt that he could get along well just being a good listener without actively taking part in class discussion. He did admit to some embarrassment at being called on in class. When asked if he would be willing to try to contribute to the next class discussion, he said that he might have nothing to say. The counselor learned that Mark had only a limited understanding of the various ways in which someone could contribute to a discussion. Beyond presenting information he saw little that he could do to contribute. It became clear also that he worried about what others, including the teacher, would say or think if he somehow said the wrong thing. He did see some value in learning to speak more in class and to feel more comfortable when doing so. He decided that he would be willing to work toward this goal.

Before trying to encourage Mark to be more active in class discussion, his counselor wanted him to learn that there are many ways of making a contribution to a discussion. The counselor used a video tape recording which a social studies teacher in the school had made the previous year showing a number of students involved in group discussion. The counselor asked Mark to watch the video tape with him and to look for different ways in which individuals contributed to the discussion. Together, Mark and the counselor identified a number of different ways of contributing, e.g., giving information, asking questions, supporting or disagreeing with a position taken by another member of the group, clarifying something someone else had said, and mediating two opposing views.

The counselor then suggested the content of a group discussion and asked Mark to ask questions or make statements which would illustrate each kind of oral participation they had identified. The counselor verbally rewarded proper responses.

In a subsequent counseling session Mark and the counselor reviewed the various ways of contributing to discussion.The counselor then played another segment of the videotaped group discussion made in the social studies class. This time the counselor stopped the tape from time to time and asked Mark to make a contribution to the discussion, trying to use a variety of ways to contribute. Again appropriate responses were rewarded. As a latter segment of the tape was played, Mark was asked to see how members of the group reacted to one another and to the experience. He was asked to determine who seemed to be enjoying the group session most. He correctly identified the active participants as those enjoying it most. He was asked to think of himself as a teacher watching the group and to think of his impressions of group members. Again he identified the active particpants as making the most positive impression on the teacher.

At the end of the second counseling session Mark agreed to try to gradually increase his oral responses in class using some of the things he had learned.

In a third counseling session Mark reported that he had spoken more in class and that he would continue working on this problem although he was not perfectly comfortable doing it yet. His teacher verified his increased participation and agreed to encourage Mark in his attempt to participate.

If the client is expected to behave differently after counseling, it will be helpful to have a model of the new behavior as a guide. You as a counselor can help clients find or develop such a model. It will be necessary also for the client to try out and practice the modeled responses. Simulation is a natural follow-up of modeling and allows controlled practice of observed model responses.

SIMULATION

Practice may not actually "make perfect," but it is important in learning new responses. The effectiveness of modeling is increased considerably if the client has an opportunity to practice the responses just observed. A convenient strategy for providing opportunities for clients to try out responses is *simulation*. Unlike modeling, which furnishes vicarious learning, simulation provides first-hand learning experiences which are necessary if new behaviors are to become part of the individual's response repertoire.

In modeling, the client is an observer; in simulation the client is an active participant. In modeling the client *sees* the responses to be learned; in simulation the client *makes* the appropriate responses under especially arranged conditions. Simulation provides a realistic though controlled situation in which new responses can be tried and perfected. It allows the client to gain skill before trying a new response in his own environment. Simulation is a way of bringing some elements of a real-life problem to the counseling setting to facilitate learning and the transfer of learning from counseling to the actual situation.

A persistent problem in counseling has been that the counselor typically sees the client only in the interview situation rather than in the settings in which the client is experiencing difficulty. This limitation poses two kinds of problems. First, the counselor must rely largely on the ability of the client to describe the relevant aspects of the problem, when in fact some individuals are unaware of the basis for their difficulty and are even unable to present pertinent cues to the counselor. A second problem is that insofar as the counseling interview is different from the real-life setting, learning accomplished in the interview is difficult to transfer to the client's situation.

It is sometimes possible for the counselor to observe the client in real-life encounters and to have the client practice new, more effective responses in actual environment. Real-life observations and tryouts are useful and should be encouraged whenever practical. Eventually, of course, new responses learned in counseling will have to be tried under actual conditions, but it is sometimes impractical to undertake preliminary learning experiences in the complex conditions of the actual environment. The real-life environment is frequently hostile to the inept responses of the learner, and learning is discouraged. One who lacks skills in social encounters may be rejected in initial attempts to interact more with others, and rather than learning social skills, he or she learns to avoid social contact. Simulation offers a safe environment for the client to experiment with new responses.

Simulation can be defined as an operational representation of the relevant features of the real situation that gives the learner a relatively safe, simplified, and germane learning environment (Meckley, 1970). Simulation actively engages the learner in the learning process. The learner plays a role in a situation in which the essential elements of an actual circumstance are reproduced. The learner responds to cues like those met or to be met in the real environment. The learner experiences the consequences of responses, but in safety.

There are many everyday examples of simulation. Much of children's play simulates adult activities and roles. Children playing house or pretending to be firemen or spacemen are engaging in low-level simulations. Although these simulations are just-for-fun, they have some utility in helping children learn to take their place in an adult world. Children's play helps them to identify adult roles. Girls play with dolls and simulate the role of mothers. Boys play with cars, trucks, and other toys identified with masculine roles. While these sex role stereotypes have had some social utility in the past, they are perhaps no longer as useful since today's views of men and women's roles are changing. Those who are interested in changing society might well be concerned about the games children play.

The high school student who practices a speech at home for the family before presenting it in the school auditorium is simulating giving a speech before an audience. Counselors-in-training practice counseling skills in simulated interviews in which one trainee plays the client and another the counselor. Simulation is widely used in training programs. Industry has developed elaborate simulators for individuals who need to learn complex skills, as in the training of astronauts or jet pilots. Many schools use less elaborate simulators to teach skills in driving a car.

Although complex equipment has been developed for particular simulations, elaborate hardware is not an essential element of simulation. Any experience in which learners play roles or pretend that conditions are other than they actually are is a simulation. A fire drill, for example, is a simulation. In its simplest form, simulation may involve just one learner pretending to be engaged in an activity—a counselor trainee practicing by herself ways to initiate a counseling interview or a boy rehearsing what to say in asking a girl for a date.

Learning under simulated conditions is not just a weak substitute for learning under real conditions. Simulation is often preferred to the actual situation for any of the following reasons:

1. Probably the most obvious reason for using simulation is that it allows us to cause events to happen. One can experience a crisis or an opportunity that one might have to wait a long time for in real life (e.g., a girl responding to a proposal of marriage).
2. Simulation allows learning to take place in a safe environment. Mistakes made by the learner have no serious or long-term consequences.
3. Time can be compressed. Experiences that would require days in real life can be simulated in minutes, and feedback to the learner can be more immediate.
4. Conditions can be simplified so that attention can be focused on one or two variables at a time.
5. Conditions can be controlled so that learning can be more easily managed than in real-life encounters.

Simulation may be necessary when new responses cannot be practiced in the actual situation in which they are eventuallly to be performed, but even when the real environment can be used, simulation still may be preferred because it can provide better initial learning experiences (Johnson, 1970).

Types of Simulation in Counseling

The type of simulation most frequently used in counseling is role playing. Role playing is, however, but one of several kinds of simulation available to the counselor. We will consider here the following types of simulations: role playing, decision-making practice groups, and problem-solving games.

Role playing. Many of the problems that individuals bring to counseling involve interpersonal skills. Initiating a conversation, replying to anger or criticism, responding to affection, and revealing opinions or feelings are just some of the areas in which people have difficulty in dealing with one another. For these and other problems, practice with new responses can often be arranged in a role-played encounter between client and counselor. Role playing was discussed earlier in this chapter as a vehicle for modeling alternate responses. Here role playing goes beyond modeling and provides the client an opportunity to practice responses with the counselor. This role-played practice has been called *behavioral rehearsal* (Lazarus, 1966). The client and counselor can simulate any number of personal encounters as experiences in which the client can try out new behaviors. One advantage of such role playing is that the simulation can be repeated a number of times while different alternative responses are tried and compared, or while one response is shaped until it has been perfected.

A behavioral rehearsal may be engaged in by the client alone. The client can speak to an imagined person or practice a desired response to an imagined situation. When overt practice is inconvenient—e.g., it may be embarrassing to talk to oneself in public—*covert rehearsal* is recommended. In covert rehearsal the client simply imagines the response that he or she would make in the situation. This kind of rehearsal is a common occurrence. We often think through an action before actually performing it. Traveling a route in our imagination before driving somewhere for the first time is a covert rehearsal. Thinking about what we will say before bringing up an unpleasant topic with a friend is also a covert rehearsal or simulation. A recommended practice sequence would be to imagine the response one wished to make, then to actually rehearse the response in a role-played simulation, and finally to try the response in the actual setting.

For an example of the use of role playing, let's look briefly at the problem Jerry brought to his high school counselor. Jerry frequently became involved in heated arguments at home. The quarrels were generally with his father and usually began with a request by Jerry to use the family car. Before the arguments were over, both Jerry and his father would bring up a long list of grievances against the other. Jerry wanted to avoid these disputes with his father if possible. The counselor suggested ways in which Jerry might change the pattern when he saw one of these arguments developing. To give Jerry practice, the counselor played the father's role in a simulated argument. Jerry played himself in the simulation and tried to use the responses the counselor had suggested. Jerry and the counselor played these roles several times with slight variations until Jerry felt sufficiently prepared to try the new responses the next time the situation arose at home.

Role playing may involve any number of participants. Counselors working with groups can develop simulations of complex social situations in which several roles interact. Elaborating on the idea of role playing Moreno (1946) has developed a major therapeutic approach called psychodrama, which utilizes several performers as well as an audience. The client engaging in role playing alone, with the counselor, or with several other people is practicing under simulated conditions to select those responses he or she would like to try in the real environment and to develop the skill necessary to perform the response in such an actual tryout.

Decision-making practice groups. When decision making becomes a counseling problem, it is complicated by the client's anxiety under pressure to make a choice. The urgency of a particular problem may make it extremely difficult for the client to learn adequate decision-making skills. Rather than waiting for a decision crisis to occur, the counselor can help clients become better decision makers long before a critical choice must be made.

Counselors should give clients as much responsibility as possible for the routine decisions made in counseling to give them experience in preparation for crucial decisions. Developing problem-solving skill is an incidental learning objective in most counseling contacts. A more direct approach to the development of decision-making skill is to anticipate critical decisions well in advance so that necessary skills can be learned and practiced before the critical problem occurs. When a decision problem can be anticipated, simulation can be useful in learning how to attack it.

For groups of clients it is often possible to anticipate problems or decisions they will face. For example, the decision of whether or not to go to college, the selection of a program of studies, the choice of a vocation, the decision of whether or not to marry, and the selection of a marriage partner are decisions commonly anticipated by developing young people. These are real decisions that must be made by most individuals and can be anticipated well in advance of the need to make the decision and before critical urgency charges them with debilitating anxiety.

When a common problem-solving or decision-making need can be anticipated for a group of clients, group practice sessions can be helpful. These groups consist of five to ten individuals in addition to the counselor. The individuals in the group are presented with a case study describing a person faced with the problem or concern. The case can be presented in a brief written description, a videotaped vignette, or simply an oral description by the counselor. The counselor leads group members in a discussion of the case. The group suggests possible actions the individual in the case might take. They identify the need for additional information and suggest how this information might be obtained. Participants are encouraged actually to locate relevant information between group sessions. Information about jobs, prerequisites for training programs, or other data pertaining to the problem presented are gathered and brought to the next group session. When additional information about the person in the case is needed, it is provided by the counselor. For example, the group may learn that an aptitude test is required for application to the college they are considering for the person in their case. Once they decide to have the subject of their case study take the test, the counselor provides a test score to serve as a basis for further deliberation by the group. As many of the elements relevant to the problem as possible are introduced in the case. The case is continued until the decision is reached or the problem is solved. Each group member can make and defend his individual decision, or a group decision can be made. The discussion leading to the decision should consider the values and goals of the subject, the alternatives available to him, the cost and probability of success of each alternative, the means for determining whether or not a choice has been a good one, and what alternatives are available if the decision made turns out to be a poor one.

These decision-making skill groups generally require several sessions for each case. Initially the group members are apt to be quick to give advice based upon their own preconceived notions or prejudices. The counselor in leading the group should elicit and verbally support careful examination of alternatives and discourage tendencies to rush into ill-considered decisions. In the cases presented it is not the particular decision reached that is important, but that it was a well-considered decision. The counselor helps not by deliberately influencing the decision one way or the other, but by giving the group a decision strategy.

Individuals participating in decision-making skill groups often identify with the subject in the case. The counselor should try to select or create a case that facilitates this identification. It is when each group member closely identifies with the case and for a moment "becomes" the subject facing a decision that this technique becomes a true simulation. The skill group gives members an opportunity to see how others in the group handle problems. The group allows each participant to try out problem-solving responses and to obtain feedback and support for well-considered responses. The deliberations made in helping the subject of the case are rehearsals to prepare each participant to better consider his or her choice when faced with a similar problem.

Case examples. A community college counselor identified a number of his students who were planning to transfer to a four-year college although they had not decided upon a definite college major. He invited eight of these students to participate in a group to examine vocational and educational goals. During the first meeting of this group, the counselor found it difficult to get individuals to talk about their plans. Some group members seemed hesitant to talk about themselves; others had not done much thinking about their plans and had little to talk about.

The counselor was disappointed in this first session, and before the second meeting of this group, he composed a case study drawn from several students he had known. The case presented Eric, a community college student capable of continuing in a four-year college but undecided about what to do. The case, including some personal history and family background, was summarized in two mimeographed pages and given to each student in the group at the next session. The following are a few brief excerpts of the group's discussion of the case:

Counselor: Let's imagine that we have been asked to help Eric plan his educational and vocational future. How should we begin?

Bill: I think he should go on to college and get his B.A. degree.

Counselor: (says nothing but looks for other suggestions because he does not want to reinforce a solution that has not been well-considered)

Nancy: I think he should get a job for a while after community college until he decides what to do.

Counselor: How can Eric decide what to do?

Janice: He could think about the advantages and disadvantages of going on to a four year college.

Counselor: Good idea!

Nancy: He could also think about the pros and cons of getting a job at least for a while before going on to more college.

Counselor: That's right!

After some discussion of the pros and cons of further education for Eric, including the likelihood of his doing well at a four-year college, the group decided that Eric should go on to college. However, there were still some problems to be discussed.

> Bill: Eric should think about some major or professional goals.
> Counselor: That's a good idea. Why can't he decide now what to major in?
> Dennis: There are a lot of opportunities, and it's hard to sort them out. I don't really know what I'd like to do because there are lots of things I haven't tried. (Note that Dennis has identified with the case and is talking about himself.)
> Counselor: That seems to be the case. Eric can't make up his mind now because he has limited information and experience. What might he do about this?

Here the discussion focused upon ways of assessing one's own abilities and interests and ways of gaining vicarious experience by reading and talking with people or direct experience through part-time jobs or volunteer work. Many good ideas were presented that might help Eric or group members explore vocational and educational opportunities. Each positive suggestion was verbally reinforced by the counselor.

This simulation took just one group session but was enough to give the group practice in handling a decision problem. The simulation seemed to facilitate further group discussion. In subsequent sessions the group members focused upon their own educational planning following the pattern they had established in the simulation.

Another counselor working in a rehabilitation facility that helped retarded individuals gain work skills wanted to make the transition from training to actual job placement easier for her clients. Thinking about the problems that other clients had experienced as new employees, the counselor wrote a case description in which these problems were encountered. This simulated case presented a brief description of the client and his new job situation and then listed six problems that he had encountered.

SIMULATED CASE

Ted Jackson had never held a regular full-time job before. He had left school after the ninth grade and had tried unsuccessfully to find a job. He is now 22 years old and has been living at home with his parents. Knowing that his parents could not support him indefinitely and wanting to get his own apartment and eventually get married, Ted needed and wanted a job. He had worked at the rehabilitation workshop for six weeks before being placed on a job at a small manufacturing plant. His job was to unload sheet metal from freight cars and help set up work for the welders.

PROBLEMS

1. He was asked to report to work the first day with work gloves, but he didn't have any money just then to buy them.
2. Ted was sent on many errands while he was new on the job and often had difficulty because he didn't know his way around the plant.
3. The plant was noisy and Ted did not always hear or understand what the foreman wanted him to do. When he didn't under- stand, he would just try to keep busy, but then found himself in trouble when the foreman returned and found the task had not been done.
4. He had a great deal of difficulty keeping up with the other employees, at first. In trying to keep pace with them he had done some sloppy work which had to be done over again.
5. A couple of times some of his fellow workers, in fun, had sent him on a wild goose chase looking for a tool that didn't exist. After learning of the joke, Ted felt foolish and didn't want to come to work again.
6. The foreman was generally easy to get along with, but sometimes would lose his patience when Ted didn't get a job done on time or didn't get it done quite right.

Having prepared the above case, the counselor brought together a number of her clients who were soon to be placed on jobs. She told them that occasionally problems were encountered on a new job and that these problems might be handled better if they could be anticipated and dealt with in a practice session. The counselor described the case to the group. She told the group about Ted Jackson, how he had received training much like theirs, and that he had been helped to get a job in a manufacturing plant. One after another the problems Ted ran into on the new job were presented and discussed. Group members were asked to suggest how Ted should have responded to each problem as it was presented. No single best answer was sought. The counselor verbally reinforced all helpful suggestions. When the list of problems had been completed, each individual in the group had experienced types of problems that might actually confront him, been given a chance to respond to the problems, received feedback, and learned how other group members had handled the problems.

You will no doubt see possibilities for using decision-making or problem-solving skill groups to help with other problems—dating, family arguments, making friends, dealing with hostility, and so forth. Whenever problems can be anticipated for a group, case studies can be developed to be used in practice sessions. The goals of practice groups are to increase individuals' experience in confronting problems so as to reduce anxiety in actual problem situations, to help members acquire a number of possible responses to specific problems, and to increase their skills in dealing with problems through practice and feedback. Here we have discussed opportunities to practice decision-making skills. A more detailed look at just what these skills are will be presented in Chapter 10.

Learning games. Most games are purely recreational. Card games, checkers, charades, and similar games are amusements that are worthwhile for both the pleasure of the activity and the challenge of the contest. Learning games are simulations that have serious purposes. Although many modern recreational games bear little resemblance to real-life activities, games originated as simulations. Today's atheltic games, for example, are distant descendants of ancient warfare and retain the elements of physical strength, speed, agility, and competition. The game of chess is also a simulation of ancient battle but emphasizes strategy rather than strength. Recreational games today may or may not simulate real situations or activities. Contract bridge has no real-life counterpart. The game of *Monopoly*, on the other hand, might be considered a simulation of certain business operations. If one wished to teach something about the relationship between the value of real estate and the income it can produce or the importance of having cash reserves, *Monopoly* might well be used as a learning game. It is, however, primarily a recreational game and only roughly simulates actual investment operations.

Although learning games are fun to play, their purpose is to teach participants rather than just to entertain them. Learning games, sometimes called serious games, are simulations in which there is competition between individuals or groups and in which there is an educational objective. A number of attempts have been made to use the enthusiasm that individuals invest in playing games to facilitate learning. Some of the outstanding work in this field has been done by Dr. James Coleman and Dr. Sarane Boocock at Johns Hopkins (Coleman, 1967; Boocock, 1966, 1967; Boocock and Schild, 1968). Learning games have been developed in which problems are realistically simulated in order to teach participants the decision processes in business management, military leadership, labor relations, and governmental and political planning. The players in these games assume roles, are given certain objectives, are confronted with obstacles, and, within the rules of the game, seek their objectives and are scored on how well they succeed. A number of learning games have also been developed to teach specific subject matter in school classrooms.

The research in the use of games to teach information and processes does not clearly indicate the superiority of this technique. Games do not necessarily teach decision-making skills or information any more effectively than other teaching methods. Games, however, do involve learners and promote interest in the learning activity and may be recommended largely on the basis that they provide an enjoyable way to learn. Games can be effective tools for counselors.

We are not discussing here the sensitivity or getting-acquainted experiences some authors have referred to as "games." Nor are we referring to "games", as described by Eric Berne (1964), that individuals play with one another in real life—e.g., insincerely being self-critical to win a compliment. Learning games are contests in which individuals or groups compete in a simulation designed to teach participants something about themselves, about others, or about a process. The participants in the game play roles and have an opportunity to see things from another's point of view.

There are several learning games on the market useful to counselors, and more are being developed all the time (Gordon, 1970; Varenhorst, 1968). We will briefly describe a few of these games to illustrate the kinds that are available.

> *Association.* Western Publishing, 850 Third Ave., New York, N.Y. A game that simulates the social and psychological effects of socioeconomic stratification. This game can be played by eight to ten participants and takes one to two hours.
>
> *Blacks and Whites.* Psychology Today Games, P.O. Box 4758, Clinton, Iowa 52732. This is a game designed to help whites understand what it means to be black in our society. It is designed for adults.
>
> *Body Talk.* Psychology Today Games, P.O. Box 4758, Clinton, Iowa 52732. Body Talk is designed to teach individuals to communicate better nonverbally.
>
> *Can of Squirms.* Contemporary Drama Service, Arthur Weriwether, Inc., P.O. Box 457, Downers Grove, Ill. 60515. There are seven games in this series, one each for elementary, junior high, senior high, college, and adult age groups and two special games for adolescents, Generation Gap and Teenage Sex Education. All seven games use the same format in which two or three member teams draw from a container a slip of paper on which is printed a brief description of a social predicament. Each team acts out the problem and a solution. Solutions are rated by peer judges and are the bases for group discussion.
>
> *Community at the Crossroads: A Drug Education Simulation Game.* Superintendent of Documents, U.S. Printing Office, Public Documents Distribution Center, Pueblo Industrial Park, Colorado 81001. This is a two to five hour game simulation of a community response to the problem of drug abuse. Participants assume roles of teachers, students, parents, and city and town leaders. Through a series of scheduled meetings, the participants

attempt to define the nature and extent of the problem, and they
determine strategies and programs for dealing with that
problem.

Consumer. Western Publishing, 850 Third Ave., New York, N.Y.
This game simulates consumer buying and teaches budgeting
and use of credit. It can be played by twelve to thirty-four
players and was designed for use with high school age students.
The game takes one and one-half to two and one-half hours.

Generation Gap. Western Publishing, 850 Third Ave., New York,
N.Y. This game gives practice in handling interactions between
a parent and an adolescent son or daughter over issues on which
they disagree. The game is designed for four to ten adolescents
and takes one-half to one hour to play.

Job Experience Kits. Science Research Associates, 259 East Erie
St., Chicago, Ill. 60611. These kits contain simulated work experiences in twenty different occupations. The kits are designed
to simulate career exploration. The kits are not true games in
that they do not involve competition among participants. Each
participant strives to achieve a criterion score rather than to out-
score an opponent. The kits are designed for high school students
and can be used with one or more participants.

Life Career. Western Publishing, 850 Third Ave., New York, N.Y.
The purpose of this game is to give participants practice in planning their educational, vocational, and marital futures. Any
number of two to four player teams can play. The game was
designed for high school age students or older, but it can be used
with junior high school students as well. The game takes two to
six hours to play.

Society Today. Psychology Today Games, P.O. Box 4758, Clinton,
Iowa 52732. This is a game that teaches participants more about
the social forces that influence individuals' lives.

Women and Men. Psychology Today Games, P.O., Box 4758,
Clinton, Iowa 52732. This game is designed to remove the false
sex stereotypes which have distorted individuals' understanding
of the other sex.

An examination of a few of these games—or better yet participation in
a learning game—will demonstrate to the reader the motivational
qualities these games possess. They can be useful in counseling, especially in dealing with anticipated problems.

Uses of Simulation in Counseling

Simulation is useful throughout the counseling process. It is useful in
helping the counselor diagnose existing or anticipated problems (Subsystem 5.0), in helping the client state a goal for counseling by discovering interests and alternatives from which goals develop (Subsystem 6.0),

in trying out and practicing new responses (Subsystem 7.0), and in assessing the degree to which a new response has been learned (Subsystem 8.0).

Diagnosing existing or anticipated problems. Clients sometimes are troubled but have no clear idea of the elements that contribute to their problem. They are unaware of the environmental cues that should signal particular responses, or they don't know how their own responses con tribute to the problem, or they miss the feedback cues that indicate the consequences of their responses. These clients just can't describe the relevant aspects of the problem, yet the counselor must have this information to be helpful.

A simulation in which the counselor and client act out the problem situation gives the counselor a relevant sample of the client's behavior that may reveal things that the client has been unable or unwilling to reveal about himself. Many clients can act out a social encounter more accurately than they can describe it. In a verbal description of a problem, the client's defenses are apt to depict the situation in a way that presents him or her in the most favorable light. In role playing, especially if the client and the counselor play their parts well, the client will be caught up in the drama and be more likely to reveal typical undisguised responses. For young children and for those who are not highly verbal or are reluctant to talk about a problem, a role enactment may present a situation more clearly then their attempt at description could.

As the counselor and client role play one or more problem social encounters, the counselor is better able to diagnose the difficulty. Perhaps it can be seen how the client's behavior is creating the problem, contributing to it, or working against its solution. If the counselor can conveniently observe the client in the problem situation itself, such an observation should be made. When direct observation is impossible or difficult, simulation allows the problem situation to be re-created under conditions that permit observation and may reveal elements of the problem. Even if the role playing does not directly reveal the relevant aspects of the problem, it can serve as a stimulus to help the client recall the vital elements.

Case example. Kevin was seeing a counselor as part of his probation on a shoplifting conviction in juvenile court. Kevin was 14 years old, an average student in junior high school, and until recently a quiet person who had never been in trouble. The counselor learned that Kevin's recent troubles, including the shoplifting, were largely due to his being influenced by other boys. Kevin admitted that these boys had talked him into participating in some things that he knew were wrong. He hadn't really wanted to shoplift but was talked into going along with the other boys. The counselor asked him how it was that he could be talked into doing something against his better judgment. Kevin said that he didn't know; he just went along. The counselor had Kevin role play a situation in which Kevin played himself and the counselor played one of Kevin's friends suggesting that they go downtown and "get some things." In the simulation it became clear to the counselor that while Kevin was reluctant to do what the others wanted, he had no alternate suggestions and finally acceded to their persuasion. The only alternatives Kevin had were to go along, which he didn't want to do, or refuse to go and be called "chicken." The role-playing simulation allowed the counselor to see the situation more clearly. He was then able to help Kevin develop alternative suggestions when faced with similar situations.

Sometimes problems can be anticipated in a simulation and dealt with before they become real problems. A role-played job interview in advance of an actual interview with a prospective employer may reveal that the client lacks the skills necessary to represent himself well in such an interview. A series of simulated employment interviews might increase the client's skill in handling these situations and reduce anxiety about participating in them.

Individuals learn to respond differently to different situations. The counselor typically sees the client as the client has learned to respond to the counseling situation. This may not tell the counselor much about how the client responds to other people under different conditions. Role-playing simulation is a way to change the situation in the counseling office so that the counselor can observe the client in a variety of circumstances. And in this way the counselor can better diagnose or anticipate problems and help the client.

Discovering interests and extending experience.   Simulation is useful in helping clients discover interests and extend their experiences to give them a broader base upon which to make decisions and to learn responses. Experiencing some of the work activities of people in various occupations, having encounters with extremely hostile individuals, behaving aggressively in particular situations, revealing affection for someone, or being discriminated against are but a few of the experiences that simulations can provide. Life provides a variety of experiences for most individuals, but some important experiences are difficult to obtain. For example, adequate and relevant prevocational experiences are difficult for young people to obtain in our highly technological society. Some individuals have missed experiences upon which interest and values can be based. It is not just a matter of trying to increase experience. Not all experience is helpful. The counselor seeks to provide experiences, real or simulated, that will provide the client with relevant information about self, others, and situations. The experience should be germane to the counseling goal for the particular client.

Trying alternate responses. A client may need to choose one response to replace an ineffective response. But there is seldom just one right way to respond in a given situation. Usually there are a number of appropriate responses, each with its possible positive and negative outcomes. Simulation allows a problem situation to be experienced a number of times, making it possible for the client to try out several alternative responses before selecting one to perfect and then attempt in the actual situation.

On becoming aware that a family disagreement is heating up into a full-fledged battle, the client might take any number of actions: (a) learn to argue the point without attacking the other individual (b) learn to listen and reflect the other's views to establish communication (c) learn to shut off the argument by changing the subject, or (d) learn to end the argument by leaving the scene. In a role-played verbal encounter with the counselor, the client could try each of these to see which had most promise of success. Perhaps in the role-played interaction another alternative would be suggested. The purpose would be for the client to learn that several alternatives exist and to get a feeling for each of several possible responses.

Evaluating the acquisition of new responses. When simulation is used as a learning device, evaluation is continuous. The counselor monitors the client's responses, gives feedback, suggests response modifications, and continues the simulation so that the client may try again to perform the desired response. When the learning sequence is undertaken in the real environment—for example, the client practices initiating conversations—an occasional role enactment in the counseling session is a good way for the counselor to monitor skill development.

Simulation in Systematic Counseling

Simulation is an effective strategy for only some clients, and then only for some of their problems. The counselor must know when simulation is appropriate and use other approaches when it is not appropriate. To be most effective, simulations should be tailored to the particular client and his specific problem. Simulation might be appropriate if: (a) an assessment of the client's performance is necessary (b) the client needs exploratory experiences to develop interests and insights (c) the client needs to try out new responses, or (d) the acquisition of new responses must be checked. Even when one of these four conditions exists, simulation is preferable only if experience in the real environment are not possible or not practical. A series of simulation is often arranged so that each accomplishes an intermediate goal and the series leads to the learning objective.

Once simulation has been chosen as the counseling strategy, several steps are necessary to develop and use this technique:

1. Identify responses and environmental components necessary in the simulation.
2. Develop the situations and the roles.
3. Brief the client on his or her role, the situational elements, and the purposes of the simulation.
4. Enact the simulation.
5. Debrief the client. Have the client recall experiences and observations. Call attention to the relevant aspects of the client's performance.
6. Reenact the simulation, if appropriate, with modifications as indicated by the first trial. Vary the simulation to promote the generalization of learning.
7. Continue the process until the learning objective is reached.

Simulation is a way of bridging the gap between the counseling and real environments. Often, learning in counseling does not transfer well to the client's world because the change from the supportive conditions of counseling to life's hard realities is too abrupt. Simulation can bring some reality into counseling and make the transition less abrupt. Fragile new responses can be strengthened in a simulated exercise and given a better chance to succeed in real-life encounters.

SUMMARY

An important way that people learn is through the observation of models. Social modeling has been used in counseling to influence client behaviors in three ways: (a) learning new responses (b) engaging in previously inhibited responses, and (c) eliminating or reducing inappropriate responses.

There are several sources of models—the client, the counselor, friends, associates, and others. Symbolic models presented on film, videotape or audiotape, or in written descriptions can also be used. Whatever mode of modeling is used, the following steps are important: (a) identifying the elements to be modeled (b) selecting or developing a model (c) preparing for observation (d) observing the model, and (e) matching the modeled responses.

A simulation is an operational representation of a real-life encounter that provides a convenient, safe, and easily managed learning environment. All simulations involve participants playing roles or pretending conditions to be other than they actually are. Role playing, decision-making practice groups, and learning games are types of simulations useful in diagnosing exisiting or anticipated problems, discovering interests, extending experience, trying responses, and evaluating the acquisition of new behaviors.

Modeling and simulation are effective strategies for showing clients appropriate behaviors and helping them rehearse and learn new responses. These strategies, however, are rarely sufficient within themselves to accomplish counseling goals. Clients often find it difficult to sustain a behavior-change effort until goals are reached. To maximize the effectiveness of the strategies discussed in this chapter, attention must be given to the conditions that maintain inappropriate behaviors and incentives that can be used to promote more appropriate responses. The next chapter does just this. Chapter 9 deals with strategies for helping clients persist in learning new, more productive responses.

9

Strategies for Motivating Behavior Change

OVERVIEW

Nearly all of us know things about ourselves that we would like to change. You, no doubt, can think of skills or knowledge you would like to have, characteristics you would like to exhibit, or habits you would like to discard. Most of us have aspects of our personality that we need to improve and that are within our power to change. Then why haven't we taken action? Why do we too easily abandon efforts toward self-improvement and relentlessly persist in behaviors we know to be disadvantageous? It is with great difficulty that we give up undesirable but habitual behaviors. Why is this so? However inefficient or self-destructive they are in the long run, these habitual responses have some utility. They bring some immediate rewards. Immediate rewards are far more compelling than benefits promised in the future. We wish that we could play a musical instrument but don't practice. We want to be more outgoing with people but hesitate to strike up conversations. We desire to be more even tempered but continue to react angrily to frustration or disappointment. Learning new responses is difficult, even painful. It is often more comfortable just to do nothing.

Knowing more productive behaviors and having opportunities to practice them does not guarantee that they will be acquired. Learning new responses can be a long and difficult effort, and the rewards of the new responses may be long delayed. One of the most difficult tasks in counseling is helping clients to remain steadfast in pursuit of their goals. Helping clients to give up the relative comfort of old responses and to expose themselves to the discomfort of learning new, potentially more rewarding, responses relies upon the principle of reinforcement.

The principle of reinforcement, which includes both reinforcement and extinction, is discussed in Chapter 9 within the context of developing strategies for motivating behavior change. In this chapter you will learn how to use reinforcement strategies to encourage the performance of certain responses and persistence in efforts toward the counseling goal. You will also learn how to use extinction strategies to reduce or eliminate undesirable responses.

INTRODUCTION

Organization

The two major sections of this chapter deal with reinforcement and extinction as counseling strategies. The first section describes how reinforcement—attention, approval, praise, and material rewards—can be used to motivate learning and encourage persistence toward the counseling goal. The section on extinction, the withholding of reinforcement, presents a number of methods for eliminating maladaptive responses. This section includes strategies for dealing with fears and avoidance responses.

Purpose

The purpose of this chapter is to help you develop techniques that you can use to motivate clients to do those things they need to do to accomplish their goals and to reduce or eliminate those responses that prevent their goal attainment.

Objectives

After reading and practicing the techniques presented in this chapter, you should be able to do the following when presented with a counseling problem:

1. Identify specific responses to be reinforced or extinguished.
2. Use verbal reinforcement to facilitate the client's participation in the counseling interview.
3. Identify reinforcers maintaining undesirable responses and reinforcers that might influence the learning of new responses.
4. Develop a contingency management program to increase or decrease a given response.
5. Develop a shaping procedure that leads the client from responses he now possesses to new and more productive ones through a series of successive approximations.

6. Reinforce imaginal or covert responses as initial approximations in a shaping process when inhibitions or fears prevent overt responses.

As you read this chapter keep in mind that the techniques discussed are available to you to help clients. The successful application of these techniques will depend upon your understanding and skill in using them. Try to find opportunities to use these techniques as you learn.

REINFORCEMENT

The principle of reinforcement may be stated as follows: the strength of a response, that is the likelihood of its recurring, depends upon its consequences. Responses that are rewarded are said to be *reinforced* and will be more likely to recur. Responses that are not reinforced will be less probable in the future. This concept is useful in understanding and changing human behavior. Those responses that bring an individual pleasure, success, recognition, and material rewards are most likely to become part of his or her habitual response repertoire. Those responses that are not rewarded fall into disuse or do not develop in the first place. If an individual takes the initiative in meeting people and encounters friendly attention and social approval, he or she will be more apt to approach people on other occasions. If the individual is ignored, the probability of again taking the initiative in social contacts will be reduced.

When working well, the reinforcement process helps individuals learn to do things that are rewarding and to deal successfully with a variety of situations. The process, in fact, does not always work well. Some individuals have severely limited experiences from which to learn effective responses. Some fail to learn well because few rewards are available to them. Others are inappropriately rewarded and learn responses that are inefficient, antisocial, and even self-destructive.

Modeling was discussed in the previous chapter as a way of understanding the development of human behavior. Models present individuals with patterns to follow. Which of these patterns will become part of the observer's personality depends upon what experience the client encounters while using them. Those that are reinforced will be retained. Those that are not reinforced will be discarded. Adequate models do not insure appropriate learning. The learner's reinforcement experience in matching a model or exhibiting unique responses shapes habitual response patterns and personality.

The principle of reinforcement is always at work strengthening some responses and weakening others. It is at work whether deliberately used or not. It may strengthen appropriate behaviors or inappropriate ones. When used as a counseling strategy, reinforcement is deliberately managed to strengthen those responses that are goal-directed and to weaken those that are counterproductive.

Much of what we know about the influence of reinforcement on learning comes from the basic research of B. F. Skinner (1953). The use of reinforcement to modify behavior is called instrumental learning or operant conditioning to distinguish it from the classical conditioning of Pavlov. It was Pavlov who demonstrated that a response elicited by one stimulus could be elicited by a formerly neutral stimulus through a process of repeated association called conditioning. Although Pavlov's research contributed to our understanding of learning, it did not explain how new responses are acquired. Skinner demonstrated that new behaviors could be learned by selectively reinforcing existing behaviors. A desired response could be taught through a process called *shaping* in which successive approximations of the desired response are rewarded until the new behavior is learned.

One of the most successful applications of Skinner's research has been programmed learning, using special texts or teaching machines (Skinner, 1961). In programmed instruction the material to be learned is divided into small steps, and questions are presented for the learner to answer throughout the program. Initially, cues are presented to insure that the learner will respond to the questions correctly. Gradually the cues are reduced until the learner can respond to the questions without cues. Reinforcement is provided through feedback that tells the learner when responses are correct. Teaching machines can also dispense tokens, candy, or toys to further reinforce correct responses.

Even without programmed instruction, systems for dispensing rewards money, toys, candy, recreational activities, or tokens that can be exchanged for these—have been used successfully in teaching those who previously have not responded to verbal entreaties to learn. Management of reinforcement contingencies, often referred to as *behavior modification,* has a great deal of research attesting to its usefulness in eliminating maladaptive behaviors and in producing goal-directed responses (Cohen, 1968; Kanfer & Phillips, 1970; Ullmann & Krasner, 1965). Teachers and parents have been taught to modify children's behavior by rewarding positive responses and ignoring negative attention-seeking behaviors. Many schools have adopted reward systems to encourage learning in students who have failed to learn under traditional incentives.

Much is yet to be discovered about how people learn, but that the consequences of a response can increase or decrease the likelihood of the response recurring has been convincingly demonstrated (Bandura, 1969;

Kanfer & Phillips, 1970). Just why reinforcement works and whether or not it is sufficient to explain all learning is still being argued, but that it does work is acknowledged.

Reinforcement in Counseling

Research supports the effectiveness of reinforcement strategies in counseling. Studies have found that what clients talk about is influenced by the response it elicits from the counselor (Krasner, 1962; Murray, 1956; Truax, 1966; Winder, Ahmed, Bandura, & Rau, 1962). The counselor's interest and attention reinforce certain client responses more than others. This happens whether or not the counselor makes deliberate use of reinforcement. Clients eventually learn what it is that the counselor wants to hear.

When deliberately used by the counselor, verbal and attentional reinforcement can effectively influence clients to talk about what is necessary to discuss if the counselor is to be helpful. The counselor's use of reinforcement can facilitate the counseling interview by encouraging the client to discuss his or her thoughts and feelings concerning the problem at hand and by discouraging, not reinforcing, defensive efforts of the client to avoid issues.

Verbally reinforcing clients for effective responses in the counseling interview has been shown to help produce more effective responses outside the interview. In one study, for example, clients who were praised and otherwise verbally reinforced for suggesting ways in which they could explore vocations actually explored more subsequent to the counseling interviews than did those who were not reinforced (Krumboltz & Thoresen, 1964).

Counselors have found it helpful to devise strategies that include some reinforcement for clients' efforts to try new responses in the real environment. Effective responses, once learned, bring their own rewards, but the learning process itself may be unrewarding or even painful. For example, one who plays the piano well is socially reinforced. Learning to play well, however, is done at some sacrifice, and many who begin lessons give up before they achieve the skill necessary to win social approval. They give up because practice is an effort, progress is slow, and rewards are too far off. Successful piano teachers give praise or other rewards for small accomplishments in learning to play in order to keep students at the task.

Many problems for which clients seek help in counseling are complex and yield slowly to solution. Learning new responses is accompanied by some discomfort, yet the client must keep at the task to achieve the goal. Counselors can help clients persist in learning effective responses by building reinforcement into the counseling strategy. Reinforcement can be used effectively in counseling by (a) identifying the response to be reinforced, (b) selecting appropriate reinforcers, and (c) having someone monitor the behavior and dispense the reinforcement at the right time.

Identifying Responses to be Reinforced

Responses to be reinforced must be clearly identified. The behavior, the circumstances under which the behavior is to be performed, and the unit of measure for the behavior must be described.

The behavior. The specific behaviors to be modified should be identified so that there is no question by the client, counselor, or someone else administering the reinforcement as to what is being reinforced. General categories that label classes of behavior—e.g., industrious, considerate, responsible—can only be reinforced as they are evidenced in specific behaviors. For example, showing up for work on time might be a specific behavior in the trait called dependability. If a student who is habitually late to school is to be rewarded for being on time, the behavior "being on time" must be clearly defined. Being in the classroom or being seated when the bell rings are both specific behaviors. The learner must understand which behavior is expected to earn the reward.

Circumstances under which behavior is performed. Certain behaviors may be appropriate at one time but not another, or appropriate in one place but not another, or under some circumstances but not others. Behaviors are to be reinforced only when they are appropriate, and the appropriate circumstances need to be clear. In school verbal responses may be reinforced in a group discussion but not in a study activity. A boy may be reinforced with attention when he cries because he is hurt but not when he cries to get his way. A girl may need to be reinforced for being more assertive in some of her interpersonal relationships but not in others.

The unit of measure. A unit of measure will have to be decided upon. Is each occurrence of the behavior to be reinforced or is persistence at some response for a period of time to be the unit of measure to be reinforced? Some behaviors are more easily or more appropriately accounted for by the frequency of their occurrence, the number of occurrences of the behavior per hour, day, or some other time interval. Contributing to a class discussion, coming to class on time, and initiating conversations are examples of behaviors that can most easily be recorded by noting how many times they occur per day or per week. Other behaviors are best accounted for by their duration in time, noting how much time is spent at the response in a given time period. Working on homework in the evenings, paying attention to the teacher, or uninterrupted time spent at some other work tasks are examples in which time spent at the responses would be the most appropriate record. If the length of time spent at the task is to be increased, rewards are made contingent on increased time on the task. A student trying to increase study time might be rewarded initially for being able to keep at the task for 15 minutes. Later it would require 20 minutes to earn the reward. Gradually the time necessary to achieve the reinforcement would be lengthened until the goal had been achieved.

Sometimes each contributing behavior cannot be reinforced nor can time spent at the task, but the result of a sequence of responses can be reinforced. Getting a job done, cleaning a room, writing a paper, or getting a "B" grade in a course may require a complex sequence of behaviors. If the reward comes at the end of the sequence, the reinforcement is somewhat removed from the actual behaviors to be increased. Immediate reinforcement is desirable, but intensive monitoring of the client is not always possible. If rewarding the end product of a series of behaviors is effective, fine. If a reward for a clean room, for example, will motivate a child to do the many things necessary to clean the room, all is well. But if this doesn't work, then the complex task may have to be broken into smaller segments. Rewards may have to be given for picking up clothes from the floor, for making the bed, and so on until the complete task is done.

Case example.   A sixth-grade teacher complained to a counselor that Jeff, a boy in her class, was always disruptive. Jeff rarely did what he was supposed to do but instead walked around the room disturbing other students. The teacher had tried to deal with the misbehavior in a variety of ways—scolding, seating Jeff near her desk, sending him to see the principal. Nothing seemed to work. The counselor suggested that all of these actions by the teacher gave Jeff special attention which was what he wanted. The teacher agreed that Jeff was seeking attention in his disruptive behavior. It was decided that the teacher would try to ignore his annoying behaviors and to verbally reinforce *productive* behaviors. A list of specific productive classroom behaviors was made— e.g., being in seat when bell rings, remaining in seat during reading, contributing to class discussion, completing written assignments, and so forth. It seemed too much to manage Jeff's behavior all day long or change many behaviors. One period, the reading period, was selected in which to influence Jeff's responses. Remaining seated and completing written assignments were two behaviors to be reinforced. Each five minutes that Jeff remained in his seat was to be verbally reinforced by the teacher. He was to be profusely praised each time he completed his written assignment in reading.

In-seat behavior in reading improved greatly with this reinforcement. However, because Jeff seldom finished his written work, his teacher had few opportunities to reinforce him for work completed. Success in increasing the number of assignments that Jeff completed was finally achieved by having the teacher verbally reinforce completion of each small part of the written assignment rather than waiting for the entire task to be done before praising him.

Selecting Reinforcers

Different people are motivated by different rewards. Even with the same individual, that which is reinforcing one time may not be the next. The counselor who wishes to use reinforcement as a counseling strategy must learn what some of the existing or potential reinforcers are for the particular individual with whom he is working. Although there are no universal reinforcers, there are some that have had general success in motivating behavior change.

Social reinforcement. This is the kind of reinforcement one person or group gives to another through verbal or nonverbal signs of approval, attention, recognition, and friendship. Praise, a smile, a nod of approval, a pat on the back, or just being near the person are examples of social reinforcement. Even negative attention—scolding or other mild punishment—can be socially reinforcing. Negative attention for some individuals is better than being ignored. Many annoying behaviors are learned and persist because they gain recognition albeit negative.

Young children depend upon adults and are generally responsive to social reinforcement from adults. Some young children and more commonly some adolescents have had unfortunate experiences with adults and do not respond well immediately to social reinforcement from them. These youths are often more responsive to peer pressure. Peer pressure, which influences all of us, is an example of social reinforcement. We want to be accepted and liked and try to do those things that will win attention and friendship. Much commercial advertising tries to associate using a product with group acceptance and social approval.

Social reinforcement is a potent motivator. It may be the most powerful influence on people's lives. A counselor who can enlist social reinforcement to help his client has a strong ally.

Information as reinforcement. To a learner, information regarding his performance can be reinforcing especially if the learning has been arranged in small steps that the learner can accomplish (Holland, 1960; Milulas, 1972). Knowing that the task has been successfully performed encourages future performance. The counselor and others trying to help can facilitate achievement of a goal by telling the client when responses are goal-directed. Keeping a progress record or graphing achievement toward a goal may also provide this kind of information. One reason for dividing the learning into small steps, as discussed in Chapter 7, is to provide many opportunities to give feedback that will reinforce further effort. Success breeds success. Knowledge that one step has been accomplished encourages the next.

Tangible reinforcement.   Tangible rewards—food, candy, toys, books, and money—have been successfully used as reinforcers. They have been especially effective with young children and with those who don't respond well to verbal reinforcement or to a particular source of social reinforcement. The use of material rewards in conjunction with initially ineffective social reinforcement can strengthen the power of the social reinforcement until that can be successfully used without tangible rewards. Praise that is given along with the material reward becomes reinforcing itself and can subsequently influence behavior even in the absence of material rewards. Probably our response to social reinforcement is learned through an initial association of material and social reinforcement.

Activities as reinforcement.   Reading, watching TV, just relaxing, or any of a number of activities can have reinforcing properties. Making some desired activity contingent upon completing a learning step has been demonstrated to be an effective way to motivate learning. In one special program, junior high school students who had made little academic progress achieved remarkably well when completion of required learning tasks permitted them to use the recreation room where they could play pool, have a soft drink, listen to music, or read magazines.

Imaginal reinforcement.   An interesting but not yet thoroughly tested means of motivating behavior change is through the use of imaginal or covert reinforcement (Kanfer & Phillips, 1970). In this technique the client must monitor his or her own behavior and think positive self-thoughts or imagine pleasant scenes as self-reward for goal-directed behavior. For example, a person trying to lose weight might imagine looking very thin each time he or she resisted a temptation to deviate from the diet. The image of looking thin would reinforce adhering to the diet. More will be said about this technique when we discuss self-management in Chapter 10.

The influence of deprivation and satiation on reinforcement.   The influence of a reinforcer is heightened if there has been a period of deprivation of that reinforcer prior to its administration (Bandura, 1969). Those who have been without social interaction for a time will usually work hard to achieve social reinforcement. Social reinforcement will be less motivating for those who have had a great deal of it recently. The husband returning home from the social pressures of his business seeking peace and quiet comes into conflict with his wife who has been without adult contact all day and wants to go out and visit friends. The husband is satiated with social contact while his wife has been deprived. An evening with friends would be a reward for the wife but an imposition for her husband.

Rewards that are readily available from other sources are poor motivators. A teacher's use of verbal reinforcement may have little influence on the boy who is popular and receives abundant social approval from his many friends. An injured worker living reasonably well on disability insurance money may be little motivated by a modest salary offer to go back to work.

An effective reinforcer is one that is desired by the client, not readily available, and capable of being managed. It must be a reinforcer that can be withheld until the desired response is made. The success of a reinforcement strategy depends on the consistency with which only goal-directed responses are rewarded.

While it is desirable in the initial stages of learning to reinforce progress frequently, a frequently used reinforcer may lose its effectiveness through satiation. A variety of reinforcers should be identified so another can be used if the client tires of one.

Token reinforcement. A token has no intrinsic value but can be exchanged for some object or privilege. Tokens are useful as reinforcers because they can be made exchangeable for a variety of rewards. If the same reward is used continually, the client may tire of it and thus its power as a reinforcer is diminished. Tokens can be exchanged for any number of things. The use of tokens allows the individual to choose from among several rewards the one he wants most at the time. Tokens thus help prevent satiation. Tokens are easily dispensed even to individuals in a group with minimum disruption of the group activity.

To be seen as valuable, tokens must be clearly associated with the rewards they can bring. The individual being rewarded must know what the tokens are worth in exchange. Some display or catalog of the rewards available and their token equivalents should be presented to the learner. Tokens can be plastic coin-like objects, small cards, slips of paper, or tickets. Some counselors give clients a card on which teachers, parents, employers, or others can sign or initial each time a response is noted rather than dispense tokens. The signatures are then exchanged for some privilege or object of value.

Reinforcing Agents

Once the response to be reinforced has been identified and the reinforcer agreed upon, someone must take responsibility for seeing that the desired response has been performed and the reinforcement administered. These tasks can be performed by the counselor, the client, or others.

The counselor.   The counselor uses verbal reinforcement—words like "right," "good," "that's the idea," and "um hum"—during the interview to encourage the client to focus on the problem and take some responsibility for it. Verbal reinforcement by the counselor also is used to encourage the client to make constructive suggestions toward the solution of his problem.

A counselor can also be a source of social reinforcement for progress made outside the interview. As the client in subsequent interviews reports attempts to use new responses, the counselor can give praise and support when warranted to motivate further attempts. Some counselors have clients phone them regularly to give brief progress reports that the counselor can verbally reinforce. In this way the reinforcement can follow the response more immediately than would be true if the client had to wait until the next counseling session.

The effectiveness of the counselor as a social reinforcer depends upon the relationship developed between the client and the counselor. An obviously disinterested counselor saying "good, good" to reinforce the client's report of progress cannot be expected to be highly effective. But the counselor who has a genuine professional interest in helping the client achieve a goal and who says "good" to let the client know that he or she has truly made a step in the right direction can be an effective reinforcer and cause change in client behavior.

The client.   A client can administer self-rewards for goal-directed behavior. A college student who finds herself watching television when she should be studying might make watching TV contingent upon first studying one hour, reading one chapter, or completing a certain number of problems.

The counselor and client can schedule a number of tasks to be accomplished by the client between counseling sessions. They can decide upon some reward, something the client would like to do, following each successfully accomplished task. The client agrees to withhold the reward until he has completed the task.

Using the client to dispense his or her own reinforcement puts a great deal of responsibility on the client but, if successful, it provides a strategy that can be used in the future without the counselor's help. Putting off some pleasurable activity until some unpleasant but necessary task is accomplished is something most people have learned to do. There are others, however, who have problems because they have not learned to do this. They may even use pleasurable activities such as eating, watching TV, sleeping, or drinking to avoid troublesome thoughts, tasks, or situations. They are rewarded for these avoidance responses by reduced anxiety and become even more inclined to avoid facing future problems. Instead of being rewarded for avoiding situations or problems, these individuals should be encouraged to make the available rewards contingent upon some step toward solving the problem or learning to handle the situation more effectively. Ultimately, the client's life must be self-managed. Learning to use self-reward to direct his or her own efforts toward a goal helps the client become self-directed. Self-management strategies will be discussed more thoroughly in Chapter 10.

Others. Teachers, parents, employers, marital partners, and friends can be used to administer reinforcement. They can help the client by observing and rewarding goal-directed behavior. It is frequently desirable to enlist the aid of others who have some stake in improved client behavior. The teacher as much as the disruptive student has something to gain in the student's achieving more acceptable social behavior. The parents and child both gain when the child learns to control a bad temper. The employee and employer both benefit as the employee learns to get to work on time or to respond better to work supervisors. These people with something at stake have an investment in the client and are frequently willing to make the effort to observe and reward desired responses. Because they have more frequent contact with the client and are important in the client's life, they can exert a powerful influence. Enlisting the help of others is frequently desirable but should be done only with the client's consent and with care to protect confidential information.

When to Reinforce

How often should reinforcement be administered? While a new response is being learned, frequent rewards are most effective (Milulas, 1972). Each occurrence of the new response or each step toward its acquisition should be reinforced if possible. Some responses are better monitored using a unit of time rather then a frequency of occurrence. Studying, for example, may be more appropriately measured by its duration than by its frequency. If an interval of time spent at a task is to be reinforced, it should be short enough to insure frequent achievement of a reward. If an extremely volatile boy must refrain from losing his temper for an entire week in order to be reinforced, he may never earn the reward. Exercising self-control for this period of time may be beyond his present capability. To be effective, reinforcement must be *dispensed* not just *promised.* The counselor must see that the learning steps are reasonable and that any progress toward the client's goal is recognized, praised, or materially rewarded.

During the initial learning period, rewards should be dispensed often and regularly in order to help the client learn to associate the response with the reward. As progress is made, reinforcement is best administered less frequently and on a variable schedule. A variable schedule of reinforcement allows a varying number of unrewarded responses to occur between those that are rewarded. In this way the client learns that as in real life not all of his best efforts will be rewarded. The variable schedule of reinforcement helps him persist in an effort over periods of time that are not rewarded and increases the likelihood that the responses learned in counseling will continue to be used once counseling is terminated. Of course, as skill increases, the client's new response should produce its own reward without the need for special supportive reinforcement.

It is best to dispense the reinforcement immediately following the response to be strengthened (Krumboltz & Krumboltz, 1972). Immediate reinforcement helps establish the relationship between the response and the reward. Immediacy is especially important for young children and for those who have not learned to have confidence in future rewards. Tokens are especially useful as immediate reinforcers that give tangible evidence of the reward but do not interrupt the learning activity as might candy or some toy.

Shaping

Sometimes the desired response cannot be immediately performed even with promised reinforcement because the individual has not learned the response. Reinforcement cannot elicit a response the client is not capable of. Offering a client rewards for actively taking part in friendly conversations will not produce results if he or she lacks the necessary social skills. Even if the desired response itself cannot be performed, some approximation of it usually can. Listening attentively to others might be a first approximation in acquiring conversation skill, for example. The approximation should include at least one of the elements of the ultimate response pattern to be learned. A series of approximations, each successively incorporating more of the desired response pattern, can be arranged to help the client acquire complex behavior patterns. The process of rewarding successive approximations until a complete response is learned is called *shaping* (Bandura, 1969; Krumboltz & Krumboltz, 1972). An example of helping someone learn a new response through shaping might be appropriate here.

Case example.   Roy had little education and had never held a job for any length of time. He had not developed the kind of work habits that he needed to hold a job. He was often late to work or absent. Once on the job, he had difficulty attending to the task and was not an efficient producer. He had lost a number of unskilled jobs.

The counselor who had been seeing Roy helped secure a job for him and enlisted the aid of Roy's new employer to help Roy become a better employee. Roy could not be expected to become a good worker immediately. Reinforcement would not be effective if it was contingent upon Roy's producing a full day's work. The counselor and employer agreed to begin by helping Roy learn to get to work on time.

Roy was paid a minimum wage for his work, but the employer agreed to pay him an additional dollar for each day that he showed up for work on time. The money was handed to him in cash with a word of praise when he arrived on time in the morning. In a short time Roy was regularly on time to work.

Roy was then told that the dollar bonus could only be earned if he not only came to work on time but also went right to work once he had checked in. It wasn't long before he was usually on the job at his work station on time. Later the reward was made contingent also on his keeping at the job without unnecessary interruption until the morning break. The length of time necessary to earn the bonus was gradually increased until the money was paid only for a full day's productive work. This shaping program was not without temporary setbacks, but in time Roy was performing on the job at an acceptable level of efficiency.

The counselor in this case had realized that asking Roy to put in a full productive day was too much to ask immediately. Getting him to work on time was the first approximation toward the goal of a full day's work. Through a series of approximations each successively closer to the eventual objective, the client's work behavior was shaped until he was productive enough to hold the job.

Use of Reinforcement in Counseling

The use of a reinforcement strategy is indicated when responses to be learned require long practice before a skill is acquired, when the initial learning attempts are painful, or when the actual rewards that come with goal achievement are far off.

The counselor must know what actual or potential reinforcement is available. During the counseling interview, the counselor should note how responsive the client is to verbal reinforcement and should learn what things or activities the client enjoys that could be used as rewards. The most powerful reinforcement that can be effectively used should be sought. Influential people in the client's life who might be enlisted to help encourage and reward progress should be identified.

The response to be reinforced should be clearly specified. The counselor, client, and others dispensing rewards must know exactly what is to be reinforced. If the response does not occur, the reinforcement must be withheld. Continual evaluation of the process must be made to assure that the strategy is working and that the rewards are being used consistently and that they maintain their reinforcing power.

Frequently clients have difficulty identifying or accepting positive or negative feedback from their social environment. For some clients the skill has not fully developed because there have been limited social interactions. For others, psychological defense mechanisms or intense focus on their own concerns have made them insensitive to social feedback. Counselors wishing to give verbal reinforcement will have to communicate it clearly, convincingly, consistently, and with some enthusiasm and emphasis or it may be missed by the client.

Case example. The following example illustrates the use of verbal reinforcement by a counselor and tangible reinforcement self-administered by the client.

Don came to the university counseling center during his junior year. He complained that there was little meaning in his life and that he could see nothing worthwhile in any future direction he might take. He felt that few people if any really knew him or cared about him. He didn't have anyone in whom he could confide. He felt alone and drifting without any direction to his life.

Don reported that he had briefly experimented with drugs but stopped because he saw that it offered no permanent value and entailed some risks. He didn't want to go back to drugs, but he could find nothing else to hang on to.

The counselor listened attentively to these negative feelings in order to better understand Don and let Don know that he cared and was willing to help if he could. After a time, however, Don was not presenting any new information but was restating his same pessimistic outlook. The counselor knew that for progress to be made the focus of the interview must change from expressions of despair to the question of what could be done to improve the situation.

The counselor at this point chose to reinforce positive, problem-solving statements and to ignore further pessimistic, self-defeating statements. The counselor used several leads to help the client change focus.

> Things seem to be terrible now. When were things better and what was your life like then?
> How would you like things to be?
> What would it take to make you think the future holds some promise for you?

As Don began to describe his life at a happier time in the past or how he would like things to be in the future, the counselor expressed interest, asked for additional details, and with other verbal and nonverbal signs of attention and approval reinforced these positive statements. Whenever the client continued to complain about how bad things were now, the counselor did not show special interest or attention. By selectively reinforcing Don with his attention, the counselor was able to help him describe several ways in which his present circumstances could be improved, any one of which might have become a goal for counseling.

The client had blamed society, the university, his parents, and other students for his general depression. The counselor used selective reinforcement to change the focus from others to self.

> O.K., things are bad. What can you do about it? You said that you would like to have friends. What does it take to have friends? What are the characteristics that people look for in a friend? How could you acquire some of these characteristics?

These leads elicited tentative suggestions from Don which were reinforced by the counselor.

> Right! That's the idea. What else could you do? Good! Is that something you might try?

The client's attempts to shift responsibility to others were not reinforced. They elicited no response from the counselor.

Selectively using social reinforcement, the counselor had helped the client take some responsibility for his own situation and to think of some possible actions to resolve the problem. A general plan was worked out to help Don become more involved with people around him and to drop some of his defenses so that people could get to know him. With the counselor's encouragement, many of the details of the plan had been suggested by Don himself.

The counselor knew that it would not be enough just to send Don from counseling with a plan. Don needed some incentive to change his behavior. He needed some incentive that would outweigh the discomfort or anxiety he might experience in trying something new.

A first step in Don's plan was to share some of the things that he had told the counselor with someone he knew at school. That was part of a strategy to help him allow people to know him. This wasn't going to be easy for him. Some reinforcement was sought that might help motivate him to carry through with this difficult task. Going to a movie to see a particular film was decided upon as a reward. Don liked movies, but felt guilty about attending them while at school because he knew that he had other things he should be doing. He had not been to a movie in a long while and had wanted to see the one then playing but had not planned to give in to this desire.

The counselor suggested that if Don took the first step in his plan to make contact with people, this would be deserving of a reward. If he would agree not to see the film until he had confided some of his feelings

to someone he knew, going to the movie would be earned and could be enjoyed without any feelings of guilt. Don agreed to do this.

The counselor asked Don to phone him early the following week to let
him know whether or not he had succeeded. If success is reported, the opportunity is presented for the counselor to reinforce the client by con-
gratulating him for his achievement. If success cannot be reported,
perhaps the step was too large or the reward wasn't powerful enough. In
either case some modification may be necessary in the plan to help Don.

Behavior Contracts

When a behavior by one individual is to be deliberately rewarded by
another, and both parties agree to the arrangement, a contract is implied. The basic essentials of a contract are that one party promises to do
something, and the other agrees to do something in return. If the boy
cleans his room, the parent will take him to a movie. If the girl does her
work, the teacher will allow her to read a magazine. If the salesman ex-
ceeds his sales quota, his employer will give him a bonus. These are informal contracts. They indicate the behavior to be performed and the
reward to be presented. Many counselors have found it useful to have the
agreements written and signed by both parties. The written document or
behavior contract makes the terms explicit and seems to give assurance
that the terms agreed to will be honored.

The behavior contract may be between the counselor and client if the
counselor has control over reinforcers. One counselor in working with
clients who want to lose weight has them give him a sum of money at the
beginning of the weight reduction program. Each succeeding week a portion of the money is returned to the client if he has lost weight. If not, the
money is given to the Heart Fund or some other charity. The conditions
are detailed in a contract signed by the counselor and client.

In developing a behavior contract, the counselor often acts as a
negotiator between two parties—student and teacher, parent and child,
or husband and wife. Interpersonal difficulties that individuals bring to
counseling often have reached the point where there is no communication
or compromise between parties. All social relationships require communication and compromise or trade-offs. The mechanisms for accomplishing these trade-offs are generally subtle and informal. When
relationships break down, these informal mechanisms are destroyed.
Communication becomes difficult. Each party fights for his own position
and refuses to listen to the other. Neither is willing to make even a small
sacrifice for the common good.

Behavior contract negotiation formalizes the trade-off process. It reestablishes communication through the counselor who facilitates the
flow of information but filters out the hostility. Each party states what he

or she wants in the situation. The counselor then works toward an agreement that allows each to gain objectives. For example, the teenage boy agrees to mow the lawn once a week, and in turn, his father agrees to allow him to use the car Saturday nights.

The behavior contract not only offers a solution for a particular problem, but it also can have more general benefits. A successful behavior contract teaches each party that the other can be depended upon and that modest sacrifice and cooperation can bring mutual rewards. In carrying out the contract, each party does something for the other, reinforces the other, and thus improves the relationship between them.

Social Value of Reinforcement

The counselor who can make effective use of encouragement, praise, and other social reinforcement can have a positive influence on others. Not only does social reinforcement strengthen the responses reinforced but it also increases the influence of the reinforcing agent. We like those individuals who are concerned with our welfare and praise and encourage our accomplishments. We are willing to make an effort to win the approval of those who reinforce us.

The ability to reinforce others is a valuable social skill for clients as well as counselors. Clients faced with interpersonal problems may profit from learning to use social reinforcement. Using positive attention and approval, they may influence others around them far more effectively than by threats or other negative measures. The parent or teacher having difficulty with a child, the wife experiencing frequent arguments with her husband, the youth unable to get along with his parents, and the person having problems making friends all might profit from learning to use social reinforcement.

Environments conducive to healthy personality development provide positive incentives to promote effective and prosocial behaviors. Counselors can help produce such environments for their clients by teaching parents, school personnel, and staffs of other social institutions to use positive incentives for motivating individuals rather than relying on punitive pressures to coerce compliance.

Reinforcement can exert a powerful influence on behavior. While it can strengthen desirable responses and motivate continued effort toward a goal, it can also promote inappropriate behavior. There are undesirable responses that resist change because reinforcement in the natural environment supports them. Incentives to change are not strong enough to overcome the powerful reinforcement maintaining these responses. A special strategy called *extinction* is needed in these cases.

EXTINCTION

Counseling goals are frequently achieved by reducing or eliminating certain responses. Unreasonable fears, unwanted habits, or unacceptable behaviors often stand between the client and his goal. Counselors need strategies to help individuals eliminate excessive fears and phobic behaviors. They need strategies to reduce or eliminate smoking, nailbiting, overeating, and other often unwanted habits. Strategies are also needed to modify annoying attention-seeking behaviors like crying, bragging, and chronic complaining.

Simply rewarding clients for not exhibiting these undesirable responses is effective in some cases. In other cases, however, a reinforcement strategy is not enough to offset the forces maintaining the undesirable responses. Unwanted responses persist because they are reinforced. They gain attention, reduce anxiety, or reward the individual in some other way. Even behaviors that in the long run are self-destructive often produce immediate rewards that reinforce their occurrence. The only way to eliminate these responses is to prevent their being rewarded.

It must be remembered that all behaviors an individual customarily exhibits, even antisocial or self-destructive behaviors, persist because they have some utility for the individual. In some way these behaviors bring attention, approval, praise, or reduce fears or anxieties. Though these responses appear to be ineffective, they may be the best the individual knows and may be at least marginally effective. Just to eliminate the behavior without replacing it with a more adaptive response is to leave the individual worse off than before. If a client's response to anxiety is an undesired behavior, the complete solution is to eliminate the undesired response and substitute a more desirable one. Extinction procedures to reduce or eliminate responses are usually accompanied by reinforcement and other strategies to help the client acquire more appropriate behaviors to replace the maladaptive ones.

The individual who engages in annoying but successful attention-getting behaviors should be helped to reduce these annoying behaviors and be helped to learn to gain attention through a variety of positive responses. Although we will focus on ways of eliminating unwanted behaviors, it should be understood that other strategies discussed before may be used at the same time to develop more productive responses.

Knowing that persistent behaviors are being rewarded in some way suggests that if the reward can be determined and prevented, the behavior will change. This is exactly what experimenters have found. If an individual engages in a behavior that has been rewarded and the rewards are withdrawn, the behavior will disappear. The withdrawal or prevention of reinforcement is a process called extinction (Bandura, 1969; Milulas, 1972). The principle of extinction states that responses that are not reinforced are less likely to recur. Extinction requires the response to be performed without its being reinforced. Each unrewarded performance of the response decreases the probability of the response recurring. A number of extinction trials may be necessary to eliminate or sufficiently reduce the response.

Behavior that has been rewarded on a variable schedule is resistant to extinction. The immediate effect of withholding the reinforcement from such behaviors may be an increased response rate or a more intense response. A parent who has often responded to a child's intentional crying may wish to extinguish this kind of crying by not attending to the next crying episode. The child may cry longer and louder in order to get the parent's attention. The response has generally worked for the child before. In time, however, the child learns that crying will not work and gives up this response that is no longer an effective attention getter.

The principle of extinction is much easier to state than to apply. It is frequently difficult to prevent an undesired response from being reinforced, but this is exactly what must be done to extinguish it. Even an occasional reward for the undesired behavior will strengthen it. In fact, this kind of occasional or variable schedule reinforcement produces behavior that is difficult to extinguish. Many antisocial behaviors persist even against threatened or actual punishment because they are reinforced intermittently. To extinguish a response, the reinforcement must be totally withdrawn. The response must occur without being reinforced. Preventing the response is not extinction. Hiding matches from children may be a good idea, but it prevents rather than extinguishes match playing. If match playing were extinguished, the child wouldn't play with them even if they were present.

Identifying the Maintaining Reinforcement

To extinguish a response, its maintaining reinforcers must be identified. The need to identify reinforcers that maintain undesirable responses was discussed in Chapter 6. How can the counselor determine what these reinforcers are? The counselor's observation of the individual in the setting where the behavior occurs or the client's observations can be used to identify the reinforcers. One should look for conditions that are associated with the onset of the behavior and the responses that are consequences of the behavior. The following questions can help the client focus on the conditions surrounding the behavior:

When and under what conditions does the response occur?
What makes the response more intense or more frequent?

What reduces it?

When you respond this way what happens?

How do others react?

How does it make you feel?

The behaviors that the client wishes to modify may bring attention, approval, sympathy, release from some duty or responsibility, reduction in guilt or anxiety, or some other reward. The reward may not be obvious. One high school student seemed to like to be sent out of class to stand in the hall. The teacher thought the expulsion from class was a punishment, but the student used the occasion to go into the restroom to smoke and made the exclusion a reward. The maxim advising us to praise in public and reprove in private does not always hold. While many enjoy public praise and want redress, if unavoidable, to be in private, a particular student may win peer approval by public reproof and may be embarrassed by public praise.

Persistent behaviors are responses that are somehow rewarded. It may be difficult, but it is important, to identify the nature of the maintaining reinforcement. A girl in counseling was troubled over her inability to make long-lasting friends. Her friendships went along fine for a while until she would say or do something to anger the friend and break off the relationship. This had happened a number of times. She could usually describe what she had done to hurt the other person, but she didn't know why she did it. What might explain this habitual behavior that seemed to have just the opposite of the desired effect, causing the girl to lose rather than make friends? The counselor knew that the girl's behavior must, in some way, be rewarding for her. After further discussion, the counselor suggested that she might have learned to be fearful of a close friendship. She could be hurt if rejected by a close friend, and rather than risk the danger of being rejected, she broke off the relationship herself. The girl agreed that this seemed to be the case and presented further evidence supporting this hypothesis. Operating on this assumption, the counselor was able to help her. Identifying the reinforcer as a reduction of the fear of being rejected was an important step in helping this client.

Many inappropriate behaviors are maintained because they are positively reinforced. That is, they bring some reward, often social attention. Many other inappropriate responses are negatively reinforced. That is, they are rewarded by the removal of some threat, fear, or anxiety. The girl who broke off friendships did so to reduce the threat of being rejected. Others have learned to be self-critical to avoid criticism from others. Any number of avoidance responses can reduce anxiety. Procrastination, phobic responses, and malingering are negatively reinforcing. They reduce anxiety or avoid threats. In order to weaken undesired responses, some strategy must be used to prevent the reinforcement from occurring. A number of such strategies will be presented.

Withholding Social Reinforcement

Some unwanted responses are reinforced unwittingly by people trying to be helpful. The mother who is overly solicitous when her child cries may thus encourage the child to become a crybaby. The teacher who only attends to a student when the student creates a disturbance reinforces disruptive behavior. Annoying or bizarre behavior is a most effective means for some people to win attention. It is difficult to ignore, yet this is just what must be done to eliminate such behavior.

Unwanted behaviors must be extinguished in the settings in which they normally occur. It may be possible to obtain the cooperation of the client's family, friends, teachers, or employers and have them withhold their attention when the client exhibits the undesirable response. If those close to the client can learn to ignore undesirable responses and be more attentive to the client's desirable behaviors, dramatic changes can occur. The person who finds that pouting, crying, or displaying anger no longer gain sympathy or power over others will abandon the response.

Extinction can take considerable time. The individual's immediate reaction to failure to receive the customary reinforcement for the old response may be to increase the intensity of the response. Crying may be louder or misbehaving more blatant, still the response must be consistently ignored. Even occasional attention to the undesired response can be enough reinforcement to maintain it. Remember that even negative attention—mild punishment or scolding—may be reinforcing. The response should be ignored or meet with decreased social interaction.

Case example.   A woman who had been seeing a community mental health counselor asked for help with her teenage son. She had a number of complaints concerning his behavior, but the most disturbing to her was his frequent outbursts of temper followed by his locking himself in his room and sulking. Responding to the counselor's questions, the mother revealed that these temper flareups were usually in response to his being refused some special request—staying out late on a school night, getting an advance on his allowance, or using the car. The counselor tried to identify the reinforcers maintaining the boy's behavior. Increased attention from his parents and occasional concessions to his demands seemed to be reinforcing his angry response to not getting his way.

The counselor suggested that hereafter the parents should carefully consider the son's requests. Reasonable requests should be granted when possible if presented in an acceptable manner. When a request was refused, the decision should be final. The parents were not to become involved in an argument with the son. The boy was to be allowed to go to his room and sulk if he chose. No attempts were to be made to coax him out or to offer concessions to him. He was to be ignored until he was able to respond normally again.

It was with some difficulty that the counselor's suggestions were followed. With effort the parents contained their own anger and ignored their son's hostility when a dispute arose. The plan was successful in substantially reducing the number of these explosive episodes during the next five weeks that the counselor worked with the mother.

Counselors can help parents, teachers, and others discourage inappropriate behaviors by withholding social reinforcement. Counselors can also use the same extinction strategy themselves. Extinction procedures can be effectively used in the counseling interview. The counselor, at times, deliberately chooses not to respond to the client's self-depreciative, pessimistic, or avoidance responses so that these negative remarks will be extinguished and more positive and productive responses can be encouraged.

Time Out

Sometimes the cooperation of others in withholding social reinforcement cannot be obtained. A class of fourth graders, for example, may not be willing or even able to ignore the attention-seeking antics of one of its members. Their spontaneous laughter at his behavior may be impossible to control. Exclusion from the group may be necessary to prevent this kind of social reinforcement from strengthening the undesirable behavior. If a behavior that formerly was maintained by social approval now leads to social isolation, the undesirable behavior will quickly be extinguished.

To temporarily isolate the individual at school the child can be seated apart from others, at home the individual can be sent to another room, and at work the person can be assigned a task with little or no social contact. Time out should not be regarded as a punishment but seen as a natural consequence of the undesirable behavior. The individual should be reinstated to the group as soon as he or she is able to do so without further disruptions.

Satiation

Some activities are rewarding in themselves and require no social approval. The child who lights matches and finds that it is fun to see them burn, like the adult who finds pornographic pictures exciting, needs no social reinforcement to encourage the activity. Should either one of these activities need to be extinguished, some means would have to be found to prevent them from being reinforced.

Satiation is one method that has been successful in extinguishing undesirable activities that are intrinsically reinforcing. The response to be extinguished is repeated again and again well beyond the point of fatigue. As fatigue sets in the repetitions become nonrewarding. These nonrewarded trials are extinction trials. They are performances which bring no reinforcement and act to reduce the likelihood of the responses recurring. The child made to continue to light matches long after it ceases to be fun will be less likely to play with matches. Continuous exposure to pornographic pictures would also reach a point of satiation beyond which further viewing would also be nonrewarding, and extinction would begin. A number of such extinction exercises might have to be arranged over a period of time to reduce the behavior to some tolerable level.

Preventing Avoidance Responses

Fears are learned and can be extinguished. One who is frightened by a vicious dog will normally have this fear extinguished as the person comes in contact with other friendlier dogs. The fear may well persist, however, if the individual avoids contact with dogs and thus does not let the fear extinguish.

When faced with an anxiety-producing situation—giving a speech, flying in a plane, or viewing blood—avoidance responses are accompanied by reduced anxiety. This psychological relief is reinforcing and helps maintain the phobic response. Most unfounded fears extinguish through subsequent safe contact with the object or situation. The phobic individual, however, never allows the fear to extinguish because he or she doesn't face the feared situation long enough to learn that is holds no real threat. Every time the situation is avoided, the individual feels relieved which makes avoidance even more likely next time.

In their early stages, fears producing avoidance can best be extinguished by preventing the avoidance behavior. As an example, school phobia is a condition in which a child through some unfortunate incident or some imagined threat fears going to school. The child may miss the school bus, complain of illness, and use all kinds of pleas with parents to stay at home. Some children have avoided school attendance for months this way. The most effective treatment has been to insist on the child attending even if it means escorting the student to school each day. Typically within two or three days, the child learns that no behavior will prevent his being taken to school and also learns that school is not an actual threat.

The folk wisdom that advises one who is thrown from a horse to get right back on so that fear won't take hold may well be applied to those who experience an initial failure or embarrassment in any activity. Once the situation has successfully been avoided, it is easier to avoid it again. It is generally better to face the situation again immediately before it becomes too difficult to do. For example, a recently physically handicapped individual may wish to avoid contact with people. Effort should be made to get the person out in public before the avoidance responses are too well reinforced to change easily. When the avoidance responses are well established, and the individual cannot be made to face the feared situation, other techniques can be employed.

Systematic Desensitization

Well-established fears can often be extinguished by employing systematic desensitization. Systematic desensitization is a special application of sequenced learning to help clients overcome debilitating fears which cannot be faced directly and extinguished (Emery, 1969; Franks, 1969). When a fear is identified that the client cannot directly face, the client and counselor develop a list of the frightening aspects of the feared situation. The list is then arranged in a hierarchy from the least frightening to the most frightening aspects. A program is planned in which the client exposes himself to the least frightening aspect on the list until it is no longer anxiety producing. He then proceeds to the next most frightening and so on until fear associated with each aspect of the situation has been extinguished.

Fear of riding in a car resulting from a severe auto accident might be extinguished by first having the client sit in a parked car for a short period each day. Next the individual might be driven around a large empty parking lot, then on a quiet rural road, a residential street, and so forth until the client again feels comfortable in normal traffic. This is a sequence of exposures to a feared situation beginning with one producing only mild anxiety. Each exposure extinguishes some of the fear and makes it easier to face the next exposure. Finally the client is able to engage in the most feared situation long enough for the fear to extinguish. This method of actually facing progressively more threatening situations is called *in vivo* desensitization to contrast it with another approach in which the encounters with the feared situation are imagined.

Rather than having live encounters with feared situations, imagined encounters can be used with good effect. A sequence of imagined situations is much more easily arranged. Here again the client and counselor work out a sequence of imagined events related to the fear and in ascending order of anxiety arousal. While the client is comfortably seated and relaxed, the person is asked to close his or her eyes and vividly imagine the least anxiety-producing scene. When the client can hold the image without raising the anxiety level, the next most anxiety-producing situation is imagined. In this manner the client works up the hierarchy backing down whenever feeling the anxiety level rising. After a number of counseling sessions and after reaching the top of the hierachy in imagery, the client should be ready to approach the situation in real life with less fear. A number of encounters with the actual situation will then be employed to further extinguish the fear.

Case example. Connie had been employed at clerical work requiring her to be on her feet a great deal until she had a severe auto accident. After a long hospitalization, she recovered but was left with a slight limp and occasional discomfort in her back. As part of her rehabilitation, she received training as an electronic assembler so that she could be employed in a job that would not require her to stand. Upon completion of this training, her counselor found her reluctant to seek employment. Connie knew that her insurance benefits would not take care of her much longer and that she would have to go back to work. She wanted to have an opportunity to meet people and did value work for that reason. However, she seemed to lack the motivation to seek a job actively. Connie avoided the issue of employment both in talking with her counselor and in her subsequent behavior. She did nothing to secure a job and made excuses for not following the job leads provided by the counselor.

The counselor could discover no positive reinforcers that might be keeping Connie home rather than seeking employment. Possible negative reinforcers were explored, and in the exploration it was discovered that Connie was embarrassed about her limp and was reluctant to leave the house.

The counselor and Connie discussed her feeling of embarrassment of walking with a limp. She was most concerned about being seen by friends who would feel sorry for her. The thought of how the disability might make her less attractive and jeopardize her prospects for marriage also increased her anxiety.

The counselor explained the desensitization strategy to Connie. A number of imaginal situations related to her fear were developed and ranked from least anxiety-producing to most anxiety-producing— walking in a quiet residential district where no one knew her, walking around a shopping center where she might meet someone she knew, walking in her neighborhood, attending a party with several friends, having someone notice and comment on her limp, having a friend notice the limp and express sympathy for her.

Once the hierarchy had been developed, the counselor had Connie sit in a comfortable chair and relax. To help her relax she was told to close her eyes and think of the most pleasant and calm scene she could imagine—e.g., lying on the warm sand at the beach on a bright summer day. While relaxing Connie was asked to imagine the first scene in the hierarchy. After holding this image a few minutes, Connie was asked to let her mind return to the calm pleasant scene. The next scene in the hierarchy was then viewed in imagination. This was continued alternating a scene from the hierarchy with the pleasant scene.

Connie was told to practice this technique herself between counseling sessions, and she appeared to have made progress for at the second session in which systematic desensitization was used, she was able to imagine the scene at the top of the hierarchy without undue stress. She was ready to venture out more in public.

A sequence of walking excursions was arranged for Connie to add an *in vivo* component to the desensitization strategy. Each day she was to go out and walk around where she would be seen. Eventually she was to talk to her friends about her accident.

The desensitization worked well in Connie's case. In a short time she was able to appear in public without anxiety and did find a job. She continued to have some concern about her attractiveness to men but decided not to work on the problem in counseling at this time.

SUMMARY

Behavior is shaped by its consequences. Responses that are rewarded are most likely to recur; responses that are not rewarded are less apt to be repeated. Clients can be helped to engage in productive behaviors and to abandon inappropriate behaviors by managing the consequences of these behaviors.

A reinforcement strategy introduces rewards to encourage the performance of desired behaviors. A number of kinds of rewards are available— social reinforcement, tangible rewards, reinforcing activities, and imaginal reinforcement. The reinforcement can be administered by the counselor, the client, or others.

The following steps are suggested in using a reinforcement strategy:

1. Identify the behavior to be reinforced or the intermediate behaviors to be reinforced in a shaping process.
2. Identify reinforcers.
3. Monitor behavior and dispense reinforcers.
4. Evaluate effectiveness of the reinforcement.

Clients often need help in reducing or eliminating inappropriate behaviors. These behaviors are of two kinds: (a) those that are maintained by positive reinforcement, and (b) those that are maintained by negative reinforcement.

Those inappropriate responses that are positively reinforced—the temper tantrums that gain attention—can be diminished by withholding the positive reinforcement. Annoying attention-seeking behaviors will extinguish when attention is withheld.

Those inappropriate responses that are negatively reinforced—avoiding asserting oneself for fear of being criticized—can be modified by preventing the avoidance of the feared but harmless situation or by gradually approaching the feared stimulus through the use of systematic desensitization. Practice approaching the anxiety-producing situation can be real, *in vivo,* or imagined. Unfounded fears will be extinguished with continued exposure to the feared but harmless stimulus.

Management of the consequences of behavior is the most tested and frequently used behavior change strategy. Reinforcement and extinction are major strategies in their own right but are also useful in combination with modeling and simulation which were discussed in Chapter 8.

Thus far we have discussed counseling strategies in the hands of the counselor that enable him to change client behavior in ways the client has indicated. In Chapter 10 the emphasis will be on teaching the client strategies that can be used to modify personal behavior and more effectively seek established goals.

10

Strategies for Becoming Self-Directed

OVERVIEW

Counseling is most often but a brief intervention in a client's life. Dramatic and lasting changes in the client or difficult goals can rarely be accomplished within the relatively brief counseling encounter. The effects of counseling are severely limited unless clients achieve increased control over their own lives. The ultimate goal of counseling is to enable clients to become the persons they want to be and to accomplish the goals they have set for themselves. Clients need strategies that they can use to extend the effects of counseling beyond the gains made while working directly with a counselor. They need strategies that they can use themselves as they confront other problems. Clients must learn to identify and analyze problems, define goals, and generate alternative courses of action that might lead to goal achievement. In effect, they must learn to be their own counselors.

Helping clients become more self-directed is preventive counseling. It prepares clients for anticipated problems rather than just responding to problem crises. It is an approach in which the counselor shares with the client his or her knowledge of human learning and behavior change strategies.

INTRODUCTION

Organization

This chapter is divided into two major sections. The first is concerned with decision making and discusses ways in which individuals can be helped to deal with problems or decisions they face. The second major section concerns self-management and presents a number of strategies to help clients monitor and change their own behavior in order to achieve the goals they desire.

Purpose

The purpose of this chapter is to help you develop skill with techniques that you can use in helping clients become more self directed and less reliant upon you in the future.

Objectives

After reading and practicing the techniques presented in this chapter, you should be able to teach clients to do the following:

1. Identify problems and specify goals.
2. Generate alternatives that lead to each goal.
3. Obtain useful information regarding alternatives.
4. Assess costs and probable outcomes of various alternatives.
5. Make tentative decisions and take actions.
6. Assess results of decisions.
7. Monitor their own behavior to identify responses contributing to or preventing solution of a problem.
8. Modify conditions in ways likely to change their own responses and make them more goal directed.

*The chapter presents ways in which you can help clients to be their own counselors. Because these methods are designed for self-use, you will have ample opportunities to try out the techniques presented to solve problems you face or to change responses you now have to more effective ones. If you can make these techniques work for you, it will be easier for you to help clients use them.

DECISION MAKING

All problems brought to counseling involve decisions and offer opportunities for counselors to help clients develop decision-making skills. A prerequisite to helping clients make decisions is that the counselor has adequate decision-making skills. We will present here a strategy for making decisions and solving problems that you can use in working with the concerns clients present to you and that you can share with clients to enable them to deal more effectively with their own problems.

All problems involve decisions, but some client concerns are primarily decision problems and are brought to counseling because clients lack a systematic way of dealing with them. Clients ask for help in deciding vocational goals, in choosing among alternative solutions to family problems, and in selecting courses of action to deal with a variety of difficult life situations. Counselors should be able to help clients make these decisions, but it is not enough just to give help with the specific decision to be made. A general goal of counseling is that clients will be better able to deal with future problems. This means that counselors not only must assist the client with the immediate problem but also must be able to teach decision-making skills to prepare the client to cope with problems in the future.

Problem solving and decision making are essentially the same. One might maintain that if no options are apparent to resolve some difficulty, *problem solving* is called for, but that once alternative actions are identified then *decision making* is needed. In fact, however, even in so-called decision situations, it is rare that all reasonable alternatives are immediately apparent. The decision of whether or not to go to college, for example, is really a question of whether to go to college or to do something else, and might more reasonably be considered a problem of what to do after high school. If further education after high school is an option, there are many kinds of schools to consider. If not to continue schooling is an option, alternatives need to be identified and considered. We choose here to ignore the fine distinctions that could be made between decision making and problem solving and consider them both to be concerned with trying to identify the most effective means of obtaining some goal. We will use the terms interchangeably in our discussion.

A Decision-Making Model

There has been a great deal written about decision making as a goal of counseling (e.g., Herr & Cramer, 1972; Krumboltz & Thoresen, 1976; Ohlsen, 1974; Shertzer & Stone, 1976). Writers generally agree that good decisions come from a sequence of steps beginning with identifying the problem, followed by generating alternatives, gathering information, and finally making a decision and trying it out. The following seven-step sequence is presented as a model for problem solving or decision making in counseling:

1. Identify the Problem
In this step the decision maker tries to identify all important aspects of the problem. Answers to the following kinds of questions are sought:
    a. What is the problem?
    b. What interferes with a solution?
    c. When does the problem occur?

   d. In what situations does the problem occur?

   e. Under what circumstances does the problem occur?

   f. Under what conditions is the problem most severe? Least severe?

   g. When does a decision have to be made or the problem have to be resolved?

   h. How much effort would finding a solution warrant?

   i. What behaviors or behavioral deficits contribute to the problem or interfere with its solution?

   j. What evidence will indicate that the problem has been well resolved?

2. Identify Values and Goals

Not all solutions to a problem will be acceptable to a given client. In this step the requirements of an acceptable solution are identified. The client's values and goals as they relate to the problem are examined so that the solution sought will be compatible with the client's values and long-term goals.

3. Identify Alternatives

In this step a list of possible problem solutions or alternative courses of action compatible with the client's values and goals is generated.

4. Examine Alternatives

At this stage information is collected regarding the costs in time, money, and effort of each proposed solution. Information is also gathered regarding the advantages and disadvantages of each proposal and the likelihood of achieving a successful solution through each possible course of action.

5. Make a Tentative Decision

While making a commitment to some action in this step, the client should be ready to reexamine the decision later if necessary. Most decisions are tentative and reversible.

6. Take Action on the Decision

In this step the decision is acted on. If the decision is of great consequence and some doubt exists about the merits of the choice made, the action taken may be a testing out of the decision rather than a full commitment. The action taken provides additional information that is fed back into the decision-making process.

7. Evaluate Outcomes

This step does not occur at a single point in time but is a continual process. If outcomes seem to be leading to the desired goals, the decision is further implemented. If not, the problem-solving process may have to identify new problem elements and new alternatives.

These are the elements in decision making. They can be organized into a workable set of procedures for helping clients deal with problems.

Applying the Decision Model in Counseling

How does the counselor decide to use decision making as a counseling strategy? A decision-making strategy is called for if the client is concerned about a choice to be made or a problem to be resolved and is unaware of alternatives, lacks information necessary to decide among alternatives, or lacks a method for systematically examining alternatives and making decisions. Even when decision making is an appropriate strategy, it is typically used in combination with other strategies previously discussed.

The client's interests, values, and goals have been identified earlier (Subsystems 5.0 and 6.0). These may need to be reviewed in counseling when a decision is to be made. Given the client's particular goals, a list of alternatives is generated. Often the client sees the problem as a choice between only two options. Frequently other alternatives exist. These need to be identified. When the possible alternatives have been identified, information is gathered on each. The desirability of each alternative is examined in terms of the client's interests, values, and goals. An estimate based on available data is made regarding the likelihood of the client obtaining his goal through each proposed alternative. The client's previous performance in situations relevant to the requirements imposed by each alternative is reviewed to assess his probability of success. A need for more information may be identified here. The cost in time, money, and energy as well as the cost of possible failure is assessed. Alternatives are given final consideration and a decision, at least a tentative one, is reached and acted on.

The decision-making process is a continuous series of actions—identifying new problems and new alternatives, compiling information, making decisions, and finally evaluating outcomes and beginning the process over again. The process is essentially the application of the scientific method to the solution of personal problems (Gelatt, 1962). It brings order to what is often a haphazard enterprise. It allows clients to exercise more control over their lives by making deliberate choices rather than taking impulsive actions later regretted or losing options by failing to make choices at all.

Learning Decision Making

Clients often come to counseling because they are faced with decisions before they have had experiences preparing them to be skillful decision makers. Skill in decision making normally develops gradually as individuals face increasingly difficult decisions and experience the consequences of the choices they have made. Lack of opportunities to make decisions or infrequent success when making choices prevents the development of skill and confidence in decision making. Many clients are inept problem solvers, reluctant to make important choices, and dependent upon others to make decisions for them. They come to counseling to have decsions made—"What should I do?" "Should I divorce my husband or not?" "What job would be best for me?" These are decisions that must be made by the client not by the counselor. Counselors can best assist these clients by helping them to become better decision makers and take responsibility for their own decisions.

Counselors can help all clients become better problem solvers by explaining the counseling strategy being used, encouraging clients to contribute to the process, and insisting that clients make the choices that are properly theirs. In working with clients' problems, counselors use a problem-solving strategy. If they make the strategy clear to clients, an example is provided that clients can apply on their own. By encouraging the client to identify problem components, list alternatives, and suggest sources of relevant information, the counselor helps the client develop decision-making skills. Counselors are apt to be too "helpful" and assume too much responsibility for developing solutions. They must be prepared to give the client as much responsibility as can be handled. Even relatively minor choices offer opportunities for the client to practice decision making.

While counseling is being terminated with a client, it is well to review the completed decision process and have the client suggest how the process might be applied in dealing with other problems. This application of learning in counseling to other aspects of the client's life is Function 9.3 of the TERMINATE COUNSELING subsystem of the Systematic Counseling model. Every counseling problem provides an example that can be used to help the client become a better problem solver. Following a decision-making strategy will not guarantee good decisions but it will assure deliberation which with practice will lead to increased skill in decision making and better decisions.

INFORMATION IN DECISION MAKING

Decision making is an information-processing operation. Information is indispensible in making well-considered decisions. Information helps the decision maker identify problems, suggest alternatives, regard some alternatives more highly than others, and in the end evaluate the decision. Counselors must be able to help clients obtain appropriate information.

The choices a person makes and the actions taken are in some measure determined by the information at hand about self and the environment. Students having difficulty with their studies can take advantage of tutorial assistance only if they have the information that such help is available. Knowing that this assistance can have positive results for them, students will be more likely to seek help than if they lack the knowledge that tutoring will do some good. A person's response to a given situation is to an extent determined by present capabilities and information about the likely consequences of alternative actions. An important function of counseling is to help clients obtain accurate and relevant information about themselves and their environment so that better decisions can be made and more effective actions taken. The counseling goal is not only to see that information is obtained but also to increase the client's ability to assess the need for information and to locate and use relevant data. More than information is needed to solve most problems, but information can be useful in identifying problems and developing solutions. And in some few cases, new information may bring about behavior change and, indeed, remedy the problem.

Self-Information

Depending upon the nature of the problems, clients may need information about their own behavior, values and interests, abilities and deficits, or how they are perceived by others. Helping individuals to better understand themselves has long been recognized as a goal in counseling (Krumboltz, 1966; Shertzer & Stone, 1974; Tolbert, 1972; Warters, 1964). We regard self-information or self-understanding to be extremely valuable, but as a means to an end rather than a goal itself. To direct one's actions effectively toward desired goals and to make well-considered decisions, accurate self-information is essential.

Often self-information can be understood only if normative data are also available. A young man whose friends generally receive "A" grades in college may accept "A" as a norm and regard his "B" grades as inferior. His grades can only be interpreted accurately if he knows what the norm actually is. He still may want better grades, but he should know the grades he has been earning are better than average if that is the case. For a woman who feels anxious speaking before groups, it may be important for her to know that this is normal and that most people feel some of this anxiety. Feelings of hostility or depression, thoughts of suicide, sexual fantasies, or imagined aggressions toward others frighten clients because they feel alone and ashamed of what they regard as abnormal behavior. The normative data that nearly everyone has had similar thoughts can reduce anxiety. Normative data are not sought as goals for the individual but as points of reference in identifying his values, interests, and abilities.

Feedback

Feedback is a special kind of information that provides data regarding the consequences of one's own actions. Feedback can be information about a response that comes directly as a result of the response itself. A direct consequence of placing one's hand on a hot stove is a feedback signal, pain, that reduces the likelihood that the response will recur. The thanks and praise one receives as a result of helping a friend are feedback that encourages further helpful behavior. It will occur to you that feedback is just another term for reward or punishment. Didn't pain punish the individual who placed his hand on the stove and praise reward the helpful person? In these two examples it is true that there is no important difference between feedback and the reward or punishment consequences of behavior. Rewards and punishments are kinds of feedback. The consequences of some responses are not so obvious. Feedback can be ambiguous or even inaccurate. An individual may continue telling stories at a party perceiving others to be truly amused when in fact they are just being polite and consider the stories a bore. Their polite attention is rewarding but provides inaccurate feedback. Valid feedback would inhibit his storytelling if the individual cared about how others actually felt.

Feedback is information one receives about the consequences of his or her responses. It may be accurate or inaccurate. It may be correctly perceived or misperceived. It may be rewarding or punishing or neither. Many counseling problems arise through misperceived, inaccurate, or unavailable feedback. Counselors should be able to help clients obtain valid feedback and accurately perceive it.

Environmental Information

The information service has traditionally been considered a guidance function (Hoppock, 1967; Isaacson, 1971; Norris et al., 1972; Shertzer & Stone, 1974). Its importance has never been greater nor its task more difficult than today. The complexities and rapidly accelerating changes in society today make it increasingly difficult, yet increasingly necessary, to make relevant information available to those who are making personal, educational, and career decisions. Counselors are challenged to help clients find career, educational, and social information.

Occupational information includes all relevant and valid data pertaining to the world of work—job opportunities, employment trends, requirements for entrance in various occupations, opportunities for advancement, hours, wages, and conditions of employment. It includes information from national, state, and local perspectives.

Educational information includes the educational and training opportunities available, requirements for admission and completion of programs, costs, financial assistance available, and the relative merits of various schools and programs.

Social information consists of data on topics such as social skills, personal appearance, health, sex, financial planning, marriage, and understanding others. This information area has become more important in recent years as counselors have become involved in helping clients with problems arising from changing and often conflicting social values. The counselor must take care not to usurp the role of attorney or the physician by giving legal or medical advice. The counselor is not an advice giver in any case. The counselor's role is to help clients locate and use information in making their own decisions.

Helping Clients Obtain Accurate Self-Information and Feedback

How can clients be helped to perceive their own behavior accurately, identify their own interests and abilities, and learn how they are perceived by other people? We shall consider a number of ways to help clients obtain accurate self-information and feedback.

Direct experience.   Of the many sources of self-information, personal experiences and self-observation are the most direct and most influential. First-hand experience is a powerful teacher. A successful learning experience will do more to improve a student's low self-concept than a pep talk by a teacher or counselor. Direct experience is an excellent way to discover interests and abilities.

In everyday living, direct experience as a source of self-knowledge has two serious drawbacks. First, although experience provides rich opportunities for some to learn and grow, learning opportunities for others are severely limited. A second drawback is that direct experience can be damaging if the individual is not able to handle it successfully. An early failure in some effort may turn the person from any future experience in that direction.

In counseling, direct experience is prescribed to extend clients' self-understanding and to help them develop interests, values, and goals. Care is taken to select and sequence the experiences so that undue failure is avoided. Occasionally a failure experience may be beneficial, but for most young people who have not yet built a stockpile of successes, a single failure may be given undue importance. For clients who have experienced repeated failures, a success is sorely needed.

Counselors should help clients build a reserve of successes to call upon to offset occasional failures. Planned direct experience should be assured of success insofar as possible.

It is especially true of developing young people that they need a wealth of opportunities to experience and learn. Clients should generally be encouraged to participate in a variety of activities available to them. For particular problems, specific direct experiences may be prescribed for clients to gain self-information. What kinds of experiences can counselors recommend to help their clients obtain information about themselves? We will list several and encourage you to think of more.

1. Sampling courses in several curricula
2. Obtaining part-time or summer employment
3. Joining and participating in an organization
4. Running for an elective office
5. Volunteering for community service
6. Trying out for a part in a play
7. Giving a party
8. Initiating a conversation in a given social setting

The value of personal experience as a source of self-information and feedback is enhanced if the clients are aware that they are seeking information and know what to look for. Clients should be provided with an opportunity to discuss their experiences and observations with the counselor. Direct experience is not always possible as a source of information. Some substitutes for actual experiences have been presented in Chapter 8 under the discussion of modeling and simulation.

Self-monitoring. When it is important to have information about a client's present behavior, self-monitoring can be used. Self-monitoring is simply keeping an accurate record of one's own behavior. Perhaps the conditions under which feelings of depression occur cannot be identified by a given female client, for example. Having her keep a diary or journal for a period of a week or more in which she records the time, place, and circumstances for each occurrence of depression might provide her with valuable information regarding the environmental conditions that influence the depression. This is just one kind of self-monitoring. A student concerned with low grades may need to record daily activities in order to get an accurate picture of how much time is given to studies. Clients whose problems are excessive worrying, sleeping, smoking, drinking, or eating may need to record the frequency or duration of these activities to obtain a base rate and provide information on the present status of the problem. Continued self-monitoring can also provide a means of evaluating the progress of counseling.

Diaries are most appropriate for recording self-observations when elements associated with some problem need to be identified. Because neither the counselor nor the client knows precisely what these elements will be, clients should be asked to describe in detail all of the circumstances surrounding each occurrence of the response of concern. Diary entries are then studied for elements common to each occurrence that might be causally related to the response. This kind of record might reveal that a client's depression is associated with family arguments, the anticipation of some unpleasant task, or some other event and provide useful information in treating the problem.

When the specific response to be observed has been identified, various means are available to keep account of its frequency of occurrence. Golf counters worn on the wrist have been used by clients to record frequencies of a given behavior over a period of time. Charts or graphs can be used to record daily or weekly frequencies of a behavior. Self-monitoring and recording behavior will be explained in more detail later in this chapter when self-management is discussed.

Instant replay.   Self-monitoring is difficult in some settings especially when the client is absorbed in a social interaction. If the client needs to make self-observations in a social encounter, the client and counselor can role-play such an encounter and record it on audiotape or videotape. The tape can be played back immediately after the interaction to give the client an opportunity to review the behavior. During the review session, the tape can be stopped, backed up, and replayed to emphasize points and to give the client ample opportunities to monitor and study responses. Kagan (1970) has pioneered in the development of this technique and has accumulated a great deal of research on its use.

This kind of instant replay has many uses in counseling. Counselors in training sometimes remark to their supervisors that the whining, complaining tone of some clients makes it unpleasant to listen to them or that other clients are so self-contradictory that it is difficult to understand what they really mean. Supervisors occasionally have suggested that the counselor trainee call the client's attention to these disturbing responses and then play back a part of the recorded counseling session to let the client hear how these responses sound. When this has been done, the effect on the client's subsequent responses has often been dramatic.

Confrontation.   The self-information processes described so far have been based on the client's own experience and observations. Self-information can also come from others. We don't often hear the truth about ourselves from others, at least not the unpleasant truth. Occasionally we will hear it from a child or from someone in anger, but usually people tell us only what we like to hear.

There are times when a client needs to know the truth about how he or she is perceived, and the counselor can be most helpful by confronting the client with an unpleasant bit of self-information. Counselors in training frequently find this hard to do. Few people enjoy pointing out other persons' faults, but then counseling isn't always pleasant. The disagreeable task can be done kindly in a spirit of helpfulness. Confrontations should focus on the inappropriate or annoying behavior, not on the person. It isn't the client who is wrong or disliked, but rather a particular bit of behavior that is annoying. Confrontation helps clients learn how their behavior affects others, but it does not negatively evaluate them as individuals.

Confrontation is frequently better accepted and more influential coming from peers rather than from a counselor. In the group treatment of chronic drug abusers, alcoholics, and public offenders, confrontation by peers is a technique often successful in cutting through the self-deception that is frequently part of the problem syndrome.

Perceptive persons are attuned to the subtle social signals that provide feedback in spite of polite attempts by others to hide real feelings. These people do not need deliberate confrontations because they have a relatively accurate assessment of themselves and how others react to them. For those who have not learned to perceive this feedback, confrontation may be an immediate need, but it is also desirable to train them to recognize subtle communications. Some suggestions for doing this were discussed in Chapter 8 through the use of modeling.

Standardized tests. Standardized tests can provide information about clients useful to them in making some decisions. Decision making involves prediction. One course of action is predicted to lead to better outcomes than another. Test information is useful in counseling to the degree that it can predict relevant outcomes. If test scores for high school students are predictive of college grades, these scores provide them with useful information in making decisions about college.

Too often test data are collected on clients without any assurance that the results can lead to better decisions. Such data collecting is a waste of time and money. The criterion for judging test information in counseling is how well it predicts relevant aspects of the future for a given client population. Test data should be used only if better decisions can be made with the test information than without (Mehrens & Lehman, 1975). To ignore useful test data would also be a serious error.

The tests demonstrated to be most predictive and useful in counseling have been aptitude tests used to predict future academic performance. These tests can be used with some confidence with clients who are like those on whom the tests were normed. For clients who are not representative of the norm group, the tests may or may not be useful. The poorest predictors among standardized tests are the personality tests. While there are special uses for some personality tests, there is little to recommend their general use in counseling.

Counselors should be able to demonstrate the validity of the tests they use. It is not enough to make the general statement that tests provide information or assist in understanding clients. The counselor must be able to state specifically what the test information should help to accomplish. The assertion that the test is effective should be based on empirical evidence.

Because test information has a scientific aura about it, clients tend to give it more credence and importance than is warranted. Some care should be taken in interpreting test results to clients. The following steps are presented as a model for test interpretation:

1. Encourage the client to discuss the decision for which the test information is to be used.

This gives the counselor a frame of reference in which to discuss the test results and a warning if the client seeks to use test scores that are inappropriate for the decision to be made.

2. Learn what the client expects of the test information.

Clients often have false expectations of tests. They may want the test results to make a decision for them. The counselor can correct false expectations by indicating the kinds of information the test provides and assuring the clients that the responsibility for making decisions is theirs.

3. Discuss with clients the kinds of information they have about themselves that might relate to the problem or decision to be made.

This allows clients to place the test information in proper perspective as one bit in a large mosaic of self-information.

4. Describe test results to the client. Explain what the scores mean. Ask questions of the client to check proper understanding.

Great care must be taken to make sure the client understands the scores, the interpretations that can be made, and the limitations of the data.

5. Encourage the client to discuss how the test information might be used.

This step further checks understanding of the test and helps the client make proper use of the results.

6. Encourage the client to suggest other ways of obtaining self-information.

The client should not believe that the test results provide ultimate answers. If the information is important, other means should be sought to validate or invalidate the test results.

Clients need accurate and relevant self-data. They need to be able to perceive the information accurately and interpret it correctly. Clients also need information about their environment in order to consider their options carefully.

Helping Clients Obtain Environmental Information

When a client is troubled by a decision, there are at least two intermediate counseling goals: (a) to help the client find relevant information and (b) to help the client become a more able information seeker. There are times when a counselor can give a client a bit of information without giving any further help. A high school senior may need to know when certain college aptitude tests are scheduled to be given. The counselor gives this information as a service to the student, but we would not want to call this service counseling. Counseling should result in some change in the client, a change that produces less dependence upon the counselor. If we can help clients learn to identify the need for information, to locate relevant information, and to interpret it properly then we are performing a counseling function.

Counselors should try to keep themselves current in areas about which their clients seek information—job opportunities, scholarships and financial aids, military service, and so forth. It would be asking too much to expect counselors to be expert in all of these areas, but it is reasonable to expect that they know how to locate sources of reliable information. The counselor needs to analyze the environment and client population carefully to learn the types of information clients might typically seek. Each counselor needs to do this because needs vary greatly with different client groups and from setting to setting.

Counselors can keep abreast of information related to problems their clients face by reading widely, maintaining active membership in professional organizations, subscribing to and reading professional journals, and attending and participating in professional meetings. Maintaining contact with the community—businesses, schools, community agencies, and service clubs—is also part of keeping abreast of information relevant to clients' needs. Perhaps most important is for counselors to keep in close contact with the populations they serve.

Direct experience.   Direct experience is an excellent source of environmental information. Part-time jobs, field trips, volunteer work, and clubs such as Scouts, 4-H, and Junior Achievement provide valuable first-hand experiences from which to learn about social and occupational environments. Many individuals have limited access to these or other direct means of expanding their experience. Counselors must be creative in discovering ways in which their clients can gain relevant first-hand information when it is needed. The following are examples of things counselors have done to help clients learn through their own experiences:

1. Helped a senior class make an employment survey of the community.

2. Instituted a series of two-week *mini courses* in cooperation with a community college staff so that clients could sample various vocational training opportunities.

3. Arranged for members of a Future Teachers club in the high school to assist teachers in the local elementary school on a volunteer basis.

4. Established a job shop to help clients make contact with employers and gain experience through temporary or part-time jobs in the community.

5. Arranged to have individuals of differing racial, ethnic, or socio-economic groups interact socially by being guests in each others' homes.

Creative counselors will think of many experiences that provide opportunities for individuals to expand their knowledge of their social, occupational, and educational environments. Hawkins (1972) recommends that high school students, both boys and girls, be given opportunities to observe and tutor nursery school children under supervision in order to see how youngsters learn and develop and to gain the skills in dealing with children they will need as parents. Through the planned direct experiences with young children, the youths would learn in ways that reading or other vicarious experiences could not match.

Prepared informational materials. Counselors must know where educational, vocational, and social information is located in the school, agency, or community. Books, pamphlets, monographs, films, filmstrips, microfilms, and audio recordings providing educational, vocational, and social information are abundant. Much printed material is available free or inexpensively through organizations or government. References to information sources are available in textbooks that are devoted to the information service in guidance (e.g., Hoppock, 1967; Isaacson, 1971; Norris et al., 1972).

For frequent information requests, the counselor may wish to develop an information bulletin, or collect relevant pamphlets to make an information packet. These frequently used materials may be kept in the counselor's office or in the counseling center. Typically, prepared informational materials will be kept in a library or resource center. Counselors should support the development of information resources in their schools or agencies. They need to identify informational deficits and recommend materials to fill voids and to update obsolete materials.

Helping Clients Use Information

Clients with decisions to make should be helped to ask relevant questions, to identify the need for information, to locate sources of information, and to evaluate and make use of appropriate data. When clients bring decision problems to counseling, the counselor should encourage them to list the kinds of questions which, if answered, would make the decision easier. An employment or vocational rehabilitation counselor may help clients make vocational choices by first assisting them to ask relevant questions concerning each option available to them. Just what constitutes a relevant question depends on the clients' values, interests, and goals.

When the questions have been asked, the next step is to determine what kind of information would provide satisfactory answers. For example, a high school senior girl trying to decide between two colleges that have accepted her applications may ask which school would she most like. What kind of information if any might answer this question? Would knowledge about the size of the two colleges, the characteristics of each student body, the communities in which the colleges are located, or some other information help her to answer her question? The client will have to decide the kinds of information that will provide the best answer.

Once the need for particular kinds of information has been identified, clients are then asked to suggest possible sources of information. Clients have many avenues for obtaining information. They may *read* suitable materials, *write* for additional information, *visit* settings for firsthand experiences, *ask* appropriate questions, and *listen* to the experiences of others. Within the counselor's school or agency, other counselors, teachers, and administrators are potential resource people with special interest and knowledge. Individuals from the community representing labor unions, businesses, community service agencies, the military services, schools, and churches can be excellent sources of educational, occupational, and social information. Successful business people, professionals, and technicians from minority groups can be sources of career planning information for all clients as well as serving as good models for minority clients. The counselor who has located a number of people in the community representing many fields of interest and expertise and who are willing to meet and share their knowledge with an individual or small group has a valuable counseling resource.

When the information has all been collected, evaluated, and applied to the decision at hand, it is the client's responsibility to make the decision. The counselor may be asked to make the decision, but since the client must experience the consequences of whatever choice is made, the decision must be the client's. The counselor has contributed by helping the client carefully consider all the available information before the choice is made. This is all that can legitimately be done.

Being able to make decisions and to outline courses of action to achieve goals are important aspects of being self-directed. But the truly self-directed person not only knows what to do but is also able to persist in a desired course of action until the goal is achieved. Many individuals have great difficulty doing the things they know they should do. A county jail inmate who had a long series of arrests told his counselor, "I know what I should do (to stay out of trouble) but I need help getting myself to do it." Several techniques for helping clients gain control over their own behavior will be discussed in the section which follows.

SELF-MANAGEMENT

Self-management, sometimes called behavioral self-control, refers to the ability of an individual to direct his or her behavior—i.e., to the ability to do those things that are goal-directed even though the effort is difficult and the rewards are long delayed or to eliminate those habitual behaviors that are undesired but are immediately rewarding. Adhering to a regular study schedule to earn better semester grades, saving money for some special purpose, jogging to increase one's life expectancy, and giving up desserts all winter and spring to be able to comfortably wear a swimsuit in the summer are all examples of self-management. Most individuals have some self-management skills, but some are better self-managers than others. There are those who manage some aspects of their lives well but have difficulties with other aspects. For a few, the lack of self-management skills presents severe problems.

There are a number of tested procedures for increasing an individual's ability to control his own behavior (Thoresen & Mahoney, 1974; Mahoney, 1974). These procedures can be taught to clients and used by them to attain the goals they seek in counseling.

Advantages of Teaching Self-Management
as a Counseling Strategy

We have previously discussed how presenting or withholding reinforcers can be used to increase goal-directed behavior. An obstacle confronting counselors who wish to use reinforcement and extinction procedures is that counselors have limited opportunities to observe the client, monitor behavior, and reward goal-directed responses. It is true that the counselor can often enlist a family member of the client, a teacher, or a fellow worker to assist in monitoring client responses and administering reinforcement. But enlisting such aid presents problems. Confidentiality cannot be maintained if others must be called upon to help. The commitment of others to assist may not be adequate to consistently attend to the task, and not all behaviors are performed publicly where they can be monitored by others.

Self-management places the observation and recording of behavior, the management of environmental variables, and the administration of reinforcers in the hands of the client. It places a great deal of responsibility on the client, but the client is often the best person to monitor his or her own responses. No one will be more motivated to attend to these behaviors than the client. Self-management strategies give clients ways to control their own behavior and offer several advantages over other behavior modification approaches:

1. Clients are motivated to persist toward their goal because they see themselves as having control over their own behavior.

2. Constant monitoring and reinforcement is possible even when the client is alone.

3. Thoughts and feelings as well as some overt behaviors can only be monitored by the individuals themselves.

4. Clients learn a strategy that they can use on their own with future problems.

5. Self-management can be taught to individuals and groups as a preventive strategy before problems arise.

Self-Management Strategies

Self-management is simply the special application of strategies we have already discussed. These strategies can be classified under four major approaches: (a) self-monitoring, (b) altering environmental stimuli, (c) learning alternate responses, and (d) altering response consequences. In addition to these strategies, we will discuss the use of covert processes in self-management.

Self-monitoring. Self-monitoring involves the self-observation and recording of specific behaviors or responses to certain conditions. Clients observe their relevant behaviors, note the circumstances under which they occur, and record their frequency, duration, or other pertinent aspects. These data are collected initially to establish a baseline and to identify relevant variables. The behavior is monitored throughout the self-management program to provide a continuous progress report and feedback that can produce behavior change. Frequently the process of systematic self-observation influences the behaviors being observed. Desired behaviors may increase and undesired behaviors decrease simply by recording them. The knowledge that behavior is changing in the desired direction lets the client know that the behavior is under self-control and reinforces further efforts to change.

Clients must be trained as observers. They need to know precisely what is to be observed and recorded. If a male client wants to lose his temper less frequently, for example, he must decide which of his responses are to indicate that he has lost his temper—raising his voice, using abusive language, breaking something, or physically attacking someone. Which of these indicates loss of temper depends upon how the client defines the target behavior and how he wishes to modify his response. He may be willing to lose control verbally but want to avoid physical violence when angry. The important thing is that the client must consistently be able to identify examples of his behavior as indicating loss of temper using his own definition.

It is usually better to record responses immediately after they occur rather than to rely upon memory. Clients can carry small cards on which to tally the frequencies of behaviors being self-monitored. Golf counters worn like wristwatches are especially useful in recording frequencies of behaviors with minimum effort. Such recording devices are particularly effective for recording behaviors that occur many times per day and can be counted accurately only by recording them as they occur. Other behaviors of concern occur much less frequently and may be unusual enough to be remembered until they can be recorded at the end of the day.

A record of the self-monitored behavior should be kept over a period of a week or more to establish a baseline and possibly to identify patterns or trends. The most frequently used method of recording is to enter each day's tally on a chart or graph. For example, a graduate student wanted to cut down on the number of cigarettes she smoked. To establish her current smoking rate, baseline, she recorded the number of cigarettes she smoked per day for a seven-day period. The record of her smoking behavior for the week is presented in Figure 10-1. The record not only showed that the student smoked an average of 22 cigarettes per day but it also suggested an increase in her smoking rate on the weekends.

In the establishment of a baseline, it may be important to know the locations in which the response occurs most frequently or the most likely time during the day, or the conditions under which the response is most apt to occur. Separate tallies may be kept to compare the occurrences of the behavior during the day with during the night, at home with at school, or under one set of circumstances with another. Just what the separate tallies should be might be suggested by the information the

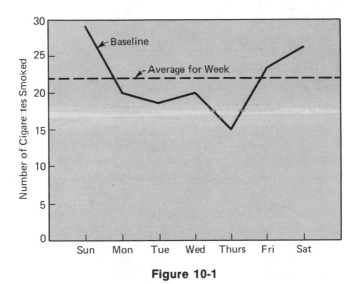

Figure 10-1

client and counselor have on hand or might be suggested from an initial daily tally over a week or ten-day period. The student's smoking behavior recorded in Figure 10-1 suggested to her that she probably smoked more on the weekends because she was with friends who smoked. To check this out she kept a separate tally of her smoking with friends and in the absence of friends for the next seven-day period. These records are presented in Figure 10-2.

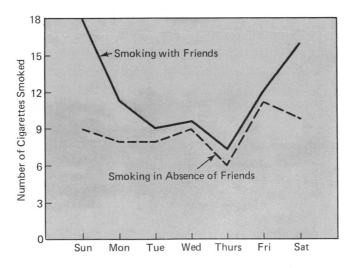

Figure 10-2

The increased number of cigarettes smoked with friends was even more significant than the graph indicates because the student estimated that most of her time was spent alone during the week and only about half of her time was spent with friends on weekends. Thus, in spite of the fact that she was alone more than she was with friends, most of her smoking occurred with friends. These data verified that her smoking was influenced by friends and suggested to her that these friends should know of her desire to smoke less. She continued to monitor her smoking while employing a number of strategies to reduce the habit including announcing her intention to friends. She was able to reduce the average number of cigarettes she smoked per day to just over five and was considering whether or not to quit smoking altogether when she was last seen by her counselor.

Self-monitoring is an essential element in self-management. It establishes a baseline against which progress can be assessed. It may indicate variables that influence the target behavior—as the influence of friends was indicated in the case of the graduate student for whom smoking was a target behavior. Self-monitoring provides continuous feedback while a behavior change program is employed. Goal-directed changes detected through self-monitoring reinforce further effort. Failure to observe change indicates the need for some modification in the strategy or in its implementation. For some behaviors that are constantly threatening to become uncontrolled, self-monitoring may have to be a life-long commitment. A successful weight control program, for example, is seldom a short-term project but requires constant self-monitoring.

Altering environmental stimuli. Behaviors are influenced by environmental stimuli. The boss may reveal a totally new personality at the company picnic. The graduate student's smoking behavior in the previous example was influenced by her social environment. Responses become associated with certain environmental stimuli. These situational factors become cues or discriminative stimuli that evoke or control particular responses. We learn that certain behaviors are appropriate in some circumstances but are most inappropriate in others. Many of the habits we have formed throughout life are triggered or influenced by environmental cues. A red traffic signal light, as an obvious example, evokes a whole chain of responses in a driver approaching an intersection. The individual can control much behavior by choosing an environment or arranging it to facilitate desirable responses.

One form of self-management is for individuals to deliberately place themselves in situations that elicit the behaviors they want to perform and that discourage the behaviors they want to eliminate. Some people are able to lead creative, active lives by continually placing themselves in positions where demands are placed on their time and talents. For example, a boy who can't bring himself to do regular physical exercise yet wants to increase his physical strength might take a summer job that demands strenuous work. A student in trouble at school for frequent fights might be able to identify situations that lead to disputes and avoid those situations as a way of reducing aggressive behavior.

Some situations are necessary to everyday life and cannot be avoided without producing severe problems. Avoiding people to reduce interpersonal anxiety is not an adequate solution. By no means can all problems be solved by avoiding situations or finding new environments. But some can. If a husband and wife find that they often fight when they play bridge and rarely fight otherwise, avoiding bridge playing may be the best way to reduce family quarrels.

Case example. Wayne McKinney, a secondary school teacher, sought counseling at the university where he was doing graduate work. He complained of being discouraged about teaching as a profession. He felt that he was merely putting in his time and not being creative or doing the job he knew that he could do. There had been few rewards for him in teaching.

In discussing this concern with his counselor, Wayne revealed that he spent considerable time during his free period at school talking with three other teachers who were also disgruntled with working conditions and who complained about their lot. He and these other teachers had initially been brought together because they had the same preparation period and usually spent part of the time talking and drinking coffee.

Wayne wanted to have a more positive attitude toward his work and find more satisfaction in it. He agreed that this was not likely to happen unless he put more effort and enthusiasm into his teaching. He could see that his colleagues were not helping him achieve these goals but were, in fact, reinforcing his complaining and lack of incentive.

A social environment more conducive to the client's goals was sought. The counselor asked Wayne to identify the colleagues he most admired, those he thought were truly interested in teaching and enjoyed their work. Several teachers were identified. The counselor suggested that Wayne spend less time with his customary associates and more with these other teachers. Wayne was confident enough in the suggestion that he arranged to have his teaching schedule changed the following semester so that his free period permitted him to associate more closely with some of the good teachers he had identified.

By the end of the second semester, he reported that his attitude had changed considerably. He was working harder and with more enthusiasm. In changing his social environment, he had left those who modeled and reinforced complaining and discouragement for a group who modeled and reinforced positive ideas and actions. He caught the positive spirit of these teachers and worked harder at his job and felt more rewarded. This change in Wayne was accomplished by finding a new social environment within the school, one that promoted the goals that Wayne had set for himself.

There are two special kinds of self-management problems associated with environmental stimuli: (a) an important response is not performed because it has not become associated with the stimuli that should cue its performance and (b) a response is performed excessively or indiscriminately because numerous inappropriate stimuli elicit its performance. In problems of the first kind, the individual is capable of performing the response but does not because he does not perceive cues or has not learned to respond to the environmental cues.

Case example.   Let's examine an example of this first problem type. A husband seldom filled out his check stub after writing a check. His wife who did the family bookkeeping complained that correct accounts could not be kept if a record of expenditures was not made. The husband wanted to help but simply forgot to fill out the stub when he made a purchase by check. He had ignored the stub so often that the checkbook or the act of writing the check had not become cues associated with filling out the stub.

To change this behavior, he took a red felt marking pen and made a star on each stub in his checkbook. From then on, each time he wrote a check, the red star reminded him to fill out the stub. He had placed cues, red stars, in his environment to signal that a particular behavior was appropriate. In subsequent checkbooks the red stars were unnecessary because by then the checkbook itself recalled to him the red star and its purpose. Thus eventually the checkbook became a natural cue for properly recording the check he had written.

Much of our behavior is performed without our being aware of it. We respond to many situations almost automatically. If we wish to change a habitual response, we need a way of intruding upon the normal chain of events. Cueing is a way of accomplishing this. A practicum supervisor told a counselor trainee that her rapport with clients would improve if she would relax and smile more. It was difficult for the trainee to act on the suggestion because as she became caught up in counseling, she forgot the supervisor's advice. As a cue to herself, she drew a smile on a small circle of paper and placed in on the wall where she would see it while talking with clients. The cue was used with some success.

Cueing is simple and clients can easily be taught to use it. The cues chosen should be attention getting and should be associated as closely as possible with the normal environmental stimuli that evoke the response when the special cue is no longer used. The red star in the earlier example met both criteria. It was an attention getter and was placed in the checkbook that would later become the cue for making the proper entry in the checkbook.

When the client can perform the desired response but forgets to do so, he can gain control over his behavior by self-cueing. This is not entirely unlike writing oneself a reminder to keep an important appointment, but it differs in one important respect. The self-cueing that we have discussed is an attempt to associate a response with environmental cues to effect a long term behavior change. It is not just an expedient way of remembering something on a single occasion. The test of the success of self-cueing is whether or not the response persists appropriately after the special cue is no longer used.

A second problem type involving environmental stimuli is one in which the response is excessively or inappropriately performed. The response is performed not only to the stimuli that should elicit it but to many other stimuli as well. Those who eat in response to appropriate stimuli eat when they are hungry, at regular meal times, and in appropriate dining areas. Those who overeat do so in response to hunger, boredom, anger, and other internal states as well as in response to various environmental stimuli. The response that should be under particular stimulus control is not. To control the response, the environmental stimuli under which the response is permitted to occur may be progressively narrowed until the response is only performed at the appropriate time and place. In this way the overeater can learn to eat only at meal times and then only in appropriate places. In this manner eating becomes disassociated with watching TV, studying, or feeling tense, and over a period of time, these environmental stimuli will no longer evoke the undesired response.

For students who daydream, listen to records, or engage in any other distracting response rather than attending to the studies they want to finish, study environments should be selected and used only for study. If daydreaming occurs, the study setting should be left immediately. Daydreaming must not be allowed to become linked to the study setting. Only study activity should be associated with the study environment. Short study periods in the designated setting should be tried to establish the proper association. By gradually increasing the amount of time spent on studies in the selected environment, the stimulus value of the setting is strengthened. The setting helps elicit the desired response.

The effort in these examples is to disassociate a response from particular stimuli. This is accomplished by gradually reducing the settings in which a response to be controlled is allowed or by selecting a setting which all responses but the controlled one are disallowed. In either case responses are brought under different and more precise stimulus control.

Interrupting response chains is another way to alter stimuli that elicit unwanted behaviors. Our own behaviors are stimuli and become cues for subsequent behaviors. A series of behaviors can be linked to target behaviors in long stimulus response chains. Think for a moment of the sequence of antecedent behaviors that are necessary for an individual to smoke a cigarette—buying the pack and carrying it conveniently, opening the pack, removing a cigarette, placing it in the mouth, replacing the pack, finding matches, lighting the cigarette, taking a puff, and extinguishing and discarding the match. Each act is linked to the next in an almost ritualistic pattern of responses. Once the pattern has been well established, its performance is nearly automatic. Occasionally smokers will light up a cigarette only to find that they already have one going in an ashtray. Some signal triggered the smoking response chain without the individuals being fully aware of it.

Firmly established response chains are difficult to break. A recommended approach is to disrupt the chain in its early stages so that the series of learned responses cannot automatically lead to the terminal response. In the smoking example, cigarettes can be carried in a different place, a different pocket or in a special case, and changed often so that new chains cannot be formed. The cigarette can be lighted differently, using the left hand if normally right handed, using matches if accustomed to a lighter, using wooden matches if book matches are habitually used. This deliberate attempt to disrupt the chain makes smoking a conscious act more easily controlled than when it was almost a reflex action. The same principle of disrupting the response chain can be effective in any habitual behavior in which a series of related responses leads to the target behavior that is to be reduced or eliminated.

The steps the client must follow in using this technique are first to identify the elements in the response chain and second to alter conditions at one or preferably more points along the chain so as to prevent the unconscious chaining of responses leading to the undesired target behavior. It is generally best to interrupt the chain early in the sequence. The responses in the chain that are furthest from the terminal response are usually the least difficult to modify.

Learning alternate responses. It is frequently possible for an individual to learn and substitute an acceptable alternate response for the undesirable one. Such an alternate response should result in the same, or nearly the same, immediate positive consequence as the undesirable response but without the long-term negative results. Reducing anxiety by deep muscle relaxation, listening to music, or working at some activity rather than drinking, nail biting, or eating are examples of the substitution of alternative responses for less desirable ones.

In using this approach, the client is helped to identify the situations in which the undesired response occurs and to develop alternate responses in each situation in which the established response is to be eliminated. Cueing may be necessary to remind the client to use the alternate response until the new behavior becomes associated with the natural environmental cues.

Altering response consequences. We have in Chapter 9 discussed how reinforcement consequences influence behavior and how reinforcement can be self-administered. Self-reinforcement is a self-management strategy when it is made contingent upon goal-directed behavior. Individuals using self rewards to modify their behavior must be able to monitor their own responses and to reward particular responses that they have determined to be goal-directed.

Case example. Brian had done well academically in high school with little effort and without developing good study habits. As a freshman at a small private college, his poor academic performance prompted him to see a counselor. In counseling he was quickly able to identify inadequate time spent on studies as the cause of his poor performance. Other possibilities were explored, but lack of study effort was verified as central to the problem. Brian found a good many things to do rather than study. One of the most time consuming of his diversions was reading about chess. He had been an avid chess player and although he didn't play often at college, he did spend a great deal of time studying the game.

Brian was asked to record the amount of time he actually spent studying each day. He then was asked to estimate how much time would be necessary for him to study to do well. (His long-range goal was to improve his grades). It was then suggested that he devise a plan in which he would use reading chess books to reward increased study time. He was to deny himself this recreational activity until he had spent a given amount of time studying. The amount of additional study time necessary to earn the reward was to be small at first and gradually increased until the study time goal was reached. Using this self-management plan, Brian was able to increase his study time and earn grades that he felt were respectable. The experience also gave him the confidence in counseling to enable him to present other problems of a personal nature to work on in consultation with a counselor.

Self-monitoring, altering environmental stimuli, learning alternate responses, and altering response consequences can be employed individually or in combination by the client in a self-management program. The counselor acts as a consultant to the client, but it is the client who makes the observations, modifies the environment, employs alternate responses, or self-administers rewards. In taking an active part in their own counseling program, clients learn strategies that they can use when subsequent problems arise.

Strategies using covert responses. Covert responses—thoughts, feelings, imagery, attitudes—are private events not directly subject to objective verification yet nevertheless they are of interest to those who study human behavior. We are concerned with two kinds of covert response. First, there are annoying or debilitating thoughts or feelings that are themselves target responses to be modified in counseling. Second, we are concerned with covert responses that may be used to modify overt behaviors. Covert responses of the first kind are negative, self-defeating thoughts, gloomy, pessimistic feelings, unproductive, self-depreciation attitudes that interfere with self-actualization. These covert responses can be eliminated or modified using special applications of learning principles.

Covert responses to modify overt behavior was encountered earlier in our discussion of desensitization using imagined images of threatening situations to extinguish specific fears and avoidance behaviors. Experimental studies and clinical experience of Cautela and other psychologists have extended the use of thoughts and imagery in effecting behavioral change (Cautela, 1971).

Thoughts as target behaviors.   Behaviors modified in counseling are usually overt responses, but occasionally it is a thought or thought pattern that is annoying the client and is the target behavior in the counseling process. A persistent worry, a feeling of helplessness, a negative self-image are covert responses that may be the focus of the client's concern. Covert responses follow the same laws of learning as do overt behaviors. Thoughts and feelings are learned and can be modified. Covert responses can be increased by reinforcement or extinguished by withholding reinforcement. Clients can be taught to increase the frequency of their positive self-thoughts, for example, by a self-management program using the following steps: (a) identify desirable self-statements, (b) monitor the frequency of these positive self-thoughts, (c) use a cue to elicit the desired covert response and (d) self-reinforce the positive thoughts.

Case example.   A woman seeing a community mental health counselor complained of feeling depressed, unloved, and worthless. She had a number of negative self-thoughts that seemed to plague her. The counselor was able to help her see that her depression was being aggravated by the negative self-thoughts that obsessed her. As a first step in her therapy, the counselor suggested that she keep a record of the frequency of positive self-thoughts she had each day. Over a week's time she recorded only three positive self-thoughts. The client was then asked to develop a positive self-statement that she could repeat to herself a number of times each day. The phrase that she chose was, "I'm a good person," and this phrase was to be repeated each time her phone rang. This approach reduced the number of negative self-thoughts per day and increased the number of positive thoughts. The procedure had an interesting side effect in that the woman's husband and children in whom she had confided regarding her therapy used the phone ringing and other occasions to tell her that she was indeed a good person. They did this sincerely with a desire to be helpful, and it was well received by the client.

The increased positive self-thoughts did not remove all the woman's problems but did seem to allow her to focus on remedial steps rather than dwell upon her troubles. Further progress was made as therapy continued.

Covert modeling.   Vividly imagining how one would like to respond in a situation can provide a model for action. The covert model may be based upon previous observations of others or remembered previous experiences in which one's own responses were effective. Covert modeling can be used to enact in the imagination a model originally presented verbally. As you are reading this, stop for a moment and imagine how you would safely exit the building if there were a fire just outside the door of the room you are now in. In your imagination you might construct several alternate models for action in such an emergency. Wouldn't having such models in advance help in an actual emergency? Each person anticipating some difficult social interaction can develop several models in imagination and choose one to use in the actual situation. Most of us daydream and imagine ourselves as we would like to be. Often the fantasies are too unrealistic to be accomplished, but many individuals have been guided by more realistic self-projected models.

The object of covert modeling is for the individual to have a clear picture of the responses desired. How well the client is able to do this will depend upon how well the self-observations and observations of others have been made and how well the observations can be synthesized into a model that is appropriate. Both of these abilities can be acquired and improved through practice.

Covert rehearsal.   Covert rehearsals differ only slightly from covert modeling. Covert rehearsal is imagining oneself performing the model response in a variety of appropriate settings. In such rehearsals in the imagination, one can try out various modifications of the modeled response and pose problems that might occur in an actual enactment of the response. Covert rehearsal allows responses to be practiced that occur infrequently in an individual's life, proposing marriage for example. It allows one to practice responses that would require special settings or equipment if the rehearsal were overt. It permits rehearsals of potentially threatening responses in safety.

Covert reinforcement.   There is some evidence that responses covertly rehearsed or actually performed can be covertly reinforced. A step toward a goal or the performance of a response to be accelerated might be covertly reinforced with a positive self-statement—"I've done well," "I'm making progress"—or a positive mental image—a self-image receiving an award or winning approval—or a feeling of well-being. The evidence supporting the effectiveness of covert reinforcement is not conclusive but the technique seems to warrant further consideration.

Many of our efforts are self-sustained because we have learned to feel good on accomplishing some task. However, some people have not often experienced success and have seldom had occasion to self-reward or think positive self-thoughts. These individuals can perhaps learn this kind of self-reinforcement and influence their own behaviors by deliberately thinking positive self-thoughts when small successes have been achieved.

Combining covert rehearsal and covert reinforcement, one might link a response with a positive consequence in imagery and have this linkage influence the performance of the response in actual circumstances. It is often difficult to manage behavioral consequences in the real life environment. If it is possible, such management can have a positive and dramatic effect on behavior. When the opportunities for a response to occur are rare and thus can be rewarded only infrequently or when positive consequences are difficult to manage, covert processes may be useful.

Covert sensitization.   Undesirable responses have been reported to be reduced or eliminated through a covert process called covert sensitization (Cautela, 1967). In this approach the client vividly imagines the performance of the undesirable responses and imagines that it is followed by an aversive consequence. Cautela has reported success with this method in treating clients with unwanted habits. Excessive drinkers, for example, are asked to imagine taking a drink and as they think of taking the first sip, they are to imagine a feeling of nausea followed by vomiting. Still in imagination, the client leaves the drink and steps outside into fresh air and a feeling of well being. Drinking is associated with nausea and turning away from a drink is linked with feeling well. The counselor presents cues to help the client make the imagined scenes as vivid as possible. The client practices these imagined scenes several times each day independently after rehearsing them with the counselor. Linking the undesirable behavior with an aversive consequence in imagination is said to be effective in reducing the actual incidence of the response. While there are many case studies attesting to the effectiveness of covert conditioning, experimental research evidence supporting this technique is lacking.

Clients in Control of Change

The approaches suggested in this section could be directed by the counselor, but it is recommended that clients be trained in their application and, in effect, become their own counselors. Using self-management strategies, clients are in control of the change process, and the counselor serves as a consultant and resource person. Early in the counseling process, it may not be possible for clients to assume full responsibility for progress, but such full responsibility is the goal of counseling. Opportunities are available even in the initial stages of counseling for clients to make decisions and actively participate in the development of a change program. These opportunities should be used to help the individual develop decision-making and self-management skills. Increased client participation is encouraged as counseling is continued.

A client capable of effective self-management is the goal of counseling. Traditionally most counselors have expected that gains made in counseling would carry over into the client's life, but few deliberately taught their clients self-control techniques. There is a good deal of current interest in teaching self-management strategies both for remedial and developmental counseling (Thoresen & Mahoney, 1974).

Self-management strategies put clients in control of the change process. Clients learn first to observe and record their own behavior then systematically to modify the environmental conditions and behavioral consequences that bring about desired changes. Continued self-monitoring tells them whether or not the strategies are working well. As they observe their behavior changing in the desired direction, they gain self-confidence by learning that they have power over formerly uncontrolled responses.

Self-management strategies can be employed for a wide variety of client problems. Behaviors can be acquired, increased, decreased, or linked to particular environmental cues through self-managed learning programs. Self-management strategies are especially useful in changing those covert or private behaviors that can only be monitored by the client.

SUMMARY

In this chapter we have discussed strategies for helping clients become self-directed. One of the most useful skills in becoming self-directed is skill in decision making. A number of aspects of this skill were identified:

1. identify the problem
2. identify values and goals
3. identify alternatives
4. examine alternatives
5. make a tentative decision
6. take action on the decision
7. evaluate outcomes

Clients should be encouraged to participate in as many decisions in counseling as possible to increase their experience and skill in decision making. For problems that are primarily decision problems, teaching decision making might be the major counseling strategy used.

To make well-considered decisions clients need accurate and relevant information about themselves and their environments. Counselors can help clients acquire self-information through direct experience, self-monitoring, instant replay, confrontation, and standardized tests.

Environmental information can be gathered through direct experience and through prepared informational materials. The client has many avenues for obtaining environmental information:

1. *reading* suitable materials
2. *writing* for additional information
3. *visiting* settings for firsthand experiences
4. *listening* to the experiences of others

Self-management strategies help clients persist toward goals they have chosen in spite of hardships and the long-delayed rewards. These strategies also help clients overcome habits that have immediate rewards but detrimental consequences in the long run. Self-management strategies can be classified under four major approaches:

1. self-monitoring
2. altering environmental stimuli
3. learning new responses
4. altering response consequences

Self-management involves the client monitoring and analyzing his or her own behavior, changing environmental conditions to optimize the probability of desirable responses, learning alternate responses to replace less desirable ones, and administering overt or covert rewards or punishment consequent to the performance of specific overt behaviors or thought patterns.

11
Evaluating Progress and Outcomes

OVERVIEW

Someone has said, "If you don't know where you want to go, you're liable to end up somewhere else." This seems reasonable enough. The implied corollary is that if you *do* know where you want to go, you'll get there and you'll know when you have arrived. Perhaps, but not necessarily. Granted that in Systematic Counseling the intended destination has been clearly determined in DECIDE GOAL AND OBJECTIVE (6.0). Granted also that the systematic counselor has a clearly marked road map, a willing passenger, and (hopefully) adequate driving skills. Moreover, carefully planned tasks have been undertaken along the way, and it therefore seems reasonable that the destination will be reached as planned. Yet, there are many turns and other obstacles to be negotiated, and the counselor and client will therefore need certain road signs or markers to steer them to their destination. The primary intent of this chapter is to help them know what signs to look for, how to read them, and how to use the resulting information.

INTRODUCTION

Organization

The principal content of this chapter is divided into seven major sections. The first two sections describe the purposes and general nature of evaluation in counseling. The third specifies in detail the various steps in the process of evaluating client performance. The fourth section describes the process of terminating counseling contact with a client. The fifth section is concerned with rationale and techniques for monitoring client progress after counseling has terminated. The sixth section describes the process of closing the case. The final section is devoted to evaluation of the counselor's own performance.

Purposes

The general purposes of the chapter are (a) to help you understand the rationale for evaluation in counseling, and (b) to provide a model procedure for conducting the evaluation process, including techniques for terminating contact with a client and for closing the case.

Objectives

Upon reading this chapter it is expected that you will be equipped to do the following:

1. List and explain the major purposes of evaluation in counseling.
2. Name the steps in the systematic approach to evaluating client performance.
3. Trace on the flowchart model for Systematic Counseling the steps involved in evaluating client performance, including the possible need for recycling.
4. State the sequence of steps involved in terminating regular counseling contact with a client.
5. State the causes of client and counselor resistance to termination, and propose a method for dealing with each.
6. Name and describe the two activities involved in transfer of learning.
7. List four ways in which the counselor can monitor client performance.
8. Describe the procedure for closing a case.
9. Explain the importance of evaluating counselor performance.
10. Name three sources of evaluation of counselor performance.

PURPOSES OF EVALUATION

There are two main reasons why counseling should be evaluated: (a) to determine client progress, and (b) to improve the counselor's effectiveness in dealing with future clients, or in further counseling activities with the present client. The counselor may also engage in formal or informal research studies to evaluate various aspects of counseling, although this is not our primary concern here.

The intent of Systematic Counseling is to enable the client to achieve the mutually agreed-upon objective stated in Function 6.4. On the way to the achievement of that objective, it is also necessary to accomplish any intermediate objectives determined in Function 7.2. Although the specific counseling strategy and accompanying steps have been completed and verified in Function 7.5, we cannot assume that the objective has been accomplished. A *systematic* review of the results of the client's performance must be conducted, including an analysis of outcomes, a decision as to whether the objective has been attained, and a decision concerning the need for additional counseling. Only after the decision is made that no further counseling is appropriate may the counselor proceed to the next subsystem, TERMINATE COUNSELING (9.0).

While the intent of counseling is to change client behavior, it is also necessary that the behavior of the counselor be examined. The counselor's behavior is one of the main instrumentalities through which client behavior is changed. The counselor must ask such questions as: Did I help the client achieve the stated objective? Did I help the client achieve the objective as efficiently as possible? What have I learned from working with this client that will help me serve future clients more effectively? It is this feedback that makes the Systematic Counseling paradigm a "closed-loop" model, i.e., what is learned about the counseling process is fed back to the counselor as a self-correcting measure to improve counseling with other clients.

NATURE OF EVALUATION

As indicated previously, the focus of evaluation in Systematic Counseling is upon client *behavior*—what the client actually does as a result of counseling. It is not upon client feelings, attitudes, or self-concept, except as these may be affected by modifications in the behavior of the client. In more traditional approaches to counseling, evaluation is often ignored completely or is based upon whether or not the client verbalizes insight into the problem. In Systematic Counseling, however, the strategy is to help the client develop more adaptive behaviors. Engaging in these behaviors may in turn lead to client insight, changes in feelings, attitudes, self-concept, and the like, but the behaviors represent the starting point for change.

A second important aspect of the evaluation process is the matter of timing. When should evaluation occur? In a sense, evaluation is a continuous process, occurring on a moment-to-moment basis throughout counseling. Everything that occurs in counseling—each counselor lead, each client response, each counselor hypothesis—should be examined in light of the overall goal for counseling. More specifically, however, careful attention should be given to the evaluation of the accomplish-ment of *intermediate* objectives as established in Function 7.2, since these objectives are preliminary steps to the accomplishment of the learning objective. Next, and most important, it is necessary to evaluate the accomplishment of the learning objective itself, as provided in Func-tion 8.2. If further counseling on the same concern or on another concern is indicated, it is then, of course, necessary to recycle and conduct the evaluation sequence again until no further counseling is appropriate. Finally, after monitoring the client's postcounseling performance and closing the case, it is necessary that the counselor evaluate his or her own performance as provided in Subsystem 12.0.

A further aspect of evaluation in Systematic Counseling is the need for external verification of what the client has learned in counseling. The true test of counseling effectiveness is what the client does *outside* the in-terview or after counseling rather than what has been done while counsel-ing is in progress. Thus, the client may report having studied more and having received higher marks on assignments, in accordance with the learning objective. However, the counselor will need to check with the client's parents and teachers before concluding definitely that the client's behavior outside the interview has improved. This, of course, should be done with the client's prior knowledge and consent. Often the client whose goal is to improve interpersonal relations with friends, teachers, or parents will perform well in a role-playing episode with the counselor in which the immediate objective is to learn skills in meeting and getting along with other people. Here again, however, the counselor will need to determine from outside sources whether the client's behavior has in fact changed in the real-life situation.

STEPS IN EVALUATION

The formal evaluation process should be conducted in the sequence in-dicated on the flowchart for Systematic Counseling, as shown in Figure 11-1. It will be noted that client performance is evaluated in Subsystem 8.0, and that counselor performance is evaluated in Subsystem 12.0, after the case has been closed.

Following the completion of the strategy and related steps as deter-mined in Function 7.5, the signal path leads to the next subsystem, EVALUATE CLIENT PERFORMANCE (8.0), and specifically to RECORD PERFORMANCE (8.1.1). This function involves recording—perferably in writing—the client's present level of performance in coping with the concern.

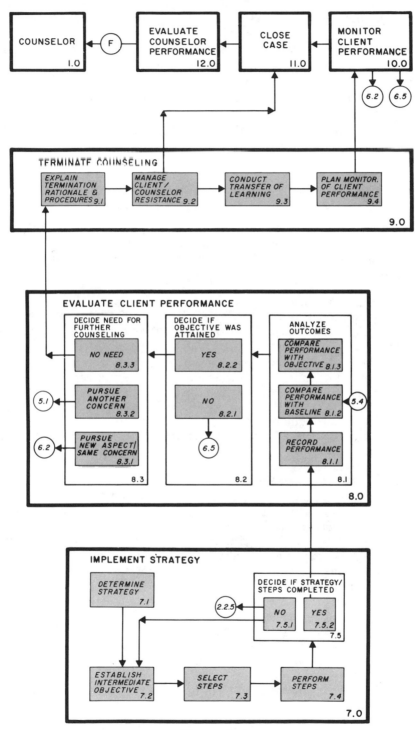

Figure 11-1

The next function, 8.1.2, is to compare the present level of performance with the baseline of concern-related behavior. This is an evaluation to determine whether any progress has been made toward remedying the difficulty or solving the problem with which the client desires help. If progress has been made, how much?

The counselor then moves to COMPARE PERFORMANCE WITH OBJECTIVE (8.1.3). This, of course, is the critical comparison. The client's current performance in the attempt to overcome the concern or problem is compared with the learning objective as established in 6.4. A YES or NO decision is then made as provided in 8.2.

If the decision in Function 8.2 is that the learning objective has been attained, it is then necessary to decide whether further counseling is needed (Function 8.3). Here, there are several alternative routes from which counselor and client must choose, as illustrated by the following examples:

1. Client A's objective has *not* been attained. Counselor and client therefore recycle to DECIDE IF CLIENT MOTIVATION IS SUF-FICIENT (6.5), and proceed through the counseling process again from that point forward.

2. Client B's objective has been attained, but the client desires further counseling on another aspect of the same general area of concern (8.3.1). In this case, counselor and client recycle to DETERMINE DESIRED GOAL (6.2). For example, if Client B has fulfilled the original objective by deciding to attend College X rather than College Y, further help may be desired in developing the skills necessary to make a favorable impression on the representative from College X who is due to visit the client's high school during the next two weeks.

3. Client C's objective has been attained, but the client desires counseling on a *new* area of concern substantially different from that of the original concern. In this case, counselor and client recycle to IDENTIFY CONCERNS (5.1) and proceed from that point forward. For example, Client C may have achieved the original objective of making a "B" average on courses for the current marking term, but may now desire help in establishing better social relationships with peers. This constitutes a switch from an academic to a personal-social concern, and therefore will require some basic exploration of the problem area before the formulation of a new learning objective is in order.

4. Client D's objective has been attained, and counselor and client agree that there is no further need whatsoever for counseling. The counselor then proceeds to terminate the counseling contact with Client D.

Using the recycling process described above, hopefully Clients A, B, and C will eventually reach the point at which Client D has arrived, i.e., they will have attained their learning objective (or will have found that it cannot be attained after repeated efforts). At that point, termination of the counseling contact is in order.

TERMINATING COUNSELING

The counselor must be concerned about efficiency as well as results. There is not enough time to continue to talk on a regular basis with a client after the job is done, since there are other clients who are also entitled to the counselor's time and help.

The process of terminating counseling may vary somewhat, depending upon the circumstances of the case. For referrals which are judged inappropriate, and for cases already in progress where it becomes clear that further counseling is impossible or inadvisable, the counselor tries to help the client find appropriate assistance (Function 2.2.5) and then proceeds to terminate counseling. Under these conditions, termination involves only EXPLAIN TERMINATION RATIONALE AND PROCEDURES (9.1) and possibly MANAGE CLIENT/COUNSELOR RESISTANCE (9.2), after which the case is closed (11.0).

More commonly, however, the occasion for termination is that the learning objective(s) have been accomplished and the decision therefore made that no further counseling is necessary. In such cases the process of terminating counseling includes two additional functions: CONDUCT TRANSFER OF LEARNING (9.3) and PLAN MONITORING OF CLIENT PERFORMANCE (9.4).

Explaining Termination Rationale and Procedures

The counselor begins the process of terminating counseling by explaining that since the objectives, if any, have been attained—or cannot be attained, as the case may be—it is appropriate to conclude regular counseling contacts. If appropriate, the counselor also explains to the client that in this concluding session they will be talking about how to apply the kinds of things learned in the counseling process to other problems which may arise, and that they will be setting up a plan for checking on the client's progress after concluding regular counseling. Of course, the counselor's explanation of the termination rationale is presented in a matter-of-fact manner. The counselor avoids any implication of rejecting the client, even if frustrated by the client's failure to decide upon or accomplish an objective for counseling. In such cases it is quite possible that the client will return committed to change if the door is left open. For example, a counselor might introduce the termination of contact as follows:

> CO: Well, Jack, now that you've raised your average grade to a B minus for the six-week period, we've almost completed our counseling.
>
> CL: Yeah . . . I figured we had.
>
> CO: Before you leave today, though, we'll be talking about what you've learned in counseling and how you can apply it to other problems you may run into. Also, we'll be setting up a plan for checking on your progress from time to time to see how your grades are coming along.

Managing Resistance

Client resistance.   Some clients, particularly those with whom a very close relationship has been developed, will indicate a desire to continue formal counseling contacts when the counselor structures termination. Resistance to termination stems from a feeling of dependency in the client's relationship to the counselor. Manifestations of resistance to termination due to dependency may include: (a) the client's saying there are other things that need to be discussed without being able to indicate other significant areas of concern; (b) asking the counselor if they can continue to "be friends" and do things socially; (c) asking if it is all right to call the counselor on the telephone; or (d) showing distress or hesitance at the prospect of discontinuing regular contacts with the counselor. In any case, the counselor recognizes and deals with these feelings with the client. Through discussing the client's dependency feelings, the counselor indicates an understanding of how the client feels but communicates the belief that the client is now able to function without the counselor's help. Continuing with the above hypothetical case, the counselor might respond as follows:

> CL: Could I drop in and see you every once in a while?
>
> CO: You mean, when we have check-up sessions to see whether your grades are holding up?
>
> CL: Well . . . I don't know . . . just to talk, I guess.
>
> CO: It seems that you feel you need to continue to talk, even though you don't have any additional concerns.
>
> CL: Well, I've sort of enjoyed talking to you. You're the only one here at school who really knows me . . . and that I feel I can talk to.
>
> CO: Well, Jack, I've been glad to be able to help you. And of course we'll get together briefly a few times to see how your grades are

coming along, but except for that it looks like you have your problem worked out.

CL: Yeah, I guess there's really nothing else I need help on. I should be able to make it all right.

CO: I believe you can, too, Jack. Of course, if somethings else comes up and you really feel you need help on it, I'll always be glad to talk to you about it.

Counselor resistance. It is also possible, of course, that the *counselor* will show inappropriate resistance to terminating contact with a particular client. This reaction may reflect the fact that the counselor finds the client's presence and behavior unusually reinforcing and is therefore reluctant to terminate that source of reinforcement. The client, perhaps less sophisticated than the counselor, may be unaware of what is happening and therefore become an unwitting ally in the prolongation of counseling. In the unfortunate event that counselor and client have become dependent upon each other, counseling degenerates into little more than a social relationship. It therefore behooves the counselor as a responsible professional to be alert for signs that counseling is being unduly prolonged, regardless of the cause, and to take the necessary steps to terminate contact without further delay.

Conducting Transfer of Learning

The next function the counselor is concerned with in the regular counseling process is conducting transfer of learning. In a sense, the counselor's ultimate goal in working with any client is to "work oneself out of a job," i.e., to equip the client with techniques and skills that have transfer value and which will therefore help in the handling of future concerns in relatively independent fashion, with minimal help from others. However, the fact that counseling has transfer value may not be realized by the client unless it is specifically pointed out. In conducting transfer of learning, the counselor discusses with the client how the client can (a) apply the behaviors learned in counseling to other situations and concerns, and (b) obtain reinforcement from other situations or people in one's environment from utilization of these new behaviors.

The client will probably need coaching to realize how the newly acquired skills or behaviors are applicable to other situations and how to utilize them to best advantage. However, the counselor can usually get the process started by giving an example or two. For instance, if the client has been working on improving a relationship with a teacher, the counselor might briefly help in examining how similar behaviors might improve relationships with parents, and the increased satisfactions this would bring. The purpose of this procedure is to provide for maximum transfer of learning from the counseling situation to the client's usual everyday situation, the real purpose of counseling. The counselor might therefore continue as follows:

> CO: Suppose you run up against another problem where you have to make a choice among alternatives, Jack. Can you see any way that you might apply what you have learned in our sessions to such a problem?
>
> CL: Maybe I could come back for more counseling.
>
> CO: That would be possible, but I was thinking more of things that you could do on your own. Remember when you first came in, we started out by trying to define very specifically just what it was that you were concerned about. After that we located some relevant information, and then we considered several alternative ways of dealing with the problem. We finally settled upon one of these strategies by looking at the advantages and disadvantages of each. So maybe if you run into another problem, you can apply some of these same techniques. See what I mean?
>
> CL: Yeah, I think so. I guess a lot of problems could be approached in that way.
>
> CO: That's right. The same basic principles would apply. And I suspect it would make you feel pretty good to solve such a problem on your own.
>
> CL: Yeah, I suppose it would.

Defining the problem carefully, locating relevant information, considering alternatives, developing specific objectives, participating in simulation exercises, following through on plans—all of these techniques have transfer value to other concerns. Conveying this relationship to the client is a very important aspect of good counseling.

Planning To Monitor Client Performance

It has been said that the road to perdition is paved with good intentions. Perhaps all clients who have attained their counseling objectives believe they will maintain their performance after regular counseling has terminated. The fact remains, however, that in some cases clients do not maintain their improved performance, but rather revert to their old, ineffectual behaviors. There are many possible causes, of course. Some clients may not be able to sustain the necessary motivation, while others may encounter unforeseen difficulties which they cannot handle without further help. It is therefore advisable, at least in most cases, for counselor and client to establish a plan for following up or monitoring the client's performance for a period of time after formal counseling has terminated.

This is accomplished in Function 9.4, PLAN MONITORING OF CLIENT PERFORMANCE.

It is conceivable, however, that in some instances it will not be appropriate to monitor client performance, and therefore that plans for monitoring should not be made. If, for example, the client's objective has been to make a choice between two courses of study, and the choice has been made and implemented, there may be no need for follow-up. In such cases, after conducting transfer of learning, counselor and client can move directly to Subsystem 11.0 and close out the case. Typically, however, follow-up will be appropriate and plans must therefore be made.

Where monitoring is considered appropriate, it is important that the client be informed of the fact that progress will be monitored, and that the client understand the manner in which it will be conducted. This knowledge may in itself provide a strong incentive for continued progress, since for most clients the counselor's interest and attention are powerful reinforcers.

One of the first considerations to be resolved is the exact nature of the follow-up activity. In most cases, brief check-up interviews with the client will be the best means of monitoring progress. On the other hand, if the client's progress can be readily ascertained through examination of records or through reports from others, it may not be necessary for the counselor to have check-up interviews with the client. Instead, the counselor may simply examine attendance records and written grade reports or ask teachers how the client is progressing. Then, at the end of the follow-up period, assuming client progress has been satisfactory, the counselor may simply make an appropriate notation in the files and discontinue the monitoring process. If such indicators suggest the need for additional client contact, however, the counselor will contact the client and offer further assistance.

Assuming that check-up interviews are deemed necessary, several considerations must be taken into account. First, the length of the follow-up period must be decided upon. This may be determined in part by the nature of the problem and the setting in which the counselor is employed. In a school situation, for example, if the client has met an objective of raising a grade to a certain level at the end of the current marking period, the follow-up period may be designated as the remainder of the semester, or perhaps the rest of the school year. The length of the follow-up period will also depend in part on the counselor's judgment of the client's ability to sustain the improved performance over time. For clients who are highly motivated or who are working on comparatively discrete and uncomplicated behaviors, a brief follow-up period may be sufficient. For those who have less motivation or who are trying to sustain a complex pattern of newly acquired behaviors, more feedback and encouragement may be needed. Consequently, a longer period of time may be necessary for appropriate monitoring.

The frequency of check-up interviews is another factor to be considered. In rare instances, it may be advisable to have check-up sessions every day, as when the client is trying to eliminate severely disruptive or aggressive classroom behaviors. In other cases, weekly or monthly checkups may be sufficient. As in choosing the overall length of the follow-up period, the frequency of checkups should be determined with due consideration for the client's ability to proceed in relatively independent fashion, as opposed to the need for more immediate feedback and reinforcement.

A related consideration is the amount of time to be devoted to each interview. In most cases, five minutes will perhaps be suffiicient, with the understanding that more time may be allotted if necessary. For example:

CO: Jack, even though you have met your objective and raised your grade point average to a B minus, I wonder if we should perhaps set up a plan for keeping tabs on your progress for a while.

CL: I don't know. . . . What kind of plan?

CO: Well, maybe we could get together for about five minutes right after you receive your mid-term marks, and then maybe at the end of the next report period. If your grades are holding up well and your study habits are okay, you could just tell me so and we wouldn't need to do anything else. But if you've run into trouble, maybe we could try to pinpoint the difficulty and work on whatever is needed to get your grades back up to par. Then, if all goes well, maybe for the rest of the year I could just look at your record at the end of each report period to see how you're doing. How does that sound?

CL: Okay, I suppose. It might help to keep me on my toes a little more if I knew I had to report to someone about it.

CO: Okay, Jack, let's plan to do that, then. Let's see, when will you have the results of your next mid-term tests?

CL: Oh . . . by about the middle of February, I think.

CO: Okay, why don't we say, then, that you'll come in to see me for your first check-up on February 20th at 9:00 a.m., okay? I'll send you a reminder notice the day before.

CL: Sounds all right to me . . . but suppose I begin to run into trouble with some of my classes before that.

CO: In that case, just let me know, and we'll get together as soon as possible. But I have a feeling you'll be able to handle it until then.

CL: Yeah, I think I will, too.

MONITORING CLIENT PERFORMANCE

An important aspect of the overall evaluation process is the counselor's followup of client progress. As Krumboltz (1968, p. 16) has observed, "The test of counseling is what people can do after they leave counseling, not what they do during counseling." It is therefore desirable to monitor postcounseling behavior to see whether or not the client follows through on the counseling objective, and for how long. The likelihood that one will follow through, of course, is substantially increased by the knowledge that one's performance is being monitored by a counselor whose interest and attention are valued.

The client's objective for counseling often represents a relatively short-term goal, such as passing all courses at the end of the current marking period, indicating a tentative choice between occupations, obtaining a job, or establishing a friendly relationship with a member of the opposite sex. It is conceivable that the client may accomplish such an objective while counseling is in progress, but may then lapse into an earlier mode of behavior after counseling has terminated. While it is perhaps unrealistic to expect a client *never* to have the same problem again, it seems reasonable that the effects of counseling should last beyond the immediate situation. This is particularly to be expected if the counselor has done a good job in CONDUCT TRANSFER OF LEARNING (Function 9.3), since it is here that the client learns how to apply the learnings acquired in counseling to future problem situations, whether of the kind which originally led to the counseling contact or not.

There are four main ways in which the counselor can monitor client progress. First, the client's postcounseling behavior can be observed, as in the halls or on the school grounds. Second, the client can be asked for a progress report from time to time, as in the check-up interviews previously mentioned. Third, information can be requested from others in the client's environment, including teachers, parents, and peers. And fourth, an examination can be made of attendance records, grade reports, and other written data compiled since the termination of counseling.

If the client encounters difficulty, it may be necessary to reinstitute formal counseling. Where lack of client motivation appears to be the cause, the counselor should recycle to DECIDE IF CLIENT MOTIVATION IS SUFFICIENT (Function 6.5). However, if the client appears to need help on a different aspect of the same general concern, it is necessary to recycle to DETERMINE DESIRED GOAL (Function 6.2) and proceed again through the counseling process from that point forward.

When a client falters, it is difficult to judge whether the lack of persistence is due to inadequate counseling or to some other cause. Two problems are seldom identical, and the client is subject to many intervening circumstances and influences, some of which may be incompatible with the continued achievement of earlier counseling goals. Regardless of the reason, if the client should fail to follow through on the goals of counseling, the counselor should make contact again and offer further assistance. The client's participation in such additional counseling is, of course, voluntary.

CLOSING THE CASE

As in terminating formal counseling, the procedure for closing the case may vary somewhat, depending upon the prior course of events. In some cases, the usual counseling process will have been "short-circuited." For example, the referral may have been judged inappropriate. Or the process of counseling may have broken down at some point along the way, as when the client repeatedly demonstrates lack of motivation to continue. In such cases, the counselor will first help the client locate appropriate assistance and will conduct the applicable portions of Subsystem 9.0, TERMINATE COUNSELING. The counselor may then initiate the process of closing the case by expressing pleasure at having talked with the client and by offering an invitation to return for further counseling if the need should arise.

More commonly, however, the process of closing the case will follow the monitoring of the client's postcounseling performance. Where follow-up interviews are involved, the counselor can explain in the last of these interviews that, since progress has been satisfactory, there is no need for further checkups. Where follow-up interviews are not involved, as when the counselor has, by prior agreement with the client, relied solely upon attendance records or grade reports and found that the client has maintained satisfactory performance, the closing of the case may be initiated by simply making an appropriate note in the files and then discontinuing the monitoring process. Or the counselor may contact the client, report the favorable findings, and state that no further followup is necessary.

Regardless of the route by which the case is closed, there are several things which should be done before the case is terminated. The counselor will usually express pleasure at having worked with the client and will invite the client to return for further counseling if the need should arise. For example:

CO: Well, Jack, since you've maintained a B minus average throughout the remainder of the semester, it looks as though it won't be necessary for us to talk about this anymore.

CL: Yeah, I guess that's right.

CO: I've really enjoyed working with you, though, and I'm confident you'll be able to handle this on your own now. However, if you do have trouble on this or any other concern in the future, I want you to feel free to come and see me about it. And, of course, I'm sure we'll bump into each other in the hall every once in a while.

CL: Thanks. I've really appreciated your help.

CO: Glad I could be of assistance, Jack. Goodbye now.

CL: Goodbye.

It is conceivable, of course, that counselor or client will show inappropriate resistance to closing the case. Here, as mentioned in the earlier discussion of MANAGE CLIENT/COUNSELOR RESISTANCE (9.2), the counselor must take steps to resolve the resistance and to close without further delay.

After taking leave of the client, the counselor will, as a matter of routine, complete the interview notes for the case. In addition, a concise summary of contacts with the client should be prepared for purposes of accountability. Such records, compiled on a number of cases over a specified time period, can then be used as one means of evaluating counselor performance. The information should include client identification data, a description of the problem presented, a detailed record of time expenditure, and a statement of outcomes. An example of such a record is given in the case of Juanita in Chapter 13.

EVALUATING COUNSELOR PERFORMANCE

As noted earlier, the immediate criterion for successful counselor performance is whether or not the client achieves the mutually agreed-upon objective(s) for counseling. Taken alone, however, this measure does relatively little to *improve* the counselor's performance with subsequent clients. It is conceivable that, given a cooperative and long-suffering client, almost any counselor—using almost any technique—can eventually effect the desired change in the client's behavior. However, the counselor is a busy person. One must be concerned with economy and efficiency as well as results. The counselor must therefore ponder such additional considerations as: (a) Did I help the client achieve the objective as quickly as possible? (b) Did I use the most effective strategy (e.g., learning new responses, or motivating behavior change) in working with this client on this particular problem? (c) Could this client have been served more efficiently by an available referral source? (d) Were my specific counseling techniques appropriate for this client? (e) Did I adhere to the flowchart model for Systematic Counseling? If I deviated, were my deviations justified? In short, what have I learned from working with this client that will help me serve similar clients with similar problems under similar conditions in the future?

The counselor may receive feedback from three main sources: the client, the counselor's own experience, and qualified others such as fellow counselors, on-the-job supervisors, and counselor educators who have observed the counselor's performance. Quite obviously, the client as the person who has the most immediate stake in the counselor's performance, is especially qualified to provide valuable feedback. The client knows better than anyone else how the counselor's techniques were perceived, whether the counselor's explanation of the counseling relationship was understood, whether the tasks assigned were manageable, whether the client would be willing to return to the counselor for help on further problems, and so on. At opportune times during or after an interview, or upon completion of the case, the counselor can seek such information from the client through direct questioning or through questionnaires devised for that purpose. Thus, the expressed reactions of the client provide an index of consumer satisfaction, an important factor in the continued success of any endeavor.

The counselor can also evaluate his or her own behavior. As suggested earlier, evaluation should be conducted on a moment-to-moment basis throughout the counseling process. The counselor should continually ask, "How am I doing with this client? Am I communicating accurately? Are we making progress? What can I do to help the client achieve the objective more effectively and efficiently?"

Aside from this continuing evaluation, after each interview the counselor should mentally complete the Performance Criteria for Systematic Counseling (see Appendix A). If, for example, counselor and client have reached VERIFY MODEL WITH CLIENT (5.6) by the end of the first interview, the counselor should review the critieria on the checklist up through that point and answer "Yes" (performance was adequate) or "No" (performance was not adequate) to each of the criterion questions. If an occasional interview has been audiotaped or videotaped, the tape can be played back and stopped at appropriate points to facilitate this type of self-evaluation.

After closing the case, the counselor should give some thought to what was done well with this particular client, what was done poorly, whether the most effective strategy was chosen, how techniques and procedures can be improved with the next client, and so on.

Depending upon job circumstances and the availability of technical equipment and facilities, it may also be possible for the counselor to enlist the help of others in the evaluation of his or her counseling. With the client's permission, fellow counselors or on-the-job supervisors can be asked to observe one's counseling by means of one-way vision facilities or videotape, or they can listen to audiotapes of selected interviews. Of course, if the counselor is in training, evaluation will be conducted by counselor educators. Again, such evaluations can be oriented around the flowchart for Systematic Counseling and the accompanying Performance Criteria.

Finally, as a counselor one should—and will—be held accountable to one's employer and to the public at large for the quality of one's performance, both in terms of counseling per se, and in terms of guidance activities more broadly defined. It is here that the summary of case data and time expenditure referred to earlier, complied over a number of cases, can be especially useful. Obviously, this type of evaluation will be more favorable to the counselor who has done an effective job of self-monitoring and has utilized the other evaluation resources that are available.

SUMMARY

This chapter has focused upon procedures and techniques necessary for the systematic evaluation of client and counselor performance. Also included were techniques for terminating formal counseling contact with a client and procedures for closing the case.

The major purposes of evaluation are to determine client progress and to improve counselor effectiveness. In Systematic Counseling, what is learned about the counseling process is fed back to the counselor, who then modifies procedures so that future clients can be served more effectively. The criterion for counseling effectiveness is client behavior—what the client does as a result of counseling. Although in a sense evaluation is a continuous process, special checkpoints are provided for the performance of major evaluation functions. The counselor should obtain external verification that the client has applied the learnings acquired in counseling.

The process of evaluation should be conducted as indicated on the flowchart for Systematic Counseling. The major steps in evaluating client performance include analyzing outcomes, determining whether the counseling objective has been attained, and deciding the need for further counseling. The counselor terminates formal counseling contact with a client by explaining the rationale and procedures for termination, dealing with resistance to termination, conducting transfer of learning, and establishing plans to monitor the client's postcounseling performance. The counselor may monitor the progress of clients by observing their behavior, by talking with them, by talking with significant others in their environment, and by examining records and reports. Findings resulting from these follow-up activities may suggest the need for further counseling. After monitoring client progress, the counselor proceeds to close the case.

After closing the case, the counselor gives special attention to the evaluation of his or her own performance. This evaluation is accomplished through self-rating on the Performance Criteria for Systematic Counseling, through introspection, and through soliciting reactions to one's performance from the client and other observers such as fellow counselors and supervisors. Data concerning all cases handled over a specified time period may be used to evaluate the counselor's performance for purposes of accountability.

12

New Directions for
Systematic Counseling

OVERVIEW

Trainees and practitioners need both theoretical foundations upon which to base their work and functional models that help them to convert theory into daily practice. During the relatively short history of the counseling movement, much more attention has been given to theory development than to providing practical models to guide the daily work of the counselor.

Systematic Counseling provides a tested model for counseling practice that explicitly describes counselor actions during all phases of the counseling process. Presently, it is designed for one-to-one application. Several extensions of this basic approach are envisioned in order that counselors might serve a greater range of client needs through a greater variety of counseling modes.

INTRODUCTION

Organization

This chapter consists of two main sections. The first section discusses reasons for and resistances to the development of counseling systems. The second section presents basic principles for the Systematic Counseling model and suggests logical extensions of this pioneering effort.

Purposes

The overall purposes of this chapter are to: (a) present reasons why many models of the counseling process have not been developed, (b) introduce typical resistive comments encountered and answers that might be given, (c) discuss the principles upon which Systematic Counseling is based, and (d) describe some logical extensions of this basic model and discuss the relevance of each.

Objectives

Upon completing this chapter it is expected that you will be prepared to do the following:

1. State at least three reasons why more models for counseling have not been developed.
2. Distinguish between theories and models as they apply to counseling.
3. Describe why a system may be useful to a person who already relates well to others.
4. Explain why the use of a system is initially an unnatural act.
5. State how a counselor can use a system to meet the wide range of client needs encountered.
6. Specify cautions to observe in merging the best parts of existing systems.
7. Explain how a system can assist the creative person.
8. Describe how a person could begin to develop a counseling system.
9. Name the principal limitations of Systematic Counseling at the present time.
10. State at least three areas in which Systematic Counseling could be extended.

MODELS FOR COUNSELING

Counselors share basic, common goals regardless of their training or their work setting. Generally, counselors are deeply concerned about people. All are attempting to translate client statements about desired states of success, happiness or acceptance, knowledge of choices, successful decision making, and other worthy goals into some frame of common understanding. All counselors, in one way or another, seek to help clients change in ways that the clients have described as desirable. All experienced counselors know how difficult it is to engage concurrently in the acts of caring, listening, responding, and assisting a client in the change process. A model, a map, a blueprint of principal counselor tasks is needed both in order to learn the counseling process and to perform counseling with a variety of clients.

Few blueprints are now available. Most that have been published are either superficial or fragmentary. Some present the counseling process in broad sweeps without providing any indication of how the specific tasks of counseling are to be accomplished. Others are focused upon highly specific skills and fail to attend to the counseling process as a totality. It seems inconceivable that the act of counseling with its proliferation into so many areas of life could remain uncharted. Only in the last decade has this effort even been undertaken.

The distinction should be noted between models for utilizing theory and theory itself. Many theories of human development and/or psychological change—rational-emotive, gestalt, trait-factor, client-centered, and behavioral, among others—have been proposed and have received varying degrees of support. Each is an attempt to conceptualize why people behave as they do. Efforts to develop and support theory have been much more ambitious and are much better known than attempts to provide a means for utilizing theory. When we speak of models or blueprints, we are referring to models of case management that suggest how theory can be implemented by the counselor—whether in training or in practice. These models, therefore, are not suggested as a replacement for theory, but rather as a vehicle for translating theory into practice.

Why has the development of models or blueprints for counseling practice not been undertaken with rigor long ago? How can a helping profession be so *un*helpful in providing a basic vehicle for practice? No single response is sufficient. Several considerations must be explored before we can begin to formulate an answer.

1. *Counseling is a relatively new profession.* Although the seeds for the profession were sown during the early years of this century, there were few practicing counselors prior to World War II. The great proliferation of training programs, grants for counselor trainees, and support for the development of counseling within the public schools did not occur until the passage of NDEA legislation in 1958. Institutional and agency counseling experienced its greatest growth even more recently. The years that have passed since our profession's expansion are few indeed when compared with the centuries that have been given to the development of principles of physics and the decades of substantial funding given to the science of human medicine.

2. *Counselors lack a clear definition and expectation.* Despite the extensive study of the counselor's role, operational consensus has not emerged. The functions performed by a counselor are largely institutionally determined and are far less uniform from setting to setting than the tasks performed by a dentist, an elevator operator, a school

principal, or an accountant. Because the role is unclear, large-scale development of models to work with the most frequently occurring concerns of clients has not emerged.

3. *Counselor training is relatively brief.* Practitioners of architecture, dentistry, law, and medicine all have completed far more extensive training programs than have counselors. This training is based upon specific systems for approaching and handling problems. Each profession has had time to develop workable systems, test them, and revise them. Trainees gain extensive experience in using these systems during training and have confidence that they will work when the trainees complete their study and begin to apply the system learned to the problems of society. By way of contrast, most of us have only learned the scope of the problems that we might face by the end of our formal training in counseling and are not yet proficient in using skills learned in a systematic fashion.

4. *Some counselors have an unscientific attitude.* We are not arguing that counseling is all science and no art. The term "art of counseling" is appropriately used to describe the practices of counselors that seem to work, although we are not certain how often or why. If we are to build an accountable profession, we must begin with personal accountability for our acts in counseling. When we work with a client, we can keep accurate records of the practices we have used and the results obtained. When we see that a given practice is consistently helpful or unhelpful, the practice can be continued or altered. Through this means of personal accountability, we can gradually reduce the "art" and increase the "science" of counseling practice.

Each of the above factors contributes to our present status. We have had relatively little time to develop models. Models that have been developed are not used as effectively as they might be because of the variance in counselor role expectation from setting to setting and the comparatively brief training programs for counselors. The brevity of training has not allowed most counselors sufficient time to learn and practice upon a vehicle for counseling, with the result that professional habit patterns are not acquired and confidence for employment of the model in posttraining practice is not secured. Further, the unscientific attitude of some counselors results in piecemeal practice in which an unsystematic approach is used, the source of error is not located and reduced, and piecemeal results are predictable.

Resistance to a Counseling System

As you talk with others in your environment about your work in Systematic Counseling, you may encounter people who are resistive to learning a systematic approach. Knowing the reason for the resistance is important. We have heard some frequently recurring comments and present them here along with our response to them. Remember, as we stressed in Chapter 1, all counselors have a system for counseling, even those who systematically insist upon being unsystematic!

1. *I don't need a system. I can already relate to people.* Relating to the client is essential. Without skill in developing a relationship, the counselor's efforts in helping are severely hampered. Clients, on occasion, seek nothing more than someone to talk with and someone who is understanding. On many other occasions, however, relating is not enough. The client may express a desire to learn something that now seems impossible, to reduce or eliminate an addictive habit, or do better at some task. All of these goals are more likely to be reached if the counselor and client have a good relationship. Of the many counselor skills involved in their attainment, relating is but one.

2. *All my life I have tried to get away from systems. I certainly don't want to impose this sort of thinking upon a client.* As detailed in Chapter 2, the term "system" has a very negative connotation for some people. It certainly is possible to find examples of systems that have been developed for socially destructive purposes. But to accept this limited connotation of the term "system" is to ignore the elaborate systems that have been developed to assist people in the areas of education, psychology, psychiatry, and human medicine, among others. Were we to free ourselves of all systems, many of the most advanced and most humane aspects of our culture would no longer be available to us.

3. *The system is too mechanical. I feel like a machine and nothing seems natural or spontaneous.* This comment might be made by a new surgical intern, a recruit for the football team, a prospective actor, a flight pilot trainee, or a graduate student in counseling. Learning any system is, by definition, a change process. During the early stages of training, the learning task is taxing, repetitive, and unrewarding. When a golfer seeks help in driving from the club pro, suggestions may be made to change the position or movement of the feet, legs, hips, arms, and head. This may result in a very *un*natural feeling and may predictably result in worse initial results than before the pro was contacted. However, as each part of the body performs its function properly, increasingly less direct attention must be paid to it. When the golfer "has it all together," the others on the course may remark, "Look at that natural swing." The golfer knows otherwise! Counselors also must go through a phase of unnaturalness until all components of the counselor and of the counseling process are coordinated and practiced in consort. As each can be performed with increased ease, a more natural feeling returns.

4. *I'm too creative to be tied down to a system. It just wouldn't work for me.* A truly creative person without a system upon which to rely has a

problem. Without a foundation upon which to build, one may be unable to express the creativity meaningfully to others. Imagine a musical composer who was unaware that a scale was comprised of seven notes and chromatic intervals. Imagine an artist who didn't know that the elements of design were governed by the principles of harmony, contrast, and proportion. The musical scale and the elements of design are the foundations for the elaborate systems within which musical composers and artists work. From early, cumbersome efforts in using their systems, they become increasingly able to perform the routine quickly and become more expressive in shading and fine artistic adjustment. Similarly, creative counselors who routinely employ a system can use creativity in adjusting the system to meet the needs of the individual client and thus become more effective practitioners.

5. *My clients aren't all the same, so I can't use a system for counseling. I have to invent a way to work with each client who comes in.* Many counselors are very taxed in meeting the wide variety of needs presented by their clients. However varied the clientele, some predictable concerns are invariably reported by several clients. Each of us must carefully consider how to best assist clients having the most predictable, or most frequently occurring, concerns. This is the beginning of a counseling system. If the system can be designed flexibly so that an increased variety of concerns can be handled through its use, the system will be more functional. Systematic Counseling, for example, includes a process for handling referrals, constructing a model of the client concerns, and deciding upon goals and objectives for counseling that is generally applicable to all clients, but provides for many different strategies that might be used with specific client concerns. When a counselor is faced with a new concern that is reported by several clients, the counselor is encouraged to develop a subsystem for coping with this concern. Once this subsystem has been devised, tested, and revised, the counselor has a reliable source of assistance rather than continually "flying by the seat of the pants."

6. *I don't use any one system. I use the best parts of several systems.* Most new systems are based upon the most effective parts of existing systems, so the statement may represent a common practice. Two concerns are worthy of exploration: (a) Have the best components of several systems been integrated into a unified whole? and (b) Are the best parts of several systems adequate, or do some new parts need to be invented because none now exist that meet the designer's need? If one could find existing parts that met all demands of the proposed system, no invention would be necessary and the parts could be integrated and used. But what if no "relationship" component were available? Both questions raised must be satisfactorily answered before a system is in workable form.

7. *I have my own system and it works.* Great! Systematic Counseling is one example of a system that has been developed, tested, and revised. However, there may be many other examples. Any counselor who has developed a system that works reliably and produces effective results has reason to be proud of the accomplishment. Hopefully, the system is in written form so that others might learn about the system and determine whether or not it would meet their needs also.

It is quite understandable that misconceptions would exist concerning the use of systems in counseling. The comparative newness of the idea alone assures that some skepticism would exist. If any of us had only a partial understanding of the system's purpose, we would tend to remain skeptical until we knew more. If our initial attempts were awkward and unrewarding, we would have added reason to doubt the utility of the idea.

An unvoiced reason for doubt needs to be considered. If we examined the system, compared it with the needs of the clientele we serve, and found the two at variance, we would not want to employ the system. However, systems are created by and for humans. Perhaps the system can be changed. Systems continually change in order to survive. Perhaps we can find a means for making the system flexible enough to meet our demands. In so doing, we must exercise care that we are not confusing the flexibility of the system with our own flexibility in using it.

A Basis for Creativity

Counseling is a creative act. Each client presents a new challenge because each client has a somewhat different background and voices somewhat different needs and desires. How, then, can we talk of a single system that will work with all clients? Doesn't a counselor need to have all possible options available in order to be of maximum assistance to the client? Of course. But having all options available and being able to use all options are quite separate matters. It is our contention that, in training and in practice, counselors need a structural map to assist them because so many processes are going on concurrently. The more specific the map, the better the base from which the counselor can operate.

Counselors are not alone in needing to have a systematic process in the forefront of their minds as they go about their tasks. Stravinsky, the noted musical composer, discussed the frustration he initially experienced when undertaking a new composition. The complete freedom afforded the composer terrorized him and he needed to retreat to a systematic means of considering how to go about his task. When this was arranged, he felt his freedom was increased:

> And yet which of us has ever heard talk of art as other than a realm of freedom? This sort of heresy is uniformly widespread because it is

imagined that art is outside the bounds of ordinary activity. Well, in art as in everything else, one can build only upon a resisting foundation: whatever constantly gives way to pressure constantly renders movement impossible. . . . My freedom will be so much the greater and more meaningful the more narrowly I limit my field of action and the more I surround myself with obstacles. Whatever diminishes constraint diminishes strength. The more constraints one imposes, the more one frees one's self of the chains that shackle the spirit. (Stravinsky, 1947, pp. 64-65)

The obstacles and constraints of which Stravinsky spoke were self-imposed. Stravinsky found that he could be creative only when he knew the boundaries within which he had to operate. In somewhat different language, the counselor has obstacles, constraints, and boundaries that must be carefully observed if the counselor is to be truly creative in working with the client. These boundaries might include the counselor's knowledge within a given area, predictable consequences of a given course of action, the usual principles of human development, and the basic laws of human behavior. All provide limits within which the counselor must operate. Only in knowing these limits and building from them can the counselor be creative.

Another aspect of creativity, counseling, and constraint is illustrated when we consider the process of learning to manage a complex system. When we begin to employ a system in counseling, the details of work are overwhelming. As we become experienced in using a system, many details of operation are more skillfully mastered and more attention can be given to the more subtle aspects of working with a client. Finally, when we are thoroughly experienced in using a system, standard procedures are performed with relative ease and most of our attention can be turned to the most subtle of nuances and the most hidden of indicators. Using a system allows us to be much more creative then would be possible unless some means for organizing complex processes were available.

A SYSTEM FOR COUNSELING

The Systematic Counseling model is the first known attempt to specify the tasks performed by the counselor at each stage of the counseling process. It covers all stages of this process from the counselor's reviewing a referral to the closing of the counseling case and the evaluation of the counselor's performance in handling it.

This system was designed to provide a rational guide for both counselor training and counseling practice. The model has been tested through the work of some 700 counseling trainees with nearly 3500 clients over an eight-year period. Clients served have been from elementary and secondary schools; community colleges, four-year institutions, and universities; social agencies, rehabilitation agencies, employment offices, correctional institutions, and homes for delinquent youth; shelter homes, half-way houses, and addictive habit centers. The range of concerns expressed has been great, but within any one subpopulation some concerns have always emerged as being common to many within that group.

Can one system work effectively with such a wide range of clients and concerns? As previously stated, it can if both the system and the counselor are flexible. By this we mean that the system is capable of accommodating a wide range of concerns, and the counselor is skilled in using the system and knows how to make the system accommodate the concern expressed.

Principles of Systematic Counseling

Our acceptance of any system is premised upon our understanding of its intent. If we are to consider Systematic Counseling as a viable system for a given setting, we need to know some of the principles upon which it is based. These principles have been presented throughout the previous chapters, but are placed here in abbreviated form for further consideration. Each principle represents a condition that we believe must exist if counseling is to be effective. Following the statement of the principle in each instance we have provided some supplementary comments that explain or support its intent. The principles are:

1. *Counseling is a voluntary act.* Neither the client nor the counselor should be compelled to continue a counseling relationship that is uncomfortable or unprofitable. Some institutions and agencies, because of the nature of their clientele, make counseling mandatory. When this practice is essential, all should be alert to any accommodation that could be made in order to make the counseling process both comfortable and profitable for client and counselor.

2. *Understanding the basis for client concerns is essential.* The counselor, in processing information provided by the client, focuses upon both affective and cognitive components. In so doing, emphasis is placed upon precision of understandings (i.e., when, where, how often, for how long, etc.). The counselor's preception of this understanding is verbally communicated to the client and then verified by the client through communication with the counselor. Without this understanding, little can be accomplished.

3. *Counseling is goal-oriented.* Both client and counselor share in setting the goals for counseling. Usually only one goal is attempted at a

time, but a series of goals may be attempted ultimately. Success in attaining one goal provides reinforcement for attempting other goals. When goals have been reached, counseling is terminated.

4. *Counseling is a learning process.* When considering how best to help a client in attaining a goal, the principles of learning are useful. Emphasis upon developing skill hierarchies and repetitive practice is essential. Principles of learning that are useful in counseling include reinforcement, extinction, modeling, simulation, and feedback, among others.

5. *Any ethical means can be used to assist the client in the learning process.* Resources in addition to the counselor are spouses, peers, parents, and teachers as well as any means of using technology for prompting, cueing, modeling, and providing feedback.

6. *All counselors have models or patterns that they use.* Many models, however, are superficial or are focused upon only a part of the counseling process. Systematic Counseling presents a logical sequence of counselor actions. It is flexible in that a wide range of concerns can be handled by counselors using it and counselors can continually add new subsystems to meet expanded needs.

7. *The counseling interview is only a "testing ground" for the use of newly learned behavior.* It is important that a client "try on" new behaviors in a safe setting and receive encouragement from the counselor concerning client performance. However, both client and counselor must remember that they are working to develop skills that can be transferred to the client's natural environment—the home, the place of work, the recreation center, the school, the street.

8. *The counselor has a responsibility for monitoring client postinterview behavior.* The effectiveness of counseling cannot be determined unless some form of record-keeping is devised that provides data concerning client behavior in the natural setting. This monitoring is designed to determine whether transfer of learning has indeed taken place and to allow the counselor the opportunity for providing brief assistance to the client if the transfer is less than desirable.

9. *Systematic Counseling is a self-corrective process.* A counselor using this process not only maintains records concerning client behavior, but also develops a means of determining whether or not the counselor is being effective. Client report, comments from fellow professionals and supervisors, and the counselor's self-assessment all are important sources of information. From this information the counselor can determine which practices and procedures have been effective with which clients. This information then can be used to select or design procedures for working with future clients more effectively.

From these principles we can note an emphasis upon client involvement in all phases of the counseling process. The client determines whether or not to participate in counseling, decides the goals to be sought through counseling, and is responsible for carrying the learning from the counseling setting into the natural environment. The counselor shares the responsibility for setting meaningful goals, has an objective understanding of the client's concern, is the initiator of the learning process devised to reach the established goals, and is responsible for arranging a viable monitoring system to determine whether or not the skills have indeed transferred into the natural setting.

In presenting the Systematic Counseling model we stress the need for a close working relationship between the client and the counselor. Each has individual responsibilities, but both work together in setting meaningful goals and devising a strategy for reaching these goals. Openness on the part of both is essential.

Extensions of Systematic Counseling

When we talk of a system for counseling, we hope that the system will provide the counselor with a general blueprint for conducting the counseling process, yet contain sufficient flexibility so that a wide range of concerns may be handled by a counselor proficient in its use. We believe that Systematic Counseling is one example of such a blueprint for practice. What, you may ask, are its limitations? Is it applicable for working with all clients in all settings? Hardly. This is the first known attempt to create a coherent printed model of the entire counseling process, and it is useful only insofar as counselors are able to make adaptations of it to fit the requirements and limitations of their own working environments.

Some adaptations can be made rather easily. Those of you who work with very young children, with institutionalized adults, or with specialized client populations (e.g., overweight people, alcoholics) can make adaptations in language, presentation, expectation, and focus that would be more relevant for your clients. This may include developing specific subsystems and adding functions that would tailor the system to the clientele you serve.

Other adaptations are less easily accomplished, but are necessary for providing the wider range of intervention strategies that are needed by the practicing counselor. Admittedly, our efforts to date have been to conceptualize, test, and revise a workable process for one-to-one intervention. This remains the cornerstone for all change processes. With the development of this cornerstone, however, the same basic steps used in the design of the Systematic Counseling model for individual intervention can be extended as models for other spheres of counseling practice. Several will be presented and the relevance of each discussed.

1. *Environmental change.* In recent years much discussion has centered upon whether counselors should assist the individual to adjust to the environment or change the environment so that it accommodates the individual. Our Systematic Counseling process is directed toward helping the individual to adjust. But sometimes this is a less helpful counselor act than addressing the workings of the environment. The environment, the institution, or society may be making unfair demands upon the individual. Counselors on such occasions need a companion map to guide their efforts in bringing about changes in environments that negatively affect individuals.

2. *Group counseling.* Group counseling provides an important vehicle for assisting some clients. Individual counseling is less complex and is probably a better skill to learn first. But the practicing counselor finds many times when the group is a better medium for change than working with the individual alone. Because of its increased complexity, a model for group counseling would be more difficult to develop, but it is needed.

3. *Consulting.* Increasingly, counselors are working with teachers, work supervisors, parents, peers, and spouses to facilitate client change. While the counselor may be effective in counseling an individual worker, for example, it is relatively unlikely that this interaction, however successful, will have a "spill-over" effect upon other workers. Such is not the case with consulting. If the supervisor or teacher could alter performance conditions, decrease learner anxiety, or set more specific learning goals, many learners would benefit and this alteration could be perpetuated by the supervisor or teacher across several years. Our existing models of consulting need to be developed into a more coherent system for meeting consulting needs so that the practicing counselor has a map to follow in working with others in the environment such as work supervisors and teachers.

4. *Family therapy.* In recent years much attention has been given to working with all family members rather than the individual. This is a demanding task. In addition to proficiency in individual intervention, the therapist must also be knowledgeable about child and adolescent development, be proficient in the use of group procedures, and have experience in marital counseling. Because of the many concurrent demands upon the therapist, a model for conducting family therapy would be a useful resource for beginning practice in this rapidly expanding area.

5. *Working with special populations.* We designed a system that we have found useful with the broad range of concerns expressed by people of many ages and educational levels. However, we recognize that counselors may be working with special populations that are outside the

range for which our system was primarily developed. We encounter counselors seeking to provide help and having only fragmentary models to draw upon as they work with severely neurotic adults, people with severe addictive habits, extremely young children, and individuals who are severely mentally retarded. Perhaps our system offers the beginnings for a model that might be useful for any and all of these counselors. Perhaps these counselors must start with a basic analysis of the process and goals confronting them and design a system that meets the needs of the clientele being served.

In each of the above instances we have worked too long without functional models. In each instance counselors can begin by assessing the most frequently occurring client needs within the client population they serve. A system can then be developed to address the most frequently reported needs of clients. As the system if refined, other client concerns can be considered for inclusion. Building a flexible system that can meet a variety of client needs is desirable. Our basic system, hopefully, can serve as a model for the development of other systems designed for some or all of the five "new frontiers" previously mentioned. From this pioneering effort, a wide range of "spin-off" models might emerge. This, we believe, would be a large step forward for the profession.

SUMMARY

Systems for counseling are in their infancy. Because of their newness we have an understandable reluctance to accept them. The system discussed throughout this text, Systematic Counseling, is not intended as a means of explaining human development or personality, but rather as a vehicle for case management to be used in conjunction with one of the existing theories of counseling.

During the eight years since its initial development, Systematic Counseling has undergone many revisions. Each revision contained fewer changes than its predecessor. This may be an indication of added stability that the system has acquired. However stable, the system as presented was intended for use only in individual counseling. We acknowledge the need for adaptations and extensions of this model to serve other client populations and to provide counseling and consulting assistance through other modes.

Finally, the model of Systematic Counseling, or any other system, is only a tool that can be used by a skillful counselor to improve the likelihood that the counselor will function in such a way that the client is helped. The test of successful counseling is really not what the counselor does or doesn't do; rather, it is whether or not the client is helped in the directions mutually agreed upon.

13

The Case of
Juanita

OVERVIEW

In earlier chapters you have been introduced to Systematic Counseling. The presentation has been necessarily didactic, since you were largely unfamiliar with the tools, techniques, and procedures of this approach. However, now that you are acquainted with the basic framework, it seems appropriate to put flesh on the skeleton and "bring it to life" by showing in detail how it can be applied to a complete case.

In chapter 8 the concept of *modeling* was described in detail. There it was shown that, under certain conditions, one of the most effective ways of learning is by observing a model. We believe that, in a book on counseling, the most effective kind of model is a transcript of a complete case, showing exactly what was said and done by both counselor and client. We hope the model case which follows will serve not only to illustrate and clarify what is meant by "Systematic Counseling," but that it will also prove useful in your own counseling practice.

INTRODUCTION

Organization

The main content of this chapter is organized in accordance with the flowchart for Systematic Counseling (see Endpapers). The initial section explains the format of the case and suggests how the case might be read to best advantage. The remainder of the chapter consists of a step-by-step presentation of the case itself, organized according to the subsystems and functions of the Systematic Counseling process.

Purposes

The main purposes of this chapter are (a) to illustrate and clarify the nature of the Systematic Counseling process, (b) to provide a model of the counseling process which readers may find helpful in their own counseling, and (c) to serve as a point of reference for specific aspects of the Systematic Counseling process.

Objectives

Upon reading this chapter, it is expected that you will be equipped to do the following:

1. Describe the process of receiving the referral and the manner in which the counselor prepares for the initial interview.

2. Name the four major content elements in the counselor's explanation of the counseling relationship.

3. Describe Juanita's major concern, including the response, temporal, and situational components, as well as the maintaining reinforcer.

4. Indicate how Juanita's learning objective met the three criteria for a sound behavioral objective.

5. Describe the combination of counseling strategies utilized to attain the learning objective.

6. Explain how teacher consultation was used in the case.

7. Describe how the counselor dealt with Juanita's resistance to termination of counseling.

8. Describe the plan followed in monitoring Juanita's performance after the termination of formal counseling.

9. List five kinds of data to be included in a case report for purposes of accountability.

10. State at least three strengths and three weaknesses in the counselor's conduct of the case.

JUANITA

This case is intended to provide a concrete illustration of Systematic Counseling. While the setting is a high school, the nature of the problem and the counseling techniques are also applicable to other school levels and to nonschool settings, e.g., rehabilitation agencies. The various steps in the counseling process with Juanita are coded and labeled in accordance with the flowchart for Systematic Counseling (see Endpapers).

The case consists of eight interviews. It is suggested that you read the first three interviews (pages 272-295) in their entirety. Interviews 4-7, which are concerned primarily with task performance and remedial operations, are summarized on pages 296-298 and then presented verbatim in small print. The detailed account of those four interviews is not essential to an overall understanding of the case, although it has been presented for those who are interested in knowing exactly what the counselor and client said and did. However, the remainder of the case, beginning with Interview 8 on page 319, should be read in its entirety.

School

Washington High is the only public high school in a Midwestern manufacturing city of 15,000 population. There are approximately 2,000 students in the school. The racial composition of the student body is 70% white, 25% black, and 5% "other," including a small number of Orientals, Latinos, and American Indians. There are three full-time counselors in the school, one for each of the three grades—tenth, eleventh, and twelfth.

Situation

It is mid-October of the school year. Donald Adams, the tenth grade counselor, has been approached in his office by Janet Holt, one of the new teachers.

Procedure

2.0: PROCESS CLIENT REFERRAL
2.1: RECEIVE REFERRAL

Ms. Holt: Don, do you know Juanita Salvado?
Counselor: No, that's not a familiar name. I've talked with only a few of the new tenth graders so far this year.

2.1.2: SCHOOL PERSONNEL

Ms. Holt: Well, Juanita is in my geometry class, and I think you may be able to help her.

2.2.1: COLLECT DATA

Counselor: What seems to be the difficulty?
Ms. Holt: I'm not quite sure, except that she seems to be a real loner. She always comes to class alone and sits at the very back of the room, several seats away from the other kids. I've never seen her speak to any of them. She seems con-

scientious about her schoolwork, but never volunteers anything. I've tried to be friendly to her, and I get the feeling she would like to be friendly, too, but that she just doesn't know how.

2.2.2: ANALYZE DATA

Counselor: So you're concerned about Juanita's shyness and apparent lack of friends. She seems to be aware of the problem, too, but doesn't seem to know how to change the situation.

Ms. Holt: Yes, and I think with a little encouragement from a counselor she might be willing to talk about it.

2.2.3.1: YES, REFERRAL APPROPRIATE

Counselor: I'll be glad to invite Juanita in to talk about this, Janet. I'll tell her about our conversation and explain how I might be able to help as a counselor.

Ms. Holt: Yes, I think that would be wise. I do hope you can help her.

2.2.4: SPECIFY CONDITIONS TO REFERRAL SOURCE

Counselor: I hope so, too. I'll try to see her in the morning. Of course, I can't guarantee that she will decide to enter counseling. That's her option. I'm sure you realize that the interviews are confidential, but I can let you know whether she decides on counseling and whether we are making progress. Also, assuming that she does decide to work with me on this and the occasion arises, would you be willing to observe her behavior further and perhaps do something in class to help?

Ms. Holt: Yes, I'll be glad to.

Counselor: Good! Now, is there anything else I should know before I see her?

Ms. Holt: Not that I can think of right now.

3.0: PREPARE FOR INTERVIEW
3.1: ARRANGE FOR APPOINTMENT

Counselor: Okay, I'll send a call slip to her first period teacher and try to see her in the morning.

Ms. Holt: Thank you very much, Don.

Counselor: And thank you for bringing this situation to my attention.

3.2.: REVIEW AVAILABLE DATA

The counselor's examination of Juanita's cumulative record folder reveals the following information:

Juanita is 16 years old and is in the tenth grade. Her parents, Paul and Dolores Salvado, are second generation Americans of Latino descent. The father, parts manager at a local automobile dealership, is a high school graduate. The mother, a high school graduate with one year of business college, has worked as a secretary but is now a housewife. Juanita has two younger brothers, ages 10 and 12. The family lives in a modest residential section of the city.

Juanita has maintained a B minus average in her schoolwork. Her standardized test scores show her to be slightly above average on both aptitude and achievement. Her interest inventory results suggest high interest in musical, artistic, social service, and clerical activities. Reports from her teachers in junior high school suggest that she is shy and a good worker. She has apparently participated in no extra-curricular activities. There is no evidence of disciplinary problems.

The next morning Juanita appears, hesitantly, at Mr. Adams' office at the appointed time. Thoughout the dialogue which follows, Co signifies that the counselor is speaking and Cl signals a remark made by the client. The numbers are used to link the counselor's remarks with the accompanying client response.

4.0: EXPLAIN COUNSELING RELATIONSHIP

Co 1: Hi, Juanita, I'm Mr. Adams, the tenth grade counselor. Have a seat here. . . . You're probably wondering why I asked you to come down to the counseling office.

4.1.1: YES, FORMAL STRUCTURE NEEDED

Cl 1: Yes, Mrs. Stevens just said you wanted to see me.

4.2.1: YES, TIME APPROPRIATE

Co 2: Ms. Holt, your geometry teacher, suggested that I talk with you. She said you are a good student in her class and that she is fond of you. She also said you appeared to be very quiet in class and that apparently you hadn't gotten to know the other kids very well. She had the feeling that perhaps you were lonely and would like to get better acquainted. . . .

Cl 2: I suppose so. . . .

Co 3: Would you like to talk this over with me?

Cl 3: I don't know. . . .

Co 4:   Have you ever talked to a counselor before, Juanita?

Cl 4:   Just a few times in junior high school, to schedule classes.

Co 5:   Maybe it would help if I explained what counseling is all about, and then you can decide whether you want to discuss these things with me. Does that sound okay?

Cl 5:   I suppose so.

4.3: DESCRIBE COUNSELING PROCESS

4.3.1: PURPOSE

Co 6:   Good. The purpose of counseling is to assist you with the things that concern you or that interest you. Some students want to make decisions about what to do after high school. Others need help with school problems—subjects and teachers. Some have problems getting along with others, such as classmates or parents. The purpose of counseling, really, is to help you with the things that are important to you.

4.3.2: RESPONSIBILITIES

Co 6:   My job as a counselor is to listen and try to understand how you feel and think about things. I won't make any decisions for you, but together we may come up with some things for you to consider in making a decision. If you make a decision, I'll help you find ways to carry it out. Your job in counseling is to help me understand how you feel and think. You also have to make decisions and carry out any tasks to help you reach your goals.

4.3.3: FOCUS

Co 6:   We usually focus on establishing some specific objectives for what you want to accomplish. If you want to do something about getting better acquainted with the other kids, we will set up a goal to work toward.

4.3.4: LIMITS

Co 6:   People participate in counseling on a voluntary basis. You may quit whenever you choose. The interviews are confidential. I don't report to anyone unless you think this would be appropriate and would give me your permission. Our interviews usually last for about 45 minutes. The number of interviews is typically anywhere from two to five. How does all this sound to you?

Cl 6:   Okay, I guess.

Co 7:   Any questions about what counseling is like?
Cl 7:   No, I don't think so.

5.0:   CONSTRUCT MODEL OF CLIENT CONCERNS
5.1:   IDENTIFY CONCERNS

Co 8:   Okay, Perhaps now you could tell me how you see this situation that Ms. Holt described.

Cl 8:   What do you mean?

Co 9:   Well, Ms. Holt said that you seemed kind of lonely and that you might be interested in getting to know the other kids better. I wonder if you see the situation the same way, or perhaps some other way.

Cl 9:   I don't think it would be possible to be friends with them—not really.

Co 10: You sound kind of discouraged.

Cl 10: I just don't think they like me.

Co 11: You haven't made friends with any of the other kids, and the reason seems to be that they don't like you. Yet, at the same time you apparently would like to be friends with them.

Cl 11: I suppose so, but I don't think they will change. They don't talk to me.

Co 12: They don't talk to you at all?

Cl 12: Not that I can recall.

Co 13: Do you talk to them?

Cl 13: No, it wouldn't do any good.

Co 14: So the situation is that they don't talk to you and you don't talk to them. Could it be that they're waiting for you to take the first step.?

Cl 14: No, they don't *want* to talk to me.

Co 15: So you don't talk to them because you feel they wouldn't respond. I wonder why they would feel that way.

Cl 15: They don't want to talk to anybody that's different from them.

Co 16: Different . . . ?

Cl 16: Yeah, unless you're a member of the majority group in this school, nobody talks to you.

Co 17: And you don't feel you're a member of the majority.

Cl 17: Well, I'm not like them. I don't look like them, I don't talk like them, and I don't act like them.

Co 18: So you feel quite different from them in several ways. Can you be more specific?

Cl 18: Well, I don't think they like anyone that's different. Like, see, I'm Latino. . . .

Co 19: So they don't like you because of your race.

Cl 19: Yeah, it seems that way.

Co 20: Well, that's one possible explanation to keep in mind. Are there any other Latino kids in your geometry class?

Cl 20: No.

Co 21: But there are some other Latino kids in school here.

Cl 21: Maybe four or five.

Co 22: How do you get along with them?

Cl 22: Okay . . . I guess.

Co 23: You sound a little hesitant.

Cl 23: Well, I only have classes with two of them.

Co 24: And do you know them?

Cl 24: Yeah.

Co 25: Would you say they're friends of yours?

Cl 25: Not . . . really. But I don't think they have anything against me.

Co 26: Would it be fair to say, then, that you don't have any real friends at school yet?

Cl 26: I suppose so.

Co 27: But you really would like to have some friends at school.

Cl 27: Yeah.

Co 28: Are there any other concerns that you can think of that you have right now? (pause)

Cl 28: None that I can think of.

5.2: SELECT CONCERN FOR COUNSELING

Co 29: Okay. I wonder, Juanita, if this matter of making friends is something the two of us could work on in counseling.

Cl 29: I suppose so.

5.3: IDENTIFY COMPONENTS OF CONCERN

Co 30: Okay, first it might help to describe the problem as fully as possible.

5.3.3: SITUATIONAL

In what kinds of situations do you feel this is a problem?

Cl 30: What do you mean?

Co 31: Well, is it just in school that you don't have friends, or is it in your home neighborhood as well, or what?

Cl 31: Oh, I have friends at home. There are a couple of girls in my block that I'm good friends with. But they don't go to school here. They're in junior high school right now. One is in the sixth grade, and the other is in the seventh.

Co 32: They're quite a bit younger than you, then.

Cl 32: Yeah.

Co 33: So, the problem of no friends occurs mainly at school.

Cl 33: Yes.

5.3.2: TEMPORAL

Co 34: How long has this been a problem?

Cl 34: A long time, I guess.

Co 35: Ever since you first started in school?

Cl 35: Um–hm, although it seems worse this year—in a new school.

Co 36: So this has been a more or less continuous concern throughout your school years, but you have felt it more this year with the shift to a new school.

Cl 36: Yes, very definitely.

5.3.1: RESPONSE, and 5.3.3: SITUATIONAL

Co 37: You mentioned earlier that the other kids don't talk to you. What other things do they do that suggest they don't like you?

Cl 37: You mean . . . like looking away from me when they pass me in the hall?

Co. 38: Yes, that could be one kind of thing. Anything else?

Cl 38: Well, they never seem to sit beside me in the cafeteria unless there are no other seats available.

Co 39: So they seem to ignore you in general, like in the hall and in the cafeteria. How about in your classes?

Cl 39: Well, they never seem to talk to me—as I mentioned before—and they don't sit near me.

Co 40: So this occurs throughout the school day. . . . How about on the way to and from school?

Cl 40: I always walk alone.

Co 41: Are there other kids who walk the same general route?

Cl 41: Yes, but they stay to themselves.

Co 42: What extra-curricular activities do you participate in, Juanita?

Cl 42: None, really.

Co 43: So that's another area where you have had no contact with the other kids.

Cl 43: Yeah . . . that's right.

5.4: ESTABLISH BASELINE OF CONCERN-RELATED BEHAVIOR

Co 44:   Let me see if I understand the circumstances surrounding this situation then, Juanita. Although you have some close friends at home, you have never had anyone whom you could realle call a friend in the school situation. This has been a continuing concern ever since you first started school. The other kids have ignored you by not looking at you, talking to you, walking with you, or sitting near you. This occurs every day on the way to and from school, in the halls, in the cafeteria, and in your classes. Is that about the way it is?

Cl 44:   Yes . . . I suppose that's pretty much the way it is. It sounds really bad . . . but I don't think it's all my fault. They just don't seem to want to be friends with me.

5.5: IDENTIFY MAINTAINING REINFORCERS

Co 45:   Juanita, you've mentioned several times how the other kids seem to feel and how they behave toward you, but you haven't said much about how you act toward them. What do you do typically in these situations?

Cl 45:   I'm not sure what you mean.

Co 46:   Well, do you wait for them to take the initiative, or do you take the initiative and then get rejected by them?

Cl 46:   What do you mean by "take the initiative"?

Co 47:   For example, do you say "Hi" first or do you wait for them to say "Hi"?

Cl 47:   Well, I don't think they would say "Hi" back to me, so I don't say it to them.

Co 48:   And how does that make you feel?

Cl 48:   I don't know.

Co 49:   Sometimes it seems that we do things—or don't do things—in order to feel better or a little bit relieved at the moment, even though in the long run our actions may make us unhappy. We may or may not be aware of this, of course. Would you agree?

Cl 49:   I think so. . . . I guess it would be easier that way sometimes.

Co 50:   Then I wonder if maybe it would be uncomfortable for you to greet the other kids first—since you don't know whether they would respond or not—or if they were to respond, what they might say. So, instead of taking that chance, perhaps you just look the other way and then you feel relieved at having gotten out of a potentially embarrassing situation.

Cl 50:   Maybe. But how do I know whether they would say "Hi" in return?

Co 51:   You don't. But on the other hand you don't know that they wouldn't return your greeting. Without taking that risk, you may never know.

Cl 51:   I suppose you're right. . . .

5.6   VERIFY MODEL WITH CLIENT

Co 52:   As I see it then, Juanita, the situation is something like this: you don't have any real friends at school, and this makes you lonely and unhappy. You would like to get to know the other kids better, but you're sort of afraid they might reject you, particularly those who are not Latino. They don't take the initiative in establishing communication, and you don't either, so it's a standoff. Is that about the way you see it?

Cl 52:   Yes . . . I think so.

6.0:   DECIDE GOAL AND OBJECTIVE
6.1:   DECIDE IF GOAL CAN BE ESTABLISHED

Co 53:   Juanita, it seems to me that this might be something we could work on together and perhaps improve the situation. Would you be willing to give it a try?

6.1.1:   YES: GOAL CAN BE ESTABLISHED

Cl 53:   Yes, I suppose so.[1]
Co 54:   Good.

6.2:   DETERMINE DESIRED GOAL

If you could change the situation, how would you like things to be?

Cl 54:   You mean, like having more friends?

Co 55:   Yes, that could be part of it. But in a long-range sense, what would you like to be able to do that would make that possible?

Cl 55:   Well . . . I suppose I would like to be able to talk easily with other people and make myself interesting enough so that I could establish good relations with anyone that I wanted as a friend.

Co 56:   Okay, so what you're really shooting for at some point out there in the future is to develop social skills that would help

[1]If she had declined the invitation to work toward increasing her social contacts at school, counseling would have been terminated with an open invitation to Juanita to see the counselor again if she wanted to work on this or other problems. If counseling with Juanita were terminated at this point, the counselor might choose to work with Ms. Holt to increase Juanita's participation in class, since the teacher brought the problem to the counselor in the first place.

you establish better relationships with other people, not only here in school this year, but at other times and places as well. In short, to be able to do this any time and any place you feel like doing it.

Cl 56: Wow! But that would be impossible.

6.3.2: YES: COUNSELOR WILL HANDLE CASE

Co 57: I know it sounds very difficult, Juanita. And you may be right—perhaps you couldn't do it in every instance. But I think some progress in that direction can be made. I'd like very much to help you do that.

6.4: ESTABLISH LEARNING OBJECTIVE

Co 57: Now, so that we'll have something manageable to work on, let's back up a bit from the overall goal that we talked about and see if we can establish an objective for counseling. This would be something that the two of us agree would be a substantial improvement over the present situation. We would need to state this as specifically as possible so that we would know whether the objective had been accomplished. See what I mean?

Cl 57: I'm not sure.

Co 58: Well, let me propose one and then you tell me whether it seems reasonable. Suppose we said that by the end of fall semester you will make friends with two of your fellow students and that one will be Latino and the other non-Latino. How does that sound so far?

Cl 58: Okay, I guess.

Co 59: Good. Now we have to spell out what it means to "make friends." And it might be well to state this in terms of the kinds of things that you would *do* with a person that would indicate that the two of you were friends.

Cl 59: I see. . . . I guess that would be the best way to find out whether I'd really made it.

Co 60: Yes, that's right, Juanita. (pause) Well, it looks like we've accomplished a couple of very important things today. We seem to have your problem pretty well pinpointed, and we've established a general goal that you want to work toward. Before we close, though, I wonder if you have any questions about what we've done so far or about what we might do in the future in counseling.

Cl 60: I don't think so. . . . I just hope I'll still feel like going through with this when I come back next time.

Co 61: I do, too, Juanita. Now, can we plan to meet again at this time next week?

Cl 61:   Yes, I think so.

Co 62:   Okay, I'll set up the appointment. But before you leave, I'd like to ask you to do something between now and our next interview. I'd like you to think about the various things that you might do with another student whom you regarded as a friend. Why don't you make a written list and bring it in next time. I'll make a list, too, and we can compare them and come up with a combined list to include in our objective. Think you could do that?[2]

Cl 62:   I think so.

Co 63:   Good! Well, I've really enjoyed talking with you this morning, and I'll be looking forward to seeing you again next week. Goodbye now.

Cl 63:   Goodbye.

During the interim between interviews, the counselor carried out his own assignment of listing the things that a student might do together with a friend. Likewise, he gave some thought to the possible wording of a formal objective for counseling and to the overall counseling strategy which he might ultimately use with Juanita. The second interview follows:

Co 64:   Hello, Juanita. Have a seat right here. Where would you like to begin today?

Cl 64:   Well, I made a list, as you asked me to. It was kind of hard, though. I really had to use my imagination.

Co 65:   That's fine. I know it's kind of difficult to make a list like that, but the fact that you made it shows that you're really working on this concern. (pause) Okay, let's take a look at your list. Well, I see you have three points listed. (Reads aloud): "1. Walking to school; 2. Eating lunch together; 3. Talking to each other in the hall or in classes." These are very good, Juanita![3] I have a few notes, too, that might help us to come up with some additional possibilities.

Cl 65:   Okay.

Co 66:   I notice that your list seems to be centered pretty much around the school day. How about at home? If your friend visited your home—or you visited your friend's home— what kinds of things might you do together?

Cl 66:   I don't know. Maybe watch television, listen to records . . . things like that.

[2]Giving the client an assignment to work on between counseling sessions establishes the fact that the client is responsible for taking goal-directed actions. Such assignments extend the effects of counseling into the client's daily life and give the counselor an opportunity to reinforce the client for goal-directed steps at the next session.

[3]The counselor reinforces positive steps taken by the client. Subsequent tasks may be more difficult, and it is therefore important to build confidence through positive reinforcement of initial steps.

Co 67: That's good. Now, suppose you and your friend went somewhere together outside of school hours. Where might you go?

Cl 67: I guess we could attend some of the events held at school in the evenings, like maybe a game or a play.

Co 68: Okay. Where would you go, other than the school building?

Cl 68: You mean like going shopping, or the movies, or something like that?

Co 69: Yes, those are all good ones. And how about stopping at a student hangout for a coke?

Cl 69: Yeah. Oh, I just thought of a couple more. We could maybe talk on the telephone or maybe study together, or just visit and talk at each other's house.

Co 70: Very good! Okay, let's see if we can get this down in writing. I'll use a sheet of carbon paper so we'll both have a copy. Suppose we say (counselor writes): "Assuming that potential Latino and non-Latino friends are available, and assuming that you have your parents' cooperation and enough material resources (e.g., money, telephone, television), you'll make friends with two of your fellow students, one Latino and one non-Latino. You'll do this by the end of the fall semester. One requirement for success in each case will be that you and the other student will spend a minimum of three hours together in one or more of the following activities during a single week:

1. Walking to and from school.
2. Talking in the hall and classroom before and after class.
3. Eating lunch.
4. Attending school functions (e.g., game, pep rally, play, dance).
5. Visiting in the home.
6. Studying schoolwork at home.
7. Listening to phonograph records.
8. Watching television.
9. Talking on the telephone.
10. Attending movies.
11. Going shopping.
12. Having refreshments at a student hangout.

A second requirement for success will be that you'll state a desire to continue your friendship with the other students." Now, how does that sound? (Gives client a copy)

Cl 70:   Okay, I suppose . . . although it looks kind of scary to see it all down in writing.

Co 71:   It does seem kind of long and demanding. (pause)

6.5: DECIDE IF CLIENT MOTIVATION SUFFICIENT

Co 71:   How do you feel about giving it a try?

6.5.2: YES: CLIENT MOTIVATION SUFFICIENT

Cl 71:   I suppose I could.

7.0: IMPLEMENT STRATEGY

7.1: DETERMINE STRATEGY (Learning New Responses, and Becoming Self-Directed)

Co 72:   Okay, we've got our objective all set. Now what we have to do is decide just how we're going to go about attaining the objective. We'll probably be doing a variety of things, but I think our overall approach should perhaps be one of starting with things that are relatively easy to do and then working up gradually to the more difficult ones. And, of course, we'll be taking steps to help you succeed with each of these things before moving on to the next. So you should have a feeling of success all along the way. How does that sound to you?

Cl 72:   Well . . . that way I wouldn't have to do it all at once.

Co 73:   No, you could take it step-by-step, sort of like learning a new operation in arithmetic. . . .And within our overall plan, we'd probably be concentrating on several kinds of activities. For one thing, you might need some ideas about how to make friends, so we could take a look at some examples—maybe some books, some tape recordings, and so on. . . . Along that same line, we might need to set up some play-acting situations where you could get some practice in what to say and do with possible friends. And, of course, you'd have to make some choices from time to time, such as which kids you wanted to be friends with, so we'd probably be working on how to make those decisions. . . . Do you think those kinds of things would be helpful?

Cl 73:   Yes . . . I'm sure they would help . . . as long as I could work up to them gradually.

7.2: ESTABLISH INTERMEDIATE OBJECTIVES

Co 74:   Fine. And in that regard, perhaps we should split up our objective into some intermediate or smaller objectives. First of all, since you're not talking to the other kids, we may need to work on developing some conversational skills.

Cl 74: Conversational skills?

Co 75: Well, for example, we might work on ways of starting a conversation, ways of maintaining a conversation, and ways of ending a conversation.

Cl 75: Oh, I see.

Co 76: Then, within our overall plan of going from simple to more difficult things, we might break this down further according to the kinds of things that you talk about. For example, we might start with what to say when greeting a person, what to say to identify yourself and get the other person to do likewise, some "small talk" topics that you might use to keep the conversation going, and then some very meaningful or personal things that friends might talk about. How does that sound?

Cl 76: It sounds okay. . . . I just hope I can do it.

Co 77: So do I, and I really think you can. Then, once you have developed the necessary conversational skills, perhaps our next intermediate objective should be to choose and establish contact with at least two kids—one Latino and one non-Latino—whom you think you would like to have as friends. Okay?

Cl 77: Yeah, but that's going to be kind of hard, because I really don't know anybody here very well.

Co 78: I can understand your concern. (pause) Of course, we'll be working on some ways of helping you decide. Do you think you'd be willing to give it a try?

Cl 78: Yes, as long as I'll be getting some help in choosing them.

Co 79: Good. I guess our last intermediate objective, then, would be to carry out some of the activities listed in our main objective with the potential friends you have selected. You'll recall that one part of your counseling objective was to spend a minimum of three hours with each of these students in one or more of the listed activities within a single week by the end of fall semester.

Cl 79: You mean like walking to school together and studying together?

Co 80: Yes, really the time could be spent in any one or more of the 12 activities we listed last week (shows client a copy of learning objective). So, you see, you really have a lot of possibilities to choose from.

Cl 80: Yeah, I suppose if I get to know them well enough it won't be too hard to spend that much time together.

Co 81: I don't think it will be either, Juanita. Another thing that could help is that they may suggest some of these activities themselves after they get to know you. So you may not have to take as much of the initiative at that point as you might think.

Cl 81:   That would be great!

Co 82:   It seems that you're feeling a little more comfortable about all this as we talk more about it.

Cl 82:   I think so.

7.3: SELECT STEPS

Co 83:   Good! Now that we have our intermediate objectives in mind, the next thing we have to do is decide exactly how we're going to go about attaining them. First of all, in regard to conversational skills, how do you think you could best learn them?

Cl 83:   I don't know. . . . Talk about it, I guess.

Co 84:   That would be one way, and I'm sure we'll be doing that as we go along. Maybe another way to get started would be to do some reading on the topic. I have a little booklet here that describes some ways of greeting people and getting the conversation ball rolling (shows booklet).[4] Could you maybe read this over between now and our next interview, and then come in prepared to discuss it next time?

Cl 84:   Sure. It looks kind of interesting, especially the cartoons.

Co 85:   Okay, fine! Perhaps we ought to stop here, then, for today. Meanwhile, in addition to your reading, maybe you can think of some other ways that we might work to improve your conversational skills. I'll think about it, too, and we'll put our heads together next time and see what we can come up with. Okay?

Cl 85:   Um-hm.

Co 86:   Good. Anything else we should talk about before we close for today?

Cl 86:   No, not that I can think of.

Co 87:   Okay, see you next week, then. Bye-bye.

Cl 87:   Bye.

Between the second and third interviews, the counselor sketched some additional steps to help Juanita attain her intermediate objectives. In broad outline, the plan was as follows:

Intermediate Objective No. 1: Develop conversational skills

Steps: a. Read booklet on conversational skills.
         b. Hear audiotape on how to meet and talk with people.

[4]If the booklet had not been available, the counselor might have had Juanita observe her classmates to identify conversational skills.

      c. Role-play with counselor.
      d. Role-play with a student.

Intermediate Objective No. 2:   *Make contact with two potential friends (one Latino and one non-Latino).*

Steps: a. Make a list of desired characteristics in a friend; rank in order of desirability.
      b. Make list of potential friends; rank in terms of possession of desired qualities.
      c. Initiate conversation with two potential friends at top of list.

Intermediate Objective No. 3:   *Participate with each person selected in one or more designated activities for at least three hours in a single week prior to the end of fall semester.*

Steps: a. Rank activities (listed in learning objective) in order of probable ease of client participation.
      b. Invite each potential friend to participate in the "easiest" activity, then the next easiest, etc.
      c. Monitor progress; take remedial steps (e.g., role-playing of techniques, selection of new potential friends, etc.), as needed.

The third interview follows:

Co 88:   Hi, Juanita. Have a seat. Where would you like to start today?

Cl 88:   Well, I read the booklet on conversational skills. It was sort of interesting. I didn't realize there were so many ways to get started in a conversation. And there were some good ideas about how to listen and to get the other person to talk.

Co 89:   So you found the booklet helpful.

Cl 89:   Yes, although I'm still not sure I could put those things into practice.

Co 90:   Right. You're worried about putting this all together, and we need to work at the parts first.

Cl 90:   Yes. . . . I think that would be better.

Co 91:   Juanita, I've tried to work out a tentative plan of steps that we might use to reach the three intermediate objectives we developed last week. I'd like your reaction to it, and then we'll change it as we feel necessary (gives client a copy of proposed steps). You've already carried out a good first step toward developing conversational skills by reading the booklet. Next, it might be helpful to listen to a tape recording which I have here in the office of two people demonstrating ways of starting, maintaining, and concluding a social conversation. Then, moving on up the ladder from easier to more demanding steps, perhaps it would be helpful to. . . (counselor continues to describe the steps for the three intermediate objectives, as outlined during the interim between the second and third interviews).

Well, what do you think? Could we go with this, would you prefer to discuss some of the parts, or would you like to change it?

Cl 91: I'm a little, uh . . . well, it just seems so much simpler when you look at the parts. I don't think . . . no, I don't really want to change anything. It really seems as though I could do those things.

7.4: PERFORM STEPS

Co 92: Good. I think you can, too, Juanita. Looking at each part does make it easier to see where we're going and why. To get started, how about listening to the tape?

Cl 92: Okay, I'd like that.

(Counselor explains the general nature of this 10-minute audiotape and points out specific kinds of things to listen for. The tape is then played in its entirety.)

Co 93: Now that you've heard some concrete examples, what are your reactions?

Cl 93: It sounded good, but I just don't think I'd ever be able to do it that well.

Co 94: I see what you mean, but you probably won't have to do it that well. The tape, which is role-played, presents a more or less ideal version. It's something to aim at, but you can probably be very successful in the real-life situation if you can make a good beginning toward some of the things presented in it.

Cl 94: Well, I can give it a try. *Any* change would be an improvement.

Co 95: Okay, now that you've heard the tape, let's role-play a few ways of greeting a person. Let's say that I'm you and you're Sue Smith, a girl in your math class. I'll turn the recorder on and we'll tape this so that we can listen back if we need to. Okay?

Cl 95: Okay.

Co 96: Let's say I approach you while you're standing at your locker in the hall and say: "Hi, I'm Juanita Salvado. I've seen you in Ms. Holt's geometry class."

Cl 96: "Yes, I've seen you, too."

Co 97: Okay, Juanita, let's see if you can tell me the kinds of things I included in my greeting.

Cl 97:   Well, you started out by saying "Hi."

Co 98:   Okay, fine. What else?

Cl 98:   Let's see . . . you told me your name.

Co 99:   Good. Anything else?

Cl 99:   Something about geometry class . . . I'm not sure.

Co 100:   Remember, I said "Hi," then I identified myself, and then I mentioned something that we had in common   in this case Ms. Holt's geometry class.

Cl 100:   Oh yeah, I remember.

Co 101:   So you see, those are three kinds of things that you could include in greeting a person whom you want to get to know. And they'll apply to almost any situation, since you can always say "Hi," "Hello," or something similar; you can always identify yourself; and if you think about it hard enough, you can nearly always hit upon something that you and the other person have in common.

Cl 101:   I see.

Co 102:   Now, suppose you try it. You're Juanita and I'm Sue.

Cl 102:   "Hi, my name is Juanita Salvado. I think we're both in Ms. Holt's geometry class during second period."

Co 103:   "Yes, I know. I'm Sue Smith. What did you think of that homework assignment we had in there for today?"

Okay, Juanita, that was really good! You did all three things: you greeted me, identified yourself, and mentioned something we had in common.

Cl 103:   I was afraid I'd leave something out.

Co 104:   But you didn't. You did very well! Now, let's back the tape up a little and see what both sessions sound like. (plays audiotape of both role-playing segments)

Cl 104:   That doesn't sound like me. Do I sound like *that*?

Co 105:   It's kind of funny how our voice can sound different to others. I always think that, too, when I hear myself on tape. But aside from that, let's consider how I sounded as Juanita, and how *you* sounded as Juanita. Did you notice any difference in volume or tone?

Cl 105:   I'm not sure. . . .

Co 106:   Let's play it again. (re-plays both segments) Notice anything new this time?

Cl 106:   Yeah, your voice was loud and clear and sounded enthusiastic. Mine was kind of quiet and dull.

Co 107:   If this had been a real-life situation, do you think the voice would have made any difference?

Cl 107:   Maybe. . . . The other person might feel you're more interested in her if you speak enthusiastically.

Co 108:   Good. Exactly! Okay, let's try it again with you as Juanita and me as Sue. This time, remember to include the three points we talked about, but try to sound more enthusiastic. (greeting incident is role-played again)

Okay, let's listen to the tape and see how we did. (plays tape) How did you sound this time?

Cl 108:   Better, I think; louder and a little more enthusiastic.

Co 109:   Yes, it was really good this time! You mentioned earlier that the booklet which you read stressed the importance of listening and getting the other person to talk. I wonder now if we could role-play some ways of picking up on what the other person says and using that as the topic for conversation.

Cl 109:   But suppose the other person doesn't volunteer anything.

Co 110:   That might happen, of course. Later, we can work on some topics you can initiate. But right now, perhaps we should see if we can find some ways of picking up on what the other person says. That would have the added advantage of showing your interest in the other person.

Cl 110:   I see. Okay.

Co 111:   All right, let's role-play again. This time I'll be Sue and you be Juanita. Let's assume that we've greeted each other and acknowledged that we're both in Ms. Holt's class. Now I'll introduce a *new* topic, and you try to pick up on it: "Gee, that was a really great movie on Channel 4 last night at eight o'clock. Did you see it?"

Cl 111:   "Yes, I did. It was good."

Co 112:   Good. You answered my question and then added something of your own. But there's another kind of thing you might want to include. Let's reverse roles and I'll try to demonstrate it. You say something about the movie, and then I'll respond:

Cl 112:   "I saw a terrific movie on TV at eight o'clock last night. Did you see it?"

Co 113:   "Yes, I did. I really enjoyed it. It sounds as though you like musicals." Okay, what did I add?

Cl 113:   Something about musicals.

Co 114:   Yes, I said something that would tend to draw you out more on the topic. I suggested that musicals might be one of your favorite kinds of movies. In that way, I invited another response from you.

Cl 114:   I see . . . the way I did it, the other person might not have said anything else. But the way you did it, it would be necessary for her to tell me something more.

Co 115: That's right. Notice also that I used an *indirect* rather than a direct question. I could have said, "Do you like musicals?" But then you could have answered simply "Yes" or "No," and I would have been stuck with having to make the next response. Of course, I could have used an *open-ended* question such as, "How do you like musicals as a general type of movie?" That might have drawn a good response from you.

Cl 115: I see. So indirect questions and open-ended questions are better.

Co 116: Yes, they're especially good during the early phases of conversation. Of course, after you get to know a person better, the exact form of the response doesn't make as much difference.

Cl 116: I suppose at that point if you know each other well, you'll find lots of things to talk about.

Co 117: Yes, that's true. (pause) You mentioned earlier that the other person might not volunteer anything, and that you might therefore have to introduce some new topics yourself.

Cl 117: Yes, I really don't think I'd know what to do if that happened.

Co 118: Okay, let's consider some "safe" topics that you can have in reserve in case you need them. These would be topics that you could use in almost any kind of social conversation, regardless of the time, place, or person you're talking with. Let's see if we can list some on paper. Can you think of what one might be?

Cl 118: Maybe the weather . . .

Co 119: Good! Yes, that's a very reliable standby. What could you say about it, for example?

Cl 119: Maybe . . . "It's a nice day, isn't it?"

Co 120: Very good! You might want to leave off the "isn't it?" part, which tends to invite a "Yes" or "No" response, but otherwise that's a good one. I suppose some additional things you might say about the weather would be: "Gee, it's nice to have some sunshine for a change," or "I think the weather reporter really goofed on the forecast for today," or "Well, it looks like winter's finally come"— things like that.

Cl 120: Yes, I think I could manage something like that if I get stuck.

Co 121: Okay, what would be another "safe" topic?

Cl 121: Maybe something about school.

Co 122: Good topic. I wonder what would be a good example.

Cl 122:   Maybe something like, "What courses are you taking?"

Co 123:   Excellent! I suppose some other examples might be: "What's your favorite subject?" "What grade are you in?" "What extra-curricular activities do you take part in?" There are a lot of topics like these that would be very appropriate, particularly since you're concerned mainly about making friends in the school setting. I wonder if there would be other topic areas that you could keep in mind.

Cl 123:   I can't think of any right now . . . .

Co 124:   Well, let's see if we can list some more. How about (continuing written list) vocational plans . . . movies . . . television programs . . . popular songs and singers . . . hobbies . . . sports . . . clothes—these might be some good ones. I'll give you this list, and as you think of any others, you might want to add them to the list, okay?

Cl 124:   Yes, that would be a good way of remembering them.

Co 125:   Now, do you think we need to role-play any of these "safe" topics?

Cl 125:   No, I don't think so. Since I have the list, I can memorize a number of them.

Co 126:   Okay then, maybe we should move on to some ways of ending or concluding a conversation.

Cl 126:   Yes, that would help, because sometimes when I'm through talking to another person I get very nervous and embarrassed about how to end it.

Co 127:   All right, let's begin by listing some possible ways. Can you think of one?

Cl 127:   Well, for one thing, the booklet I read said you can always mention something else that you have to do.

Co 128:   Yes, that's a good one. You can mention another commitment or appointment that you have to get to very soon, such as being in class before the bell rings, or getting home in time for dinner. Any other ways you can think of?

Cl 128:   Oh, the booklet also pointed out that the other person may have another commitment that you know about. And you can end the conversation by calling attention to it.

Co 129:   Yes, that's right. If you know the other person has a commitment or an appointment, you can call attention to it and then close the conversation. Besides enabling you to conclude the conversation, this method also demonstrates your concern for the time of the other person. Can you think of any other ways?

Cl 129.   No, I don't think so.

Co 130:   Well, the two ways we've already talked about are sort of indirect ways of closing, since the reason given for closing is that you or the other person has to stop in order to fulfill another commitment. But how about a more direct method—one in which you simply state that you have enjoyed talking with the other person and then say, "See you tomorrow," or "I'll be calling you," or something like that?

Cl 130: Yes, I suppose that would be another way.

Co 131: And, you know, regardless of the particular approach you use, there are some other things you can do to make closing easier. For example, you can glance at your watch, get up out of your chair if you are seated, reach for your coat, move toward the door, and so on.

Cl 131: I see. . . . All of those things would be signals to the other person that I have to go.

Co 132: Exactly. And most people will pick up on such signals. And there's another thing that occurs to me. Once you've made up your mind to go, it's important to go ahead and do it—politely, but briefly. Don't drag it out so that you and the other person become self-conscious about it and you then have to initiate a closing maneuver all over again.

Cl 132: I see. I know that my parents have trouble with that when they're ready to leave somebody's house where they've been visiting. Sometimes it takes them half an hour to get out the door!

Co 133: I can see what you mean. (pause) And one other thing—it's usually a good idea to provide a "bridging" remark which indicates that you expect to see the other person again. For example, you might say, "I'll see you tomorrow," or "I'll call you next week," or "I'll be looking forward to seeing you at my house next Monday night."

Cl 133: Yes, that would make it clear that you weren't just dropping them.

Co 134: That's right. (pause) Now, you indicated earlier that closing a conversation would probably be difficult for you. So I wonder if we should role play some ways of closing.

Cl 134: Yes . . . I think that would be a good idea.

Co 135: Okay, suppose we set the situation up this way. Let's say that you're Juanita and I'm Sue. We have walked home together from school and have stopped and talked for about half an hour in front of your house. I live several more blocks down the street. You feel the need to close because you have to go shopping for groceries with your mother. Remember the kinds of things you want to include. First, one of the three types of closing which we talked about. Second, a remark which indicates that you've enjoyed talking to me. Third, a "bridging" remark. And fourth, any body movements or gestures which are appropriate, such as looking at your watch, moving toward your house, and so on. Think you can do that?

Cl 135:   I'll give it a try.

Co 136:   Good! Okay, as Sue I say to you: "Gee, I hope Ms. Holt doesn't assign any homework this weekend. If she does, I don't think Mom and Dad will let me go to the slumber party."

Cl 136:   "I hope she doesn't too. (glances at watch) Oh, I almost forgot! Mom wanted me to help her get the groceries at four o'clock. Wish we could talk some more, but I'll have to go in now. Bye-bye."

Co 137:   "Bye. See you tomorrow morning." That was really good, Juanita. You included everything but one. Know what it was?

Cl 137:   No . . . I don't think so.

Co 138:   Well, remember, I said I'd see you tomorrow morning?

Cl 138:   Oh yeah, I forgot the bridging remark, and you put it in.

Co 139:   Right, but you did well! Okay, let's try it again, but let's say that you decide to use a commitment of *mine* that you know about as the reason for closing the conversation. Let's say that I have told you earlier in the day that my piano lesson has been changed from Tuesday to today at 4:15 p.m. and that I have apparently forgotten about it while talking to you after school in front of your house. Okay, here we go—as Sue I say: "Gee, I hope Ms. Holt doesn't assign any homework this weekend."

Cl 139:   "I hope not, too. (glances at watch) Say, it's almost four o'clock. It's been fun talking, but I don't want you to miss your piano lesson."

Co 140:   "Say, that's right! Thanks for reminding me."

Cl 140:   "Drop by and pick me up on the way to school tomorrow. Bye-bye."

Co 141:   "Okay, see you then. Bye!" Juanita, that was just great! You included everything.[5]

Cl 141:   Yeah, neither of those was very hard, because I had a good reason for closing. But suppose I can't think of any special reason.

Co 142:   Okay, let's say that you have no particular commitments and that you are aware of none which the other person has. You're just plain tired of talking! Now, let's role-play that one. We can use the same basic situation. You and Sue have been talking for a half-hour in front of your house after

---

[5]Note the frequent use of verbal reinforcement. It encourages Juanita to learn and to gain the confidence necessary to try these new skills in actual situations.

school, and you just simply want to end the conversation and go on inside your house. (pause) You seem a little hesitant. . . . Would you like me to demonstrate that one first?

Cl 142: Yes, that's the one I feel the shakiest about.

Co 143: Okay, you be Sue and make some kind of remark about the geometry class. Then I'll try to respond as Juanita.

Cl 143: "Say, all that homework in Ms. Holt's class is getting me down."

Co 144: "Yeah, me too. Maybe she'll let up a little bit after we get through this unit we're working on now. (glances at watch, shifts books, and starts toward 'house') I've enjoyed talking, Sue, but I think I'd better go in now. Pick me up in the morning and maybe on the way to school we can talk about it some more, okay? (smiles) Bye now."

Cl 144: "Okay, see you then, bye."

Co 145: How was it?

Cl 145: Good. I think you included everything. You also started to move away, which was a good signal for me. Also, the way you worded what you said, I don't think it would have hurt my feelings or anything.

Co 146: Okay, let's reverse roles for a moment and you try it.

Cl 146: Okay, I'll do my best.

Co 147: Then here we go. As Sue, continuing a long conversation on the same topic, I say: "I don't know why teachers—especially English and math teachers—assign so much homework. You'd think they'd realize we have other classes besides theirs."

Cl 147: "I don't either. (glances at watch) It's been fun talking, Sue, but I really have to go in, now. I'll see you in the morning, though, okay? We'll walk to school together."

Co 148: "Okay, maybe we can talk some more about it then. Bye." That was pretty good, Juanita, but let's back the tape up and listen to it again.

(plays last two role-played segments)

Any reactions?

Cl 148: Well, one difference was that you were more enthusiastic as Juanita than I was. . . . And you mentioned that we could continue talking about the topic the next morning.

Co 149: Right. In real-life situations you might want to include those points, too. But you did very nicely! I think you're really showing a lot of progress!

Cl 149: Well, I think I've learned some things to say, and also the practice has helped. But practicing with you wasn't very hard. I still don't know whether I could do it with anyone else. . . .

Co 150:   That's a very good point, Juanita. I think you can, but I'm
sure you'll feel more confident and maybe learn more by doing it with other kids. For this reason, I'd like you to practice between now and our next interview with someone in
your own age group. Can you think of anyone that you
could do that with?

Cl 150:   No. . . . I can't think of anyone.

Co 151:   How about one of your brothers?

Cl 151:   But they're younger than I am.

Co 152:   Yes, but maybe your oldest brother . . . he's 12 years old,
isn't he?

Cl 152:   Yes, I suppose he would do it. He's more outgoing than I
am, so he might think it would be fun.

Co 153:   Okay, good! And if that doesn't work out, I wonder if you
could practice with your mother. You see, really, while it
would be better to practice with another young person, the
practice itself is the main thing.

Cl 153:   Oh yes, I'm sure she would. She's always wanted me to be
more outgoing with people.

Co 154:   Okay, fine! Then, let's say that during the next week you
will practice the following things. I'll write this down and
give you a copy: (writes)

1. Greeting another person.
2. Picking up on what the other person says.
3. Introducing safe topics of your own.
4. Ending the conversation under the three conditions that
we discussed.

Think you could do that?

Cl 154:   Yes, I think so.

Co 155:   Okay, there's one more thing I'd like you to do. Could you
think a little about the kinds of characteristics you desire in
a friend, so we could talk about that also next time?

Cl 155:   What do you mean by "characteristics"?

Co 156:   Well, it could include things like physical appearance, personality, interests, hobbies, and so on.

Cl 156:   Okay, I'll think about it. Should I make a written list?

Co 157:   Yes, that would be fine. (pause) Incidentally, it occurs to
me that we might be able to set up some additional role-
playing possibilities for you here at school, if you would
think that would be helpful. Ms. Harper, the speech and
drama coach, is always looking for possible "acting" jobs
that her students can get involved in to gain experience. If

you like, as a homework assignment on my part I could ask her to suggest one of the girls in her class who might be willing to role play some social situations with one of my counselees. Think you might like to do that?

Cl 157: That might be a good idea. . . . But I'm not sure I could do as well as a drama student, though.

Co 158: I can understand your feeling, but I'm sure Ms. Harper would suggest someone who would be very easy to work with. And, of course, the two of you would be doing each other a favor. You both need the practice. This would give you an opportunity to have a role-playing partner more nearly your own age, and a drama student would probably sound more realistic and convincing in her role because of her training.

Cl 158: Could I maybe think about it . . . and let you know next time? Meanwhile, you could ask Ms. Harper if she has someone in mind who might be willing to do it.

Co 159: Okay, fine! I'll sound Ms. Harper out on the general idea, but I won't mention your name and won't make contact with the other student unless you tell me next time you want to go ahead with it, okay?

Cl 159: Yes . . . that would be fine. I think I'll have a better idea about whether I'll need more practice after trying it with my brother and possibly with my Mom.

Co 160: Good idea. (pause) Is there anything else we should talk about today before we close?

Cl 160: No, I don't think so.

Co 161: How do you feel now about your progress on your objective about making friends?

Cl 161: Well . . . I'm learning. It still looks like a big job, but I think I can maybe do it. Taking it in small steps, one at a time, really helps.

Co 162: Good! I think you're making great progress! I've really enjoyed our session today. I'll see you next week at the same time, then. Goodbye for now.

Cl 162: Goodbye, and thanks.

During the interim between the third and fourth interviews, the counselor carried out his own homework assignment by contacting the speech and drama coach and obtaining the name of a female drama student who had a study hall the same period as Juanita and who might be willing to role play designated social situations with her.

You have now read a verbatim account of the first three interviews. It is assumed that by this point you have grasped the flavor of the interac-

tion between Juanita and Mr. Adams. As you can see, they have begun
PERFORM STEPS (Function 7.4), which is ordinarily the longest part
of any counseling case. Juanita is no exception; Interviews 4–7 are also
concerned with Function 7.4. The remaining portions of the Systematic
Counseling process will begin with Function 7.5 in the eighth and final
interview.

If you would like to know exactly what the counselor and client said
and did in Interviews 4–7, a complete transcript is provided in the small
print which begins on page 298. On the other hand, if you are primarily
concerned with understanding the broad scope of the case and do not
care to know the details, you may wish to read the following brief summary of Interviews 4–7 and then proceed directly to page 298, where
Interview 8 will be presented in its entirety.

Summary of Interviews 4–7

In Interview 4 the client reported success with both parts of her
homework assignment. She had practiced the designated aspects of
social conversation with her oldest brother and with her mother. She had
also made a written list of 10 characteristics which she desired in a
friend. In the interview she ranked these characteristics from most important to least important. She also developed a list of potential Latino
girlfriends and ranked them on the basis of the list of desired
characteristics. She then made and ranked a similar list of potential non-
Latino girlfriends. At the end of the interview, as homework Juanita
agreed to: (a) role play selected aspects of social conversation for at least
a half-hour each day with Gail, a student suggested to the counselor by
the the speech and drama coach; (b) greet and carry on a conversation for
at least five minutes with Maria, her top-ranked potential Latino friend;
and (c) greet and converse for a minimum of two minutes with Karen,
the most preferred non-Latino possibility.

In the fifth interview, Juanita reported that the practice with Gail had
helped considerably and that she had met and talked for more than the
assigned length of time with Karen. However, she had been rebuffed by
Maria, which left her baffled and discouraged. Much of the interview
consisted of a brain-storming session with the counselor about possible
reasons for the failure with Maria, followed by role playing of alternative
approaches which might be used with her. Juanita then ranked, according to ease of participation, the activities which were listed earlier in
her learning objective. As her next homework assignment, Juanita agreed
to: (a) have lunch with Karen in addition to talking with her as before,
and to keep a record of time spent with her; (b) continue practicing with
Gail, primarily on new approaches which might be tried with Maria; and

(c) approach Maria again, attempt a reconciliation, and hold a five-minute conversation with her. As his own homework assignment, Mr. Adams was to tell Ms. Holt, the geometry teacher and referral source, about Juanita's progress thus far in counseling. He was also to ask Ms. Holt to observe Juanita's interaction with other students in class, particularly Karen, and to ask her to place Juanita and Karen in the same small group for special class projects.

In interview 6 Juanita reported more than satisfactory progress with Karen, having eaten lunch with her on three occasions and talked with her in the halls and classroom for a total of two hours. However, she had been rebuffed a second time by Maria, despite continued practice beforehand with Gail. After considering several additional alternatives concerning Maria, Juanita decided to drop her and switch instead to Carlotta, her second choice as a potential Latino girlfriend. As homework she agreed to: (a) continue to practice with Gail, particularly in terms of how to approach Carlotta; (b) contact Carlotta and talk with her for at least two minutes; and (c) increase the time spent with Karen to three hours in the next week. To facilitate Juanita's relationship with Carlotta, the counselor agreed to ask Ms. Holt to put Carlotta into the same small group with Juanita and Karen for an upcoming class project.

In the seventh interview Juanita reported more progress than she had made at any previous point. She had continued to practice social conversations with Gail for one-half hour each day. She had introduced herself to Carlotta and talked with her for five minutes, as opposed to the assigned two minutes. Ms. Holt had put Juanita, Carlotta, and Karen into the same small group, and the arrangement was working well. In an unanticipated development, the three girls had studied for two hours at Karen's house. Moreover, Juanita had exceeded her goal with Karen, having spent four hours and 50 minutes with her during the past week, as opposed to the assigned three-hour minimum. During the interview she agreed to continue her previous activities with Karen and to move down the list further and talk with her on the telephone. She agreed to practice this unfamiliar activity with Gail first. The counselor and client next agreed on a set of activities to be pursued with Carlotta during the coming week. The goal for the week was now to meet the main part of the original objective for counseling, i.e., to spend at least three hours separately with each of her new friends—Karen and Carlotta. It was agreed that if this objective were met, the next interview would probably be the last regular meeting on this problem with the counselor. Juanita's specific homework assignment with Karen was to spend at least three hours with her in a combination of the following: talking in the hall and in the classroom, eating lunch, walking to and from school, and talking on the telephone (after practicing with Gail). With Carlotta, Juanita agreed to spend a minimum of three hours by attending a basketball game, having refreshments at a student hangout after the game, and browsing at a music store one afternoon and listening to records.

Having read the above highlights of Interviews 4–7, you may wish to turn to page 319 and begin reading the final interview. If you prefer to know the details of the intervening sessions, please continue instead with Interview 4, which was as follows:

7.4: PERFORM STEPS (cont'd)

Co 163:   Hi, Juanita. Have a seat. Where would you like to start today?

Cl 163:   Well, my brother and I practiced quite a bit. I think it helped, but after a while he got kind of tired and wouldn't be serious about it. So then I asked my Mom, and she went through everything with me several times.

Co 164:   Now that you've had some additional practice, how do you feel about your conversational skills?

Cl 164:   I think I'm doing better. It's a lot easier to get started now. And I usually can think of a way to end the conversation. But sometimes I get bogged down in the middle and run out of things to say.

Co 165:   So even though there's been some improvement, you still may need additional practice.

Cl 165:   Yes, I think so, especially on the middle part where I have to keep things going.

Co 166:   Well, last week after we finished talking I contacted Ms. Harper, and she suggested the name of one of the girls in her drama class who she thought might like to do some role-playing of social situations. I haven't contacted the student yet, but if you like I'll be glad to get in touch with her and find out if she would like to take part. Ms. Harper seemed to think there would be no doubt, since the drama students are looking for any practice they can get.

Cl 166:   I've thought it over since last week . . . and I think I'd like to do it, although I'm sure it won't be easy.

Co 167:   Perhaps not, but I'm sure the other student will be very understanding and helpful.

Cl 167:   When would we do it?

Co 168:   Well, I know that the other student has a study hall the same period as you do, so it could probably be worked out during study hall. (pause) I'll go ahead and contact her, then, and if she's willing I'll call both of you in during your study hall period this afternoon and we'll set it up. I can explain the situation to her and help the two of you set up the roles. I can also observe for a few minutes if you like.

Cl 168:   Okay . . . but suppose she doesn't want to role play with me?

Co 169:   If that occurs, I'll see Ms. Harper again and we'll find someone else. But she seemed sure this student would be willing.

Cl 169:   Okay.

Co 170:   Now, did you do the rest of your homework for today—the list of qualities you would like in a friend?

Cl 170: Yes. (shows list to counselor) It was kind of fun to do this. I really let myself go! I came up with 10.

Co 171: Fine! Let's see what we have here (reads aloud from list): "Interesting personality," "good-looking," "similar interests," "not stuck-up," "likes rock music," "same age," "Latino," "good student," "female," "lives near me." That's a very good list, Juanita![6]

Cl 171: Well, it may be too ideal. . . . I'm not really sure I could find anyone with *all* those qualities. But I guess it wouldn't hurt to try.

Co 172: Then maybe you would be satisfied if you could find someone who had several of them?

Cl 172: Yes, I think so.

Co 173: Okay. As I said, I think your list is good. There are a couple of the items that I'm not sure I understand, though. Can you tell me what "interesting personality" means to you?

Cl 173: I don't know. . . . Someone who has interesting ideas, I guess.

Co 174: What kind of ideas?

Cl 174: Well, someone who has lots of ideas. Not someone who's got a one-track mind. . . . Maybe someone who is interested in a lot of things—like music, movies, sports, clothes—things like that. . . . And someone who has a sense of humor.

Co 175: Okay, fine. That clears it up quite a bit. It sort of overlaps a little with the third item—"similar interests"—doesn't it? So maybe we've really clarified what you mean by both "interesting personality" and "similar interests."

Cl 175: Yeah, I guess so.

Co 176: There's just one more that I was wondering about—what does "good student" mean?

Cl 176: Someone who makes good grades.

Co 177: And "good grades" would mean . . .?

Cl 177: Well, I suppose . . . B's or better. My grades are okay, but I think I could do better if I could study with someone who's making grades at least as high as mine.

Co 178: Okay, I think we've got these characteristics pretty well pinned down, Juanita. (pause) As you said before, though, you may not be able to find someone who has all of those qualities. So I wonder if we could maybe pick out the most important ones. Maybe we could rank them from "most important" to "not so important." How does that sound?

Cl 178: Okay. I think I could pick out the main ones without too much trouble. . . . I think "female," "Latino," and "interesting personality" are very important. Also, "similar interests" and "not stuck up."

Co 179: All right. Those are the most important ones, then. You'll recall that our objective was for one of your new friends to be Latino. So maybe we could put that at the top, with the understanding that

---

[6]The list of characteristics not only gives Juanita a way of observing people but also provides a model for her. It suggests characteristics which others might want in her.

you would also work on making friends with at least one person who isn't Latino. Okay?

Cl 179: Yeah, I remember. I think it would be easier to start with someone of my own race.

Co 180: Okay, fine. We'll put "Latino" at the top of the list, then. (writes) Now, how would you rank the other four?

Cl 180: Well, I suppose "female" would be second. . . . I think I'd feel more comfortable with a girl right now. And I guess "interesting personality" and "similar interests" would be next.

Co 181: (writes items 2–4) Okay, and that would leave "not stuck up" as fifth. That means "not conceited," I assume.

Cl 181: Yes. I don't like people who act like they're better than anyone else.

Co 182: Okay. (continuing written list) Now, can you rank the remaining five items? That would be numbers 6 through 10.

Cl 182: Well, I suppose a person's looks don't really mean so much, so maybe that one could be last. . . . And I guess "likes rock music" isn't really as important as most of the others, so maybe that could be next to last. . . . (pause)

Co 183: Okay, fine. You're sort of starting from the lower end of the list and working up. That leaves three more: "same age," "good student," and "lives near me." How would you rank those?

Cl 183: Well, it's kind of hard to say, but I suppose "lives near me" would be the most important, since I live farther away from school than most students do, and my Dad usually has the car with him.

Co 184: Okay. (writes) That will be number 6. . . .

Cl 184: And I guess "good student" would come next, and then "same age."

Co 185: Fine, Juanita! Now, we've got the list. Here's a copy for you. (reads aloud)

1. Latino
2. Female
3. Interesting personality
4. Similar interests
5. Not stuckup (not conceited)
6. Lives near me
7. Good student
8. Same age
9. Likes rock music
10. Good looks

Now that you see them all written out, would you like to switch any of them around?

Cl 185: No . . . I don't think so.

Co 186: Okay, can you think of any other characteristics that you would like to add to the list?

Cl 186: Not right now. Maybe I'll think of some later. Could I add them on then?

Co 187: Sure. But meanwhile, we can work from this basic list. Now that we know what kinds of things you're looking for in a friend, perhaps we should try to come up with a few names of girls that you might like to have as friends.

Cl 187: Yeah, and that's going to be hard because I don't really know very many people here.

Co 188: But you do know the names of a few people that you would like to get to know better.

Cl 188: Yes, a few . . . .

Co 189: Okay, let's take the girls of Latino ancestry first. Can you name one that might be a possibility?

Cl 189: Well, there's Maria Hernandez. I've talked to her a couple of times, but I can't really say that we're friends.

Co 190: Okay, Maria Hernandez would be one. (writes) Can you think of another?

Cl 190: Maria has a friend that I met once. I think her first name is Clemencia; they call her "Clem." I don't know her last name.

Co 191: All right, that's fine. (adds Clem's name to list) Anyone else? (pause)

Cl 191: There's a new girl in Ms. Holt's geometry class who I think is Latino. Her name is Carlotta, I think. I've never talked to her, but she seems like she would be a nice person to know. (pause) The only other Latino girl anywhere near my age that I can think of would be Paula Gonzalez. She's in the twelfth grade. I've never talked with her, but Mom knows her mom.

Co 192: Okay. (writes last two names) That makes a list of four Latino girls. Maybe we should switch over now to non-Latino girls, and we can come back to the first list if you think of anyone else.

Cl 192: That's okay . . . but I can't think of any non-Latino girls that I really know.

Co 193: But there are some you'd like to get to know. . . .

Cl 193: Yes. . . . There's this girl—Linda Crawford—who sits in front of me in English class. I've worked on small projects in class with her a couple of times, and she's been very nice to me. But I've never talked with her except for those times.

Co 194: All right, let's put her on the list. (writes Linda's name) How about someone else?

Cl 194: Well, there's a girl in Ms. Holt's class that lives near me. I've seen her on the way to school at times. I've never really talked with her, but she seems nice and we've smiled at each other a few times. I think her name is Karen.

Co 195: Okay. (adds Karen's name to list) One advantage would be that Karen lives near you.

Cl 195: That's right. . . . Oh, I almost forgot—in phys. ed. class there are a couple of girls that I know somewhat. Most of the time we end up on the same team when we play softball. We're not very good athletes, so we usually get assigned as outfielders and sometimes we just stand out there and talk instead of playing our positions. It's kind of fun except when someone hits a ball out there. Then we really have to scramble.

Co 196: They sound like excellent possibilities, Juanita. What are their names?

Cl 196: Irene and Chris.

Co 197: Okay. (writes names) That makes four names of Latino girls and four of non-Latino girls. Are there any other names that we could add to either list?

Cl 197: Yeah . . . probably. But I can't think of any better ones right now.

Co 198: Okay, now that we have our two lists of names, what do you think should be our next step?

Cl 198: Narrow the list down, I guess.

Co 199: Exactly! Suppose we do it in much the same way that we decided which qualities in a friend were most important to you—that is, by ranking them in order of their overall appeal. And we can use the ranking of personal qualities as a guide. Shall we start with the Latino girls?

Cl 199: Yeah, that would be good.

Co 200: Okay, now let's look back at our list of desired characteristics in a friend (shows list of 10 characteristics) and our list of potential Latino girlfriends—Maria, Clem, Carlotta, and Paula. Now, how could we go about comparing the girls in terms of these characteristics?

Cl 200: Maybe . . . by just writing their names across the top of the list of characteristics and then writing "Yes," or "No" for each item.

Co 201: Good idea! (writes four names across top of list) Okay, suppose you take a few moments and check the qualities that each girl has.

(long pause while Juanita completes task)

Cl 201: Okay . . . I think I've finished. The only thing is, I don't know whether some of the characteristics apply to a particular girl or not. I really don't know the girls that well. So I had to put in a number of question marks.

Co 202: That does make it more difficult. But let's see what you have. (counselor examines list, which appears as follows):

		Maria	Clem	Carlotta	Paula
1.	Latino	Yes	Yes	Yes	Yes
2.	Female	Yes	Yes	Yes	Yes
3.	Interesting personality	Yes	Yes	Yes	?
4.	Similar interests	Yes	?	?	?
5.	Not stuck-up	Yes	Yes	Yes	?
6.	Lives near me	No	No	No	No
7.	Good student	Yes	?	Yes	Yes
8.	Same age	Yes	Yes	Yes	No
9.	Likes rock music	?	?	?	?
10.	Good looks	Yes	No	Yes	Yes

This looks very interesting, Juanita. (pause) And it seems like maybe a rather clear ranking of the four names can be derived from it, don't you think?

Cl 202: Yeah . . . it looks like Maria would come out first . . . and then Carlotta, then Clem. As I said before, I really don't know Paula at all, so she would have to be last.

Co 203: All right, so our ranking of potential Latino friends would be: (writes)

1. Maria
2. Carlotta
3. Clem
4. Paula

Now, shall we do the same thing for the non-Latino girls?

Cl 203: Yes . . . I can try.

Co 204: Okay, suppose we use the same procedure. Here's another copy of the desired characteristics. I'll write the names of the girls across the top, just as we did before. (writes names of Linda, Karen, Irene, and Chris) Now, see if you can rate whether or not they have the characteristics. (long pause while client completes task)

Cl 204: Okay, here it is. (hands sheet to counselor) It wasn't too hard, but again I had to guess in some places. (the list appears as follows):

		Linda	*Karen*	*Irene*	*Chris*
1.	Latino	—	—	—	—
2.	Female	Yes	Yes	Yes	Yes
3.	Interesting personality	Yes	Yes	Yes	Yes
4.	Similar interests	?	?	Yes	No
5.	Not stuck-up	Yes	Yes	Yes	Yes
6.	Lives near me	No	Yes	No	No
7.	Good student	Yes	Yes	?	No
8.	Same age	Yes	Yes	Yes	Yes
9.	Likes rock music	?	?	Yes	?
10.	Good looks	Yes	Yes	No	No

Co 205: (examining list) That looks good, Juanita. The order may not be as clear as on the other one, though. It looks like Karen is number 1 and Chris is number 4, but it seems pretty close between Linda and Irene for second place.

Cl 205: Yeah . . . I see what you mean. They both have six "Yes's." But I think Irene has pretty much the same interests as I do, and I think that's very important. I'm not really sure about Linda. But on the other hand, she's a good student, and Irene's not. But then, I know Irene likes rock music. So I guess at this point maybe Irene should be number 2, mainly because I think her interests would fit in better with mine.

Co 206: Okay that's fine. That means that our ranking of potential non-Latino friends would be: (writes)

1. Karen
2. Irene

3. Linda

4. Chris

Now, how does that look?

Cl 206: I think it looks okay. It certainly gives me a basis to get started.

Co 207: Fine! Juanita, I see our time for today is coming to a close. Before we stop, though, let's make sure we have an understanding about what we're both supposed to do between now and our next interview. I'm going to call you and the drama student into the office this afternoon during your study hall. At that time I will explain the situation to her and we'll set up the two roles. Then the two of you can go into the group counseling room, which is vacant at the time, and practice. There's a tape recorder in there, so you can also tape your conversations and listen to them. I'll observe for a few minutes, and then leave you and the other student on your own. If she is willing, do you think the two of you could role-play for at least half an hour every day between now and our next appointment?

Cl 207: I suppose so. . . . All the practice I can get would help.

Co 208: Good! If you can do an acceptable job in your role-playing sessions, we will have completed our first intermediate objective—to develop conversational skills. Today, of course, we've been working mainly on our *second* intermediate objective—to make contact with two potential friends. Only one more thing on that objective remains to be done. And that brings me to the second thing I'd like you to do before our next interview. Do you suppose you could initiate a conversation with Maria and another one with Karen during the week?

Cl 208: What would that involve?

Co 209: Well, I believe you said you've already talked with Maria a few times. . . .

Cl 209: Yes . . . it shouldn't be too hard with her.

Co 210: So let's say that you will greet her and carry on at least a five-minute conversation with her, okay?

Cl 210: Yeah. . . . I think I could do that.

Co 211: But you've never really met Karen?

Cl 211: No, not really.

Co 212: So, how would it be if we said that you would greet Karen, introduce yourself, and carry on at least a two-minute conversation with her?

Cl 212: Well . . . I suppose I could use some of the things we used in our role playing last week to talk about.

Co 213: That's right. And then, of course, you and the drama student can practice on that, too, with her taking the role of Karen, and perhaps Maria also. Think you could do that?

Cl 213: I think so, especially after I get some more practice in role-playing.

Co 214: Okay, fine, Juanita! I think you're making excellent progress! How do you feel about it?

Cl 214:	Well, I feel a lot more confident. But I guess a better indication will be how I make out with Maria and Karen.
Co 215:	That's right, but I feel confident that you can make a go of it. You may have a little difficulty, but if you do we can talk about it next time and see if we can come up with some additional ways to deal with the situation.
Cl 215:	Okay, I'll try it. It's good to know that I can get more help if I need it.
Co 216:	Well, if we're all set, I'll see you this afternoon with the drama student, and we'll have our next interview this time next week, okay?
Cl 216:	Okay, I'll see you then.
Co 217:	Goodbye, Juanita.
Cl 217:	Goodbye.

That afternoon the counselor made the necessary arrangements with the study hall supervisor and met with Juanita and Gail, the drama student suggested by Ms. Harper. Juanita and Gail seemed to like each other, and the role-playing got off to a good start, centering around techniques for greeting another person, maintaining the conversation, and concluding the conversation under various conditions previously practiced with the counselor. After observing for 10 minutes and making a few brief suggestions, the counselor left Gail and Juanita to practice on their own, with the understanding that they would continue to role-play social situations each day during study hall for the next week. The fifth interview with Juanita follows:

Co 218:	Hi, Juanita. Come in and have a seat. Where would you like to start today?
Cl 218:	Well, there are a lot of things to report on. . . . For one thing, Gail has been a lot of help. And she's such a nice person! We practiced every day for at least half an hour—more on a couple of occasions. I'm nowhere near as good as she is, but I find that I can learn a lot by watching how she plays her roles. She's really cool.
Co 219:	So you're finding your sessions with Gail enjoyable as well as helpful.
Cl 219:	Definitely. And she's very understanding, just like you predicted. She always compliments me if possible, and she's very patient when I goof.
Co 220:	That's great, Juanita! (pause) Now, how about Maria and Karen?
Cl 220:	Well, it went okay with Karen, I think. I really surprised myself. Gail and I had really worked hard to get ready for that one. It just so happened that Karen and I both arrived early for Ms. Holt's class last Friday, and there were only a few students in the room at the time. So when she smiled at me, like she usually does, I smiled back and said, "Hi, I'm Juanita," and she sort of took it from there. She introduced herself in return, and asked me a question about something or other, and we were still talking when Ms. Holt walked in, which was probably a good five minutes later.

Co 221:   Juanita, that's absolutely terrific! I'm really proud of you!

Cl 221:   And then, I talked with her a couple more times, too. And oh—it's funny, you know, when I made out my list I didn't know whether she liked rock music, and I've found out she does! So we've talked about that, mainly.

Co 222:   It really sounds like you and Karen are off to a great start. Now, what about Maria? You surprised me a little by not reporting on her first.

Cl 222:   Well, you know, it's really funny. I thought it would be much easier with Maria, especially with her being Latino and everything, but was I wrong! It wasn't anything I could really put my finger on, but I'm just not sure we could hit it off.

Co 223:   Can you think back and tell me exactly what the two of you said, as well as you can recall?

Cl 223:   Well, on the way to my first period class I noticed her talking to another girl in front of her locker. I stopped and said, "Hi, Maria, are you going to be walking home this afternoon?" But she just turned and sort of glared at me and said, "Hello, Salvado." Then she went right on talking to the other girl.

Co 224:   I see. And what did you do then?

Cl 224:   Well, I stood there for a moment. . . . I'm sure my face must have been red. . . and then I just went on to class. It was really disappointing, because of all the people I had listed, I thought she would be the easiest to talk to.

Co 225:   It was crushing to be turned away. . . .

Cl 225:   Yes . . . I never expected that kind of treatment.

Co 226:   Did you have any other contact with her during the past week?

Cl 226:   I saw her a couple of times, but I didn't approach her.

Co 227:   I see.(pause) Juanita, I wonder if we could maybe brainstorm for a bit and see if we can list some possible reasons why Maria may have responded the way she did.

Cl 227:   Well . . . I suppose she might have been upset about something.

Cl 228:   Any idea what that could have been?

Cl 228:   I don't know, unless maybe she and the other girl were talking about something kind of private that they didn't want anyone else to know about.

Co 229:   Okay, that's one possibility. Can you think of any others?

Cl 229:   Well, she might have been in a hurry or something and didn't want to be interrupted for that reason. It was just a couple of minutes before the bell rang.

Co 230:   All right, that's another one. Are there any other possibilities you can think of?

Cl 230:   I suppose she could have just been in a bad mood that morning . . . like, maybe she had an argument with her parents before leaving for school, or she didn't get a good night's sleep, or something like that.

Co 231:   Okay, those would all be possibilities, too. Anything else?

Cl 231: No . . . I really can't imagine anything else, unless . . .maybe I've misinterpreted her actions toward me in the past, and she hasn't ever liked me.

Co 232: Well, we have a number of possibilities listed here. I gather that you feel the last one isn't very realistic . . . that is, she's never acted this way to you before, so this one occasion wouldn't necessarily mean she has never liked you.

Cl 232: Yeah . . . I suppose that's kind of wild . . . I guess we could eliminate that one.

Co 233: All right, assuming that she may still be a reasonable possibility as a friend, then could it be that you maybe misinterpreted her behavior? That is, could it be that she was saying in effect, "Don't butt in while I'm talking to another person," or "I'm in a hurry to get to class," or "I've had a bad morning; don't bug me"? Do any of those messages sound reasonable?

Cl 233: I guess they're "reasonable," but I don't think they're very polite. . . .

Co 234: No, I agree with you that they weren't polite. (pause) But at the same time, it seems that you still might like to cultivate a friendship with Maria. Is that so?

Cl 234: I suppose it would be worth another try, but I certainly wouldn't be looking forward to it.

Co 235: Then, since you don't want to write off Maria—at least not yet—I wonder if it would be helpful to look at some ways that you might respond to such situations in the future—whether with Maria or anyone else?

Cl 235: I guess so. . . . I sure wouldn't want to feel that uncomfortable again.

Co 236: Fine. And then we might want to explore some ways that you could use to maybe patch things up with Maria. Would you be interested in doing that?

Cl 236: Yes. . . . I suppose I could try.

Co 237: Okay, can you think of how you might have responded differently in the situation with Maria with less chance of drawing a negative response from her?

Cl 237: I'm really not sure. I suppose I could have just smiled at her or waved to her, or something like that, and not tried to talk to her at the time.

Co 238: Okay, that's one alternative that might be appropriate in some situations. But suppose you really wanted to speak to her. How could you have done that and maybe not received a negative reaction?

Cl 238: I really don't know. . . . (pause)

Co 239: Well, I believe you said you greeted her with something like, "Hi, Maria, are you going to be walking home today?" Is that right?

Cl 239: Yes, something like that.

Co 240: Okay, suppose you had only said, "Hi, Maria," and not added the question? Do you see any difference there?

Cl 240: Yeah . . . I think so. When I asked her the question, I guess maybe
she had to decide whether to answer the question or to continue
her conversation with the other girl.

Co 241: That's right. And if she was on edge, or in a hurry, or talking about
something very private—or a combination of those things—maybe
her response just sort of popped out in a moment of frustration.

Cl 241: Maybe, but I certainly didn't mean any harm!

Co 242: I know you didn't, Juanita, and I'm not defending Maria. She did
respond inappropriately. But since you want to be able to handle
these kinds of situations more effectively, whatever the other
person's response, I guess we have to concentrate mainly on your
behavior.

Cl 242: Yeah . . . I guess you're right.

Co 243: Okay, but assuming that a situation like this does arise again and
you do get a negative response, what could you do rather than just
turn away?

Cl 243: I don't know. . . .

Co 244: Okay, pretend you're Maria and I'm you, and let's role play the
situation for a moment. You're busy talking to someone else and I
come up and say: "Hi Maria, how about walking home together
this afternoon?"

Cl 244: (turns and glares) "Hi, Salvado." (turns back)

Co 245: "Oh, I'm sorry I interrupted. I'll see you later, Maria." Okay,
Juanita, what did I do?

Cl 245: You apologized for interrupting.

Co 246: Good. What else?

Cl 246: You said you'd see me later.

Co 247: Okay, fine. Of course, Maria could still take offense even if you did
it that way, but it seems less likely. (pause) Shall we switch roles
now and you try it?

Cl 247: Okay.

(The situation is re-enacted with Juanita playing herself and the
counselor playing the part of Maria)

Co 248: Very good, Juanita! You did fine. Do you think you could use an
approach like that if you find yourself in that situation again?

Cl 248: Yeah, I think so. Before, I was so anxious to talk to Maria that I
didn't even think about the possibility that I might be interrupting.

Co 249: Fine. (pause) But this disagreeable episode with Maria did take
place. Now I'm wondering what you might do to patch things up
with her. Shall we work on that for a moment?

Cl 249: Yes, I'd like to do that. I guess I would have to apologize to her in
some way, but I really don't know what to say.

Co 250: All right. Maybe we should role play again. I can be you, and you
be Maria. Let's say that you catch Maria leaving the building
after school, and the two of you are alone. As Juanita, I say: "Hi
Maria, could I talk to you for a minute?"

Cl 250: "Make it quick, because I've got to be getting home."

Co 251: "If you're in a hurry, I don't want to keep you. I could call you on the phone tonight if that would be more convenient."

Cl 251: "I'm not going to be home tonight. We might as well do it now."

Co 252: "Okay, I appreciate your taking the time. I just wanted to apologize for butting into the conversation the other day in front of your locker. I realized later that I shouldn't have interrupted."

Cl 252: "Juanita, you knew the bell was about to ring, and you saw I was talking to someone else! Besides, I wasn't feeling well that morning. It really ticked me off!"

Co 253: "I realize how you must have felt. I sincerely regret the interruption, and I do hope we can be friends."

Cl 253: "Well, maybe."

Co 254: Okay, Juanita, I think you did a good job of playing Maria. Now, what are your reactions to the conversation?

Cl 254: You really played it cool! You didn't get mad even when I was kind of nasty to you.

Co 255: That's right. I tried to keep my cool and not be drawn into an argument. That was very important. Think you could do that?

Cl 255: I don't know. I guess I could give it a try.

Co 256: Okay, let's do it again. This time you be yourself, and I'll be Maria.

Cl 256: Okay.

(Incident is role-played again, with roles reversed)

Co 257: You did fine, Juanita! Do you think you could do that with Maria in real life?

Cl 257: Maybe I could. I might need more practice, though.

Co 258: Is that something that you and Gail could work on this week during study hall period?

Cl 258: Yes, that's a good idea.

Co 259: All right, Juanita. Could we say, then, that after getting some additional practice you will approach Maria again before our next interview?

Cl 259: Yes, I could do that.

Co 260: Good! If all goes well, you will have selected a minimum of two potential friends, as called for in your overall objective for counseling. If not, we may have to move down the list to Carlotta, okay?

Cl 260: Okay. But I'll do my best to make it with Maria.

Co 261: All right. (pause) I guess at this point we're ready to move ahead with our third intermediate objective. Remember what that was?

Cl 261: I'm not sure. . . .

Co 262: (reads from written plan) Well, you were going to "participate with each person selected in one or more designated activities for at least three hours in a single week prior to the end of fall semester."

Cl 262: Oh yeah, I remember. And there were some steps listed under that.

Co 263: Yes, first you were going to take the activities that we listed earlier and rank them in terms of how easy you think they would be to participate in. I have the list of activities here. (shows list) There are 12 of them, as you can see. Would you like to rank them now?

Cl 263: Yeah, it might be kind of hard, but I think I can do it.

Co 264: All right, why don't you just take a few minutes and write a number opposite each one, starting with "1" for the easiest activity and ending with "12" as the hardest.

 (long pause while client completes ranking)

Cl 264: Okay, I think I've finished it. (hands list to counselor) It wasn't too hard to pick the easy ones or the difficult ones, but there's not much difference between the ones in the middle; they were harder to rank.

 (The ranking appears as follows)

1. Talking in the hall or classroom before and after class
2. Eating lunch
3. Attending school functions
4. Walking to and from school
5. Listening to phonograph records
6. Talking on the phone
7. Attending movies
8. Having refreshments at a student hangout
9. Going shopping
10. Studying at home
11. Watching television
12. Visiting in the home

Co 265: (examining list) Yes, the intermediate items are usually harder to place. (pause) Can you see any patterns or trends in your ranking of these activities?

Cl 265: No. . . . I don't think so.

Co 266: Well, it seems that the first few activities are concerned with the school setting, while the last few would take place at home—your home or the other girl's home.

Cl 266: Yeah, I see what you mean. . . . Maybe that's because I would feel more comfortable in a setting like school, where I'm used to seeing the other person. I've never really gotten together with other girls in my home or theirs. . . . . That would involve being alone with them in a situation where I'd have to carry more of the responsibility for the conversation. Other kids wouldn't be around to help.

Co 267: That's right. . . . So, in general you'd feel more comfortable with activities taking place in the school setting. . . . But you would also be willing to try some of the others?

Cl 267: Yes, to some extent. But I'd rather start with the activities near the top of the list.

Co 268: All right, fine. Now, with Karen you've already started on the first activity, and you seem to be doing fairly well. As a homework assignment, how would you feel about adding the second activity—eating lunch together in the school cafeteria?

Cl 268: Okay . . . that would be fun. I think I could do it.

Co 269: Fine! And, of course, you could continue to talk with her in the halls and classroom before and after class, as you've been doing.

Cl 269: Oh yes, that wouldn't be any problem.

Co 270: All right. And since your ultimate goal with Karen is three hours a week in one or more of the activities, maybe it would be a good idea to start keeping a record of the time you and Karen spend together. That will give us both a better idea of how you're coming along on your objective. Think you could do that?

Cl 270: Yes, it might be kind of fun to do that, and then increase it each week.

Co 271: Fine. Incidentally, I believe you mentioned a while back that Karen is also in Ms. Holt's class with you. I wonder if it would help if I asked Ms. Holt to pair the two of you up for any small group work that you may be doing. When she first talked with me about you, she said she would be willing to do anything she could to help.

Cl 271: Yes, that would be fine. She sometimes splits us up into groups for working on certain kinds of problems, or for preparing special reports. That would be great!

Co 272: Okay, and since it sometimes helps to have someone else observe our behavior to see how we're doing, would it be okay if I ask her how you're coming along with Karen and the other students in that class? This wouldn't involve prying into your affairs or anything like that, but just observing and maybe making some suggestions that might help.[7]

Cl 272: That would be okay. I really like Ms. Holt. I wouldn't think she was spying or anything.

Co 273: Okay, I'll talk with her, then. Now, as we said earlier, you're also going to practice with Gail, mainly on how to deal with Maria, and then you're going to try to patch things up with Maria.

Cl 273: Yes, that's probably going to be harder than spending more time with Karen, but I'll do my best.

Co 274: Okay, Juanita. (pause) How do you feel about your progress up to now?

Cl 274: I feel pretty good about it, generally. . . . I really think I'm improving. I've already done some things I never thought I'd be able to do, although I realize I still have a long way to go.

Co 275: I think you're doing fine, too! (pause) Now, is there anything else we need to talk about today?

Cl 275: No. . . . I don't think so.

[7]This gives the counselor an objective measure of Juanita's progress and perhaps represents a different and useful perspective.

Co 276: Okay, then, I'll see you next week. I'll be looking forward to hearing how you make out. Goodbye for now.

Cl 276: Bye, and thanks for your help.

Following the interview, the counselor contacted Ms. Holt and informed her in very general terms of Juanita's progress in counseling. He asked her to observe Juanita's relationships with the other students in geometry class, particularly Karen. He also inquired into the feasibility of placing Juanita and Karen in the same small group for special class projects. Ms. Holt seemed delighted with Juanita's progress and readily agreed to the counselor's requests. Before school on the morning of the next interview, the counselor again saw Ms. Holt and learned that Juanita and Karen were in fact talking regularly before class and that they usually left the room together when class was dismissed. Juanita was observed on one occasion speaking to Linda as well. While no small group activity had been used the past several days, Juanita and Karen were to be placed in a small group of five students for work on a special project later in the week. The sixth interview with Juanita follows:

Co 277: Hi, Juanita. Where would you like to start today?

Cl 277: Well, I'm not sure. . . . It's really not a clear-cut picture. (pause)

Co 278: You sound kind of uncertain . . . and maybe a little discouraged.

Cl 278: Well, yes, I am. I think Karen and I are doing okay. I ate lunch with her three times in the last week, and we continued to talk in the halls and so on. And I practiced with Gail quite a bit, but . . . I don't know. . . .

Co 279: So, you have some good news to report about you and Karen, but the rest is kind of discouraging. . . .

Cl 279: Yeah . . . Gail and I practiced on how to make up with Maria, but when I tried it with Maria herself, it just didn't go well at all.

Co 280: Would you like to tell me what happened when you contacted Maria?

Cl 280: Well, I came up to her as she was leaving the building after school last Thursday and apologized for interrupting the conversation in front of her locker. I really did my best, just as Gail and I had practiced it, but Maria was just as snooty and distant as ever.[8]

Co 281: Do you have any idea why she might have reacted that way?

Cl 281: Not really. She just seemed very irritated about the whole thing.

Co 282: So, you really felt that you did your very best, and she still didn't respond favorably.

Cl 282: That's right, and I'm not sure that she ever would, regardless of how hard I tried. I can only do so much, and then it seems it's up to her. (pause)

---

[8]Not every systematic plan works well. Clients must be prepared for some failures in learning new responses.

Co 283: Well, it seems that you're facing a decision here, Juanita. Within the framework of your objective for counseling, several possibilities come to mind. You could continue to approach Maria in pretty much the same way, hoping that you can make friends with her. Or, you can possibly work on some new ways of approaching her. Or, finally, you can move down your list of potential Latino friends and try to establish a friendship with Carlotta. Does that make sense?

Cl 283: Yeah, I guess so. . . .

Co 284: Okay, let's take a look at each of these alternatives. As I said, you could try again with Maria, apologizing to her about that incident in front of her locker and hoping that she will eventually respond in a positive manner. How do you feel about that?

Cl 284: Frankly, I don't think it would work. She's really stubborn, and I doubt that more of the same on my part would have any effect, except maybe to make things worse.

Co 285: So, are you saying that maybe we should rule out that alternative?

Cl 285: Yes, I don't see any point in it.

Co 286: All right, let's consider the second possibility. How would you feel about working on some new ways of approaching Maria?

Cl 286: What kind of ways?

Co 287: Well, for example, you could forget about making another apology and instead invite her over to your house to watch TV or listen to rock music, or something like that. Or, you could confront her very directly and tell her how you feel about the way she's been treating you—strangely enough, that seems to defuse the anger in some people and open the way to communication. Those would be a couple of possibilities, and I suspect we could also think of some others.

Cl 287: No, I really don't think it would be worth it. For one thing, I really wouldn't know how to go about doing those things. I know I could practice with you, and maybe with Gail, but I just don't think I want to spend that much time trying to make it with Maria. She's not the only Latino girl in this school!

Co 288: Okay, so you really don't think that approach would be worth the time and effort. (pause) I guess that brings us to the third alternative—moving down the list to Carlotta, your second choice for a Latino girlfriend. How do you feel about doing that?

Cl 288: Well, even though it would mean starting over with someone else, I think I'd rather do it. . . . Of course, I really don't know Carlotta. She's in Ms. Holt's class, like Karen, but I've never talked to her.

Co 289: So you think you'd prefer to switch to Carlotta. (pause) Do you think you know how you might approach her?

Cl 289: Well . . . yeah, pretty much the same way I did with Karen and Maria, I guess.

Co 290: Okay, as I recall, your beginning task with Karen was to greet her, introduce yourself, and carry on at least a two-minute conversation. Do you think you could do that with Carlotta between now and our next interview?

Cl 290:   Yes, I think so. Maybe I could practice with Gail before I try it with Carlotta.

Co 291:   Good idea. (pause) Incidentally, I talked with Ms. Holt this week, and told her in a very general way what we had been doing in counseling. She was really pleased with your progress. And she said you and Karen were hitting if off well with each other. She also mentioned that she planned to put you and Karen in the same small group for some kind of special activity coming up in a few days.

Cl 291:   Say, that would really be great!

Co 292:   Yes, I knew you'd be pleased. And I wonder . . . you know, since Carlotta's also in that class, I could ask Ms. Holt to put her in the same group with you and Karen. Would you like me to do that?

Cl 292:   That might be a good idea . . . but I guess that means I should probably carry out my other task with Carlotta first.

Co 293:   Yes, I think you're right. Do you think you and Gail could work this afternoon on how you might approach Carlotta? Then, maybe you could introduce yourself to her and talk with her tomorrow. . . . I think Ms. Holt said the groups will be ready to go the next day.

Cl 293:   Okay, I'm sure Gail would be willing. She's really been glad to help in any way possible.

Co 294:   Fine. Let's do it that way, then. (pause) Now, I know you talked with Karen quite a bit last week, and I believe you said you had lunch with her three times. About how much time did you spend with her, altogether?

Cl 294:   Well, I kept a record, as you suggested. It came out to about two hours, counting lunch times.

Co 295:   That's great, Juanita! Then you're already accomplishing nearly two-thirds of your final minimum goal with Karen!

Cl 295:   Yeah, it really feels good to know I'm making progress.

Co 296:   All right, what do you think you and Karen should do this week, and how much time can you reasonably spend together?

Cl 296:   Well, I think we'll probably go right on having lunch together, and that would take up quite a bit of time.

Co 297:   Okay. And how about moving down the list of activities to something else as well? (shows list to client)

Cl 297:   I don't really know of any school functions this week, so I guess that one's out. . . . But, you know, Karen lives in the same general neighborhood as I do. Maybe we could walk to school together.

Co 298:   Good idea! (pause) And since you've found out that she likes rock music, how would you feel about inviting her to your house to listen to some records?

Cl 298:   Well, maybe. . . . But as I said before, I've never really had anyone come to my house like that. . . .

Co 299:   Okay. Maybe that's one you can keep in reserve, and do it if it seems appropriate at the time. But, could we say that you'll try to increase your total time with Karen to at least three hours? And

	that you'll do this by talking with her before and after classes, eating lunch with her, and walking to and from school with her?
Cl 299:	Yeah . . . I think I could do that.
Co 300:	Okay, let's see if I can summarize our tasks for this week, then. You're going to continue to practice with Gail, contact Carlotta and talk with her for at least two minutes, and increase your time with Karen to at least three hours. Meanwhile, I'll see Ms. Holt today and ask her to put Carlotta in the same small group with you and Karen. Now, how does that sound?
Cl 300:	That's a lot of things to do, but I think I can do it. It's funny . . . it doesn't seem like so much when it's gradually increased like this.
Co 301:	No, that does make it easier. (pause) I gather that you're feeling pretty good about your overall progress now.
Cl 301:	Well, yes, except for Maria. But, in a way, it's a relief not to have to think about talking to her.
Co 302:	Do you think you might be able to approach her again at a later time, after she cools off a bit?
Cl 302:	Well . . . maybe. But I'm not even going to think about that now.
Co 303:	Okay, Juanita. (pause) Is there anything else we need to talk about today?
Cl 303:	No, I think we've covered quite a few things. Now I just have to go out and do them.
Co 304:	Well, let's stop for today, then. I think you're doing fine, and I'll look forward to seeing you next time. Goodbye.
Cl 304:	Bye, see you next week.

After concluding the interview with Juanita, the counselor contacted Ms. Holt and asked her to put Carlotta, Karen, and Juanita into the same group for the special class activity scheduled to begin two days later. He also asked her to observe the interaction among members of the group, especially between Juanita and Carlotta. Ms. Holt readily agreed. The seventh interview with Juanita follows:

Co 305:	Hi, Juanita. Where shall we begin today?
Cl 305:	With Carlotta, I guess. Gail and I practiced first, then I saw Carlotta the next day just before Ms. Holt's class and introduced myself to her. She's kind of shy like me, but she seems really nice. We talked for about five minutes, which I guess is a little more than the goal I set last time.
Co 306:	That's right, Juanita! Your goal was a minimum of two minutes, and you talked for five minutes. That's just great! (pause) Incidentally, Ms. Holt told me she would put you, Carlotta, and Karen into the same small group in geometry class. How did that work out?
Cl 306:	Fine! We're doing special projects, and the three of us are hitting if off great. Karen is more outgoing than Carlotta and I, and she draws us into the conversation. But the best part is that we got together and studied one evening at Karen's house.

Co 307:   You did? That's great, Juanita! How much time did the three of you spend studying together?

Cl 307:   Oh . . . about two hours, I guess. And then my Dad came for me and we drove Carlotta home.

Co 308:   That's fine. Say, do you realize how far down your list of activities "studying at home" is?

Cl 308:   Pretty far, I think.

Co 309:   Well, let's see (producing list). . . . It's actually number 10, out of 12 items. That means it's really one of the most venturesome activities listed. True, you did it with two other girls instead of one, but you did it, and that's the important thing.

Cl 309:   Yeah, it was actually kind of fun. But there were three of us to carry the conversation. I don't know how I would react with just one other person.

Co 310:   Perhaps you could think about working up to that. (pause) Well, it seems like you're off to a good start with Carlotta. Now, not counting the time the three of you spent together, how much time would you say you spent with Karen?

Cl 310:   Well, we had lunch together every day last week. . . . That's about two and a half hours. And we walked home twice together, and one morning we walked to school together. That would be about one and a half hours doing that. And then we talked in the hall for about 10 minutes each day.

Co 311:   Okay, let's see . . . that would make a grand total of four hours and 50 minutes. And your goal for this week was to spend a minimum of three hours with Karen. So you exceeded your goal by almost two hours. And that's not counting the time you and Karen spent with Carlotta studying. That's really great!

Cl 311:   Yeah, it really feels good when I'm able to meet my goal.

Co 312:   It makes me feel good, too, because I knew you could do it. (pause) Do you recall your overall objective for counseling?

Cl 312:   Yeah, I think so. The main part was that I was going to spend at least three hours with each of my two friends in a single week doing the kinds of activities on the list.

Co 313:   That's right. And you've already spent more than three hours in a week with one of them. Now, as soon as you've done that with *both* of them in the same week, you'll have met the main part of your objective. How would you feel about tackling that for this week?

Cl 313:   Well . . . it wouldn't be any problem with Karen. I don't know about Carlotta, but I think I'd like to give it a try! If I don't make it, I can always try again, can't I?

Co 314:   Sure. But I have a hunch you just might do it. (pause) Now, perhaps we should talk about which activities you'll try with each person. Shall we consider Karen first?

Cl 314:   Okay.

Co 315:   All right. So far, you've been talking with her in the hall or classroom, eating lunch with her, and walking to and from school with her. (pause) How would you feel about continuing with these activities and maybe moving down the list to another activity that you haven't engaged in yet? (shows list to client)

Cl 315: Well, let's see . . . maybe talking with her on the phone would be a good one to try. I've really never used the phone very much.

Co 316: Okay, that sounds like a good one. Do you feel that you would be comfortable doing that, or would you maybe need some practice first?

Cl 316: I think I'd like to practice first. For one thing, if one of her parents answered, I wouldn't really know what to say.

Co 317: Okay, is that something you and Gail could practice on?

Cl 317: Yeah . . . I'm sure Gail would be willing to help.

Co 318: And how much time would you plan to spend with Karen on the phone?

Cl 318: Well, I could maybe call her at least three times, and we could spend about 10 minutes on the phone each time.

Co 319: All right. That would make a half-hour. That leaves at least two and a half hours more to spend with Karen. How would you like to spend that time?

Cl 319: Actually, I think I could fill out the rest of the time in the same things that she and I did together last week. I mean, we could continue talking together at school, and walking to and from school together. And I'm sure we'll go right on eating lunch together.

Co 320: So then, you'll spend a minimum of three hours with Karen. You'll do this by continuing the same three activities you engaged in before, plus talking on the telephone. (pause) Now, what about Carlotta?

Cl 320: Well, I was just thinking . . . maybe the three of us could eat lunch together—Carlotta, Karen, and I. . . . But I guess that wouldn't count, would it?

Co 321: I think it would be a good idea to do that, Juanita. But I guess when we drew up your original objective we had in mind that you would be spending a minimum of six hours with your new friends—three hours each. Isn't that right?

Cl 321: Yeah, I think so. But I think I will ask Carlotta to eat lunch with Karen and me. I'll just have to think of some other activities. (long pause) Oh, I can think of one . . . basketball season just started a couple of weeks ago, and I think Carlotta's a sports fan. So maybe we could go to the game Friday night!

Co 322: Okay, that's an excellent idea. And that would take . . . about an hour and a half?

Cl 322: Yeah, I think so.

Co 323: All right. You still need another hour and a half. What else can you do together?

Cl 323: I really can't think of anything. . . .

Co 324: Well, let's look at the list of activities again (shows list). . . . I suspect a lot of the kids will stop somewhere for something to eat after the game. . . . How would you feel about inviting Carlotta to stop at one of the student hangouts for refreshments?

Cl 324:   I guess we could do that. . . . There's a snack shop about two blocks from here that some of the kids stop at after school. . . . We might try that.

Co 325:   Say, that would really be wonderful! How long would it take to walk there after the game and have something to eat together?

Cl 325:   Oh, about 30 or 45 minutes, I guess. I could probably get my Dad to pick us up there and drive Carlotta home. So, counting that, I suppose it would be closer to 45 minutes.

Co 326:   All right. That leaves another 45 minutes. Do you have any idea how you could spend that time?

Cl 326:   I'm really trying . . . but I just can't seem to think of anything.

Co 327:   How would you feel about browsing with her in a music store one afternoon after school? Maybe you could listen to some records together for the remaining 45 minutes.

Cl 327:   Well . . . maybe. I think she likes the same kind of music I do. We talked about that a little over at Karen's house last week. I suppose we could try that.

Co 328:   And if you do spend three hours with her, as well as three hours with Karen, you'll have met your objective. How would you feel about that?[9]

Cl 328:   That would really be great! It would give me a real feeling of accomplishment.

Co 329:   Well, if you do accomplish your objective, next week will probably be our last interview.

Cl 329:   I see. . .

Co 330:   Now, can you review what you're going to do between now and our next interview?

Cl 330:   Well, I'm going to spend a minimum of three hours with Karen. We'll be talking in the hall and in the classroom before and after classes, eating lunch together in the school cafeteria, and walking to and from school together. We're also going to spend some time talking on the telephone, but I'm going to practice that with Gail first. I'll also try to spend at least three hours with Carlotta. Hopefully, we'll go to the basketball game Friday night and have refreshments at the snack shop afterwards. Then, one afternoon after school we'll try to browse at a music store and listen to some records.

Co 331:   That's a good plan, Juanita. It's possible, of course, that Carlotta may have other plans that would prevent her from participating in some of those activities. For example, suppose she can't go to the game Friday night. What would you do?

Cl 331:   I think there's another game on Tuesday night. Maybe we could go to that one instead.

Co 332:   Good idea, Juanita. You should consider the activities you mentioned as tentative. Then, you can substitute any others from your

---

[9]The emphasis on the time spent with each friend rather than the quality of the relationships may seem inappropriate, but it is a way of measuring experiences with friends. Contact with others must be made and maintained before one can work to improve the quality of social relationships.

list that you think are appropriate. As long as you spend three hours or more with each person, it doesn't really matter which activities from the list are used. (pause) Now, is there anything else we need to talk about today?

Cl 332:   No . . . I don't think so.

Co 333:   All right, then. I'll see you next time. Bye for now.

Cl 333:   Goodbye, and thanks again.

The following is the eighth and concluding interview with Juanita, held on December 5, just prior to the end of fall term:

Co 334:   Hi, Juanita. Where should we begin today?

Cl 334:   I really don't know where to start. There are so many things to report.

7.5:   DECIDE IF STRATEGY/STEPS COMPLETED

Co 335:   Well, suppose we start with a review of what we've done and see if we've covered all the steps we planned. You'll recall that our overall strategy for helping you to make more friends was to start with things that were relatively easy and then work up gradually to more difficult things.[10]

Cl 335:   Yeah, I remember. We started easy and then added on more things to do each week.

Co 336:   That's right. And you'll remember that you had three smaller objectives within the framework of your overall objective for counseling. And under each of those smaller objectives we had some steps to perform. The first small objective was to develop your conversational skills. And under that you were going to read a booklet on conversational skills, hear an audiotape on how to meet and talk with people, and role-play social conversations with me and with another student.

Cl 336:   Yeah, that's where Gail came in, and she's really helped a lot.

Co 337:   Yes, I know. . . . Then, your second small objective was to make contact with two potential friends. To reach that objective you were going to make a list of characteristics desired in a friend and then rank them in terms of the desired qualities. Finally, you were to initiate a conversation with two potential friends. Your third small objective was to participate with each person selected in one or more of the activities on the list for at least three hours in a single week before the end of fall semester. To attain this last

---

[10]The strategy is reviewed because it is a useful plan that Juanita may be able to use when faced with other problems.

small objective you were to rank the activities in your overall objective according to ease of participation. Then you were to invite each potential friend to participate in the easiest activity, then the next easiest, and so on. We were to keep tabs on your progress and take remedial steps as needed. (pause) Now, have we done all of those things?

Cl 337: Yes . . . I think we have. I had some trouble in some places, so I had to role play and then try again. And, of course, there was that thing with Maria—we had to substitute Carlotta. But I think those kinds of things were allowed for in the list of steps.

Co 338: Yes, they would come under remedial steps. (pause) So, as far as you can tell, you've carried out the overall plan we set up.

Cl 338: Yes, I think I have. I can't think of anything that was left out.

8.0: EVALUATE CLIENT PERFORMANCE
8.1: ANALYZE OUTCOMES
8.1.1: RECORD PERFORMANCE

Co 339: I can't either, Juanita. (pause) Now, let's see if we can record very specifically how you're doing at this point. First of all, what kinds of things did you do this past week with Karen, and how much time did you spend with her?

Cl 339: Well, we did all the things that were in my plan for the week. We continued to talk at school, and we had lunch together three times in the cafeteria. We also walked to school together three times, and we walked home together twice. And I practiced phone conversations a couple of times with Gail, like you suggested, and then called Karen four evenings during the week.

Co 340: That's good, Juanita. And how much time did you spend with Karen altogether?

Cl 340: I kept notes on it. . . . I've got a summary right here (shows counselor written tabulation, which appears as follows):

Karen

Talking at school	50 minutes
Lunch—3 times	1 ½ hours
Walking to or from school—5 times	2 ½ hours
Talking on phone—4 times	50 minutes

TOTAL 5 hours, 40 minutes

Co 341: Say, that's really great! You nearly doubled your minimum goal! (pause) Okay, now, what did you do with Carlotta?

Cl 341: Well, it turned out that Carlotta had to go shopping with her folks on Friday night, so we weren't able to go to the game then. But we *did* go to the game Tuesday night. And we stopped for a few minutes at the snack shop and had cokes and hamburgers. Then my Dad picked us up and drove us home. Then, one afternoon we stopped by Music Haven—the record store—and listened to some records for a while. And twice I had lunch with Karen and Carlotta together, although I didn't count that.

Co 342: Well, it sounds as though you did everything you planned to with Carlotta.What was the total amount of time spent with her?

Cl 342: I've got a record of that, too (shows counselor written tabulation, appearing as follows):

Carlotta

Basketball game -2 hours
Snack shop and riding home - 1 hour
Music Haven - 1 hour, 15 minutes

TOTAL   4 hours, 15 minutes

Co 343: So, you went well beyond your minimum goal with Carlotta, too. That's an excellent record, Juanita! (pause)

Cl 343: Yeah . . . I was really proud of myself.

8.1.2: COMPARE PERFORMANCE WITH BASELINE

Co 344: And that represents quite a change from what you were doing when you first came for counseling. At that time, although you had some close friends in your home neighborhood, you had no one whom you could really call a friend at school. You had very little contact with the other kids. They ignored you, and you ignored them, although deep down you really wanted to be friendly with them. This happened daily, both at school and on the way to and from school. In other words, you had no interaction of a friendly, social nature with any of your fellow students. Is that about right?

Cl 344: Yes, it sounds awful . . . but that's the way it was.

Co 345: But now—that is, during the past week—you've spent a total of nine hours and 55 minutes with two friends whom you didn't know at all when you came for counseling. You spent part of this time interacting with them in class, in the hall, in the cafeteria, and on the way to and from school. You also spent some time with one of them attending a game at school in the evening. In addition, you talked with one of them on the phone four times, and made a visit to a music store with the other one. Is that an accurate summary of what you're doing in terms of social interaction with your fellow students?

Cl 345:   Yes, that's just about all of it . . . except that I've also gotten to know Gail fairly well, too. Although she's been helping me learn how to make friends with other people, I think I can say that we're friends, too. And another thing . . . in Ms. Holt's class I've been working closely with Karen and Carlotta. I had never done anything like that before.

8.1.3:   COMPARE PERFORMANCE WITH OBJECTIVE

Co 346:   So there were some additional gains that you hadn't planned on. (pause) Now, let's take a look at your progress in terms of your objective for counseling. Do you recall what your objective was?

Cl 346:   By the end of fall semester I was going to make friends with two students here at school. . . . And one was supposed to be Latino and the other non-Latino.

Co 347:   Right! And how were we going to determine whether you had been successful?

Cl 347:   Well, I was supposed to spend at least three hours with each person in a single week, doing the kinds of things that we listed.

Co 348:   Right again! That was the first thing we were going to look for. And what was the second?

Cl 348:   I . . . don't think I remember. . . .

Co 349:   You were going to state a desire to continue your relationship with your new friends.

Cl 349:   Oh yeah, I remember now.

Co 350:   And do you want to continue being friends with them and continue doing the kinds of things we listed?

Cl 350:   Oh sure! They're really great—both Karen and Carlotta. And of course, Gail—I want to spend some time with her other than just in role playing. She's really helped me a lot.

8.2:   DECIDE IF OBJECTIVE WAS ATTAINED

Co 351:   All right, Juanita. Would you say, then, that you've attained your objective?

8.2.2: YES, OBJECTIVE ATTAINED

Cl 351: Yes, very definitely. I've made friends with two girls—Karen and Carlotta. And as I said before, I think Gail and I are friends, too. . . . And, beyond that, I think my overall behavior and feelings in relation to the other kids have changed. I'm not as "stand-offish" as I was before with other kids. I feel more confident in meeting them and talking with them.

8.3: DECIDE NEED FOR FURTHER COUNSELING

Co 352: That's really great, Juanita! I had a feeling you could do it all along. (pause) Now, do you have any other concerns you want to discuss?

Cl 352: Do you mean . . . anything else about making friends?

Co 353: Well, either about that general area, or any other concern that you might want to discuss.

8.3.3: NO NEED

Cl 353: No, I can't think of anything else right now. . . .

Co 354: Right now you're pretty happy with having made friends. (pause) But I'm wondering if, in the course of our working together, you might have thought of other things you might want to work on—perhaps concerning school, home, your personal habits. . .

Cl 354: I know what you mean. . . . I've thought a lot about counseling and really think it's helped me. . . . I just don't believe I have anything else to work on now, though. . . .

9.0: TERMINATE COUNSELING
9.1: EXPLAIN TERMINATION RATIONALE AND PROCEDURES

Co 355: (pause) Well, in that case it looks like this will probably be our last session for now. You seem to have things worked out nicely. Before you leave today, though, there are a couple of things we still need to do. First, we'll be talking about how you can apply some of the things you've learned in counseling to other problems that you might run into in the future. And second, we'll set up some plans for checking on your progress from time to time to see how you're doing.

Cl 355: But . . . we won't be having regular appointments any more. . . .

Co 356:   No, not unless you have something else you want to work
            on. (long pause)

Cl 356:   I guess that's okay, but. . . I've really looked forward to
            coming in each week and talking to you. No one has ever
            really listened to me before. . . .

9.2: MANAGE CLIENT RESISTANCE

Co 357:   It's kind of uncomfortable to think about not meeting like
            this and continuing to talk about your concern.

Cl 357:   Well . . . yeah, sort of. (pause) I really don't know what I
            would do if something went wrong between me and Karen,
            or me and Carlotta. . . .

Co 358:   So, even though you've accomplished your objective, you're
            somewhat uncomfortable because you aren't sure things
            will keep on going well between you and your new friends.
            And you think maybe it would help if you could keep on
            seeing me like this.

Cl 358:   Yeah . . . I guess so.

Co 359:   Can you give me an example of what might go wrong
            between you and the other girls?

Cl 359:   Well . . . nothing specific. . . . We just might not get
            along . . . .

Co 360:   Are there any techniques or skills that you've learned over
            the past several weeks that you feel you need further prac-
            tice on?

Cl 360:   No . . . I think I've learned them pretty well.

Co 361:   Can you think of any other skills or techniques which we
            haven't covered that you might need?

Cl 361:   No . . . I can't think of any.

Co 362:   So, then, it's kind of a vague discomfort that some situation
            will arise that you might not be able to handle. Yet, you
            can't really think of what such a situation might be like,
            and you seem to be fairly well-equipped in terms of the
            general techniques and skills required.

Cl 362:   Yeah, I suppose so. . . . I guess I can handle it on my own. If
            it got really bad, I could always come back to see you about
            it, though, couldn't I?

Co 363:   Sure you could. Of course, we'll probably be having brief
            check-up sessions from time to time for a while. So that
            would give us an opportunity to work on any difficulties you
            might run into in the near future. However, if serious diffi-
            culties should ever arise, I would want you to feel free to

contact me at once. But I have a good deal of confidence in your ability to handle this on your own.[11] (pause)

Cl 363: Okay, I'll certainly try.

9.3: CONDUCT TRANSFER OF LEARNING

Co 364: Another thing we need to do, Juanita, is very closely related to what we've just been talking about. As you think back over how we dealt with your concern, can you think of how you might be able to use some of the same methods and techniques to solve other problems on your own?

Cl 364: You mean, like coming back to see you if I have another problem?

Co 365: That might be one way—coming in to see a counselor. But I was thinking more of things that you could do on your own. You see, one of the purposes of counseling is to help students develop ways of learning new behaviors, solving problems, and making decisions that extend beyond the immediate problem they are working on in counseling. Does that make any sense to you?

Cl 365: Yeah . . . I think so. Like, maybe it's a good idea to set up a long-range plan like we did for working on a problem.

Co 366: Good, that's certainly part of it—developing a systematic plan for dealing with the problem. But before you can do that, what do you have to do?

Cl 366: I'm not sure. . . .

Co 367: Well, let's think back to when you first came to see me back in October. At that time you were rather unhappy in that you didn't have any friends at school. And do you remember what you thought the reason was?

Cl 367: Yeah . . . I thought it was because of my race, since there are just a handful of Latino students at this school.

Co 368: Right. At that time you thought the reason for your problem was something beyond your control. And what did we do then?

Cl 368: Well, you kind of exploded that idea by asking me how many Latino friends I had at school. And I really didn't have any.

Co 369: So, what did the problem turn out to be?

Cl 369: Mainly, it was that I didn't know how to go about making friends.

[11]The counselor wants to be available but does not want Juanita to be overly dependent upon him.

Co 370:   Exactly! So, one of the first things we did was to clarify the nature of the problem—that is, we found out just what the problem was.

Cl 370:   Yeah, I guess that's very important. Otherwise, you could end up working on the wrong problem.

Co 371:   That's right. So, do you see that one of the first steps in solving a problem would be to find out exactly what the problem is? And that this would apply not only to problems involving relationships with other kids, but to other kinds of problems as well?

Cl 371:   Yeah, I see what you mean. . . .

Co 372:   Okay, after we clarified just what the problem was, what did we do?

Cl 372:   We set up a plan for solving the problem.

Co 373:   Right. And as part of the plan we first set up an objective that we wanted to reach. And we stated it in terms of the kinds of things you wanted to be doing when you finished counseling. And how did we decide to work toward that objective?

Cl 373:   Well, first we broke it down into some little objectives to make it easier. Let's see . . . first I was to develop some conversational skills, then I was to make contact with two possible friends, and then the third thing was that I was going to spend a certain length of time with them in certain activities.

Co 374:   Very good! And after we decided on the smaller objectives, what did we do?

Cl 374:   We made a list of things I was going to do to attain each of the little objectives—like reading, role playing, listing the things I desired in a friend, listing potential friends, and so on. Things like that.

Co 375:   Okay, good. So we developed a very clear plan of operation—and we wrote all of the steps down so we could keep track of what we were supposed to do—that's very important.

Cl 375:   Yes, that helped quite a bit.

Co 376:   And then, after you had done all of the steps we planned, we compared your performance with your objective. And as it turned out, you performed very nicely and more than attained the objective. (pause) Do you remember what we did when you ran into trouble at one point?

Cl 376:   You mean, with Maria?

Co 377:   Yes.

Cl 377:   Well, we tried to analyze reasons for what happened and then we practiced how to deal with her differently . . . but somehow that didn't work out.

Co 378: That's right. So what did we do then?

Cl 378: We listed some alternative ways of meeting that part of the objective, and then I decided to try to make friends with Carlotta instead.

Co 379: Good. In other words, you developed a back-up plan and used that instead. (pause) Now, can you see how you might use some of these same techniques in dealing with other problems?

Cl 379: I think so.

Co 380: Okay, can you review the major steps?

Cl 380: Let's see . . . first find out just what the problem is . . . then set up a goal to work for, then break the goal down into smaller goals with tasks for each one . . . .

Co 381: And then, after you've carried out your plan, compare your progress with your objective.

Cl 381: Yeah, I guess a lot of problems could be solved in that way.

Co 382: And I imagine it would make you feel pretty good to solve such a problem on your own. . . .

Cl 382: Yeah, I'm sure it would. It would make me feel more confident of myself.

Co 383: And then there would usually be other kinds of rewards involved—like gaining friends, or making higher grades, getting along better with your folks, or getting into the college of your choice, and so on.

Cl 383: Yes . . . like, right now I've got at least two new friends and I'm certainly enjoying school more. And my parents are really happy about it, too.

9.4 PLAN MONITORING OF CLIENT PERFORMANCE

Co 384: Fine, Juanita! Now, there's one more thing we need to do before we close. A few minutes ago you mentioned that you might possibly run into some difficulty in maintaining your improved relationships with the other kids. So I'm wondering if perhaps we should set up a plan for reviewing your progress once in a while. Then, if we find that you're getting along okay, that would be just great. But if we find you're having some difficulties, we could talk about the situation and try to get things worked out.

Cl 384: Well . . . I'd probably feel a lot more comfortable if we did something like that. But I guess I don't really know what would be involved.

Co 385:   Actually, there could be several possibilities. For one thing, we could get together for brief check-up interviews—say, about once a month. We probably wouldn't need to talk for more than five minutes or so. We could do that maybe for the next three months.

Cl 385:   I think I'd like that. . . . That way, I wouldn't feel like I had to handle it entirely on my own . . . at least not at first.

Co 386:   That's right. Of course, I'm pretty sure you won't really need any new help, but in case you do, we could take whatever steps are needed. Another thing . . . you know, sometimes we become so involved in our own behavior that we can't really observe it as well as someone else can. So I'm wondering how you'd feel if I asked Ms. Holt how you're doing from time to time.

Cl 386:   Oh, that would be okay. I really like her, and I'm sure she'd be glad to do it.

Co 387:   Fine, Juanita. And, of course, I'm sure I'll see you occasionally around school, so maybe I could make some observations, too. I wouldn't be snooping or spying or anything like that, but just noticing how you seem to be interacting with the other kids.

Cl 387:   That would be all right, too. You're probably more familiar with my situation than anyone else, so you'd really know what to look for.

Co 388:   Okay, fine. Now, there's one more way of following up on your progress that I think might be helpful. At the end of each report period, in addition to assigning grades, the teachers make brief written comments about how their students are doing in class—you know, things like work habits, class conduct, and so on. And one of the things they usually comment on is something called "social relationships," which has to do with how well a student gets along with the other kids. So maybe it would be a good idea for me to take a look at those reports for a while to see how all your teachers think you're doing. . . .

Cl 388:   Yeah, I've heard about those reports. I guess they've never said anything terribly bad about me. At least, I've never heard about it if they have. (pause) Okay, I guess it might help to find out how they think I'm doing. I'm pretty sure about what Ms. Holt would say, but I don't know about the others. (laughs)

Co 389:   Okay, good, Juanita! Suppose we say, then, that we'll check on your progress in four ways. First, you can observe your own behavior and tell me how you think you're doing. We'll do this once a month for the next three months. Second, I'll ask Ms. Holt from time to time how your're getting along. Third, whenever I see you with the other kids in the hall or the cafeteria or on the school grounds, I'll make a mental note about how you seem to be doing. We can then compare notes in our short check-up interviews. And fourth, I'll check the written teacher comments at the end of the next report period. Then, if things are going well when we have our third check-up session, perhaps we can say that your problem has really been taken care of and we won't need to check on it any further.[12]

Cl 389:   Yeah . . . I think it sounds okay. It should really keep me on my toes, knowing that I'm going to have to report on what I've done, and that other people will be observing me also.

Co 390:   Okay, then . . . let's see (consults appointment book) . . . suppose we set up our first check-up session for January 15th at 8:15. That would be just a few minutes before first period begins. And we'll plan to spend about five minutes together at that time. Can you make it then?

Cl 390:   Yes, that would be fine.

Co 391:   Then we're all set. . . . Well, I've certainly enjoyed working with you over the past couple of months, Juanita, and I'm really happy about your progress! I think you have things pretty well worked out now, and I'll be looking forward to seeing you next month.

Cl 391:   I want to thank you for all your help.

Co 392:   It was a pleasure to work with you, Juanita. Bye now.

Cl 392:   Goodbye.

10.0   MONITOR CLIENT PERFORMANCE

In accordance with the plan established in Function 9.4, Mr. Adams monitored Juanita's progress for the next three months. The primary vehicle for this was the brief check-up interviews which he and Juanita had agreed upon. At these meetings, which were typically no more than five minutes in length, Juanita stated that she had continued to be friends with Karen and Carlotta, although she had not always spent as much time with them as when she was working on her counseling objective. She also reported that she had met two other girls whom she considered "friends," although not to the same extent as Karen and Carlotta. She and Maria usually said "Hello" to each other, but their relationship had not progressed further. In mid-February, she reported that she had joined the Mathematics Club, a group sponsored by Ms.

[12]Lack of follow-through beyond counseling is where many counseling efforts fail. The counselor in this case helped ensure further progress through continued monitoring.

Holt. This was the first extra-curricular activity in which she had participated.

At opportune times, Mr. Adams checked with Ms. Holt, who reported that Juanita had continued her friendly behavior with other students in class and that she was a moderately active contributor in meetings of the Mathematics Club. On the whole, Ms. Holt considered her progress to be quite satisfactory and stated that she was a "changed girl" as compared to when she was first referred for counseling.

In addition to his brief, scheduled meetings with Juanita, Mr. Adams also made a point of observing her behavior informally as she interacted with other students in the halls and cafeteria. Here, he noted that she was usually found in the company of other girls, though it appeared that she was more of a listener than an active participant in conversation. She was never observed speaking to a boy, nor did she report any contacts with males during her check-up interviews.

Finally, Mr. Adams examined Juanita's records at the end of the next marking period, as was his custom for all tenth graders, and found that her grades had remained at a B minus level. However, the brief written comments furnished by her teachers had changed from remarks such as "Quiet" and "Reserved," to "Improved in her relationships with others" and "Occasionally contributes to class discussions."

Thus, although there were no dramatic changes during the follow-up period, Juanita maintained the gains made earlier during formal counseling and was apparently making continued progress.

11.0: CLOSE CASE

Mr. Adams now proceeded to close out the case of Juanita. In the third and final check-up interview, which had been held in mid-March, he had again expressed pleasure at having worked with Juanita and had verbally reinforced her for sustaining and enhancing her earlier gains in the area of social relationships. He had also assured her of his confidence in her ability to make continued progress. Finally, he had invited her to consult with him in the future in case she needed further help on social relationships or on any other concern which might develop. In that interview Juanita seemed considerably more self-confident and showed no signs of resistance to terminating contact with the counselor.

Accordingly, Mr. Adams completed his case notes. He also informed Ms. Holt of Juanita's progress and of the fact that he was no longer working with her. Finally, Mr. Adams made a record of his work with Juanita for purposes of accountability. Such information, recorded on small index cards, would be used by the school principal and the central administration as one means of assessing his effectiveness at the end of the year. Juanita's card appeared as follows:

Counselor: Adams, D.
Client: Salvado, Juanita   Female, Age 16, Grade 10
Problem: Lack of friends at school
Time:
    Interviews: 4 hr.   (eight 30-min. weekly
                                            sessions, Oct. 17-Dec. 5)

    Follow-up: 15 min.   (three 5-min. monthly
                                           sessions, Jan. 15-Mar. 15)

    Consultation: 1 hr.

    Planning: 30 min.

    Case notes: 1 hr.
            TOTAL   6 hr., 45 min.

Outcome:
        December: 2 reported friends; verified by teacher and
                    counselor observation.
        March: Continued progress; 2 more friends; joined Math
                 Club; more class participation.

12.0:   EVALUATE COUNSELOR PERFORMANCE

Mr. Adams was obviously pleased with Juanita's performance. She had indeed attained her objective. She had acquired four friends, whereas she had had none when she came for counseling. She seemed happier and more contented in school. Moreover, she had acquired some skills and understandings which seemed likely to promote continued improvement in her social relationships. Finally, she had stated that she was highly pleased with her counseling experience.

Nevertheless, Mr. Adams realized that the client's progress and satisfaction were only one index of his effectiveness as a counselor. Other questions remained to be answered. Did he adhere to the Performance Criteria for Systematic Counseling (Appendix A)? Were the techniques, objectives, and strategy used best suited to this case? What did he learn from this case that would help him counsel more effectively with similar clients in the future?

Partial answers to some of these questions had been obtained at earlier stages in the process of counseling with Juanita. From his first contact with Juanita, Mr. Adams had viewed evaluation of his own performance as a continuous process which would extend throughout and beyond the process of formal counseling with her. Accordingly, he had tried to adopt a constructively critical attitude toward whatever he had said to her on a moment-to-moment basis. In addition, while writing his case notes following each interview he had devoted a few moments to analyzing what he had done well, what he had done poorly, and how he might improve in his subsequent interviews with Juanita.

Now, having completed his contacts with the client, Mr. Adams sought to examine his work in three main areas: (a) adherence to the flowchart for Systematic Counseling and the accompanying Performance Criteria; (b) suitability of techniques, objectives, and strategy; and (c) identification of ways to improve counseling with other clients having similar problems in the future.

With regard to the first area, he reviewed the flowchart and the Performance Criteria and concluded that, on the whole, he had closely followed the format for Systematic Counseling. The only area that he could think of where he might have deviated was his failure to mention the maintaining reinforcer for the problem behavior when verifying the model of the client's concern in 5.6. Since the maintaining reinforcer is a crucial part of the client's problem, it should be mentioned in the counselor's summary remarks where an attempt is made to obtain the client's verification of the concern.

In terms of his counseling techniques, however, Mr. Adams felt in retrospect that he had unduly controlled the interview sessions with Juanita. Especially during the early interviews, he felt that he had talked too much and had failed to draw Juanita out sufficiently concerning the nature of her problem. In Systematic Counseling it is to be expected that the counselor will do much of the talking in the early phases of contact with a client, particularly when explaining the nature of the counseling relationship. However, when discussing client concerns, the client should be given much more initiative and should be allowed to explain the concern(s) in considerable detail. This he felt he had not done. Perhaps he had too quickly settled on the problem as solely one of lack of skills, and had not given due consideration to the possibility of racial bias. Perhaps, in addition to helping Juanita develop social skills, he should have undertaken some sort of programmatic effort to promote greater harmony among the diverse racial groups in the school. In the long run, such an effort might have benefited other students as well as Juanita.

In setting the learning objective (6.4), the counselor had exercised a rather heavy hand. He might better have given Juanita more of the responsibility for setting up the objective, as opposed to doing it for her and then asking her approval. The counselor should always keep in mind that a major objective is to foster independent and responsible behavior on the part of the client. That is, throughout counseling the client should be encouraged to assume as much responsibility as possible under the circumstances. The appropriate amount, of course, is difficult to determine; it may vary from one client to another and perhaps from one problem to another. But Mr. Adams felt that he had erred on the side of assuming too much responsibility and giving the client too little.

He felt that, in view of Juanita's severely limited social skills, the chosen strategy—a combination of learning new responses and becoming self-directed—had been appropriate. Specifically, modeling and simulation techniques were used to help Juanita learn new responses, while instruction and practice in decision making helped her become more self-directed. The intermediate objectives also seemed well-suited to the problem, except that the final one was essentially identical with the learning objective (6.4) and was therefore not really "intermediate." The intermediate objectives should consist of a graded series of lesser objectives, and the final one should lead up to, but stop just short of, the ultimate objective for counseling.

In summary, aside from the need to adhere more closely to certain portions of the flowchart and the Performance Criteria, Mr. Adams felt there were two main areas in which he had learned something from counseling with Juanita which would help him do a better job in working with future clients. First, he resolved to take a somewhat less active role in directing the course of the interview, allowing the client to talk more and to assume more responsibility for proposing solutions and making decisions. Second, he would try to remember that, in some cases, a particular client's concern may reflect a broader problem in the school environment, and that group work or other preventive approaches may be appropriate as a complement to individual counseling.

SUMMARY

The Case of Juanita includes eight complete interviews illustrating the application of Systematic Counseling to an interpersonal concern. Although the entire transcript of the case is presented, it is possible to grasp the essential elements by reading Interviews 1-3, the summary of Interviews 4-7, and the final interview.

The setting for the case is a high school in a small Midwestern community. Juanita, a 16-year-old sophomore of Latino descent, was referred to the counselor by her geometry teacher, who was concerned about

Juanita's shyness and lack of friends. The learning objective developed with Juanita provided that she would acquire conversational and other social skills that would enable her to become friends with two of her fellow students by the end of the semester.

The strategy utilized by the counselor involved a combination of learning new responses and becoming self-directed. Specific procedures included modeling, simulation, and decision making. Modeling of appropriate behavior was presented in a number of ways, including printed materials, audiotape, and role playing. Simulation was also used extensively, in that Juanita tried out new social behaviors through role playing with a variety of people, including the counselor, fellow students, and members of her family. Decision making entered prominently into the case as Juanita deliberated upon the characteristics she wanted in a friend, and in her choice of two potential friends. To facilitate the attainment of the learning objective, a graded series of intermediate objectives and steps was developed, ranging from easy to difficult.

The case presents several additional features. First, although Juanita was a highly motivated client who attained her learning objective, many of the difficulties with which a counselor must deal are illustrated, e.g., Juanita's reluctance to face the nature of her problem; the slow, painstaking progress through the performance of steps (Function 7.4); the unresolved difficulty with one of her potential friends; and her resistance to termination of counseling. Second, in addition to the more common type of counselor-client interaction, verbatim accounts of role-playing sessions and teacher-counselor consultation are provided. Third, a format for recording case data for purposes of accountability is presented. Finally, following the closing of the case, the counselor reviews his own performance and determines ways in which he can improve his counseling with subsequent clients.

APPENDIX A

PERFORMANCE CRITERIA FOR SYSTEMATIC COUNSELING

Directions to Counselor:

1. Complete a separate copy of the Criteria for each client whom you counsel during this term.
2. Please fill in appropriate blanks on the Criteria *prior to meeting with your supervisor.* (These blanks are indicated by an asterisk.) You may attach additional sheets if needed. Also, please indicate decisions made in handling the case by checking the appropriate boxes (✓) in the margin.

Subsystem 1.0 - Counselor

As a counselor, you are obligated to assume certain professional responsiblities when you enter into a counseling relationship. You are no longer *just* a graduate student and private citizen of worth and dignity. You are also a recognized professional counselor who is certified by our society to provide unique services to members of our communities. You will be viewed as a person who possesses certain skills, knowledge, and attitudes. This subsystem (1.0) of Systematic Counseling focuses on the attitudes of the counselor who is preparing to enter a counseling relationship. Other subsystems will focus on the skills and knowledge needed during the counseling process.

An attitude is an enduring, learned predisposition (state of readiness) to behave in a consistent way toward a given class of objects. It is by the consistency of response to a class of objects that an attitude is identified. Thus, the criteria for evaluating your counseling attitudes will necessarily be your performance during the entire counseling process. It is suggested, however, that you review the following concepts *prior* to entering into a counseling relationship. They will help you develop an appropriate *state of readiness* for counseling.

1. As a counselor you must respect the worth and dignity of the client regardless of the client's behavior, attitudes, creeds, race, or socioeconomic status.
2. You must work to develop a sound relationship with the client. You must remember that you have the responsibility for developing a *counseling* relationship which has additional qualities beyond those of trust, understanding, and respect. It is a relationship in which your professional skills and knowledge are utilized in order to help the client attain personal goals.
3. You must constantly examine your own needs for reinforcement to determine if the counseling relationship is fulfilling your needs at the expense of client progress toward goal attainment.
4. You must always assist the client to examine the psychological dimensions of what he or she is thinking, saying, and feeling. This means that you must be sensitive to all dimensions of behavior: verbal, nonverbal, cognitive, affective, and psychomotor.
5. You must be willing to expend the time and effort (reading, study, consultation) to gain additional skills and knowledge in order to be of appropriate assistance to clients. Less than 100 percent effort should be a signal to you to engage in self-examination as to the cause of your lack of motivation.
6. You must be thoroughly familiar with the flowchart for Systematic Counseling.
7. You must remember that you are a social model and therefore represent the entire counseling profession. If you do a poor job, you invite the public to question the competence of all counselors.

Subsystem 2.0 - Process Client Referral

*What subfunction of 2.1 was the referral source?_____
You must present evidence that the functions of 2.2 (ANALYZE APPROPRIATENESS OF REFERRAL) were performed.

Criteria for 2.2.1 (COLLECT DATA)

You must present evidence that data were collected concerning the reasons for client referral. Evidence to show that such data were collected must be in the form of a written summary of records, reports of observations of the client by you or the referral source, and/or reports of interviews with the referral source. (Not applicable to self-referral.)

*List the evidence which shows that 2.2.1 was performed:

> Supervisor's comments. Is the evidence adequate?

Criteria for 2.2.2 (ANALYZE DATA)

Your analysis must identify the problem and the conditions attendant to the problem. These must be stated in behavioral terms. For example, "Jim fights on the playground before school. The frequency of Jim's behavior is three to four times per week and has persisted since the start of this school year," or "Jill is seventeen years of age, has never had a date, and is not permitted to date by her parents. She has been asked to go to the junior prom and wants help in securing the permission of her parents."

*List your analysis of the problem and its conditions:

> Supervisor's comments: Is the analysis adequate?

Criteria for 2.2.3 (DECIDE IF REFERRAL IS APPROPRIATE)
Criteria for a YES decision (2.2.3.1)

( ) a. Any educational or vocational problem that requires information and/or decisions that can be made through the use of the decision-making process is an appropriate referral.

( )   b. Any interpersonal or intrapersonal conflict that involves overt behavior responses that are recognized as inappropriate by referral sources is an appropriate referral if: (1) the frequency of the responses can be reduced to 10% or less for a given situation within 10 hours of counseling time, and (2) you can present evidence to your supervisor that you have the intervention resources at your disposal to assist the client to decrease the frequency of responses.

*List the approximate amount of time you will have to spend with the client and how you anticipate that this time will be spent:

*List the intervention resources at your disposal (e.g., persons, techniques, material resources, etc.):

Supervisor's comments: Was the referral appropriate?

If YES decision (2.2.3.1), you must present evidence which shows that 2.2.4 was performed.

Criteria for 2.2.4 (SPECIFY CONDITIONS TO REFERRAL SOURCE)

Evidence must be a written report of the conditions under which the referral was accepted. For example, was the referral source informed of the confidentiality requirements? If the referral source will assist you with the case, was the source specifically informed of his or her role? Was the referral source given directions on how to arrange for the client to make an appointment? (Not applicable to self-referral.)

*List evidence which shows that 2.2.4 was performed:

Supervisor's comments: Is the evidence adequate?

( ) *If a NO decision (2.2.3.2) was made, state why the referral was not accepted:

Supervisor's comments: Did the counselor use logical reasoning in terms of 2.2.3.2?

If a NO decision (2.2.3.2) was made, you must show evidence that 2.2.5 (ASSIST IN LOCATING APPROPRIATE ASSISTANCE) was performed.

Criteria for 2.2.5 (ASSIST IN LOCATING APPROPRIATE ASSISTANCE)

*Give the name of the agency or individual to whom the referral source was directed. The specific qualifications of the agency or individual must be stated:

Supervisor's comments: Was adequate assistance rendered in locating an appropriate referral source?

Criteria for Termination of Case Referred to Another Agency or Individual.

Upon completion of 2.2.5 (ASSIST IN LOCATING APPROPRIATE ASSISTANCE), you must input to 9.1 (EXPLAIN TERMINATION RATIONALE AND PROCEDURES). You must present evidence that the client understands that, although another individual or agency will be providing assistance with this particular concern, the client can return to see the counselor if assistance is needed with other problems. You must then input to 9.2 (MANAGE CLIENT/COUNSELOR RESISTANCE). Criteria for 9.2 are specified on page 357 of this checklist. You must next input to 11.0 (CLOSE CASE). Note that termination *under these conditions* involves moving *directly* from 9.2 to 11.0, rather than going through 9.3 (CONDUCT TRANSFER OF LEARNING), 9.4 (PLAN MONITORING OF CLIENT PERFORMANCE), and 10.0 (MONITOR CLIENT PERFORMANCE).

Supervisors's comments: Was the case terminated appropriately?

Subsystem 3.0 - Prepare for Interview

Criteria for 3.2 (REVIEW AVAILABLE DATA)

*In the following space you must present evidence that you have reviewed any available data prior to the initial interview. Acceptable evidence consists of a written summary of client interests, achievements, personal background, and test information. If such information was not available, you must state why it was not.

> Supervisor's comments: Is the review of available data adequate?

Subsystem 4.0 - Explain Counseling Relationship

Criteria for 4.1 (DECIDE IF FORMAL STRUCTURE NEEDED)

( )Criteria for YES decision (4.1.1)

All referrals who are being seen by you for the first time must be provided with formal structure even though they have been interviewed previously by another counselor.

( ) Criteria for a NO decision (4.1.2)

    a. The client has been seen previously by you, when structure was provided, *and*

    b. The client responds immediately when invited by you to discuss his or her concerns.

> Supervisor's comments: Did the counselor make an appropriate
> decision?

Criteria for 4.2 (DECIDE IF TIME IS APPROPRIATE)

( ) Criteria for a YES decision (4.2.1)

The client does not respond to your invitation to discuss his or her concerns and/or shows symptoms of anxiety such as: blushing, shifting weight in the chair, looking away from you, gripping the chair, wringing hands, playing with objects, or slow, hesitant speech.

( ) Criteria for a NO decision (4.2.2)

The client responds immediately when invited by you to discuss his or her concerns. Structure then is provided during 5.0 (CONSTRUCT MODEL OF CLIENT CONCERNS), or 6.0 (DECIDE GOAL AND OBJECTIVE), or at the termination of the interview.

> Supervisor's comments: Did the counselor make an appropriate decision?

If YES decision (4.2.1) was made, you must present evidence that 4.3 (DESCRIBE COUNSELING PROCESS) was performed.

Criteria for 4.3.1 (PURPOSE OF COUNSELING)

You must explain the purpose of counseling. For example, "The purpose of counseling is to assist you with the things that concern you or those that interest you. Some students want to make decisions about what to do after high school; others need help with school problems, subjects, and teachers. Some have problems getting along with others, such as classmates or parents. The purpose of counseling, really, is to help you with the things that are important to you."

> Supervisor's comments: Was 4.3.1 adequate?

Criteria for 4.3.2 (RESPONSIBILITIES)

The responsibilities of the counselor and the client must be defined. For example, "My job as a counselor is to listen and try to understand how you feel and think about things. I won't make decisions for you, but together we may come up with some things for you to consider in making a decision. If you make a decision, I will help you find ways to carry it out. Your part in counseling is to help me understand how you feel and think. You also have to make decisions and carry out any tasks to help you reach your goals."

> Supervisor's comments: Was 4.3.2 adequate?

Criteria for 4.3.3 (FOCUS)

You must state the focus of counseling. For example, "In counseling we usually focus on establishing some specific objectives for what you want to accomplish."

```
Supervisor's comments: Was 4.3.3 adequate?



```

Criteria for 4.3.4 (LIMITS)

You must define the limits of counseling: (a) the voluntary basis of counseling, (b) confidentiality, and (c) time limits. For example, "People participate in counseling on a voluntary basis. You may quit whenever you choose. The interviews are confidential. I don't report to anyone unless you would think this would be the thing to do and give me your permission. Our interviews usually last for about 45 minutes, if you need this much time. The total number of interviews is typically from two to five."

```
Supervisor's comments: Was 4.3.4 adequate?



```

Subsystem 5.0 - Construct Model of Client Concerns

Criteria for 5.1 (IDENTIFY CONCERNS)

You must invite the client to discuss his or her concerns. You must recognize any difficulty experienced by the client in responding to the counseling environment and take steps to increase the frequency of client responses in describing his or her concerns. For example, one step might be as follows: "You seem to have some difficulty in talking with me. How can I make it easier for you to talk about the things that are on your mind?" You must check out your awareness of the client's concerns by means of restatement, reflection, and summary statements of the data received from the client.

*State the identified concern(s):

Supervisor's comments. Was 5.1 adequate?

Criteria for 5.2 (SELECT CONCERN FOR COUNSELING)

You must help the client select a concern for counseling. If the client has several problems, you should assist the client in identifying the concern having the highest priority. One problem should be considered unless two concerns are closely related. As it is important for the client to experience success in the shortest possible time, you should help the client order his or her priorities in terms of the probability of attainment of different objectives.

*State the concern selected for counseling. If more than one concern has been identified, rank the concerns in order of priority:

Supervisor's comments: Was 5.2 adequate?

Criteria for 5.3 (IDENTIFY COMPONENTS OF CONCERN)

a. 5.3.1 (RESPONSE)

You must determine the terms used by the client to describe the problem and then help the client to specify the observable and measurable aspects of the concern.

*State the response components of the concern:

Supervisor's comments: Was 5.3.1 adequate?

---

b. Criteria for 5.3.2 (TEMPORAL)
   You must assist the client to describe when the behavior occurs, how long it has occurred, and if there is any pattern or sequence to the problem.
*State the temporal components of the concern:

Supervisor's comments: Was 5.3.2 adequate?

---

c. Criteria for 5.3.3 (SITUATIONAL)
   You must assist the client to describe where or under what circumstances the problem becomes apparent.
*State the situational components of the concern:

Supervisor's comments: Was 5.3.3 adequate?

Criteria for 5.4 (ESTABLISH BASELINE OF CONCERN-RELATED BEHAVIOR)

You must report one or more of the following baselines, depending upon the type of concern presented by the client: frequency, duration, and amount of behavior, utility of information, and the conditions that exist at the time of occurrence of the behavior.

*State the baseline of concern-related behavior:

Supervisor's comments: Was 5.4 adequate?

Criteria for 5.5 (IDENTIFY MAINTAINING REINFORCERS)

You must assist the client to identify those tangible or intangible reinforcers that maintain his or her problem behavior.

*State the maintaining reinforcers:

Supervisor's comments: Was 5.5 adequate?

Criteria for 5.6 (VERIFY MODEL WITH CLIENT)

In a summary statement, you must check out and clarify the hypotheses which you have formulated during the interview. You must secure the client's verbal agreement that your model is essentially correct. If this agreement cannot be secured, you must recycle to 5.1 to determine where the discrepancies between your concepts and the client's thinking and feelings are.

*Summarize the verified model of the concern:

```
┌─────────────────────────────────────────────────────────────────┐
│                                                                   │
│ Supervisor's comments: Was 5.6 adequate?                          │
│                                                                   │
│                                                                   │
│                                                                   │
│                                                                   │
│                                                                   │
│                                                                   │
└─────────────────────────────────────────────────────────────────┘
```

Subsystem 6.0 - Decide Goal and Objective

Criteria for 6.1 (DECIDE IF GOAL CAN BE ESTABLISHED)

( ) Criteria for YES decision (6.1.1)

The client has verified your model of the concern, enters willingly into a discussion of the problem, and shows little or no reluctance to continue in counseling.

```
┌─────────────────────────────────────────────────────────────────┐
│                                                                   │
│ Supervisor's comments: Was the appropriate decision made?         │
│                                                                   │
│                                                                   │
│                                                                   │
│                                                                   │
│                                                                   │
│                                                                   │
└─────────────────────────────────────────────────────────────────┘
```

( ) Criteria for a NO decision (6.1.2)

The client demonstrates through verbal and /or nonverbal behavior that he or she is in too anxious a state to work on the problem, feels the problem is of too little importance, or needs additional structuring on the need for goals.

Supervisor's comments: Was the appropriate decision made?

If a NO decision (6.1.2) was made, you must present evidence that 6.7 (DISCUSS NEED FOR GOALS IN COUNSELING) was performed.

Criteria for 6.7 (DISCUSS NEED FOR GOALS IN COUNSELING)

There must be verbal evidence that you provided the client with information about the necessity of establishing goals. If necessary, you must recycle to 5.1 (IDENTIFY CONCERNS) or input to 2.2.5 (ASSIST IN LOCATING APPROPRIATE ASSISTANCE) if an acceptable goal cannot be identified.

Supervisor's comments: Was 6.7 adequate?

Criteria for 6.2 (DETERMINE DESIRED GOAL)

*You must help the client to specify the desired long-term outcome or resolution of the problem. This provides a general direction in which you and the client can move and constitutes a broad framework within which a realistic learning objective can eventually be determined. For example, "What you would like to do, ideally, is to overcome your shyness to the point that you could enter a conversation freely with other people at any time and any place without feeling discomfort." Write the desired counseling outcome:

Supervisor's comments: Was 6.2 adequate?

Criteria for 6.3 (DECIDE IF COUNSELOR CAN/WILL HANDLE)
( ) Criteria for a YES decision (6.3.2)
  Use criteria previously provided for a YES decision when receiving a referral. See 2.2.3, page 337.

Supervisor's comments: Was the appropriate decision made?

( ) *If a NO decision (6.3.1) was made, you must state below why you cannot/will not handle the case:

Supervisor's comments: Was the counselor's decision appropriate?

Criteria for 6.4 (ESTABLISH LEARNING OBJECTIVE)
  *You and the client must verbally reach a contract to work toward a learning objective that: (a) is stated in behavioral terms, (b) indicates a criterion of minimum performance, and (c) indicates the

conditions under which the behavior is to be demonstrated. Write this objective below:

Supervisor's comments: Was 6.4 adequate?

Criteria for 6.5 (DECIDE IF CLIENT MOTIVATION SUFFICIENT)
( ) Criteria for a YES decision (6.5.2)
  You must receive verbal agreement that the client is ready to decide upon a strategy for reaching the learning objective.
  * State the evidence:

( ) Criteria for a NO decision (6.5.1)
  The client is unwilling to verbally commit himself or herself to working on the problem.
  * State the evidence:

Supervisor's comments: Was the appropriate decision made?

If a NO decision (6.5.1) was reached, you must present evidence that 6.6 (DISCUSS REASONS FOR INSUFFICIENT MOTIVATION) was performed.

Criteria for 6.6 (DISCUSS REASONS FOR INSUFFICIENT MOTIVATION)

One or more of the following must be mentioned in the discussion of motivation: time, money, anxiety, commitment, client responsibility for his or her own behavior.

Supervisor's comments: Was the discussion adequate?

( ) If a NO decision (6.5.1) continues to be made after performing 6.6, you must show evidence that you made an input to 2.2.5 (ASSIST IN LOCATING APPROPRIATE ASSISTANCE).

Supervisor's comments: Was the input to 2.2.5 appropriate?

Subsystem 7.0 - Implement Strategy

Criteria for 7.1 (DETERMINE STRATEGY)

One or more of the following broad strategies must be selected for attaining the learning objective: (a) Learning New Responses, (b) Motivating Behavior Change, (c) Becoming Self-Directed.

*State the broad strategy selected:

Supervisor's comments: Was the chosen strategy (or strategies) appropriate?

Criteria for 7.2 (ESTABLISH INTERMEDIATE OBJECTIVES)
You and the client must verbally agree on a sequence of intermediate objectives which will enable the client to reach the learning objective.
* State the intermediate objectives:

1.

2.

3.

4.

Supervisor's comments: Was 7.2 adequate?

Criteria for 7.3 (SELECT STEPS)
You and the client must verbally agree on a statement of operational steps which will lead to the accomplishment of the intermediate objectives. Guidelines are as follows, categorized according to the three major strategies:
( )a. Learning New Responses
There must be evidence that you and the client have developed a learning sequence for acquiring the new response. This learning sequence will generally include procedures for helping the client understand the situational and behavioral elements of the new response, practice sessions to develop skill, and planned opportunities for the client to try out the response in an actual setting.
( )b. Motivating Behavior Change
There must be evidence that the appropriate reinforcers have been identified, that their systematic presentation or with-

drawal can be adequately managed, and that the planned modification of reinforcement contingencies is likely to produce behavior change.

( )c. Becoming Self-Directed

1. Decision Making

   There must be evidence that the client's goals have been identified and that at least three alternatives for reaching the client's goals are to be examined. Evidence must be provided that you and the client have developed specific procedures for obtaining and using information in clarification of goals and in examining alternative ways of achieving goals.

2. Self-Management

   There must be evidence that procedures have been planned to enable the client to monitor his or her own behavior and to manage environmental stimuli so as to promote desired behavior change.

*Summarize the steps used:

Supervisor's comments: Were the steps appropriate?

Criteria for 7.5 (DECIDE IF STRATEGY/STEPS HAVE BEEN COMPLETED)

Criteria for a YES decision (7.5.2)

There must be evidence that the strategy determined in 7.1 and the accompanying steps have been completed. Examples of appropriate evidence include oral reports from you and the client, and oral or written reports from others who have observed the client's behavior.

Criteria for a NO decision (7.5.1)

The client has failed to perform the necessary steps, or has performed them in a superficial or otherwise inappropriate manner. Or, the intermediate objectives and operational steps are in need of revision.

(NOTE: Because 7.3-7.5 is a crucial and often prolonged stage of the counseling process, provision has been made so that you and your supervisor can recycle three times if necessary).

*1. State the date (_____) and reasons for a NO decision:

If a NO decision (7.5.1) was made, you must recycle to 7.2 (ESTABLISH INTERMEDIATE OBJECTIVES) and proceed again from that point forward. If after repeated attempts the strategy/tasks have not been completed, you must input to 2.2.5 (ASSIST IN LOCATING APPROPRIATE ASSISTANCE).

Supervisor's comments: Was adequate evidence presented?

---

*2. State the date (_____) and reasons for a NO decision:

Supervisor's comments: Was adequate evidence presented?

---

*3. State the date (_____) and reasons for a NO decision:

Supervisor's comments: Was adequate evidence presented?

Subsystem 8.0 - Evaluate Client Performance

Criteria for 8.1 (ANALYZE OUTCOMES)
Criteria for 8.1.1 (RECORD PERFORMANCE)
There must be verbal evidence that indicates the performance of the client.
*Summarize the client's performance:

Supervisor's comments: Was 8.1.1 adequate?

Criteria for 8.1.2 (COMPARE PERFORMANCE WITH BASELINE)
There must be verbal evidence that the client's performance was compared with the baseline established in 5.4.

Supervisor's comments: Was 8.1.2 adequate?

Criteria for 8.1.3 (COMPARE PERFORMANCE WITH OBJECTIVE)
There must be verbal evidence that the client's performance was compared with the learning objective.

Supervisor's comments: Was 8.1.3 adequate?

Criteria for 8.2 (DECIDE IF OBJECTIVE WAS ATTAINED)
( ) Criteria for a YES decision (8.2.2)
The objective established in 6.4 was attained as verified by data from 8.1.3.
( ) If a NO decision (8.2.1) is made, you must show that you structured for input into 6.5 (DECIDE IF CLIENT MOTIVATION IS SUFFICIENT).

Supervisor's comments: Was 8.2 decision appropriate and was the counselor's action adequate?

Criteria for 8.3 (DECIDE NEED FOR FURTHER COUNSELING)
( ) Criteria for 8.3.3 (NO NEED)
There must be verbal evidence that you and the client agree that no additional counseling is needed at this time.
( ) Criteria for 8.3.2 (PURSUE ANOTHER CONCERN)
There must be verbal evidence that you and the client agree that additional counseling is needed and that a new objective for counseling should be established. You must show that you structured for input into 5.1 (IDENTIFY CONCERNS).
( ) Criteria for 8.3.1 (PURSUE NEW ASPECT/SAME CONCERN)
There must be verbal evidence that you and the client agree that a new objective is needed for the problem on which you have been working. You must show that you structured for input into 6.2.

*State the concern to be pursued (if 8.3.2 or 8.3.1 was selected):

Supervisor's comments. Was 8.0 decision appropriate and was the counselor's action adequate?

Subsystem 9.0 - Terminate Counseling

Criteria for 9.1 (EXPLAIN TERMINATION RATIONALE AND PROCEDURES)

You must show that plans for terminating counseling were discussed. These plans may include a tapering off or a reduction in the frequency of sessions. You must explain that since the objectives, if any, have been attained—or cannot be attained, as the case may be—it is appropriate to conclude regular counseling contacts. If applicable, you must also explain that you and the client will be talking about how to apply the kinds of things learned in the counseling process to other problems which may arise, and that the two of you will be setting up a plan for checking on the client's progress after regular counseling is concluded.

Supervisor's comments: Was 9.1 adequate?

Criteria for 9.2 (MANAGE CLIENT/COUNSELOR RESISTANCE)

You must show that any resistance to termination was discussed, such as: client dependency upon you or behavior that indicates problems of anxiety in managing environmental situations. You must show that you have reinforced behavior that indicates client movement toward independence and assertive action. Likewise, you should avoid unduly prolonging the counseling contact as a result of your own behavior, as shown, for example, by initiating or maintaining lengthy social conversation after the client's concerns have been resolved.

Supervisor's comments: Was 9.2 adequate?

Criteria for 9.3 (CONDUCT TRANSFER OF LEARNING)

There must be evidence that you discussed with the client how he or she can apply the skills learned in counseling to other concerns and situations. You must discuss how any reinforcement received in the counseling relationship can be obtained from other environmntal stimuli.

Supervisor's comments: Was 9.3 adequate?

Criteria for 9.4 (PLAN MONITORING OF CLIENT PERFORMANCE)

In nearly all cases, it is advisable to monitor the client's progress for a reasonable period of time after formal counseling has terminated. If monitoring is considered appropriate, you must inform the client that his or her progress will be monitored and must explain the manner in which monitoring will be conducted. The monitoring procedure will typically involve one or more of the following: (a) observing the client's behavior directly; (b) asking the client how he or she is progressing, usually in brief checkup interviews; (c) requesting information from others who are familiar with the client's performance; and (d) examining records and other written data concerning the client's behavior.

If monitoring is not considered appropriate (e.g., the client is moving immediately from the community and will not be available for further contact), you should omit Function 9.4 and input to 11.0 (CLOSE CASE).

Was monitoring considered appropriate?

( ) YES

( ) NO

*If a NO decision was made, explain why monitoring was not considered appropriate:

Supervisor's comments: Was an appropriate decision made, and was appropriate action taken?

Subsystem 10.0 - Monitor Client Performance

You must show that the plan previously established in 9.4 (PLAN MONITORING OF CLIENT PERFORMANCE) was carried through. Evidence must include a written summary of follow-up data and/or a taped interview confirming that the plan was carried through to completion and that the client's progress remained satisfactory.

*Place written evidence below:

( ) If the client fails to maintain satisfactory progress because he or she has encountered difficulty with a different aspect of the same general concern, you must recycle to 6.2 (DETERMINE DESIRED GOAL).

( ) If the client fails to maintain satisfactory progress but has encountered no new difficulties, you must recycle to 6.5 (DECIDE IF CLIENT MOTIVATION IS SUFFICIENT).

Supervisor's comments: Was evidence of adequate monitoring presented? If not, did the counselor make appropriate provision for recycling?

Subsystem 11.0 - Close Case

You must show that you closed the case appropriately. Where a final follow-up interview with the client is involved, you should (a) express your pleasure at having worked with the client, (b) invite the client to return for further counseling if the need should arise, and (c) resolve any client or counselor resistance to closing the case.

You must then complete your interview notes for the client's file and must prepare a brief summary of your work on the case for purposes of accountability. The accountability summary must include client identification data (name, age, grade, etc.), a description of the presenting problem, a record of the time spent in each major type of activity (counseling, follow-up, consultation, planning, record-keeping, etc.), and a statement of counseling outcomes at the end of regular counseling and at the end of the follow-up period.

* Place the accountability summary below:

Supervisor's comments: Was the case closed appropriately?

Subsystem 12.0 - Evaluate Counselor Performance

Alone, as well as in conference with your supervisor, you are to examine *four* areas of your performance:

a. counseling outcomes
b. counselor attitudes
c. counselor knowledge
d. counselor behavior

Data from recordings, records, the Performance Criteria, and supervisor feedback will provide suggestions for the improvement of your performance during counseling.

References

Air Ministry. *The origins and development of operations research in the Royal Air Force.* Air Publication 3368. London: Her Majesty's Stationery Office, 1963.

American Association of School Administrators Commission on Administrative Technology. *Administrative technology and the school executive.* Washington, D.C.: American Association of School Administrators, 1969.

American Personnel and Guidance Association. *Guidepost,* July 4, 1974, pp. 4-5.

Bandura, A. *Principles of behavior modification.* New York: Holt, Rinehart & Winston, 1969.

Berne, E. *Games people play.* New York: Grove Press, 1964.

Bertalanffy, L. von. General systems theory—A critical review. *General systems,* 1962, *7,* 1-20.

Bertalanffy, L. von. *General system theory.* New York: George Braziller, 1968.

Bertalanffy, L. von. General systems theory and psychiatry—An overview. In W. Gray, F. J. Duhl, & N. D. Rizzo (Eds.), *General systems theory and psychiatry.* Boston: Little, Brown, 1969.

Boocock, S.S. An experimental study of the learning effects of two games with simulated environments. *American Behavioral Scientist,* 1966, *10,* 8-18.

Boocock, S.S. The life career game. *Personnel and Guidance Journal,* 1967, *46,* 328-334.

Boocock, S.S., & Schild, E. O. (Eds.) *Simulation games in learning.* Beverly Hills, Calif.: Sage Publications, 1968.

Bourdon, R. D. Imitation: Implications for counseling and therapy. *Review of Educational Research,* 1970, *40,* 429-457.

Buckley, W. F. *Sociology and modern systems theory.* Englewood Cliffs, N.J.: Prentice-Hall, 1967.

Buckley, W. F. Society as a complex adaptive system. In W. F. Buckley (Ed.), *Modern systems research for the behavioral scientist.* Chicago: Aldine, 1968.

Bugental, J. F. T. The challenge that is man. *Journal of Humanistic Psychology,* 1967, *7,* 1-9.

Campbell, R. E., Dworkin, E. P., Jackson, D. P., Hoeltzel, K. E., Parsons, G. E., & Lacey, D. W. *The systems approach: An emerging behavioral model for career guidance.* Columbus, Ohio: The Ohio State University Center for Vocational and Technical Education, 1971.

Carkhuff, R. R. *Helping and human relations* (2 vols.). New York: Holt, Rinehart & Winston, 1969.

Cautela, J. R. Covert sensitization. *Psychological Record,* 1967, *20,* 459-468.

Cautela, J. R. Covert conditioning. In A. Jacobs & L. B. Sachs (Eds.), *The psychology of private events: Perspectives on covert response systems.* New York: Academic Press, 1971.

Churchman, C. W. *The systems approach.* New York: Dell, 1968.

Clarke, D. L. *Analytical archaeology.* London: Methuen, 1968.

Cogswell, J. F. Proposed systems simulation research studies for CLASS: The counseling function. FN-(L)-6083. Santa Monica, Calif.: System Development Corporation, December, 1961.

Cogswell, J. F. The systems approach as a heuristic method in educational development—An application to the counseling function. SP-720. Santa Monica, Calif.: System Development Corporation, March 5, 1962.

Cogswell, J. F., & Estavan, D. P. Explorations in computer-assisted counseling. TM-2582/000/00. Santa Monica, Calif.: System Development Corporation, August 6, 1965.

Cohen, H. L. Educational therapy: The design of learning environments. In J. M. Shlien (Ed.), *Research in psychotherapy.* Washington, D.C.: American Psychological Association, 1968.

Coleman, J. S. Games: New tools for learning. *Scholastic Teacher,* 1967, *51,* 9.

Cook, D. R. *A systems approach to the development of pupil personnel services. An operating manual.* Boston: Northeastern University, January, 1973. (ERIC document reproduction service no. ED 074 419)

Davidson, S., & Roy, R. H. A case study in newspaper operation. In C. D. Flagle, W. H. Huggins, & R. H. Roy (Eds.), *Operations research and systems engineering.* Baltimore: Johns Hopkins Press, 1960.

DeGreene, K. B. (Ed.) *Systems psychology.* New York: McGraw-Hill, 1970.

Easton, D. *A framework for political analysis.* Englewood Cliffs, N.J.: Prentice-Hall, 1965.

Emery, J. R. Systematic desensitization: Reducing test anxiety. In J. D. Krumboltz & C. E. Thoresen (Eds.), *Behavioral counseling: Cases and techniques.* New York: Holt, Rinehart & Winston, 1969.

Ford, D. H., & Urban, H. B. *Systems of psychotherapy: A comparative study.* New York: Wiley, 1963.

Franks, C. M. (Ed.) *Behavior therapy: Appraisal and status.* New York: McGraw-Hill, 1969.

Gagné, R. M. (Ed.) *Psychological principles in system development.* New York: Holt, Rinehart & Winston, 1962.

Gelatt, H. B. Decision-making: A conceptual frame of reference for counseling. *Journal of Counseling Psychology,* 1962, *9,* 240-245.

Gibson, R. E. The recognition of systems engineering. In C. D. Flagle, W. H. Huggins, & R. H. Roy (Eds.), *Operations research and systems engineering.* Baltimore: Johns Hopkins Press, 1960.

Glaser, R. (Ed.) *Training research and education.* New York: Wiley, 1965.

Gordon, A. K. *Games for growth.* Palo Alto, Calif.: Science Research Associates, 1970.

Gordon, J. E. *Personality and behavior.* New York: Macmillan, 1963.

Gray, W., Duhl, F. J., & Rizzo, N. D. (Eds.) *General systems theory and psychiatry.* Boston: Little, Brown, 1969.

Gray, W., & Rizzo, N. D. History and development of general systems theory. In W. Gray, F. J. Duhl, & N. D.. Rizzo (Eds.), *General systems theory and psychiatry.* Boston: Little, Brown, 1969.

Grinker, R. R. (Ed.) *Toward a unified theory of human behavior.* New York: Basic Books, 1956.

Hall, A. D., & Fagen, R. E. Definition of system. In W. F. Buckley (Ed.), *Modern systems research for the behavioral scientist.* Chicago: Aldine, 1968.

Hawkins, R. P. It's time we taught the young to be good parents (And don't you wish we'd started a long time ago?). *Psychology Today,* November 1972, pp. 28-30.

Hays, D. G. Model for designing a district testing program. Fullerton, Calif.: August 13, 1969. (Unpublished graphic analog)

Herr, E. L., & Cramer, S. H. *Vocational guidance and career development in the schools: Toward a systems approach.* New York: Houghton Mifflin, 1972.

Holland, J. G. Teaching machines: An application of principles from the laboratory. *Journal of Experimental Analysis of Behavior,* 1960, *3,* 275-287.

Hoppock, R. *Occupational information.* New York: McGraw-Hill, 1967.

Hosford, R. E. Determining effective models for counseling clients of varying competencies. Unpublished doctoral dissertation, Stanford University, 1966.

Hosford, R. E. Behavioral counseling: A contemporary overview. *Counseling Psychologist,* 1969, *1*(4), 1-33.

Hosford, R. E., & Ryan, T. A. Systems design in the development of counseling and guidance programs. *Personnel and Guidance Journal,* 1970, *49,* 221-230.

Isaacson, L. E. *Career information in counseling and teaching.* Boston: Allyn & Bacon, 1971.

Johnson, R. A., Kast, F. E., & Rosenzweig, J. E. *The theory and management of systems.* New York: McGraw-Hill, 1963.

Johnson, R. G. Simulation techniques in career development. *American Vocational Journal,* 1970, *45*(6), 30-32.

Kagan, N. Multimedia in guidance and counseling. *Personnel and Guidance Journal,* 1970, *49,* 197-204.

Kanfer, F. H., & Phillips, J. S. *Learning foundations of behavior therapy.* New York: Wiley, 1970

Kelly, G. A. Humanistic methodology in psychological research. *Journal of Humanistic Psychology,* 1969, *9,* 53-70.

Kemp, C. G. Existential counseling. *Counseling Psychologist,* 1971, *2*(3), 2-30.

Kershner, R. B. A survey of systems engineering tools and techniques. In C. D. Flagle, W. H. Huggins, & R. H. Roy (Eds.), *Operations research and systems engineering.* Baltimore: Johns Hopkins Press, 1960.

Khailov, K. M. The problem of systemic organization in theoretical biology. In W. F. Buckley (Ed.), *Modern systems research for the behavioral scientist.* Chicago: Aldine, 1968.

Krasner, L. The psychotherapist as a social reinforcement machine. In H. H. Strupp & L. Luborsky (Eds.), *Research in psychotherapy* (Vol.II). Washington, D.C.: American Psychological Association, 1962.

Kremyanskiy, V. I. Certain peculiarities of organisms as a "system" from the point of view of physics, cybernetics, and biology. In W. F. Buckley (Ed.), *Modern systems research for the behavioral scientist.* Chicago: Aldine, 1968.

Krumboltz, J. D. Behavioral goals for counseling. *Journal of Counseling Psychology,* 1966, *13,* 153-159.

Krumboltz, J. D. A behavioral approach to group counseling and therapy. *Journal of Research and Development in Education,* 1968, *1*(2), 3-18.

Krumboltz, J. D., & Krumboltz, H. B. *Changing children's behavior.* Englewood Cliffs, N.J.: Prentice-Hall, 1972.

Krumboltz, J. D., & Thoresen, C. E. The effect of behavioral counseling in group and individual settings on information-seeking behavior. *Journal of Counseling Psychology,* 1964, *11,* 324-333.

Krumboltz, J. D., & Thoresen, C. E. (Eds.). *Behavioral counseling: Cases and techniques.* New York: Holt, Rinehart & Winston, 1969.

Krumboltz, J. D., & Thoresen, C. E. (Eds.) *Counseling methods.* New York: Holt, Rinehart & Winston, 1976.

Laszlo, E. *System structure, and experience.* New York: Gordon & Breach Science Publishers, 1969.

Lazarus, A. A. Behavioral rehearsal vs. non-directive therapy vs. advice in effecting behavior change. *Behavior Research and Therapy,* 1966, *4,* 209-212.

London, P. *Behavior control.* New York: Harper & Row, 1969.

Loughary, J. W. *Counseling in secondary schools.* New York: Harper, 1961.

Loughary, J. W. System analysis as a research and development method. In Experimental Designs Committee of the Association for Counselor Education and Supervision (Ed.), *Research guidelines for high school counselors.* New York: College Entrance Examination Board, 1966.

Loughary, J. W., Friesen, D., & Hurst, R. Autocoun: A computer-based automated counseling simulation system. *Personnel and Guidance Journal,* 1966, *45,* 6-15.

Mahoney, M. J. *Cognition and behavior modification.* Cambridge, Mass.: Ballinger, 1974.

Meckley, R. F. Simulation in leadership training. *American Vocational Journal,* 1970, *45*(6), 26-27.

Mehrens, W. A., & Lehmann, I. J. *Standardized tests in education.* New York: Holt, Rinehart & Winston, 1975.

Mesarović, M. D. Foundations for a general systems theory. In M. D. Mesarović (Ed.), *Views on general systems theory: Proceedings of the second systems symposium at Case Institute of Technology.* New York: Wiley, 1964.

Milulas, W. L. *Behavior modification: An overview.* New York: Harper & Row, 1972.

Moreno, J. L. *Psychodrama.* New York: Beacon House, 1946.

Murray, E. J. A content-analysis method for studying psychotherapy. *Psychological Monographs,* 1956, *70* (13, Whole No. 420).

Norris, W., Zeran, F. R., Hatch, R. N., & Engelkes, J. R. *The information service in guidance: For career development and planning.* Chicago: Rand McNally, 1972.

Ohlsen, M. M. *Guidance services in the modern school.* New York: Harcourt Brace Jovanovich, 1974.

Patterson, C. H. A current view of client-centered or relationship therapy. *Counseling Psychologist,* 1969, *1*(2), 2-25

Patterson, C. H. *Theories of counseling and psychotherapy* (2nd ed.). New York: Harper & Row, 1973.

Pepinsky, H. B. The selection and use of diagnostic categories in clinical counseling. *Applied Psychology Monographs,* 1948, *6*(15).

Pierce, S., Ripp, G., Thelander, B., Tonetti, J. P., & York, K. Career development plan. Unpublished graphic analog, Albany, N.Y.: New York State Bureau of Guidance, January, 1972.

Rabow, G. *The era of the system.* New York: Philosophical Library, 1969.

Ramo, S. *Cure for chaos.* New York: David McKay, 1969.

Rapoport, A. Foreword. In W. F. Buckley (Ed.), *Modern systems research for the behavioral scientist.* Chicago: Aldine, 1968.

Rogers, C. R. *Client-centered therapy.* Boston: Houghton Mifflin, 1951.

Roy, R. H. The development and future of operations research and systems engineering. In C. D. Flagle, W. H. Huggins, & R. H. Roy (Eds.), *Operations research and systems engineering.* Baltimore: Johns Hopkins Press, 1960.

Ryan, T. A. American Educational Research Assocation 1969 presession: Systems approach in counseling and counselor education. *Final report.* Washington, D.C.: American Educational Research Association, 1969.

Saettler, P. *A history of instructional technology.* New York: McGraw-Hill, 1968.

Shannon, E. E., & Weaver, W. *The mathematical theory of communication.* Urbana, Ill.: University of Illinois Press, 1949.

Shertzer, B., & Stone, S. C. *Fundamentals of counseling.* Boston: Houghton Mifflin, 1974.

Shertzer, B., & Stone, S. C. *Fundamentals of guidance.* Boston: Houghton Mifflin, 1976.

Silvern, L. C. *Systems engineering of education I: The evolution of systems thinking in education.* Los Angeles: Education & Training Consultants, 1965.

Silvern, L. C. LOGOS: A system language for flowchart modeling. *Educational technology,* 1969, *9*(6), 18-23.

Skinner, B. F. *Science and human behavior.* New York: Macmillan, 1953.

Skinner, B. F. Teaching machines. *Scientific American,* 1961, *205,* 90-102.

Stewart, N. R. Decision making in systematic counseling. East Lansing, Mich., August 8, 1972. (Unpublished graphic analog)

Stewart, N. R., & Fiedler, L. J. Information-seeking in systematic counseling. East Lansing, Mich., January 26, 1971. (Unpublished graphic analog)

Stewart, N. R., Jensen, G., Leonard, P., & January, V. Systematic counseling supervisory process. East Lansing, Mich.: August 8, 1972. (Unpublished graphic analog)

Stravinsky, I. *[Poetics of music in the form of six lessons].* (A. Knodel and I. Dahl, trans.).Cambridge: Harvard University Press, 1947.

Super, D. E. *Computer-assisted counseling.* New York: Teachers College Press, 1970.

Thoresen, C. E. Being systematic about counselor training: Some basic steps. Paper presented at the meeting of the American Personnel and Guidance Association, Detroit, April, 1968. (a)

Thoresen, C. E. The "systems approach" and counselor training: Basic features and implications. Paper presented at the meeting of the American Educational Research Association, Chicago, February, 1968. (b)

Thoresen, C. E. Relevance and research in counseling. *Review of Educational Research,* 1969, *39*(2), 264. (a)

Thoresen, C. E. The systems approach and counselor education: Basic features and implications. *Counselor Education and Supervision,* 1969, *9*, 3-17. (b)

Thoresen, C. E. Behavioral humanism—A direction for counseling and research. Paper presented at the meeting of the American Educational Research Association, New York, February, 1971.

Thoresen, C. E., & Mahoney, M. J. *Behavioral self-control.* New York: Holt, Rinehart & Winston, 1974.

Tolbert E. L. *Introduction to counseling* (2nd ed.). New York: McGraw-Hill, 1972.

Truax, C. B. Reinforcement and nonreinforcement in Rogerian psychotherapy. *Journal of Abnormal Psychology,* 1966, *71*, 1-9.

Tyler, L.. E. *The work of the counselor* (3rd ed.). Englewood Cliffs, N.J.: Prentice-Hall, 1969.

U.S. Office of Education. *Computer-based vocational guidance systems.* OE-25053. Washington, D.C.: U.S. Government Printing Office, 1969.

Ullmann, L. P., & Krasner, L. *Case studies in behavior modification.* New York: Holt, Rinehart & Winston, 1965.

Varenhorst, B. B. Innovative tool for group counseling: The life career game. *School Counselor,* 1968, *15*, 357-362.

Walker, D. F. Toward more effective curriculum development projects in art. *Studies in Art Education,* 1970, *11*, 3-13.

Warters, J. *Techniques of counseling.* New York: McGraw-Hill, 1964.

Wiener, N. *Cybernetics.* New York: Wiley, 1948.

Winder, C. L., Ahmed, F. Z., Bandura, A., & Rau, L. C. Dependency of patients, psychotherapists' responses, and aspects of psychotherapy. *Journal of Consulting Psychology,* 1962, *26,* 129-134.

Wolberg, L. R. *The technique of psychotherapy.* New York: Grune & Stratton, 1967.

Yelon, S. L. Toward the application of systems analysis to counselor education. *Educational Technology,* 1969, *9* (3), 55-60.

Name Index

Ahmed, F.Z., 182

Bandura, A., 148, 149, 150, 157, 181, 182, 186, 190, 197
Berne, E., 171
Bertalanffy, L. von, 19, 34, 36, 37
Boocock, S.S., 170
Bourdon, R.D., 148
Buckley, W.F., 21, 36
Bugental, J.F.T., 28

Campbell, R.E., 46
Cautela, J.R., 232, 234
Churchman, C.W., 40
Clarke, D.L., 36
Cogswell, J.F., 42, 43
Cohen, H.L., 181
Coleman, J.S., 170
Cook, D.R., 46
Cramer, S.H., 208

Darwin, C., 35
Davidson, S., 39
DeGreene, K.B., 34, 36, 38
Duhl, F.J., 36
Dworkin, E.P., 46

Easton, D., 36
Emery, J.R., 202
Estavan, D.P., 43

Fagen, R.E., 21
Fiedler, L.J., 46
Ford, D.H., 11
Franks, C.M., 202
Friesen, D., 43

Gagné, R.M., 36, 42n
Gelatt, H.B., 210
Gibson, R.E., 21
Glaser, R., 42n
Gordon, J.E., 170

Gray, W., 36
Grinker, R.R., 36

Hall, A.D., 21
Hawkins, R.P., 220
Hays, D.G., 45, 46
Herr, E.L., 208
Hoeltzel, K.E., 46
Holland, J.G., 185
Hoppock, R., 213, 220
Hosford, R.E., 45, 46, 149, 157
Hurst, R., 43

Isaacson, L.E., 213, 220

Jackson, D.P., 46
January, V., 46
Jensen, G., 46
Johnson, L.B., 39
Johnson, R.A., 21
Johnson, R.G., 163

Kagan, N., 216
Kanfer, F.H., 181, 182, 186
Kast, F.E., 21
Kelly, G.A., 27
Kemp, C.G., 26
Kershner, R.B., 21
Khailov, K.M., 34
Krasner, L., 181, 182
Kremyanskiy, V.I., 34
Krumboltz, H.B., 190
Krumboltz, J.D., 149, 157, 182, 190, 208, 212, 249

Lacey, D.W., 46
Laszlo, E., 37
Lazarus, A.A., 164
Lehmann, I.J., 217
Leonard, P., 46
London, P., 28
Loughary, J.W., 43, 44, 95

Subject Index

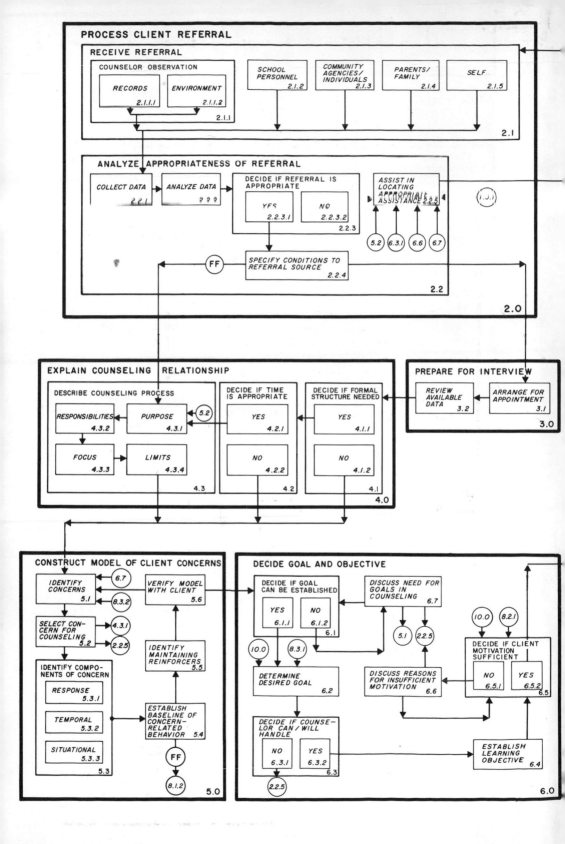